AN ENCYCLOPEDIA OF

WOMEN'S WRESTLING

AN ENCYCLOPEDIA OF

WOMEN'S WRESTLING

100 PROFILES
OF THE STRONGEST
IN THE SPORT

★ *LaToya Ferguson* ★

STERLING
New York

STERLING
New York

An Imprint of Sterling Publishing Co., Inc.
1166 Avenue of the Americas
New York, NY 10036

ISBN 978-1-4549-3120-1

Distributed in Canada by Sterling Publishing Co., Inc.
c/o Canadian Manda Group, 664 Annette Street
Toronto, Ontario M6S 2C8, Canada
Distributed in the United Kingdom by
GMC Distribution Services
Castle Place, 166 High Street, Lewes,
East Sussex BN7 1XU, England
Distributed in Australia by NewSouth Books
University of New South Wales, Sydney, NSW 2052, Australia

For information about custom editions, special sales,
and premium and corporate purchases, please
contact Sterling Special Sales at 800-805-5489 or
specialsales@sterlingpublishing.com.

Manufactured in China

10 9 8 7 6 5 4 3 2 1

sterlingpublishing.com

For picture credits, see page 267.

CONTENTS

ITS

Foreword

It seems surreal to me to even be writing this. When I started wrestling, in Ireland in 2011, independent wrestling—especially for women—was hardly even a thing. The internet wasn't as available then, so I knew of very little wrestling outside WWE. But I was a huge fan of the product and I stumbled upon a wrestling school. I thought I would give it a go, with no idea of ever even doing a show in mind, no concept of being a character or how to build on myself. I did it as a way of getting fit, and I found I made a lot of friends with a similar passion. Before I knew it, I had started doing shows around the country; I was shocked to find myself in that position. Still, though, the shows were catered to children, and the idea of getting outside Ireland or making it more than a fun hobby was nonexistent. I was one of the only female wrestlers in the country; I had big dreams but never dared to dream any of them would come true.

Then things started to change. The wrestling scene changed.

A world outside WWE started to unfold, as independent wrestling started to gain a huge following in Ireland and the UK. I decided it was time to change things up for myself and invented a new character, moving away from the basic create-a-women's-wrestler "Kazza G" that I had been wrestling with so long—and would have fit in perfectly in WWE's Divas era—and created "The Session Moth," a nonstop partier of a character. This was my chance to have fun with myself and to change things, as women had never really gotten to do comedy wrestling this seriously before. It was brand new and exciting and a complete swerve from the typical "women's wrestler" gimmick. Because of the boom in the independent scene, more people liked seeing things they didn't see on TV, and there was a certain freedom I felt in doing stuff that hadn't been done before and not taking myself so seriously. I still trained hard, as hard as I could, because if all these doors were going to start opening up for me, I was going to do everything I could to make it last and keep it fresh.

I have been wrestling as the "Session Moth" for four years now, and I have had the chance to explode all over Europe and eventually got to take my character to Japan with STARDOM and to the United States. The fact that, from starting with virtually no independent wrestling scene in Ireland and as the only female student in my wrestling class to getting to travel the world and be known enough to even be considered to write this forward, shows what a gigantic change there has been over the years in professional wrestling. It used to be that the only way to make a career in wrestling—especially as a woman—would be to sign with WWE; you had to have the right look, the right promo, the right skill. Now, after creating a character that is so far removed from the "right" way of things, I have managed to make a career, based solely on independent booking and independent self-promotion. Independent wrestling is alive and well, and women's wrestling is thriving, no matter where you are.

—Session Moth Martina

Introduction

"What we do is entertainment. We are extreme athletes.
Gymnasts have routines, but it doesn't demean anything
they're doing on the bars. We tell a physical soap opera
under the most difficult conditions. We have all sizes out
there taking a beating on their body. We are traveling
280 days out of the year and in a different hotel bed
every night. The talents of most of the people in this
ring are quite underrated at a media level, but there are
22 million people who switch this on every week and enjoy
the hell out of it. We are the ultimate variety show."

—JOANIE "CHYNA" LAURER, 2001

It might seem simple enough on the outside, but wrestling has always been a complex concept. It's a sport, but it's not quite a sport. It's a TV show, but not always and not exactly. It's fake, but it's not quite fake. Sometimes it's real, but there's a level to how real it is as well. Long gone are the days of true kayfabe (pig Latin for "be fake," though the actual origin of the term is not 100% known), as the popular belief is no longer that the people facing off in the ring have legitimate gripes with each other. But still, the stigma of wrestling continues. It's "soap operas for dudes," people say, which is either supposed to make men feel fine about watching it or feel even guiltier for watching it. As for the women, what about them?

Professional wrestling is a performance art. In fact, it might be the truest, grandest performance art left. Fast-forward past the Greco-Roman and amateur origins of professional wrestling, it's all one big grift: performers working the marks, as they were. For all the evolution of professional wrestling, the carnie speak, from which so much of its terminology and ideology is derived, pretty much stuck. This is why the illusion of professional wrestling was such a serious point for so many years—and still is in some ways, just in *different* ways—as well as the reason why so many people have a problem with professional wrestling being "fake." No one ever complains about *Game of Thrones* or *The Walking Dead* being "fake" or asking the audience to suspend their disbelief. But when it comes to professional wrestling, the expectation of reality and full transparency suddenly becomes a criteria for a particular brand of entertainment that has never been about full transparency. Actually, maybe that's it: maybe people still think they're being grifted. According to the July 2001 *Guardian*: "Good wrestlers are like ballet dancers: they need perfect coordination and balance so that when they leave the ground they can land exactly as they intend to."

One of the most popular sayings when it comes to professional wrestling is, "Well it ain't ballet." However, professional wrestling is perhaps more comparable to ballet than just about any other performance art. It's something Darren Aronofsky even realized when he originally wrote *The Wrestler* and *Black Swan* as companion pieces. Professional wrestling, above all else, is entertainment. Professional wrestling fans for years may have been upset with Vincent Kennedy McMahon for branding professional wrestling as "sports entertainment," but considering the simple meaning of such a term, nothing could describe it any better.

> **Note:** In the "Notable Matches" section of each profile, the (c) symbol stands for "champion." It notes who, as of the beginning of the match in question, is the incumbent champion. The information in the main profiles is current as of the date of writing (August 2018). The profiles will be updated with future editions.

The list of professional wrestlers and wrestling promotions is almost endless, and that's no different when you compartmentalize them into women's wrestling and wrestling promotions specifically. But in 2018, the ability to find women's wrestling and wrestlers was even easier than ever. There's the WWE Network, which features a near complete—yet still ever-expanding—library of professional wrestling from the World Wrestling Federation/World Wrestling Entertainment (WWF/WWE), World Championship Wrestling (WCW), Extreme Championship Wrestling (ECW), and all the other professional wrestling territories that McMahon purchased back in the day. There are also independent promotions that focus solely on providing women's wrestling at the highest possible level.

Admittedly, there is a certain amount of fetishism and eroticism that can come with the sub-set of women's professional wrestling, even though that's also true of men's professional wrestling (despite the lack of focus in mainstream promotions). *Playboy* was a large part of WWE (née WWF's) identity when it came to its women's (née Divas) division in the 1990s and early 2000s, with entire feuds and character pushes often times being built around them. But as wrestling pro-gressed in all other aspects—and the rise of the Internet, honestly—so did a desire to see women get the same treatment as the men in the ring. In fact, as the year winds down, WWE has just hired a handful of women that people couldn't have reasonably dreamed they would have signed even 5 or 10 years ago. This encyclopedia will prove as a resource for the rich, robust past and present of women's professional wrestling, which has become one of the biggest draws in modern professional wrestling in recent years. Hopefully, this will be an empowering source and resource for readers, regardless of actual wrestling fandom . . . even when it has to acknowledge things (which are now anomalies in the mainstream wrestling world) like Lingerie Pillow Fights in order to truly show how professional wrestling has evolved and changed for the better.

From its carnie upbringings to its role as one of the most prolific brands of living, breathing performance art, professional wrestling probably won't be going anywhere soon, if ever. While the image of professional wrestling to outsiders is usually still that of the muscle-bound men of the 1980s—like Hulk Hogan and "Macho Man" Randy Savage—professional wrestling has never been more diverse. But that image update should also be considered when it comes to the feminine side of the business too. With regard to women's professional wrestling , the *Playboy* models from the mid-to-late 1990s couldn't be farther from the norm for them these days either. Nor were they really ever accurate when it truly came to women's professional wrestling throughout the ages, from those humble carnival days on.

Disclaimer: This is not the entire history of women's professional wrestling. This is far from a complete compendium of women's professional wrestling. That is a task that would be too great to take on in these limited pages and would require far more than 100 entries. And to be perfectly honest, this is also a somewhat contemporary and mainstream look at women's professional wrestling. In fact, it just scratches the surface. But conveniently, just by scratching the surface, there's still so much to learn about these warriors, these wrestling Goddesses and Knockouts and Divas, these women of power. So consider this a starting point, an entryway into the fascinating and unbelievable world of women's wrestling.

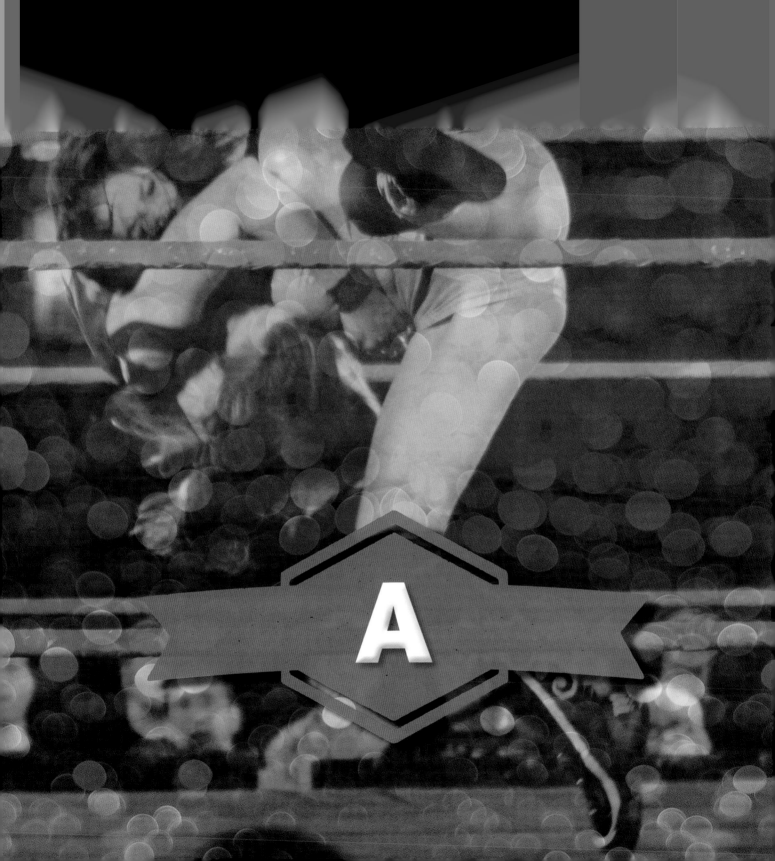

★ ACT YASUKAWA ★

YEARS ACTIVE: 2012–2015

TRAINED BY: Fuka Kakimoto

BILLED FROM: Misawa, Aomori, Japan

ACCOMPLISHMENTS: 1x Artist of STARDOM Champion (with Natsuki Taiyo & Saki Kashima) · 2x Wonder of STARDOM Champion · 2012 STARDOM Technique Award · 2013 Goddesses of STARDOM Tag Tournament (with Kyoko Kimura) · 2013 STARDOM Fighting Spirit Award · 2015 STARDOM Fighting Spirit Award

AKA: Act Ranger · member of Oedo Tai

NOTABLE MATCHES: Act Yasukawa vs. Dark Angel (c) at STARDOM Season 14 Goddesses In Stars 2013 - Night 4, for the Wonder of STARDOM Championship (November 4, 2013) · Act Yasukawa (c) vs. Kairi Hojo at STARDOM 3rd Anniversary Show, for the Wonder of STARDOM Title (January 26, 2014) · Act Yasukawa vs. Yoshiko (c) at STARDOM Queen's Shout, for the World of STARDOM Championship (February 22, 2015) · Act Yasukawa vs. Kairi Hojo at STARDOM Appeal The Heat, for the #1 Contendership to the World of STARDOM Championship (October 11, 2015)

★ Short but memorable, Act Yasukawa's professional wrestling career can be described as both inspirational and tragic. As a youth, Yasukawa suffered from ADD and depression, the latter of which only grew worse (and near fatal) after a doctor diagnosed her as "a bad, lazy kid who pretends to be sick to get out of going to school." She was also nearly blind in her right eye. After an eventual failed suicide attempt and during her recovery, Yasukawa found herself drawn to the world of acting. But even that new passion was met with its own hurdles, as Yasukawa was diagnosed with Graves' disease—a thyroid disorder which led to intense weight loss—and

found it difficult to get the roles of strong, "action heroes" that she longed to portray.

But eventually she did achieve that goal, being cast in a 2011 stage production called *Wrestler Girls* alongside model-turned-wrestler Yuzuki Aikawa. Aikawa was training to become a wrestler at this time, and Yasukawa was drawn to that; so when the STARDOM promotion's General Manager Fuka Kakimoto, invited her to audition to become a wrestler (after meeting Aikawa), she jumped at the chance: "I felt like this was probably my last chance to become a fighter in real life, so I took it. I felt like it was destiny, my chance to fulfill my dream."

Three months into training, Yasukawa got sick again and was told by her doctor not to wrestle, but she refused to give up on her dreams of being a fighter. So she fought her sickness—taking a medicine that would help her symptoms but would also leave her infertile—and continued her training, even incorporating her impairment into her wrestling gimmick by wearing an eye patch over her right eye and designing her ring gear with one pants leg, highlighting her asymmetry. She even started to come to the ring with a bottle of rum; but Yasukawa made clear she wasn't trying to be a wrestling pirate. Instead, she was paying homage to a samurai named Date Masamune who was also from northern Japan and wore an eye patch. As for the rum? "It's just because I like alcohol," she explained. "I chose rum specifically because it has color and a smell, so fans know that when I walk to the ring, I'm drinking the real thing."

Despite her work as a heel in STARDOM, Act Yasukawa quickly became a fan favorite upon her debut in 2012. In fact, in some ways, it was because of that heel persona, as she would even spit rum onto fans, only for other fans to chant "Act! Act!" in an attempt to receive the same treatment. And that popularity soon translated into championship wins, as she won her first wrestling championship in January 2013, the Artist of STARDOM Championship—a trios tag team title—alongside Natsuki Taiyo and Saki Kashima. This triumph was short-lived, however, as the trio had to vacate the title three months later due to Yasukawa suffering an injury to her cervical spine. Yasukawa returned to STARDOM that June, eventually winning her first singles title—the Wonder of STARDOM Championship—in November. Regarding her time as Wonder of STARDOM Champion, Yasukawa said: "I feel that the holder of Wonder of STARDOM Championship is responsible for energizing the crowd. While the red belt [World of STARDOM title] represents strength, the white belt [Wonder of STARDOM title] represents spirit and energy."

She held the championship until 2014, having to vacate it due to another battle with Graves' disease. However during that time off, Yasukawa had a successful cataract surgery to repair the vision in her right eye and continued to be part of STARDOM shows, selling merchandise and working on ring crew (setting up and taking down the ring before and after the shows). Returning to the ring in early December 2014, Yasukawa eventually won the Wonder of STARDOM Championship back the next month at the STARDOM 4th Anniversary Show, making her the first person to hold the title more than once. So far, only Mayu Iwatani and Io Shirai holds the same distinction.

Then in February 2015, in her first match for the STARDOM's highest honor (the World of STARDOM Championship), Act Yasukawa found herself challenging Yoshiko, a wrestler she had once promised in an interview to "overcome some day." However, Yasukawa never got the chance to even attempt to achieve her dream goal, as the match—which became known as *Seisan* Match or "Ghastly Match" in Japanese media—immediately became a betrayal of professional in-ring trust in the form of a brutal shoot (an actual, unscripted) beating from Yoshiko. As soon as the bell rang, the much larger Yoshiko attacked Act Yasukawa with stiff shots to Yasukawa's face—especially targeting her surgically repaired eye—with the referee intervening and pulling apart the two women. At that point, Yasukawa's face was swollen and bloody; but the match was continued, only for Yoshiko to continue stiffly beating on Act Yasukawa. This time, the match ended with

wrestler Yasukawa's friend and tag team partner Kyoko Kimura throwing in the towel from ringside. But even as the match officially ended, the women had to be physically pulled apart in order to put an end to things. Throughout the entire "match," Yasukawa fought to turn it into a proper wrestling match and shouted "I'm a pro wrestler!" and "I want to do pro wrestling" as she was dragged from the ring by her fellow wrestlers to the backstage area. At the hands of Yoshiko, Yasukawa suffered broken nasal and cheek bones, as well as a fractured orbital bone, which required another month in the hospital to recover from surgery. Fighter that she was, Yasukawa again returned to in-ring competition that September but was forced to retire at STARDOM's final show of the year as a result of the lingering effects (she was prevented from ever seeing in her right eye again) of her match with Yoshiko.

To this day, the actual motive behind Yoshiko's attack is unknown. Rumors of professional jealousy and a desire not to lose the championship to Yasukawa have swirled, with the general belief being that Yoshiko legitimately wanted to end Act Yasukawa's career as a result of said jealousy. Yet, as a result of this incident, Yoshiko was subsequently stripped of the World of STARDOM Championship and suspended from the promotion. She announced in May 2015, that she would be retiring, just a couple of weeks after her mentor, Nanae Takahashi, quit the company. The retirement ceremony took place that June; however, unlike Yasukawa, that "retirement" was short-lived: Yoshiko debuted in Takahashi's new wrestling promotion, SEAdLINNNG, in January 2016. She has since continued to wrestle in other all-women's wrestling promotions in Japan.

Despite her career being cut short, Act Yasukawa at least got to end it on her own terms, winning a tag team match with her Oedo Tai teammate Kyoko Kimura. After retirement, Act Yasukawa has continued to work for STARDOM as a manager for Oedo Tai, as well as returning to acting and even modeling. Despite her wrestling career being cut short by a nightmare, Act Yasukawa truly got to see her dreams come to reality.

★ AJA KONG ★

YEARS ACTIVE: 1986–present

TRAINED BY: All Japan Women's Pro-Wrestling (AJW) Dojo · Jaguar Yokota

BILLED FROM: Tokyo Tachikawa

ACCOMPLISHMENTS: 1x AJW Champion · 1x AJW Tag Team Champion (with Naboko Kimura) · 1x All Pacific Champion · 2x AJW World Women's Wrestling Association (WWWA)_ World Single Champion · 4x WWWA World Tag Team Champion (1x with Grizzly Iwamoto, 2x Bison Kimura, 1x with Amazing Kong) · 1992 Japan Grand Prix · 1996 Japan Grand Prix · 1992 Tag League the Best (with Kyoko Inoue) · AJW Hall of Fame Class of 1998 · 1x Queen of ARSION Champion · 1x Twin Star of ARSION Champion (with Mariko Yoshida) · 1x KO-D 6-Man Tag Team Champion (with Danshoku Dino & Makoto Oishi) · 3x DDT (Dramatic Dream Team) Pro-Wrestling Ironman Heavymetalweight Champion · 3x All Asia Athlete Women's (AAAW) Single Champion · 3x AAAW Tag Team Champion (1x with Maumi Ozaki, 1x with Devil Masami, 1x with Amazing Kong) · 1x HUSTLE Super Team Champion (with Margaret) · 1x JWP Joshi Puroresu Tag Team Champion (with Sachie Abe) · 1x Ladies Legend Pro-Wrestling (LLPW) Tag Team Champion (with Amazing Kong) · 3x OZ Academy Openweight Champion · 4x OZ Academy Tag Team Champion (1x with Hiroyo Matsumoto, 1x with Kaoru Ito, 1x with Sonoko Kato, 1x with Hikaru Shida) · 2010 OZ Academy MVP Award · 1x SENDAI Girls' World Champion · Wrestling Observer Newsletter Hall of Fame Class of 2006

AKA: Aja Shishido · AmeErika · Erika · "The Daughter of King Kong" · 1/2 of Double Kong · 1/2 of W Kong · member of Gokuaku Domei · 1/2 of Jungle Jack · member of Jungle Jack 21 · 1/2 of Super Maniacs

NOTABLE MATCHES: Jungle Jack (Aja Kong & Bison Kimura) vs. Gokumon-to (Bull Nakano & Grizzly Iwamoto) at AJW Survival Shot (August 19, 1990) · Aja Kong vs. Bull Nakano (c) at AJW Wrestlemarinepiad 1990, for the WWWA World Title in a Steel Cage match (November 14, 1990) · Jungle Jack (Aja Kong & Bison Kimura) vs. Gokumon-to (Bull Nakano & Kyoko Inoue) at AJW, in a Hair vs. Hair match (January 11, 1991) · Jungle Jack (Aja Kong & Bison Kimura) vs. Manami Toyota & Esther Moreno at AJW (April 29, 1991) · Aja Kong & Bull Nakano vs. Eagle Sawai & Harley Saito at AJW Dream Slam 1 (April 2, 1993) · Manami Toyota vs. Aja Kong at AJW Doumu Super Woman Great War ~ Big Egg Wrestling Universe, in a V*TOP Five Star Tournament First Round match (November 20, 1994) · Aja Kong, Bertha Faye, Tomoko Watanabe, & Lioness Asuka (with Harvey Wippleman) vs. Alundra Blayze, Kyoko Inoue, Sakie Hasegawa, & Chaparita Asari at WWF Survivor Series 1995, in a 4-on-4 Survivor Series Elimination match (November 19, 1995) · Aja Kong vs. Meiko Satomura (c) at SENDAI Girls' Pro Wrestling, for the SENDAI Girls' World Title (April 8, 2016) · Aja Kong vs. Chihiro Hashimoto at SENDAI Girls' Pro Wrestling (April 6, 2017)

⭐ Considered one of the best monster heels in the industry—as well one of the names that defines *joshi puroresu*—Aja Kong has seen and done it all. Born to a Japanese mother and an African American father in the military, Aja Kong (born Erika Shishido) had an uphill battle in a sport where her gender would already be an uphill battle. After all, the Japanese census claims that 98.5 percent of Japan's population is ethnic Japanese. And as her father left her family when she was five, there was also the discrimination over being a child of divorce and to a single mother. Seeing professional wrestling as an outlet for her anger as a youth, Shishido was instantly drawn to and inspired by beloved tag team The Crush Gals, who were absolute megastars in Japan during the 1980s and 1990s. In 1986, at the age of 16, she started training at the AJW Dojo under the tutelage of Jaguar Yokota. She was one of 500 girls who came to try out for the wrestling promotion, and she was also one of the only eight to make it.

Now, as a professional wrestler, that same mixed heritage that gave her a different look from her peers helped her stand out. In fact, despite the fact that she wanted to play a babyface character—a hero, a good guy—it was the higher-ups at AJW who decided she would play the heel—the bad guy—because of her "otherness." Finally that outlet for her anger could manifest itself into her wrestling persona, as she took all that hatred from Japan and turned it into her character's hatred toward Japan. No one else was doing that, nor were they rocking the signature blonde mohawk Shishido also came to be known for. And Erika Shishido would not just be a heel: she'd be a monster heel.

Almost immediately after making her AJW debut, Shishido joined Gokuaku Domei (aka Atrocious Alliance), a heel faction led by Dump Matsumoto, one of The Crush Gals' biggest rivals. It was this partnership that allowed Shishido to perfect her heel character, considered a mix between both Matsumoto and (then New Japan star) Big Van Vader. (Vader even used Shishido's character as inspiration for his own in Japan.) This lasted until Matsumoto retired in 1988, but Shishido reunited with Gokuaku Domei stable-mate (and AJW class of 1986

peer) Nobuko Kimura two years later to form the team Jungle Jack. With this, Erika Shishido became Aja Kong (and Nobuko Kimura now Bison Kimura). Eventually, the Jungle Jack stable added other women wrestlers, including Debbie Malenko, Kaoru Ito, Mika Takahashi, Sakie Hasegawa, and Madusa Miceli (aka Alundra Blayze). The original Jungle Jack pairing made Aja Kong a star, as she and Kimura engaged in a two-year feud with their former Gokuaku Domei teammate Bull Nakano and her heel stable Gokumon-to. Jungle Jack's feud with Nakano led to Kong and Kimura winning AJW's WWWA World Tag Team Championship titles two times, as well as to the losing end of a Hair vs. Hair match in 1991. As leaders of their respective stables, however, Kong and Nakano also faced off in singles championship competition. Then in November 1992, Kong got some revenge for the Hair vs. Hair match and put an end to Nakano's three-year reign as AJW's WWWA World Single Champion. Aja Kong's first reign as WWWA World Single Champion went on to last two and a half years, and by 1994 she was considered a key draw in AJW and consistently main evented the company's major shows all the way to her departure in 1997.

Kong had a cup of coffee in the WWF (as it was called at the time), debuting and dominating in a WWF Women's four-on-four elimination tag team match at the Survivor Series pay-per-view in 1995. After that impressive performance as the sole survivor on her team, Kong was poised to feud with Alundra Blayze as the top contender for the WWF Women's title in 1995. She even appeared on two episodes of WWF *Monday Night RAW*, winning both matches (and breaking the nose of her opponent in one). But after Blayze was released from the company (and took the championship with her)—despite being booked to defend her title at 1996's Royal Rumble pay-per-view—women's wrestling in WWF took a drastic turn away from this particular brand of athleticism and dominance, and Kong's services were no longer needed.

In 1997, Aja Kong founded her own all-women's wrestling promotion called ARSION (short for Hyper Visual Fighting

ARSION). ARSION's first show took place in 1998, but behind the scenes issues led to Kong departing the company in February 2001, literally: She walked out of an in-progress tag team match and announced that she was quitting. ARSION officially shut its doors in the summer of 2003, but Yumiko Hotta took over the promotion and renamed it AtoZ (which closed in 2006).

Post-ARSION, Aja Kong worked as a true independent wrestler both in Japan and eventually the United States. In Japan, she became mentor and tag team partner to African American wrestler Amazing Kong. Facing Amazing Kong in Amazing Kong's Japanese debut at joshi promotion GAEA Japan in 2004, the two formed a tag team that same night called W Kong. That same year, they won GAEA's AAAW Tag Team Championship; in fact, they won tag team championships in both AJW and Ladies Legend Pro-Wrestling. They even became tag team champions for the HUSTLE professional wrestling promotion in 2006 under the ring names Erika and Margaret—employing comedy gimmicks in which they wore tutus—and were the last team to hold the WWWA World Tag Team Championship title before AJW closed in 2005. In 2011, Aja Kong returned to the United States to partake in the CHIKARA wrestling promotion's JoshiMania. Kong competed all three nights of the event, but it was on night 1 where she main evented in a wrestling dream match against Sara Del Rey. She returned to the States again to wrestle an eight-woman tag team match at SHIMMER Volume 74 in 2015, as part of a send-off for Tomoka Nakagawa's retirement. These days, Aja Kong can still be found dominating at the SENDAI Girls' and OZ Academy wrestling promotions. After 30 years in the business, the lyrics to her entrance theme in AJW, "Jungle Emperor," really say everything that needs to be said about Aja Kong:

> "God -made the Devil just for fun
> When He wanted the real thing
> He made Aja Kong!"

★ AJ LEE ★

YEARS ACTIVE: 2007–2015

TRAINED BY: Azrieal · Jay Lethal · Mo Sexton · Florida Championship Wrestling (FCW)

BILLED FROM: Union City, New Jersey

ACCOMPLISHMENTS: 1x Queen of FCW · 1x FCW Divas Champion · 2012 Pro Wrestling Illustrated (PWI) Woman of the Year · 2013 PWI Woman of the Year · 2014 PWI Woman of the Year · #2 in 2014 PWI Female 50 · 1x WSU Tag Team Champion (with Brooke Carter) · 2009 Women Superstars Uncensored/National. Wrestling Superstars (WSU/NWS) King and Queen of the Ring (with Jay Lethal) · 3x WWE Divas Champion · 2012 Slammy Award for Diva of the Year · 2014 Slammy Award for Diva of the Year · 2012 Slammy Award for Kiss of the Year (with John Cena)

AKA: Miss April · April Lee · 1/2 of The Chickbusters

NOTABLE MATCHES: AJ Lee vs. Serena (c) at FCW, for the Queen of FCW title (February 14, 2010) · AJ Lee vs. Naomi at WWE NXT Season 3 (November 23, 2010) · AJ Lee vs. Kaitlyn (c) at WWE Payback 2013, for the WWE Divas Championship (June 16, 2013) · Kaitlyn & Dolph Ziggler vs. AJ Lee & Big E Langston at WWE SummerSlam 2013 (August 18, 2013) · AJ Lee (c) vs. Natalya at WWE TLC 2013, for the WWE Divas Championship (December 15, 2013) · AJ Lee (with Tamina) vs. Kaitlyn at WWE Main Event (January 8, 2014) · AJ Lee (c) vs. Natalya at WWE Main Event, for the WWE Divas Championship (March 11, 2014) · Nikki Bella vs. Paige (c) vs. AJ Lee at WWE Night of Champions 2014, in a Triple Threat match for the WWE Divas Championship (September 21, 2014) · Nikki Bella vs. AJ Lee at WWE *Monday Night RAW* (March 16, 2015)

★ In May 2009, April Jeanette Mendez signed with FCW, WWE's developmental brand at the time. AJ was the first woman in two years with any wrestling experience—after Natalya Neidhart

in motels, friends' houses, or the family car) in New Jersey. In fact, one of the moments that's often brought up when it comes to AJ's lifelong passion for wrestling is a WWE video of her when she was 13 years old, crying as she met her idol Lita in 2001.

April enrolled in wrestling classes when she was 20 years old, wrestling under the ring name "Miss April" in independent promotions. In October 2008, she joined WSU, going on to win the 2009 WSU/NWS King and Queen of the Ring tournament with her trainer, Jay Lethal, in (coincidentally) April of that year. A month later, April signed that WWE developmental contract. Spending two years in FCW, AJ Lee became the first woman to win the developmental promotion's two women's titles, the Queen of FCW title and the FCW Divas Championship.

AJ made her soft WWE main roster debut in season three—the Divas season—of WWE's original game show version of *NXT*. Over the course of that 13-week season, AJ Lee developed an on-screen relationship with her *NXT* Pro mentor, Primo, as well as an on-screen and off-screen friendship with fellow *NXT* competitor and season winner Kaitlyn. While she quickly became a fan favorite due to her genuine passion for professional wrestling, her geek girl cred, and her signature Converse shoes, the behind-the-scenes culture for WWE Divas in this era still wasn't the most progressive. In AJ's autobiography, she wrote that the head of talent relations at the time told her "nobody wants to have sex with you." AJ Lee certainly didn't fit the stereotypical mold of the cliché Diva, but that didn't keep the fans from rooting for her. However, with the concept of sex appeal translating to a point of marketability under that particular mindset, AJ Lee was soon eliminated from *NXT* (placing third in the season), despite being told she was getting the most fan votes each week.

After her elimination from *NXT* toward the end of 2010, AJ returned to developmental and wouldn't make her official main roster debut until May 2011, debuting on *SmackDown* as part of a Divas tag team with Kaitlyn. While it was never an official WWE tag team name, the two quirky Divas referred to their pairing as "The Chickbusters." Mentored on-screen by Natalya,

in 2007—to be signed to a developmental deal for the company. It was a good thing that she took a chance on herself—she saved up and spent $1,500 to even attend the WWE tryout camp in Tampa, Florida, which led to her signing. According to April, "I began saving my money. I just thought, whether I get signed or not, they just need to see me. . . . Fate must've taken over, because I was so skinny and didn't know how to do my hair and makeup."

It may not have been just fate though. Later known as AJ Lee, this woman's tenure in WWE eventually helped pave the way for the Divas Revolution and Women's Evolution. However, before she was signed, April was just a girl who had dreamed of being a WWE Diva herself since she was 12 years old. Inspired by Lita—a "WWE Diva" also known for her alternative approach to what exactly that meant—April found wrestling to be an escape from the struggles of her every day family life (whether that be living

The Chickbusters feuded with Alicia Fox, Rosa Mendes, and Tamina for the next couple of months. Simultaneously, Lee (as well as Kaitlyn) returned to *NXT* to pull duty in season five, *NXT Redemption*. At that point the series became less of a competition and more of a bizarre narrative experiment that lasted 67 weeks until the present-day version of *NXT* was formed. Lee feuded with her former *NXT* season three competitor Maxine and was romantically paired with Hornswoggle, two storylines that were only acknowledged on *NXT*, despite *NXT* acknowledging that AJ Lee was on the *SmackDown* roster. However, on *SmackDown*, The Chickbusters ended up feuding with their mentor as Natalya eventually turned heel and formed The Divas of Doom with Beth Phoenix in August. The Chickbusters feuded with The Divas of Doom for a couple of months and lost, effectively splitting up the team (though AJ and Kaitlyn's relationship would be a key facet of their characters).

The end of 2011 was when it all changed, as AJ Lee was paired with WWE Superstar Daniel Bryan in what would soon begin her breakout year and unprecedented push in this era of the WWE. The storyline centered on Daniel Bryan's turn to the dark side as he became the World Heavyweight Champion, eventually using his girlfriend (Lee) as an excuse, a human shield, an emotional punching bag. (And when approached by Kaitlyn and Natalya, who worried about her in this relationship, the now "mentally unstable" Lee physically lashed out at them.) This led to WrestleMania XXVIII and the now famous "kiss heard 'round the WWE Universe," Bryan's good luck kiss to AJ Lee before he defended the WWE World Heavyweight Championship. Unfortunately, this kiss ended up working as a distraction that caused Bryan to lose the championship in a record-setting 18 seconds. Soon, the men Daniel Bryan feuded with—CM Punk and Kane—became caught in AJ Lee's web of desire. Or mind games, as the question regularly became: "What is AJ thinking?" The question was also one of who AJ should end up with, a question that led to the hashtag option of #AJALL. Eventually, AJ kicked Bryan to the curb and became the general manager of *RAW*, but she still remained in the spotlight. Of course, Lee's "mentally unstable" behavior eventually cost her the position, this time landing her in a bizarre love triangle between WWE megastar John Cena and playboy Dolph Ziggler. Eventually, AJ Lee chose Ziggler, officially turning heel for the first time in her WWE main roster career and forming a powerful trio (with Big E Langston as Lee and Ziggler's muscle). In time the power trio led to AJ Lee capturing her first Divas Championship—feuding with and torturing her former best friend, Kaitlyn, in order to do so and participating in the first-ever Divas in-ring contract signing segment—and Ziggler becoming the World Heavyweight Championship. But as was AJ Lee's way, the Lee/Ziggler romance couldn't last forever.

From "girl next door to vengeful vixen," AJ Lee continued not to fit the typical Diva mold—and at 5 foot 2 inches, her diminutive stature stood out even more in terms of her differences—but it was that aspect of her wrestling persona that smashed open doors for her and paved the way for future women's wrestlers in the company. In 2013, a WWE.com article about WWE Superstars who could become the "Face of the WWE" notably included only one WWE Diva in the conversation: AJ Lee. At the time, merchandise on par with the male Superstars on the roster (even something as simple as a t-shirt) was nigh invisible for WWE Divas. Except for AJ Lee, as that WWE.com article noted: "Fact is, no Diva has commanded attention quite like AJ Lee. T-shirts, watches, iPhone cases, hoodies, even baby bibs—her likeness is on more products than Yogurt from *Spaceballs*." In a way, AJ Lee's meteoric rise to the top of the Divas Division—as well as just as a major focus in weekly WWE television—was an anomaly. At the beginning of 2014, she became the longest-reigning Divas Champion, surpassing Maryse as the previous record holder. She then went on to defend the title at WrestleMania XXX in the Vickie Guerrero Divas Invitational (a 14-Diva match, with one fall to a finish), marking both the first time the Divas Championship had been defended at WrestleMania since its introduction in 2008 and the only time it would ever be defended on the company's flagship pay-per-view.

A great deal of AJ Lee's character translated from her own behind-the-scenes feelings of detachment and antagonism from her fellow Divas. This allowed her to cut a "worked shoot" promo better known as a "pipe bomb"—a promo in which the character played on both real frustrations and criticisms that blurred the line of a wrestling work, originally famously executed by AJ Lee's real-life significant other CM Punk in 2013 on an episode of *RAW*. Face-to-face with the Divas Division—specifically the cast members of E! reality series *Total Divas*—AJ spoke about how she had been the one to have "shattered glass ceilings," "broken doors," and in her words, "saved your Divas Division," while the rest of them were just concerned with being famous. While the promo itself was reported to have adversely affected her already shaky backstage relationship with her peers, AJ Lee still maintained her high status in the division on-screen and among the WWE Universe. It was also one of several moments toward the end of her run that made her time behind-the-scenes more contentious among her peers. When AJ won the WWE Slammy Award for 2014 Diva of the Year, during her acceptance speech, she said she hoped that then developmental Divas Bayley, Charlotte, or Paige would be next year's winner . . . intentionally neglecting to mention any of her colleagues on the roster.

But it wasn't just her fellow Divas that AJ would put on blast: In February 2015, AJ Lee took an unscripted shot at Stephanie McMahon on Twitter, calling out a tweet from McMahon about wage equality and women's rights as an empty gesture, as the female roster "have record-selling merchandise & *have* starred in the highest rated segment of the show several times . . . yet they receive a fraction of the wages & screen time of the majority of the male roster." That same night, after a seconds-long Divas wrestling match on *RAW*—after NXT Women's Division had changed the way people looked at women's wrestling in WEE—#GiveDivasAChance started trending worldwide on Twitter. It was a matter WWE couldn't ignore this time, as Vince McMahon even tweeted: "We hear you. Keep watching. #GiveDivasAChance."

AJ Lee retired in April 2015, five days after winning her Divas tag match at WrestleMania 31. Then in September 2015, Nikki Bella (who AJ had made submit for the win in that WrestleMania 31 match) went on to surpass AJ Lee's record-setting Divas Championship reign at 301 days. AJ Lee's championship reign may no longer be in the record books, but few could argue that her impact hasn't lasted.

After retiring, AJ announced that she was in the process of writing a memoir. The book—*Crazy Is My Superpower: How I Triumphed by Breaking Bones, Breaking Hearts, and Breaking the Rules*—was released in April 2017 and made it to the *New York Times* Best Sellers list. (Then, that same December, it was announced that her book was being developed into a scripted television series.) In the memoir, AJ revealed that her retirement was a mix of the discovery that she had permanent damage to her cervical spine and a feeling of being "caught in the middle" between WWE and now husband CM Punk after he walked out on the company. (The kicker was that WWE sent Punk his release papers on his and AJ's wedding day.) It also chronicled AJ Lee's struggles with bipolar disorder and her dysfunctional, emotionally abusive upbringing and how, through it all, she didn't let that stop her from achieving her dreams. And that she did.

★ ALEXA BLISS ★

YEARS ACTIVE: 2013–present

TRAINED BY: WWE Performance Center

BILLED FROM: Columbus, Ohio

ACCOMPLISHMENTS: #29 in 2016 PWI Female 50 · 3x WWE RAW Women's Champion · 2x WWE SmackDown Women's Champion · Women's Money in the Bank (2018) · #2 in 2018 PWI Female 50

AKA: "Five Feet of Fury" · "The Goddess of WWE" · "Little Miss Bliss" · "The Wicked Witch of WWE" · 1/2 of Team Rude · 1/3 of Team In Your Dreams

NOTABLE MATCHES: Alexa Bliss vs. Alicia Fox at NXT, in an NXT Women's Championship Tournament First Round match (May 8, 2014) · Blake, Murphy, & Alexa Bliss vs. Enzo Amore, Colin "Big Cass" Cassady, & Carmella at *NXT* (June 17, 2015) · Alexa Bliss vs. Carmella vs. Nia Jax at *NXT*, for the #1 Contendership to the NXT Women's Championship (May 25, 2016) · Alexa Bliss vs. Bayley at *NXT* (July 6, 2016) · Alexa Bliss vs. Carmella vs. Becky Lynch vs. Naomi vs. Nikki Bella at WWE Backlash 2016, in a 6-Pack Challenge for the inaugural WWE SmackDown Women's Championship (September 11, 2016) · Alexa Bliss vs. Bayley (c) at WWE Payback 2017, for the WWE RAW Women's Championship (April 30, 2017) · Alexa Bliss vs. Sasha Banks (c) at WWE *Monday Night RAW*, for the WWE RAW Women's Championship (August 28, 2017) · Alexa Bliss (c) vs. Mickie James at WWE TLC 2017, for the WWE RAW Women's Championship (October 22, 2017)

⭐ "Little Miss Bliss" Alexa Bliss is proof that big personalities absolutely come in small packages. Coming from a cheerleading and bodybuilding (having performed in the Arnold Classic) background, the woman formerly known as Alexis Kaufman is used to the bright lights of athletic competition. But coming up with a compelling character is something completely different.

Having signed a developmental contract to NXT (to train at the WWE's Performance Center) in May 2013, Bliss found herself doing a few little spots for WWE before officially debuting on NXTV. She was first spotted in the celebration of Paige as *NXT*'s inaugural Women's Champion and also worked as ring announcer for an episode of *NXT* before the end of 2013. Then she had the honor of being one of the NXT Women cast as extras in Triple H's WrestleMania XXX entrance in 2014, alongside Sasha Banks and Charlotte. But before that, Alexa got the chance to show her stuff in front of the WrestleMania Axxess crowd, competing in a losing effort against Paige for the NXT Women's Championship.

It was the month after WrestleMania that she made her official television in-ring debut, in a tournament for the then vacant NXT Women's Championship. There, she introduced her glittered up, fairy-like babyface character to the NXT Universe. Commentary

for Bliss's entrance and the match painted the picture early with Bliss. "She told me she's a graduate of the University of Bliss with a major in bedazzling," quipped one commentator. The rest of the match—which was an impressive initial outing for Bliss—featured a bunch of comparisons to describe her: "Pint-sized." Of course, "fairy." And she was compared to everything from "Tinkerbell" to "Polly Pocket" to "Thumbelina."

Eventually, Bliss's own entrance theme would start off with the words that best described Bliss's character at the time, from her own mouth: "Glitter, Glitz, Sparkle, Bliss." But she also found herself in the underdog role on *NXT*, regularly facing off against much more established opponents and losing to them. That is, until March 2015, when she ended up in a mini-feud with the NXT

Women's Championship at the time, Sasha Banks. After beating Banks in a non-title match (by count-out) on an episode of *NXT* filmed in Bliss's hometown of Columbus, Ohio, Bliss earned a title match against the champ. The next week, Sasha Banks retained her championship against Bliss, but Bliss got to show her ability on a bigger stage. Everything changed, however, when Bliss turned heel just a couple of months later, joining forces with NXT Tag Team Champions Blake and Murphy in their feud against fan favorites Enzo Amore, Colin Cassady, and Carmella. At the time, wrestling critics and fans alike were wondering how someone considered such a natural babyface like Bliss could work as a heel, especially as part of a team who were struggling to find an identity (despite their championship gold). Yet Alexa ended up transforming into one of the most praised heels on the roster for her ruthlessness and facial expressions, a far cry from the lover of glitter she once was. A year later, Alexa Bliss left Blake and Murphy in the dust. And she was just getting started.

For the rest of her time in NXT, Alexa Bliss remained a heel, but she still came up short in championship bouts. Her feud with Bayley over the NXT Women's Championship led to a main event title match during a November 2015 episode of *NXT,* but even with her entrée in other number 1 contender matches, Bliss always came up short. But despite the NXT Women's Championship eluding her, that did not define her, as Bliss ended up being one of the few *NXT* talents to get drafted to the main roster in the 2016 WWE draft. Drafted to SmackDown LIVE, Alexa Bliss soon debuted a new Harley Quinn–inspired look for her character (after past cosplay looks such as Freddy Krueger and Iron Man in *NXT*). By December that same year, Alexa Bliss became the new (and second ever) SmackDown Women's Champion. During her time on the SmackDown roster, Alexa became the first-ever two time SmackDown Women's Champion and went into WrestleMania 33 as champion (despite her second reign being ended by Naomi).

Alexa Bliss made history again in April 2017 when the WWE Superstar Shake-up moved her to RAW and she became the RAW Women's Champion that same month—officially making her the first WWE Superstar to win both of WWE women's titles.

Since her humble, glitter-filled beginnings in NXT, Bliss has become the first competitor to become both a two time WWE SmackDown and two time WWE RAW Women's Championship (and has since become a three-time RAW Women's Champion). She main evented *RAW* against Sasha Banks—the same woman she lost to in her first televised stab at the NXT Women's Championship—and achieved her second RAW Women's Championship reign as a result of that match. She also joined the cast of E! WWE reality series *Total Divas* in its seventh season alongside her best friend and fellow main roster competitor, Nia Jax. In her short (no pun intended) career, Alexa Bliss has often been considered "the next Trish Stratus," the next woman to become an all-time great both in the ring and in terms of character starting right from the ground up. Given her accomplishments thus far—including retaining her RAW Women's Championship in the first-ever WWE Women's Elimination Chamber match—that comparison is an understandable one.

★ ALICIA FOX ★

YEARS ACTIVE: 2006–present

TRAINED BY: Ohio Valley Wrestling (OVW) · FCW

BILLED FROM: Ponte Vedra Beach, Florida

ACCOMPLISHMENTS: 1x OVW Women's Champion · #17 in 2010 PWI Female 50 · #43 in 2011 PWI Female 50 · #36 in 2012 PWI Female 50 · #35 in 2013 PWI Female 50 · #25 in 2014 PWI Female 50 · #44 in 2015 PWI Female 50 · 1x WWE Divas Champion

AKA: Victoria Crawford · Tori · "Foxy" · 1/3 of Team Bella · 1/2 of Foxsana · 1/3 of Team In Your Dreams

Alicia Fox vs. Eve Torres (c) vs. Gail Kim vs. Maryse at WWE Fatal 4-Way 2010, in a Fatal 4-Way match for the WWE Divas Championship (June 20, 2010) · Alicia Fox vs. Emma at NXT (February 5, 2014) · Alicia Fox vs. Paige at WWE Superstars (November 20, 2014) · Alicia Fox vs. Paige at WWE Main Event (June 2, 2015) · Alicia Fox & Noam Dar vs. Sasha Banks & Rich Swann at WWE Extreme Rules 2017, in a Mixed Tag Team match (June 4, 2017)

★ As of 2018, Alicia Fox is the longest tenured female performer on the WWE Roster. But back in 2006, she was Victoria Crawford, a model for Venus Swimwear in Jacksonville, Florida. It was through that modeling that WWE's then Head of Talent Relations John Laurinaitis "discovered" her, picking both her and the Diva who would be known as Kelly Kelly out of a fashion catalog and signing them to WWE after the fact. Years after the fact, Fox would consider that hiring decision an "experiment" on WWE's end to see if they could even teach models how to wrestle.

After spending two years in WWE developmental both at OVW (in Louisville, Kentucky) and FCW (in Tampa, Florida), Alicia Fox officially made her main roster debut in June 2008 on *SmackDown*, introduced as the wedding planner for Vickie Guerrero and Edge's wedding. Of course, since wrestling weddings never quite go as planned, at the wedding, Triple H (who was feuding with Edge over the WWE Championship at the time) revealed footage of Edge and Alicia Fox kissing the day before. During Edge and Triple H's title match at the next pay-per-view, The Great American Bash, Fox interfered in an attempt to help Edge . . . but only ended up causing Edge to accidentally spear Vickie and fail at his attempt to regain championship gold.

Alicia Fox then disappeared for three months, only to pop up on WWE's version of ECW as the manager to new babyface Superstar DJ Gabriel. Why a wedding planner would eventually end up being a wrestling manager (and then a wrestler) is a question only wrestling can answer. In fact, WWE.com's official description of such a concept in Alicia Fox's biography does just

that: "After she was caught canoodling with the groom, however, Alicia wisely crawled into a foxhole somewhere before re-emerging as a bona fide Superstar." While Alicia's nuptial-based beginnings have since become a long forgotten aspect of her character, the on-screen explanation for the DJ Gabriel connection at the time was that she had moved her wedding planning business to England during that three month span, and that's when she met Gabriel.

Still, Fox became the first (and only) African American Divas Champion, an opportunity she had not gotten the chance to relive again before the Divas Championship was retired at WrestleMania 32 in 2016. That reign was only 56 days, and upon defending the title against Melina in the former champion's mandatory rematch, Fox came up short. Outside of title contention, Alicia Fox ended up as a mentor for *NXT* season three rookie Maxine . . . but since Maxine was the second competitor eliminated, Fox was like a Diva without an island, regularly competing against other mentors and rookies on the season but not really having a place. Post-*NXT* season three, on the main roster, Fox allied with Tamina and Rosa Mendes in order to feud with The Chickbusters (AJ Lee and Kaitlyn), but once she and her team lost that feud, Alicia Fox was now a face again. (A running joke amongst fans was that Alicia Fox would be a face or heel depending on the week and the match necessity.) This led to her being a victim of The Divas of Doom (Beth Phoenix and Natalya), and despite her championship past, she spent the majority of her time in 2012 and 2013 on the losing end of her matches. This eventually led to a storyline in 2014 where Alicia Fox would respond to each loss with a post-match tantrum, harassing the commentary team and ringside production crew. The saying "crazy like a fox" became synonymous with Alicia Fox's character at the time, even in backstage WWE App vignettes, where that behavior fueled a nearly year-long story between Alicia Fox and the object of her romantic obsession, WWE interviewer/commentator Tom Phillips.

In the fall of 2014, Alicia Fox joined the cast of E! Network's *Total Divas* for the reality series' third season. As a result, during the summer of 2015, as Paige attempted to rally the Divas Division to band together against *Total Divas* stars The Bella Twins (and Divas Champion Nikki Bella), Alicia joined forces with the Bellas, effectively forming "Team Bella." This coincided with the main roster debuts of three of *NXT*'s top women (Charlotte, Becky Lynch, and Sasha Banks) and the formation of two other teams to feud with Team Bella and among each other: Team B.A.D. (Naomi, Tamina, and Sasha Banks) and Team PCB (Paige, Charlotte, and Becky Lynch). The original *Monday Night RAW* segment introducing these new Divas featured Stephanie McMahon calling for a "revolution" in the Divas Division, but despite the initial excitement of these debuts and the Divas (eventually dubbed "Superstars" instead of "Divas" at WrestleMania 32) finally getting proper screen and in-ring time, the forced teams—for example, Alicia Fox essentially had to assume a role as a bonus Bella—and branding aspects of the Divas Revolution wore thin. By March 2016, Team Bella was over and Alicia Fox was a face again for a brief period of time. At WrestleMania 32, Fox was on the winning team in a 10-Diva tag team match of Team Total Divas against the makeshift Team B.A.D. and Blonde.

WHY A WEDDING PLANNER WOULD END UP BEING A WRESTLING MANAGER IS A QUESTION ONLY WRESTLING CAN ANSWER.

Fox decided not to return to *Total Divas* in its sixth season and has since stated she "didn't like the way she came off" on the show, describing it as looking "like a crazy young drunken nut" at that point in her life. Still, the "crazy" moniker continued to be part of her on-screen WWE person. After the 2016 WWE Draft, Fox was drafted to RAW. Again, Alicia Fox's character found itself in an aimless path—though she did have a mini-feud with new main roster Superstar Nia Jax, which she lost—until she was romantically paired on-screen with Cedric Alexander, a member of RAW's (along with its supplemental show, *205 Live*) Cruiserweight Division. The *205 Live* storyline led to a love triangle between Alexander, Fox, and the lecherous Noam Dar. Eventually, Alexander dumped Fox, turning her heel in the process and causing her to ally with her new boyfriend, Noam Dar. Fox was adamant that "no one" breaks up with her, so she forced Dar to feud with Alexander—as well as Alexander's best friend, Rich Swann—eventually leading to an "I Quit" match that Alexander beat Dar in. After that, Dar dumped Fox, and Fox returned to her regular *Monday Night RAW* duties in the Women's Division.

Then, after nine years on the main roster, Fox got her first piece of official WWE merchandise in the form of a t-shirt. She also ended up as captain of (the winning) Team RAW for the women's elimination tag team match at Survivor Series 2017. "Crazy like a fox," Alicia Fox's WWE career has been an interesting one. Alicia Fox remains the longest tenured full-time female performer on the entire WWE roster.

 ALLIE ★

YEARS ACTIVE: 2005-present

TRAINED BY: Rob "El Fuego" Etcheverria · Squared Circle Training · Ashley Sixx · Derek Wylde

BILLED FROM: Toronto, Ontario, Canada

ACCOMPLISHMENTS: 2x Total Nonstop Action (TNA) Impact Wrestling Knockouts Champion · 1x Classic Championship Champion · 1x Great Canadian Wrestling W.I.L.D. Champion · 2009 Ontario Indy Wrestling Awards Female Wrestler of the Year · #1 in 2009 Ontario Wrestling's Indy Elite (OWIE) Top 30 · 2013 2CW Girls Grand Prix 2 · #8 in 2015 PWI Female 50 · #15 in 2016 PWI Female 50 · 1x Pro Wrestling Xtreme Women's Champion · 1x WSU Champion · 1x SHIMMER Tag Team Champion (with Kimber Lee) · 1x SHINE Tag Team Champion (with Kimber Lee) · 2x Classic Championship Wrestling Women's Champion · 2017 Impact Wrestling Turkey Bowl (with Eddie Edwards, Richard Justice, Fallah Bahh, and Garza Jr.)

AKA: Cherry Bomb · Allie Impact · 1/2 of The Kimber Bombs · Laura Dennis · 1/3 of Team Sailor Moon · 1/2 of The Fitness Power Couple · 1/3 of TV Ready · member of Team Big League · 1/2 of Ditz and Glitz · member of The Lady Squad · SMASH Wrestling's Resident Vampire Slayer · "The Demon Slayer" · 1/2 of Demon Bunny

NOTABLE MATCHES: Cherry Bomb & Pepper Parks vs. The World's Cutest Tag Team (Candice LeRae & Joey Ryan) at SMASH Wrestling Challenge Accepted (November 23, 2014) · Cherry Bomb vs. Mickie James at 2CW Christmas Chaos (December 27, 2014) · The Kimber Bombs (Cherry Bomb & Kimber Lee) vs. Courtney Rush & Vanessa Kraven at SMASH Wrestling Super Showdown III (August 23, 2015) · Cherry Bomb vs. Courtney Rush at SMASH Wrestling Any Given Sunday 4 (March 20, 2016) · Cherry Bomb vs. Leah Vaughan vs. Courtney Rush at SMASH Wrestling Forest City Rampage (April 9, 2016) · Cherry Bomb (c) vs. Allysin Kay at WSU Unshakable, for the WSU World Championship (May 14, 2016) · Team Canada (Allie, KC Spinelli, & Taya) vs. Team USA (Cheerleader Melissa, Santana Garrett, & Sienna) at Lucha Libre AAA Worldwide (AAA) Lucha Libre World Cup (Women's Division) - Night 2, in the Lucha Libre World Cup (Women's Division) Third Place match (June 5, 2016) · Team Slap Happy (Heidi Lovelace & Evie) vs. The Kimber Bombs (Kimber Lee & Cherry Bomb) (c) vs. BaleSpin (KC Spinelli & Xandra Bale) vs. Fly High WDSS (Kay Lee Ray & Mia Yim) at SHIMMER Volume 84, in a Four Corners Elimination match for the SHIMMER Tag Team Championship (June 26, 2016) · Allie vs. Rosemary at SMASH Wrestling Super Showdown IV, in a No Disqualification match (August 21, 2016) · Allie (USA) vs. Rosemary (CANADA) at SMASH Wrestling CANUSA Classic 2016, in a Steel Cage match (October 22, 2016) · Allie (c) vs. Mercedes Martinez at WSU 10th Anniversary Show, for the WSU World Championship (February 11, 2017) · Allie (USA) vs. Gail Kim (CANADA) at SMASH Wrestling CANUSA Classic 2017 (December 3, 2017)

★ Every tale has two sides, and that is true of Laura Denis's wrestling career. The first side is Cherry Bomb, the villainous mean girl independent wrestler who became entwined in a blood feud with the "different" Courtney Rush. The second is Allie, the annoying, yet naïve assistant to Maria Kanellis-Bennett turned ultimate underdog and best friend with the demon assassin Rosemary. Both are technically the same woman—and the same goes for Courtney Rush and Rosemary—but depending on when and where, you would never know from their personalities.

Trained by the now defunct Squared Circle Training wrestling school in Toronto, 18-year-old Laura Dennis was given the professional wrestling name "Cherry Bomb" by her head trainer, Rob Etcheverria. Debuting in 2005, Cherry Bomb mostly worked the Canadian and Northeastern United States independent promotion circuit at places like Pure Wrestling Association, Capital City Championship Combat, Great Canadian Wrestling, Northern Championship Wrestling (nCw). Unfortunately, in September 2007, Cherry Bomb suffered a neck injury during a match, putting her on the shelf until March.

Following her injury, Cherry Bomb began wrestling in bigger Independent promotions, from Ring of Honor (ROH) to the

"TV Ready" (or #TVReady) trio. Cherry Bomb also debuted at SHIMMER Women Athletes in the fall of 2008, but it wasn't until 2013 (in SHINE) that she formed her memorable heel tag team with Kimber Lee, The Kimber Bombs (originally known as Team Combat Zone). The Kimber Bombs eventually won the SHINE Tag Team titles at SHINE 25 and won the SHIMMER Tag Team titles (which they held for over a year) a month later at SHIMMER Volume 72.

During their reign of supremacy, The KimberBombs faced off against Courtney Rush and Vanessa Kraven in a tag team match at SMASH Wrestling's Super Showdown III, taking Kraven out with their SHINE Tag Team Championship belts and beating a defenseless Rush (who Cherry Bomb had already been feuding with) unconscious. But they didn't just stop there, and Cherry Bomb cut Rush's hair while Kimber Lee held her down. Little did anyone know what an iconic feud would come as a result of this attack. What followed were multiple videos leading up to the next event of "a very different" Rush, seemingly "possessed" and who would eventually see Cherry Bomb in all of her opponents during matches. Cherry Bomb ended up suffering from a broken collarbone a couple of weeks after the original haircut incident and wouldn't show her face in SMASH again until that November, in a pre-tape video airing during one of Courtney's matches. Mocking Courtney for looking "a little bit different," she flaunted the ponytail she'd kept as a trophy. Then later that month, Cherry Bomb showed up in person during another one of Courtney's matches, in a sling from collarbone surgery but still 100% ready for a battle of barbs. This time, Cherry Bomb made clear that she wasn't scared of the "crazy" and "pathetic" Courtney Rush—in fact, she called herself "a trillion

women's promotion SHINE to promotions in Japan. After debuting in WSU in 2010, she won the WSU Championship against LuFisto. She held that title from May 2015 to February 2017 (for 644 days), losing it to the longest reigning champ in WSU history, Mercedes Martinez, after claiming to be the most dominant champion in the company's history and a symbol of the future, unlike Mercedes, the past. (Funnily enough, she started her reign as Cherry Bomb and ended it as Allie.) But it was her work in SHIMMER, Combat Zone Wrestling (CZW), and SMASH Wrestling where the sadistic, egotistical mean girl (to put it lightly) character became synonymous with Cherry Bomb. She joined CZW in 2012 alongside her real-life boyfriend (now husband) Pepper Parks, where the two of them eventually worked as the heel pairing of The Power Fitness Couple before joining forces with fellow CZW wrestler BLK Jeez to form the times better" than Rush. And once she was healed up, she was coming for Rush, not the other way around.

As the best villains are the ones who think they're the heroes of their stories, Cherry Bomb's continued poking of the bear—or demon, in this case—with Courtney was impressive, if not absolutely ill-advised. Cherry Bomb officially returned to SMASH in January, accompanying Kimber Lee to the ring for a match against Courtney Rush. Rush beat Kimber Lee in a match, leading Cherry Bomb to bust out a stake-cross (à la her admitted inspiration, Buffy the Vampire Slayer) to take down the possessed foe. Rush then threatened to chop off Kimber Lee's hair—to which the audience chanted "CUT IT OFF" and "CHOP"—and a surprisingly empathetic Cherry Bomb pleaded with her to stop "tormenting" innocent people so they could finish this one-on-one, without weapons. In what momentarily looked like a possible face turn for Cherry Bomb, she immediately went back on her word as soon as Kimber Lee was released and attempted to stake Rush . . . which was presented by Rush spitting a mysterious mist in her eyes. The next month Cherry Bomb and Courtney Rush got into a pull-apart brawl in the ring—where Cherry Bomb threw her shoe at Rush—not wanting to wait until the former was medically cleared to wrestle. But they did and met in the main event of SMASH's March event Any Given Sunday 4, a match that Cherry Bomb came out to the Buffy The Vampire Slayer theme song for and ended in disqualification but certainly didn't end the feud. Instead, coming full circle, the two women went face to face at Super Showdown IV—a year after the feud escalated to this level—now under their TNA Impact Wrestling ring names, Allie and Rosemary (the demon that possessed Courtney Rush). But that still wasn't enough, and the two women faced off once more in SMASH Wrestling's first Steel Cage match, two months later. The demon defeated the slayer, and all was finally right in the world.

But going back a few months before the end of the war between the slayer and the demon, Cherry Bomb made her official TNA Impact Wrestling debut in the spring of 2016, as Allie. (While Pepper Parks made his debut for the company as well, in the summer and as a face named Braxton Sutter.) Despite over a decade of experience under Cherry Bomb's belt, for the purposes of the storyline, Allie had absolutely none. The annoying—but eager to please—Allie was the apprentice to new Impact Wrestling hire and the self-proclaimed "First Lady of Professional Wrestling" Maria Kanellis. Allie was dedicated to "Miss Maria," always trying her best to do a good job and please her boss, only to constantly be talked down to by Maria, Maria's muscle Sienna, and eventually, Maria's rich friend Laurel Van Ness. Because of the way Maria and the rest of The Lady Squad treated Allie, she slowly started to gain the support of the Impact Wrestling fans, but it wasn't until she accidentally won the TNA Knockouts Championship (from Sienna) in a five-way match—which she was put in in order to stack the odds in Sienna's favor—that she officially made her face turn. However, the next week, Maria made her drop the championship to her in a "match," forcing her assistant to lie down and essentially gift her the championship. For months, Allie was tortured by Maria, Sienna, and Laurel, but she found some semblance of peace in her budding friendship and flirtation with Braxton Sutter. Sutter even began "training" Allie to wrestle, as the Allie character required Cherry Bomb to underplay her wrestling ability (an act she's called "incredibly challenging"). However, Laurel decided she wanted Braxton for herself, so she and Maria schemed to force him to date her and eventually propose to her.

In one of the most memorable segments in TNA history, at the wedding of Laurel Van Ness and Braxton Sutter—which Maria forced Allie to attend as the ring bearer—Braxton broke things off with Laurel and professed his love for Allie, a move that Allie reciprocated and that sent Laurel Van Ness into a mental tail spin. Maria would try to fire Allie the next week, but in a moment of empowerment, Allie quit. Moving forward, Laurel Van Ness and Sienna would attempt to get revenge on Allie—who would have preferred to focus on her task of having a real Knockouts Championship reign—only to be thwarted by an unlikely new ally on Allie's side: "The Demon Assassin" Rosemary. Longtime followers of both Allie/Cherry Bomb and Rosemary/Courtney Rush couldn't believe what was happening, but the newly formed friendship known as "Demon Bunny" combined two of Impact Wrestling's most beloved personalities, as polar opposite as they were. Such is the strangeness of professional wrestling.

★ ALLISON DANGER ★

YEARS ACTIVE: 2000–2013

TRAINED BY: International Wrestling Association (IWA) Cruel School · Steve Corino · Rapid Fire Maldonado · Mike Kehner

BILLED FROM: The City of Angels

ACCOMPLISHMENTS: 1x Independent Wrestling Federation Tag Team Champion (with Rapid Fire Maldonado) · 1x International Catch Wrestling Association (ICWA) Ladies Champion · 1x New Breed Wrestling Association (NBWA) Women's Champion · #21 in 2008 PWI Female 50 · 1x Pro Wrestling WORLD-1 Women's Champion · 1x WCEW/ThunderGirls Divas Champion · 1x WXW Women's Tag Team Champion (with Alere Little Feather)

AKA: Allison Corino · Lt. Desiree Storm · 1/2 of The Dangerous Angels · 1/2 of Regeneration X · member of The Prophecy · member of The Smooth Criminals · 1/2 of You Can Call Me Al

NOTABLE MATCHES: Allison Danger vs. Rebecca Knox at SHIMMER Volume 3 (February 12, 2006) · Allison Danger vs. Rebecca Knox at SHIMMER Volume 6, in a Pure Wrestling Rules match (May 21, 2006) · Allison Danger, Rain, & Ranmaru vs. Daizee Haze, Mickie Knuckles, & Sumie Sakai at CHIKARA Tag World Grand Prix 2006 - Night 3 (February 26, 2006) · Allison Danger vs. Sara Del Rey at ROH The Fifth Anniversary Special: Liverpool (March 3, 2007)

· Allison Danger vs. Sara Del Rey vs. Daizee Haze vs. Lacey (with Rain) at Full Impact Pro (FIP) Hot Summer Nights - Night 1, in a Four-Corner Survival match (June 29, 2007) · The Dangerous Angels (Allison Danger & Sara Del Rey) & Daizee Haze vs. The Minnesota Home Wrecking Crew (Lacey & Rain) (with The YRR) & Amazing Kong at FIP Hot Summer Nights - Night 2 (June 30, 2007) · The Dangerous Angels (Allison Danger & Sara Del Rey) vs. Cheerleader Melissa & MsChif at SHIMMER Volume 17 (April 26, 2008)

★ Allison Danger resented professional wrestling at first. The younger sister of ECW legend Steve Corino, as a kid, Steve would practice wrestling moves on her, which is typically the perfect recipe to leave a poor taste of the sport in someone's mouth. While Allison eventually found something to enjoy about wrestling in the form of the glamorous Miss Elizabeth, Allison found it hard to truly connect to the sport without other girls her age to talk to about it. When she was older, however, she was able to appreciate the sport, and if not for her older brother following his professional wrestling dreams and making it in ECW, Allison might not have entered the business herself. While "Allison Danger" might not be a household name, her importance to the women's independent wrestling scene cannot be undersold.

As Allison would attend her brother's shows, Steve would introduce her to the talent in the locker room. It was there that she met and befriended ECW star Francine, a friendship that soon led to Allison's debut in the wrestling business. Upon attending an IWA Reading (in Pennsylvania) show in May 2000 as a guest of Francine's, another ECW star, The Sandman, asked Allison to fill-in as his valet (as his usual valet, his wife, was unavailable). Allison agreed after Francine encouraged her to do so, and from that point on, she was in the wrestling industry. According to Allison, it was Steve who gave her the "Danger" surname. "When I came in, I used just the name Allison. My brother added the Danger part so my name wouldn't sound boring." Steve was also the one to point her in the direction of the proper wrestling school and even pitched in teaching her himself, as he wanted her to do it right if she was going to do this at all. Danger worked some shows on IWA Reading, as well as on ring crew, and had her first-ever match alongside her trainer Rapid Fire Maldonado in a mixed tag team match.

After appearing on the first ROH show ever (in 2002) as a manager (Danger's preferred nomenclature, over "valet") for The Christopher Street Connection and taking a bump through a table, ROH booker Gabe Sapolsky turned what was supposed to be a one-time deal for Danger into a regular gig. She eventually went on to manage top ROH heel Christopher Daniels and his team, The Prophecy, first feuding with a faction led by her brother called The Group. The Prophecy eventually broke up in 2004, as members BJ Whitmer and Dan Maff turned face and fired Allison Danger as their manager—which led to her enacting revenge by putting a bounty on their heads. After that feud with her former stable mates, Danger briefly feuded with Daizee Haze in early 2005—at a time when women's wrestling in ROH was an absolute rarity—before she left the promotion. (She returned later that year along with Christopher Daniels—who had been written out of ROH to leave for TNA at the beginning of 2004—and remained in the company as his manager, until he left again in 2007.)

In 2005, Danger also cofounded the SHIMMER wrestling promotion out of Chicago alongside wrestling jack of all trades and idea man Daze Prazak. In a sense the all-female version ROH, SHIMMER was formed as a haven for serious women's wrestling, an alternative to the Divas-centric approach to professional wrestling. In addition to commentating alongside Prazak on SHIMMER shows, Danger also competed on them. In fact, Danger was the opponent for a wrestler named Rebecca Knox—who has gone on to a bigger stage as Becky Lynch in WWE—in her debut SHIMMER match. Danger (alongside former foe Daizee Haze) would go on to feud with Knox in the promotion, though the feud was cut short by a severe injury on Knox's part.

Injuries and an eventual pregnancy would end up getting in the way of Danger's in-ring duties for the company, but even then, she would still attend on commentary, as a manager, or whenever she was needed in the promotion. It was announced on April 9, 2013 that Allison Danger would be retiring as an active wrestler after SHIMMER Volume 57. After the match, in which she and Leva Bates (known together as Regeneration X) faced Ayako Hamada and Cheerleader Melissa, Danger revealed the reason behind her retirement: having suffered a stroke that past January and informed of the heightened chance of future strokes, lesions were found on her brain, forcing her to retire as an in-ring competitor. As a matter of fact, Danger didn't even know about the lesions until two hours before she flew out for that particular SHIMMER weekend of shows. Still, Danger remains an integral part of SHIMMER, as well as a strong proponent and matriarch of independent women's wrestling.

★ ALLYSIN KAY ★

YEARS ACTIVE: 2008–present

TRAINED BY: Mathew Priest · Bill Martel · Blue Collar Wrestling Alliance (BCWA)

BILLED FROM: Detroit, Michigan

ACCOMPLISHMENTS: 1x Absolute Intense Wrestling (AIW) Women's Champion · #8 in 2017 PWI Female 50 · 1x WSU Tag Team Champion (with Sassy Stephie) · 1x Global Force Wrestling (GFW) Women's Champion · 2x TNA/GFW/Impact Wrestling Knockouts Champion

AKA: Allysin Kay · "AK-47" · "Mount Crush" · Beth Moore · Maria Maria · member of Valkyrie · 1/2 of Made In Sin · member of The Lady Squad · 1/3 of The Midwest Militia · 1/2 of Team Be Jealous · member of Flexor Industries · Sienna the Savage

NOTABLE MATCHES: Allysin Kay (with Chest Flexor) vs. Mia Yim at AIW Girls Night Out 6, in an Unsanctioned match for the vacant AIW Women's Championship (August 3, 2012) · Made In Sin (Allysin Kay & Taylor Made) vs. Shazza McKenzie & Davina Rose at SHINE 4 (October 19, 2012) · Allysin Kay (c) vs. Athena at AIW Girls Night Out 12, in a No DQ Falls Count Anywhere match for the AIW Women's Championship (March 29, 2014) · Allysin Kay vs. Cherry Bomb (c) at WSU Unshakable, for the WSU World Championship (May 14, 2016) · Team USA (Sienna, Cheerleader Melissa, & Santana Garrett) vs. Team Canada (Allie, KC Spinelli, & Taya) at AAA Lucha Libre World Cup (Women's Division) - Night 2, in the Lucha Libre World Cup (Women's Division) Third Place match (June 5, 2016) · Allysin Kay (TNA) vs. Madison Eagles (c) (SHIMMER) vs. Taylor Made (c) (SHINE) vs. Ivelisse (with Amanda Carolina Rodriguez) at SHINE 35, in a 4 Way match for the SHINE Championship/SHIMMER Championship/TNA Knockouts Championship (June 17, 2016) · Sienna (c) vs. Allie vs. Marti Bell vs. Madison Rayne vs. Jade at TNA Impact Wrestling Turning Point 2016, for the TNA Knockouts Championship (August 25, 2016) · Allysin Kay vs. Chelsea Green at SHINE 42 (May 12, 2017) · Sienna (c) vs. Rosemary at GFW Impact Wrestling, in a Last Knockout Standing match for the GFW Knockouts Championship (July 27, 2017)

⭐ In December 2008, six months into her training at BCWA in Detroit—which opened a year prior, in 2007—Allysin Kay had her debut match. However, it would be a little longer before she wrestled outside of BCWA, eventually debuting in Beyond Wrestling (in March 2010). Having wanted to be a professional wrestler since she was nine years old—she was a big Lita fan growing up—Kay had no problem wrestling women or men. She just wanted to wrestle. Upon debuting in Beyond, the world of independent wrestling seemingly opened up to Kay, soon debuting in AIW, Main Event Championship Wrestling, CAPW, and WSU (which officially broke her out of her Midwest wrestling scene bubble).

This new wrestling world (which eventually led to even bigger exposure in promotions like SHIMMER, SHINE, and ROH)

led Kay to a feud with Jessicka Havok—who defeated Kay in her debut AIW match—across these various promotions. And while Havok came out on top in the feud, she and Kay eventually realized just how similar they were. As a result, they formed a tag team called "Team Be Jealous," choosing to direct their energy at destroying others instead of themselves. Eventually, Team Be Jealous evolved into a trio (including Sassy Stephie) forming in WSU called "The Midwest Militia," with Kay and Stephie winning the WSU Tag Team Championship in March 2012—only finally losing the championship two years later.

By 2013, Kay was incorporating (what her character considered to be) class into her repertoire, coming out to the ring with peacock feathers, keeping her pinkies up in even the highest pressure of situations. It's the gimmick most wrestling fans aware of her associate her with. As the AIW Women's Champion, Kay's ego had only gotten bigger, proclaiming that she was the best wrestler in the entire world. And for everyone who didn't believe her—especially in AIW—she had a signature machete (which Kay would eventually go on to auction off years later) to help prove them wrong.

BY 2013, KAY WAS INCORPORATING CLASS INTO HER REPERTOIRE. IT'S THE GIMMICK MOST WRESTLING FANS ASSOCIATE HER WITH.

However, that certainly proved to be an uphill battle, as Kay first had to get past Mia Yim to become the champion. Their feud began back at AIW Girls Night Out 5 in 2012, in a match Yim won . . . as well as one in which Yim actually broke Kay's nose. (As a result, Kay began wearing a pink mask to the ring.) A few months later, at Girls Night Out 6, the two women duked it out in an Unsanctioned match (where fans brought the weapons, including a plastic AK-47) to determine the new AIW Women's Champion. Kay won that match with the help of her Flexor Industries stablemates, but wanting to prove that she could beat Yim on her own, there was a rubber match a few months later at Girls Night Out 7 . . . inside of a steel cage. Again, Kay won, proving her supremacy as the AIW Women's Champion. She'd hold onto the championship until Girls Night Out 12 in the spring of 2014, losing it to Athena in a No Disqualification match (and failing to recapture it from her in the No Disqualification rematch).

In the spring of 2016, it was announced that Allysin Kay had been signed to an Impact Wrestling contract. She debuted as Maria Kanellis-Bennett's new muscle, "Sienna," during Kanellis-Bennett's Knockouts Championship feud with Jade (aka Allysin Kay's longtime rival, Mia Yim) and Gail Kim. As part of Maria's Lady Squad (eventually alongside Laurel Van Ness, as well), Sienna eventually won the Knockouts Championship that summer, at the Slammiversary pay-per-view, losing it a couple of months later to Maria's put-upon assistant Allie in a Five-Way match. (As a result, Maria would force Allie to lie down and lose the championship to her.) After Maria's departure from the company in early 2017, Sienna remained close with Laurel Van Ness—who had suffered a psychotic break after a failed wrestling wedding—and opposed to Allie—who she blamed for Laurel's state—while also feuding with the new authority figure in the form of Karen Jarrett. That spring, Impact Wrestling introduced wrestler Kevin Matthews as Sienna's cousin, "KM," and Kongo Kong, as a monster Sienna programmed to help Laurel get revenge on Allie. She also won the Knockouts Championship for the second time that year, losing it months later at the Bound For Glory pay-per-view to a retiring Gail Kim (who Sienna had wanted to destroy the legacy of).

In January 2018, Sienna was rushed to the hospital after a round of Impact tapings, where they discovered she had a blood clot in each of her lungs. But even in the hospital, she kept her class: pinkies up all the way.

★ ALUNDRA BLAYZE ★

YEARS ACTIVE: 1984–2001

TRAINED BY: Brad Rheingans · Eddie Sharkey · AJW Dojo

BILLED FROM: Milan, Italy

ACCOMPLISHMENTS: 3x WWF Women's Champion · WWE Hall of Fame Class of 2015 · 2x IWA World Women's Champion · 1989 AJW Tag League the Best (with Mitsuko Nishiwaki) · 1x American Wrestling Association (AWA) World Women's/Ladies Champion · 1x International World Class Championship Wrestling (IWCCW) Women's Champion · 1988 PWI Rookie of the Year · 1x WCW Cruiserweight Champion

AKA: Madusa · "Made in the USA" · Madusa Miceli · member of The Diamond Exchange · member of Team Madness · member of The Dangerous Alliance

NOTABLE MATCHES: Madusa Miceli (with Nick Kiniski) vs. Candi Devine at AWA, for the vacant AWA World Women's Championship (December 27, 1987) · Madusa, Kaoru Maeda, & Mika Takahashi vs. Aja Kong, Bison Kimura, & Grizzly Iwamoto at Universal Pro-Wrestling (June 7, 1990) · Madusa Miceli vs. Luna Vachon at TWA Summer Sizzler II (August 3, 1991) · Madusa Miceli & Eddie Gilbert vs. Luna Vachon & Cactus Jack at TWA Autumn Armageddon II, in a Hair vs. Hair Mixed Tag Team match (September 21, 1991) · Alundra Blayze (c) vs. Bull Nakano (with Luna Vachon) at WWF SummerSlam 1994, for the WWF Women's Championship (August 29, 1994) · Alundra Blayze (c) vs. Bull Nakano at AJW Doumu Super Woman Great War ~ Big Egg Wrestling Universe, for the WWF Women's Championship (November 20, 1994) · Madusa vs. Akira Hokuto at WCW Starrcade 1996, in the WCW World Women's Championship Tournament Finals (December 29, 1996)

★ Madusa (like "Made in the USA") Miceli was the first woman to be crowned PWI's Rookie of the Year, as well as the first foreign wrestler to sign a contract with AJW. Yet when she started training under Eddie Sharkey and wrestling in 1984 on the independent wrestling scene, she was only making $5 a match, wrestling four nights a week. That was a far cry from the nursing job as a home health aide she left to pursue this career, but it ended up being worth it (even though she first lost her house and car as a result of that pursuit). Two years later, business picked up in a major way for the woman known as Madusa Miceli, as she started wrestling in AWA, immediately feuding with Sherri Martel and eventually taking her spot once Martel left the promotion. Martel's departure also left the AWA World Women's Championship vacant, allowing Miceli to defeat Candi Devine for the belt (in her first shot at the title) to close out 1987. As champion, Miceli would also manage AWA World Heavyweight Champion Curt Henning, eventually joining him (before he left for WWF) in the stable The Diamond Exchange. Losing the championship a little less than a year after winning it, to Wendi Richter, Miceli enlisted her Diamond Exchange brethren to help in her feud with Richter. This led to a mixed tag team match on AWA's first and only pay-per-view, SuperClash III.

This type of domination was seemingly par for the course when it came to Madusa Miceli's wrestling career. Miceli's first wrestling tour of Japan—for six weeks in 1989, in which she held the IWA World Women's Championship for a day—quickly turned into a three-year deal at AJW and her becoming part of Aja Kong's dominant Jungle Jack stable. With this deal came a new kind of notoriety, outside of the standard wrestling territory form. There were Madusa posters, Madusa action figures, a *Who's Madusa?* CD (in which she sang in Japanese) and music videos to accompany it—the sky was the limit. After that, she was signed by WCW as a member of (and "Director of Covert Operations" for) Paul "Paul E. Dangerously" Heyman's faction, The Dangerous Alliance. There she mostly served as a Rick Rude's valet, but she eventually got her chance to show her in-ring stuff once more when she made the jump to WWF.

Miceli was brought into the WWF to revive the Women's Division in 1993—three years after the WWF Women's

Championship had first become vacant—under the ring name Alundra Blayze (as she owned the trademark for "Madusa Miceli"). As part of this rebirth of the division, Blayze pushed for the WWF to bring in new women for her to compete with and to expose to the American wrestling audience. This led to the signing of Blayze's former AJW colleague Bull Nakano as her major rival in the company. Blayze and Nakano had a women's championship match at WWF SummerSlam 1994—with Nakano managed by Luna Vachon, Miceli's old Tri-State Wrestling Alliance (TWA) rival—in which Blayze retained, yet she lost the rematch in November at the Tokyo Dome, at the historic AJW Big Egg Wrestling Universe show. Alundra Blayze would go on to win the WWF Women's Championship two more times in 1995, but her third championship reign wasn't exactly a joyous one. The way the story goes, WWF released Blayze that December due to budget cuts. After her departure, the Women's Division entered a dark ages of sorts—at least, in terms of athletic competition—as the championship remained vacant until 1998.

Blayze then returned to WCW, a week after she was released from WWF, immediately firing the first shot in the Monday

Night Wars (the infamous feud between WWF and WCW at the time) by throwing her WWF Women's Championship belt in the trash on live television and saying, "That's what I think of the WWF Women's Championship belt." (Years later, Miceli would admit to regretting her decision to perform the act—which she also claimed was the result of Eric Bischoff pushing hard for the idea.) She also returned to the Madusa moniker, making clear that Madusa was her name, not "Alundra Blayze." Again, a major promotion wanted to build its Women's Division around Madusa, and as a result, the WCW Women's Championship was created in December 1996. Madusa even brought in her rival Bull Nakano as competition again. But Madusa never won the championship, and it was retired in September 1997, not even a year old. And while Madusa's second stint in WCW lasted longer and allowed her to wrestle more than her first one, it didn't exactly set the wrestling world ablaze—even though she became the first woman to win the WCW Cruiserweight Championship during her run. While she was with the company, she was able to train women at WCW's training school, The Power Plant, including future WCW and WWF/WWE women such as Torrie Wilson, Stacy Keibler, and Molly Holly.

Miceli left WCW and retired from professional wrestling altogether in 2001, citing a combination of the news that WWF owner Vince McMahon was going to buy WCW and the changing in direction of women's wrestling at the time to T&A-based gimmick matches (like the Bra & Panties match or the Lingerie Pillowfight match). Having entered the world of monster trucks in 1999, Miceli made that her post-wrestling career.

In spring of 2015, Miceli entered into the WWE Hall of Fame under the Alundra Blayze moniker, alongside "Macho Man" Randy Savage, Kevin Nash, and Rikishi, to name a few. The announcement of this induction was a surprise, as Miceli had essentially been blacklisted from the WWE for the previous 20 years because of her trash can moment on WCW. But on that stage, at WrestleMania 31 weekend, she brought out a trash can to finally take out the WWF Women's Championship that

was once so greatly disrespected and bring it "where it belongs" after all these years. Then, in the fall of 2015, she became the American commissioner of the Japanese *joshi puroresu* promotion World Wonder Ring STARDOM (STARDOM, for short), getting back to her roots in a sense.

Since her induction, Alundra Blayze has appeared in other WWE programming, such as the Mae Young Classic as well as an episode of the WWE Network original program *Table For 3* (with fellow former WWE women's wrestlers Ivory and Molly Holly) and as a participant in the battle royal at WWE's first-ever all-women's pay-per-view, Evolution. The WWE Network also released an Alundra Blayze documentary called *TrailBlayzer* about Miceli's work in professional wrestling and monster truck driving. After 20 years of being painted as the villain in WWE's history, that has to mean a lot. But to quote Miceli herself: "The way I see it is who gives a heck if you fall down, just try again. Look, my life has been filled with failure, upon failure, upon failure. But, from my experience, success is built upon failures."

★ ANGELINA LOVE ★

YEARS ACTIVE: 2000–present

TRAINED BY: Rob "El Fuego" Etcheverria · Squared Circle Training · DSW · OVW · Bill DeMott · Lance Storm

BILLED FROM: Toronto, Ontario, Canada

ACCOMPLISHMENTS: 2009 PWI Woman of the Year Runner-up · 2010 PWI Woman of the Year Runner-up · #2 in 2009 PWI Female 50 · #2 in 2010 PWI Female 50 · 1x Pro Wrestling Pride Women's Championship · 6x TNA Knockouts Champion · 1x TNA Knockouts Tag Team Champion (with Winter) · 2015 TNA Global Impact Tournament (with Team International)

AKA: Angel Williams · Angel · Canadian Angel · member of La Legión Extranjera (The Foreign Legion) · member of The Embassy · member of The Beautiful People · 1/3 of Mi Pi Sexy (Mi∇⊖)

NOTABLE MATCHES: The Beautiful People (Angelina Love & Velvet Sky) & Awesome Kong (with Raisha Saeed) vs. Gail Kim, ODB, & Taylor Wilde at TNA Hard Justice 2008 (August 10, 2008) · Angelina Love vs. Awesome Kong (c) vs. Taylor Wilde at TNA Lockdown 2009, in a Six Sides of Steel Cage match for the TNA Knockouts Championship (April 19, 2009) · Angelina Love vs. Awesome Kong (c) at TNA Sacrifice 2009, for the TNA Knockouts Championship (May 24, 2009) · Angelina Love vs. Gail Kim (c) at TNA Impact Wrestling, in a Last Knockout Standing match for the TNA Knockouts Championship (August 20, 2014) · Christina Von Eerie vs. Su Yung vs. Nicole Matthews vs. Angelina Love at DEFY Wrestling DEFY4 GIGANTIC - Night 1, in a 4 Way Elimination match for the inaugural Women's Tacoma Cup (June 29, 2017) · Angelina Love & Davey Richards vs. Alisha Edwards & Eddie Edwards at Impact Wrestling Slammiversary XV, in a Full Metal Mayhem match (July 2, 2017)

⭐ Before she was the leader of TNA's The Beautiful People, Angelina Love was just a wrestling fan from Toronto, Canada. Inspired by the work of Shawn Michaels—as opposed to his rival, Canadian's beloved Bret Hart—she was known as the wrestling girl at school, even being voted "Most Likely To Become a Wrestler" in her high school yearbook. After she graduated, she asked a friend who was ring announcing at independent wrestling promotions in the United States for advice on how to get started in local Ontario wrestling promotions. She ended up training at Rob "El Fuego" Etcheverria's Squared Circle Pro Wrestling in 2000, getting her start on the Canadian independent wrestling scene as "Angel Williams." Williams started as a valet/manager, first to "Dangerboy" Derek Wylde, then eventually for future fellow TNA Wrestling colleagues Chris Sabin, Eric Young, and Scott D'Amore, among others. Her work as a valet even led to her being voted Impact Wrestling Federation's "Manager of the Year" in her debut year. But Williams wanted to do more than just stand ringside for the wrestlers: She wanted to be a wrestler.

Williams wouldn't make her official in-ring debut until the summer of 2002, but two years later, she ended up being scouted by WWE and offered a tryout. After the initial tryout, WWE had her come in to train a bit at OVW and even work a *RAW* and *SmackDown* taping. A month later, the then 23-year-old Williams was offered a developmental contract with the company, courtesy of a "Merry Christmas, we're signing you" phone call. Reporting to Deep South Wrestling (DSW), located in McDonough, Georgia, she still wrestled under the ring name Angel Williams. But unfortunately for Williams, her time in WWE—even as just a developmental star—wasn't the fairytale end to her girlhood dream of wrestling superstardom. Again, Williams found herself on the valet side of things, managing wrestler Johnny Parisi her first summer in DSW. But in September 2005, she finally had her first match in developmental, against (and beating) future WWE Women's and Divas Champion Michelle McCool. She went on to feud with a fellow Rob Etcheverria trainee, Shantelle Taylor, whom she would later go on to feud with again in TNA (with Williams under the name Angelina Love and Taylor as Taylor Wilde).

At the end of February 2006, Williams had to get knee surgery to repair a torn ACL and ended up being on the shelf for seven months. According to Kevin Matthews, who was in developmental the same time as Williams and has been outspoken about Bill DeMott's abuse of power as a head trainer, the injury was sustained as a result of DeMott forcing an already hurt Williams to do 40 up and overs until her patella tendon snapped. Once she returned to DSW that November, she feuded with the promotion's kayfabe General Manager Krissy Vaine, a wrestler who abused her power and had other Divas interfere in Williams's matches to send her a message. The feud led to Vaine and Williams learning to co-exist and becoming co-GMs together. At the same time, Angel Williams was constantly on the verge of being called up to the WWE's main roster; things just didn't turn out that way, for one reason or another. When she originally returned from the injury, she managed the tag team The Gymini and was supposed to come up to the main roster with them, but once they tanked in their first appearances in WWE, they were released from their contracts at the beginning of 2007 and Williams was stuck in developmental. There were also earlier talks of Angel Williams working as JBL's consultant on *SmackDown*, but the combination of her injury and Jillian Hall impressing Vince McMahon prevented that idea from coming to fruition. And proving that anything truly can happen in the WWE, Angel Williams eventually was going to make her main roster debut on *SmackDown*—as Matt Hardy's new girlfriend—to the point where she was seated in the crowd for the segment, only to be told right before it was supposed to happen that the segment got cut and Vince had rewritten the entire show.

Luck apparently just wasn't on Williams's side during her time in WWE developmental. In April 2007, DSW shut down, and Williams (along with her fellow developmental colleagues) was moved to Louisville, Kentucky, to train at OVW. Her OVW debut was that May, in a dark match against Serena . . . and that was it. Two days later, Angel Williams was released from her developmental contract. Rumor has it WWE had a problem with her braids—and that she refused to take them out—and her look, but no confirmation has been made on the actual reason. Williams has since been vocally open about the possibility of signing with WWE, but she has also said that her time in developmental "was a traumatic wrestling experience" where she "was never really given a chance," given the culture of training and WWE Divas at the time.

Post-WWE developmental, Williams returned to Canadian indies like Elite Canadian Championship Wrestling (ECCW). She also made her Mexican wrestling debut in AAA, where she was introduced by fellow TNA alumni Konnan as "Canadian Angel"—a new guest member of the stable La Legión Extranjera (The Foreign Legion)—during the summer of 2007. But she wouldn't be in Mexico long, as she was contacted by TNA—having wrestled some performance enhancement matches in 2004, before she got signed by WWE—to become a part of their Knockouts Division. That year, her first match involved her participating in a 10-woman Gauntlet for the Gold to crown the inaugural TNA Knockouts Champion (at Bound For Glory, TNA Impact Wrestling's equivalent of

WrestleMania). A month later, she found herself in a four-way match (at Genesis) competing for the championship against Gail Kim (the champion), ODB, and Roxxi Laveaux.

Williams came up short both times, but her luck finally turned around immediately after, as she joined up with the newly named Velvet Sky (formerly Talia Madison) as Angelina Love. Both the Love and Sky characters were named after actual porn stars, an intentionally titillating choice that also led to the babyface duo being known as "Velvet-Love Entertainment." Velvet-Love Entertainment lasted for a year until their heel turn, which is when The Beautiful People came in. With this, Love and Sky had characters other than "hot girls," as they took inspiration from Paris Hilton, Nicole Richie, and *Mean Girls*. It started toward the end of their face run, as fellow Knockout Roxxi Laveaux (their first feud) warned them of a premonition she'd had about them being in danger. Not heeding Roxxi's warning, they instead offered her a makeover. When Roxxi wouldn't accept the makeover, they snapped, becoming The Beautiful People, enemies of all things "ugly." This all came to a head—literally—at Sacrifice 2008 when Angelina Love interfered in the Ladder match portion of the Makeover Battle Royal. As Angelina Love had come in third place—meaning she was the last participant in the Battle Royal not to end up in the Ladder match—to ensure that she would not get her head shaved and Roxxi would, she interfered in the match to make sure Gail Kim would win (as Kim had won a Shears-On-Pole match for immunity on an episode of TNA *Impact!*). The Beautiful People would then go on to mock Roxxi and celebrated with her shaved off hair, which was only the beginning of their shallow behavior. Eventually, they would put paper bags on the heads of their fallen opponents and spray hairspray in their faces to win matches, in addition to enlisting other members such as Kip James as their "fashionist" Cute Kip and Madison Rayne, a pledge to The Beautiful People's newly formed "sorority," Mi Pi Sexy (Mi∇⊖). Again, in the form of Mi Pi Sexy, The Beautiful People went with the easy titillation, though TNA never quite acknowledged the sorority name as an official aspect of the characters—even with all of the hazing and initiation rituals they put Madison Rayne through.

With The Beautiful People by her side, Angelina Love won the Knockouts Championship against her stable's nemesis, Taylor Wilde, and then champion Awesome Kong in a 3-Way Six Sides of Steel Cage match. She continued to hold onto the championship thanks to interference from Sky, Rayne, and Kip . . . until a few months later, on an episode of TNA *Impact!*, as she defended the championship against Tara, without the help of The Beautiful People. She would win back the championship that same month at Victory Road 2009, thanks to Madison Rayne seducing the referee. However, Love would lose the championship again the next month and then be released by TNA that September, due to visa issues. Once she was able to return in the beginning of January, she returned as a babyface,

feuding with The Beautiful People (including her replacement in the group, Lacey Von Erich) and even teaming with Tara, her former rival. After winning the Knockouts Championship for the third time, however, in a "Lockbox elimination match" (in which the lockbox Love won the championship), Tara slowly turned heel on her, striking as soon as Love lost the Knockouts Championship again (this time to Madison Rayne). Unfortunately for Love, before the feud could really get started, an arm injury two days after Tara turned on her put her on the shelf for a month, and it wasn't until a month after she was cleared that she'd return to TNA.

By August 2010, Angelina Love would win the Knockouts Champion two more times (making it five reigns), as well as reunite with Velvet Sky (against Madison Rayne) to reform The Beautiful People. And then that fall, after losing the Knockouts Championship to Tara, Love would enter into a bizarre (and ultimately, incomplete) storyline with the debuting Knockout (and supposed fan of Love's) called Winter. For a month, Winter appeared in backstage vignettes with Love, as seemingly a figment of her imagination, until she finally showed up to save Love during a backstage brawl between Knockouts. A month later, Angelina Love and Winter would win the TNA Knockouts Tag Team Championship from Madison Rayne and Tara. During this time, however, The Beautiful People had not yet broken up again, and Velvet Sky accused Winter of trying to break them up. That would soon come to fruition though, as Velvet Sky would accidentally cost Love and Winter the tag belts, and Winter would reveal a form of mind control over Love in the form of drink she'd called "medicine." This would officially turn Love heel again, as Winter's control forced Love to feud with Sky and attack anyone Winter saw as a threat. Eventually, Angelina Love chose to do Winter's bidding without the "medicine," but the story petered out after that, with no firm conclusion or feud between the two as a result of this mind control—a move that many fans considered the death knell of her career in TNA. By July 2012, Love was out of TNA for real this time.

She returned in 2014 for another heel Beautiful People reunion with Sky—which saw an alliance with the roster's male equivalents, The BroMans—and even became a six-time Knockouts Champion—second only to another pioneer of the Knockouts Division, Gail Kim—in the process. Then in the fall of 2015, The Beautiful People (with Madison Rayne) reunited again, this time as faces against The Dollhouse, who were essentially the newer model. But this last reunion was cut short by Love's actual pregnancy, and her contract with TNA expired in spring of 2016. Love's fourth and most recent return to TNA was during its brand to Impact Wrestling/Global Force Wrestling (GFW) in the first half of 2017, this time specifically for her feud between her then husband Davey Richards and his former tag team Eddie Edwards. This feud involved Eddie's wife, Alisha Edwards, getting involved and ultimately led to a tag team Full Metal Mayhem match at Impact Wrestling's Slammiversary XV between the two couples. After Slammiversary, she left the company once more and continued on with her work on the independent scene as Angelina Love. To this day, Angelina Love is considered one of the founding members of TNA Impact Wrestling's Knockouts Division.

★ ASUKA ★

YEARS ACTIVE: 2004-present

TRAINED BY: Yuki Ishikawa · WWE Performance Center

BILLED FROM: Osaka, Japan

ACCOMPLISHMENTS: 5x DDT Pro-Wrestling Ironman Heavymetalweight Champion · 1x JWP Joshi Puroresu Openweight Champion · 2013 JWP Joshi Puroresu Best Bout Award (vs. Arisa Nakajima, on December 15) · 2013 JWP Joshi Puroresu Enemy Award · 1x Kuzu Pro Diva Champion · 1x NEO Japan Ladies Pro Wrestling Tag Team Champion (with Nanae Takahashi) · 2011 Osaka Joshi Pro Wrestling One Day Tag Tournament (with Mio Shirai)

· #1 in 2017 PWI Female 50 · 2x Pro Wrestling WAVE Tag Team Champion (1x with Ayumi Kurihara, 1x with Mio Shirai) · 2011 Pro Wrestling WAVE Catch the WAVE · 2011 Pro Wrestling WAVE Dual Shock WAVE (with Ayumi Kurihara) · 1x Reina Joshi Puroresu World Tag Team Champion (with Arisa Nakajima) · 1x Reina World Women's Champion · 2014 Reina World Tag Team Championship Tournament (with Arisa Nakajima) · 2x (and inaugural) SMASH Diva Champion · 2011 SMASH Diva Championship Tournament · 1x NXT Women's Champion · 2016 NXT Year-End Award for Female Competitor of the Year · 2018 WWE Women's Royal Rumble

AKA: Kana · Kana-hime · Ramen Woman · Sekai no Kana ("World Famous Kana") · Skull Reaper Kana · 1/2 of Triple Tails.S · 1/3 of Triple Tails · member of Passion Red · "The Empress of Tomorrow"

NOTABLE MATCHES: Kana vs. Syuri at SMASH.4 (June 25, 2010) · Kana vs. LuFisto at SHIMMER Volume 44 (October 2, 2011) · Kana vs. Sara Del Rey at CHIKARA Klunk In Love (October 8, 2011) · Kana vs. Arisa Nakajima (c) at JWP Joshi Puroresu Pure Slam 2013, for the JWP Openweight Title (August 18, 2013) · Kana vs. Meiko Satomura at Kana Pro Mania (February 25, 2014) · Kana & Naomichi Marufuji vs. Meiko Satomura & Minoru Suzuki at Kana Produce ProMania Reach (June 16, 2014) · Asuka vs. Emma (with Dana Brooke) at NXT TakeOver: London (December 16, 2015) · Asuka (c) vs. Bayley at NXT TakeOver: Brooklyn II, for the NXT Women's Championship (August 20, 2016) · Asuka (c) vs. Billie Kay vs. Peyton Royce vs. Nikki Cross at NXT TakeOver: San Antonio, in a Fatal 4-Way match for the NXT Women's Championship (January 28, 2017) · Asuka (c) vs. Nikki Cross vs. Ruby Riot at NXT TakeOver: Chicago, in an Elimination Triple Threat match for the NXT Women's Championship (May 20, 2017) · Asuka vs. Nikki Cross at NXT, in a Last Woman Standing match for the NXT Women's Championship (June 28, 2017)· Asuka (c) vs. Ember Moon at NXT TakeOver: Brooklyn III, for the NXT Women's Championship (August 19, 2017)

★ Nobody is ready for Asuka." In WWE, that was the catchphrase—the battle cry—that seemed like it would never be disproven. For over two years, no other woman had been able to stop Asuka, even when they appeared to be as close to her equal as possible. But the question in modern WWE also became: *Does Asuka have an equal?*

Getting her professional wrestling start in 2004—as Kana—she was originally drawn to professional wrestling by the work of male wrestlers, not female. To name a few, The Great Muta, Tiger Mask, Yoshiaki Fujiwara, Antonio Inoki, Nobukiko Takada, and Minoru Suzuki greatly inspired Kana. (And in the case of Suzuki, that adoration would lead to quite the uncomfortable intergender wrestling match.) These competitors were notable for their innovation in the sport of professional wrestling, especially in the form of strong style, "catch-as-catch-can" wrestling, and even bringing a more Mixed Martial Arts approach to sports entertainment. These were the wrestlers who brought realism and authenticity to a "fake" sport, and their influences can be felt in this woman's own wrestling style. With that in mind, it also makes sense that Kana chose to be trained by Yuki Ishikawa, founder of the short-lived Battlarts wrestling promotion (which ran from 1996 to 2011): Battlarts had an emphasis on strong style and a more contact-heavy approach to professional wrestling. Kana even wrestled on the final Battlarts show, in a singles match against Aki Shizuku.

She debuted and wrestled primarily in AtoZ, the offshoot of the Aja Kong-founded ARSION *joshi puroresu* promotion. AtoZ was around from 2003 to 2006, and like the promotion, Kana first called her professional wrestling career quits in 2006. She retired that March, due to chronic nephritis (a kidney disease), returning to her other passion and opening her own graphic design agency. But the retirement was short-lived, as Kana surprisingly returned to the ring in September the next year. This time, there was no sign of her stopping. In October 2009, she would earn her first wrestling championship alongside fellow Passion Red faction member Nanae Takahashi for the NEO Japan Ladies Pro Wrestling Tag Team Championship. They would only hold the titles for two months, and NEO would close by the end of 2010, but given Kana's newfound passion for wrestling, she wasn't wrestling just in one place

this time around. She just wouldn't be wrestling anywhere Nanae Takahashi was working—such as STARDOM, which Takahashi cofounded—as Kana would leave Passion Red in the beginning of 2010, due to a legitimate feud with her tag team partner. In fact, this tension even led to the two of them turning a promo into a shoot argument in the heat of the moment, with Takahashi slapping Kana. That would be the end of Passion Red. After NEO closed, Kana became a regular (while still working in other promotions without fully committing to just one) in the Pro Wrestling WAVE promotion, and that's where she formed the heel faction Triple Tails with the joshi sister duo of team Mio and Io Shirai. Once Io left the faction to work as a singles wrestler, Kana and Mio worked as the tag team Triple Tails.S.

"NOBODY IS READY FOR ASUKA."

But a major part of the reason behind Triple Tails' inception was as a result of Kana finding herself on the wrong side of the joshi community—not from her in-ring antics but because of something outside the ring. Again, calling on her preference for men's wrestling over women's wrestling, Kana wrote what was known as her "Joshi Manifesto," an article for Japan's *Weekly Pro-Wrestling* publication. In the article, she offered five "suggestions" to change women's wrestling (specifically joshi) for the better. The manifesto essential boiled down to the concept of calling for joshi wrestlers to stop wrestling like girls and to get out of the business if they're not at a certain quality level. Despite the somewhat reasonable (albeit harsh) argument behind these suggestions, considering Kana's lack of veteran experience and propensity to wrestle an even stiffer style than the already stiff joshi talent pool (which Nanae Takahashi originally called her out for, thus causing the rift between them)—and the fact that she had previously retired from wrestling, no matter how short the time and for why—the reaction was far from positive among the movers and shakers in Japan's *joshi puro* scene. Eventually, the heat from the manifesto was used as fuel for storylines for Kana. In fact, if anything, the scorn she inspired from writing the piece only made her a hot commodity, even if it initially made her persona non grata on the joshi circuit. Especially since the manifesto would allow her heel character to play even more superior compared to women's wrestlers; after all, the best wrestling characters are simply the wrestler's personality turned up to 11. After the manifesto dropped, Tajiri brought her into Japan's new SMASH promotion (not to be confused with Canada's SMASH Wrestling promotion)—arguably, she wrote the article specifically as a way to become the top heel in SMASH—where she would be known as "The World Famous" Kana. She would even read from her "Joshi Manifesto," out loud, at SMASH events. The rest was Triple Tails history.

Kana would also book her own joshi events under both the Kana Pro (from 2010–2015) and Triple Tails.S (in 2011) banners, with the former leading to Kana competing against Minoru Suzuki in the aforementioned hard-to-watch intergender tag team match, as well as teaming with him months later in an intergender tag team match against another one of her wrestling inspirations, Yoshiaki Fujiwara. Kana made her American wrestling debut at SHIMMER Volume 41 (in October 2011), against Mia Yim, again bringing her disrespect for women's wrestling up, as she didn't believe anyone in SHIMMER could go toe-to-toe with her. This continued, as she defeated Sara Del Rey—arguably the best women's wrestler in America at the time—at SHIMMER Volume 42, but she didn't have the same luck at SHIMMER Volume 43, as she lost a #1 Contendership match to Cheerleader Melissa. At SHIMMER Volume 44, however, though she beat LuFisto, it was here that she finally showed respect to another woman on the roster. Kana and LuFisto would go on to become a tag team on-and-off in SHIMMER, though their few shots at the SHIMMER Tag Team Championships never led to tag team gold.

In the summer of 2015, Kana appeared in the audience at NXT TakeOver: Brooklyn (with her name written in a typo as "Kanna"), and her signing with WWE was all but confirmed. A few days later, it was actually confirmed, which led to a press conference in Tokyo for the official announcement. When NXT on-screen General Manager introduced Asuka on NXT TV, he called her perhaps "the greatest signing in NXT history." While the "Asuka" name appeared to be a tip of the hat to famed joshi legend—as well as former AtoZ booker and 1/2 of The Crush Gals—Lioness Asuka, Asuka's own admitted preference for male wrestling means that isn't exactly so (despite WWE.com and NXT commentary suggesting it's an homage). The true reason for the choice in name change stemmed from the fact "Asu" in "Asuka" translates to "Tomorrow" or "Future," which also explains why Asuka is known as "The Empress of Tomorrow" and her entrance theme is titled "The Future." In a tweet announcing her debut at NXT, Triple H called her "the newest face of the future."

Asuka's first feud in NXT was against the devious duo of Emma and her sidekick Dana Brooke, who believed the NXT Women's Division was all about them. During this feud, Asuka quickly took down Brooke, while Emma tried her best to avoid suffering the same fate. Unfortunately, Emma fell to Asuka at NXT TakeOver: London at the end of 2015, though she at least put up more of a fight than Brooke in the process. Emma would get a rematch in an episode of NXT in 2016, but she still came up short, this time with championship goals in the eyes of Asuka. In April 2016, Asuka beat Bayley at NXT TakeOver: Dallas to win the NXT Women's Championship, effectively proving that Asuka's particular brand of domination wouldn't be stopped, not even by the eternal positive mental attitude of Bayley. Even more surprising though was when Bayley failed to win back the championship at NXT TakeOver: Brooklyn II (when the previous year's Brooklyn show was essentially Bayley's star-making performance), crushing the dreams of the eternal underdog coming back from behind. Instead, this was only the beginning of Asuka's seemingly unstoppable dominance in NXT and WWE as a whole. People from within NXT, WWE's main roster, and even outsiders would challenge Asuka, but no one would come close. And even when they came close, it still wasn't close enough.

On May 14, 2017, Asuka officially reached a milestone, with her undefeated streak in NXT outlasting Goldberg's historic WCW undefeated streak at 174-0 (Goldberg's was 173-0). Going through women like Bayley, Emma, Dana Brooke, Deonna Purrazzo, Nikki Cross, Ember Moon, Liv Morgan, and many, many more, Asuka's own NXT Women's Championship reign lasted for 510 days, until she relinquished the championship after NXT TakeOver: Brooklyn III (due to a kayfabe collarbone injury) that August. For quite some time, the word around the wrestling news and rumor circuit was that Asuka would never be brought up to the main roster, that (because of her age) she would simply be the face of NXT's Women's Division for the rest of her WWE career. However, as it turned out, talent was a far more important factor, and after two years in NXT, Asuka made the jump to the main roster, debuting on WWE *Monday Night RAW* in October (after debut vignettes started airing in September). It was a long time coming and one that also spoke to the strong state of NXT's Women's Division outside of Asuka: Apparently Triple H begged Vince McMahon not to bring Asuka up to the main roster during the 2016 *RAW/SmackDown* draft, claiming that he needed her as "an anchor" to NXT, to keep it from being "doomed."

In a 2011 interview Kana told her fans around the world they should "keep [their] eyes firmly on [her]." It's hard to dispute that she's more than followed through on her promise of greatness. 2015 saw Dave Meltzer, the foremost professional wrestling journalist, argue that Asuka was possibly "the best worker in WWE, man or woman." Two years later, she became the first Japanese wrestler to get the coveted #1 spot in Pro Wrestling Illustrated (PWI) Female 50 (since its conception in 2008). Then in 2017, in the first-ever live edition of WWE *Monday Night RAW* on Christmas Day, the still undefeated Asuka declared that she would be participating in the inaugural WWE Women's Royal Rumble match at Royal Rumble 2018 (which she won). Assured, cocky, and amused by her opponents, Asuka

went from a top heel as Kana to something more transcendent as Asuka. She's even been called the female Brock Lesnar. What that means exactly? As she continues to promise any and all of her competitors: "Nobody is ready for Asuka." Except for maybe Charlotte Flair, who finally broke Asuka's streak at the grandest stage of them all, WrestleMania 34.

★ AWESOME KONG ★

YEARS ACTIVE: 2002–present

TRAINED BY: School of Hard Knocks · Jesse Hernandez · Kumiko Maekawa · Noah Denker

BILLED FROM: Tokyo, Japan

ACCOMPLISHMENTS: 1x WWWA World Single Champion · 1x WWWA World Tag Team Champion (with Aja Kong) · 2003 Japan Grand Prix · 1x AWA Superstars of Wrestling World Women's Champion · ChickFight IX · 1x GAEA Japan AAAW Tag Team Champion (with Aja Kong) · 1x HUSTLE Super Tag Team Champion (with Erika) · 1x LLPW Tag Team Champion (with Aja Kong) · 1x National Wrestling Alliance (NWA) Midwest World Women's Champion · 2x NEO Japan Ladies Pro Wrestling Tag Team Champion (1x with Haruka Matsuo, 1x with Kyoko Kimura) · 2004 OZ Academy Tag Tournament (with Chikayo Nagashima) · #1 on 2008 PWI Female 50 · 2008 PWI Woman of the Year · 1x Pro Wrestling World-1 Women's Champion · 1x Resistance Pro Wrestling (RPW) Women's Champion · 2x TNA Knockouts Champion · 1x TNA Knockouts Tag Team Champion (with Hamada) · 2011 Cauliflower Alley Club Women's Wrestling (Active) Award · 2015 TNA Queen of the Knockouts Tournament

AKA: Amazing Kong · Kia Stevens · Vixen · Kharma · Margaret · "The Mean Queen" · "Queen Kong" · 1/2 of Double Kong · 1/2 of W Kong · member of Daffney's All Star Squad (Daff's A.S.S.) · member of The Dollhouse

NOTABLE MATCHES: Amazing Kong vs. MsChif at SHIMMER Volume 9 (April 7, 2007) · Amazing Kong vs. Tyler Black at NWA Midwest (September 22, 2007) · Awesome Kong vs. Gail Kim (c) at TNA Turning Point 2007, for the TNA Knockouts Championship (December 2, 2007) · Awesome Kong vs. Gail Kim (c) at TNA Final Resolution 2008, in a No Disqualification match for the TNA Knockouts Championship (January 6, 2008) · Awesome Kong (c) vs. Gail Kim vs. ODB at TNA Destination X 2008, in a 3-Way Dance match for the TNA Knockouts Championship (March 9, 2008) · Amazing Kong vs. Mercedes Martinez at SHIMMER Volume 23 (May 2, 2009) · Amazing Kong vs. LuFisto at SHIMMER Volume 27, in a SHIMMER Championship #1 Contendership match (November 8, 2009) · Amazing Kong vs. MsChif (c) vs. LuFisto at SHIMMER Volume 28, in a 3-Way Elimination match for the SHIMMER Championship (November 8, 2009) · Awesome Kong vs. Tara at TNA Turning Point 2009, in a Six Sides of Steel Cage match (November 15, 2009) · Awesome Kong & Hamada vs. Sarita & Taylor Wilde (c) at TNA Impact Wrestling, for the TNA Knockouts Tag Team Championship (January 4, 2010) · Awesome Kong vs. Taryn Terrell (c) vs. Gail Kim at TNA Impact Wrestling, in a 3-Way Dance match for the TNA Knockouts Championship (March 20, 2015)

⭐ When it comes to the modern-day monster heel, the name Kong comes to mind. No, not Aja Kong: Awesome Kong or Amazing Kong, depending on which era of her work you're discussing. Today, most people may know this Kong as Kia Stevens, one of the stars of hit Netflix series *GLOW*. On *GLOW* she's Tammé, a mother looking for a new sense of purpose, in the form of *GLOW*'s top heel, Welfare Queen.

But before she was playing a professional wrestler on television, Stevens was hoping to become a wrestler . . . also on television. Her journey toward professional wrestling officially began on the second season a television series called Discovery Health *Body Challenge*, as the then social worker worked to lose weight in order to get the ideal body for a career in professional wrestling. (Stevens had previously tried out for the second season of WWE's competition series *Tough Enough*, where she

was told she was too fat to be a WWE Diva.) During the six-week program, the Discovery Health producers set up a surprise meeting for Stevens with Chyna, one of the female wrestlers (the other being Lita) who inspired her to follow her dreams of wrestling in the first place. After the show, she began her wrestling training at Jesse Hernandez's School of Hard Knocks. A few weeks after she'd taken her first bump, she tried out for AJW (despite not being overly familiar with Japanese women's wrestling), as they were looking for new talent, and thus the legend of Kong truly began.

At her tryout, Stevens impressed enough the AJW brass with her raw talent for them to invite her to further training in the AJW Dojo. With this, Stevens would move to Japan full-time, training nonstop (both in wrestling and mixed martial arts) while also learning Japanese and truly assimilating into the culture, a process Stevens would later go on to call after the fact "the most rigorous routine I've ever experienced in my life." She would also say, "They wanted to bring me down, to build me up. And they wanted to see how much I would take, and I took it all." In the process, Masatsugu Matsunaga gave Stevens her new ring name: Amazing Kong. Over a year after starting her professional wrestling career and coming to Japan, Amazing Kong would win AJW's WWWA World Single Championship, defeating Ayako Hamada (a woman who she would go on to team with in TNA).

The intent was for Amazing Kong to become the new monster heel on the joshi puro block, filling the void of Aja Kong in AJW while also playing on that same otherness of a large African American woman in a native Japanese world—only even more so this time around. And when it came to filling that void, the AJW brass meant that literally: AJW would technically announce Aja Kong for their match cards (by listing "A. Kong"), only for Amazing Kong to come out and wrestle instead. This is where the fluency in Japanese came in, because Amazing Kong was able to parse that if Aja Kong took offense to this bait and switch and saw it as disrespect on Amazing Kong's end, Amazing Kong would need to accept whatever punishment ever came her way if she met the veteran, for fear of being blacklisted from the world of joshi.

While Amazing Kong was supposed to be a "replacement" for Aja Kong, she actually became the mentee and tag team partner of the veteran wrestler. After her debut match at GAEA Japan in 2004—against Aja Kong—Amazing Kong became tag team partners with the veteran that same night, officially forming the team W Kong (aka Double Kong). In fact, the two Kongs had actually met prior to this particular event, as they'd finally run into each other—at a restaurant—and Aja Kong both stopped to chat with Amazing Kong and paid for Amazing Kong and a friend's lunch. They'd go on to win the AAAW Tag Team Championship in GAEA, as well as the tag team championships of both AJW and Ladies Legend Pro-Wrestling. They even became tag team

champions for the HUSTLE professional wrestling promotion in 2006 under the ring names Erika and Margaret—employing comedy gimmicks in which they wore tutus—and were the last team to hold the WWWA World Tag Team Championships before AJW closed in 2005. Amazing Kong also main evented the final GAEA Japan show in 2005, in a winning effort teaming with Ayako Hamada and Mayumi Ozaki.

Because of her success in Japan, it was only a matter of time before Amazing Kong returned to her native land to wow American audiences. She debuted at SHIMMER Volume 5 in 2006, against Nikki Roxx, and faced her again at SHIMMER Volume 14, putting her on a five-match winning streak and into contention for the SHIMMER Championship. This would lead to the dream match at SHIMMER Volume 15, with Kong challenging Sara Del Rey for the championship—a match she'd "lose," but only by count-out. Up until 2009, the only times Amazing Kong would "lose" in SHIMMER competition would either be via count-out, via disqualification (as Kong of course had a temper), or through someone else being pinned or forced to submit in a multiwoman match. Kong's stint in SHIMMER also led to her working in ROH, SHIMMER's sister promotion; after an initial debut in 2007, she feuded with Sara Del Rey (during Del Rey's teaming with the Kings of Wrestling) in ROH in 2010. And the road to SHIMMER/ROH led to the NWA, as the then AWA World Women's Champion Kong entered a champion vs. champion title feud with MsChif, the NWA World Women's Championship. She won the initial title vs. title match against MsChif, becoming a dual champion, and then won the rematch against MsChif— after losing the AWA World Women's Championship—only for MsChif to finally win the championship nearly a year later, due to a count-out (thanks to a special stipulation).

While WWE was talking about the Divas Revolution and women main eventing shows in 2015, TNA was doing it for real back in 2007, as it rebranded its Women's Division as the Knockouts Division. Upon being signed, Amazing Kong would now become Awesome Kong (for branding purposes), and she would be considered an integral part of the Knockouts Division. To this day, her feud with Gail Kim in TNA is known as the definitive feud of the company's Knockouts Division. Her heyday in TNA was also known for its role in providing definitive proof that women's wrestling could be taken seriously if treated seriously: At this time, the Knockouts segments would bolster ratings for entire episodes, consistently being the highest rated segments. In 2008, she began inviting "fans" to face her in the ring. It was a concept at first considered by fans to be TNA running out of ideas for Kong after the Gail Kim feud, only to be revealed as a way to debut the wrestler Taylor Wilde and have Kong feud with her. Unfortunately, in 2010, a new creative regime would take over behind-the-scenes at TNA—Eric Bischoff, alongside Hulk Hogan—and a physical backstage altercation between Kong and radio shock jock Bubba the Love Sponge (a close friend of Hogan's) led to Kong being sent home from the tapings. That same day, Kong reportedly asked for her release from TNA, and the company wouldn't grant said release—but they would suspend her when she refused to work on TNA's United Kingdom tour. That suspension, and upon Kong's filing of a lawsuit against Bubba the Love Sponge in February 2010 (for an alleged threatening phone call), led to Kong's release from her TNA contract the following month.

But where one door closed, another opened, as Awesome Kong then signed with WWE at the end of 2010 and made her debut (skipping developmental completely) on the May 2011 WWE pay-per-view Extreme Rules (after a month of vignettes hyping her debut) as Kharma, attacking Michelle McCool after a match. Kharma continued to attack the "Barbie dolls" of the Divas Division for weeks, until the May 23, 2011 edition of WWE *Monday Night RAW*, in which she interrupted a Divas tag team match . . . and broke down into tears. On the next RAW, she cut an in-ring promo explaining her lifelong dream to join the WWE and the long road it took to get there—but at the moment, she was about to experience another one of her lifelong dreams, in the form of motherhood. Kharma vowed to be back

after her pregnancy, and after The Bella Twins interrupted to mock her, Kharma also promised that she'd be coming for them when she came back. In January 2012, Kharma made her surprise return at the Royal Rumble—in the annual Royal Rumble match as the rare woman to compete in the men's match—but she was not back full-time and was released from WWE that July, with the Royal Rumble being her only match in WWE. As for her pregnancy, after an initial report from TMZ of Kia Stevens giving birth to a healthy baby boy, the story was retracted, as Stevens admitted she had lied and the baby didn't survive birth. Stevens would later also admit that her release from WWE was due to her inability to return to action in a reasonable time frame after this trauma.

> AWESOME KONG'S HEYDAY IN TNA WAS KNOWN FOR PROVIDING DEFINITIVE PROOF THAT WOMEN'S WRESTLING COULD BE TAKEN SERIOUSLY IF TREATED SERIOUSLY.

The end of 2012 saw Kong return to action as Amazing Kong, with her spending 2013 working in SHINE, SHIMMER, RPW, and CHIKARA, among others. She'd also return to both TNA and Japan in 2015, with the latter leading her to wrestle in Nanae Takahashi's new wrestling promotion, SEAdLINNNG (where she would even reform W Kong). At the end of 2015, SEAdLINNNG announced in a statement that Awesome Kong was retiring from professional wrestling due to health issues. Soon after, Kong followed up with a clarification that she wasn't quite done yet, stating: "Amazing Kong is retired from wrestling, but Awesome Kong has further obligations to attend." Those obligations would of course include her contract with TNA Wrestling, which was set to expire that upcoming January (which negotiations would determine whether or not Awesome Kong was done too). However, those obligations also ceased to exist just before her contract expired, after a physical altercation in the women's locker room, in which Kong reportedly attacked Reby Hardy a week before the latest TNA UK tour.

While Kong is not tearing up the wrestling world the way she did in her prime, after almost a year out of the ring, Amazing Kong wrestled at Empire Wrestling Federation's (EWE) 21st Anniversary. She then wrestled a couple more special attractions matches in 2017, one against one of the hottest acts on the indies at the time in Deonna Purrazzo and one against Taya Valkyrie, an Impact Wrestling Knockout and Lucha Underground star. While Kia Stevens has focused more on playing a wrestler on TV these days with Netflix's *GLOW*, there's clearly still room for Kong in the wrestling world.

★ AYAKO HAMADA ★

YEARS ACTIVE: 1998–2018

TRAINED BY: Aja Kong · Mariko Yoshida · Gran Hamada · Gran Apache

BILLED FROM: Tokyo, Japan

ACCOMPLISHMENTS: 2x WWWA World Single Champion · 1x WWWA World Tag Team Champion (with Nanae Takahashi) · 2003 STARDOM Tag League the Best (with Nanae Takahashi) · 1x Queen of ARSION Champion · 1x Sky High of ARSION Champion · 2x Twin Star of ARSION Champion (1x with AKINO, 1x with Michiko Omukai) · 1x ARSION P*Mix Tag Team Champion (with Gran Hamada) · 1x AAAW Single Champion · 1x AAAW Tag Team Champion (with Meiko Satomura) · 1x Azteca Karate Extremo (AKE) Women's Champion · 1x International Wrestling Revolution Group (IWRG) Intercontinental Women's Champion · 1x AAA Reina de Reinas Champion · 1x NEO Japan Ladies Pro Wrestling Tag Team Champion (with Kaoru Ito) · #18 in 2011 PWI Female 50 · 1x Pro Wrestling WAVE Single Champion · 3x Pro Wrestling WAVE Tag Team Champion (with Yuu Yamagata) · 2013 Pro Wrestling WAVE Dual Shock WAVE (with Yuu Yamagata) · 2015 Pro Wrestling WAVE Dual Shock WAVE (with Yuu Yamagata) · 2013 Pro Wrestling WAVE Catch the WAVE Best Bout Award (vs. Ryo Mizunami, on May 26) · 2015 Pro Wrestling WAVE Catch the WAVE Best Performance Award (with the Wonderful World Fairy Family) · 2007 SENDAI Girls' Pro Wrestling Battlefield War Tournament · 1x SENDAI Girls' Pro Wrestling World Champion · 1x SHIMMER Tag Team Champion (with Ayumi Kurihara) · 2003 Tokyo Sports Joshi Puroresu Grand Prize · 2x TNA Knockouts Tag Team Champion (1x with Awesome Kong, 1x with Taylor Wilde) · 1x Universal Wrestling Association World Women's Champion · 1x World Wrestling Association (WWA) World Women's Champion

AKA: Hamada · "Super Estrella" · Arisin Z · Dadae Takahashi · Dokuron Z · member of Black Dahlia · member of CAZAI · member of La Legión Extranjera · 1/2 of HamAKINO · 1/2 of Las Aventureras

NOTABLE MATCHES: Ayako Hamada vs. Sara Del Rey at SHIMMER Volume 28, in a No Disqualification/No Count Out match (November 8, 2009) · Hamada & Awesome Kong vs. Sarita & Taylor Wilde (c) at TNA Impact Wrestling, for the TNA Knockouts Tag Team Championship (January 4, 2010) · Ayako Hamada vs. Jessie McKay vs. Sara Del Rey SHIMMER Volume 34, in a 3-Way match (September 11, 2010) · Hamada vs. Ayumi Kurihara at SHIMMER Volume 38 (March 26, 2011) · Ayako Hamada vs. Meiko Satomura at SENDAI Girls' Women's Wrestling Big Show in Sendai ~ Meiko Satomura 20th Anniversary Show, for the SENDAI Girls' World Championship (October 11, 2015) · Ayako Hamada vs. Taya (c) at AAA Rey De Reyes 2017, for the AAA Reina de Reinas Championoship (March 19, 2017) · Ayako Hamada (c) vs. Taya at AAA, in a Street Fight for the AAA Reina de Reinas Championship (April 21, 2017)

★ Suffice it to say, Ayako Hamada was thrust into greatness fairly early on in her career. A second-generation wrestler, she followed in the footsteps of her father (who also had a hand in training her), Gran Hamada, and her older sister, Xóchitl Hamada. Born and raised in Mexico, the tough as nails Ayako Hamada first started wrestling when she was just 17 years old, in Japan's ARSION promotion, and won her first championship—the Twin Star of ARSION Championship (with AKINO)—less than a year later. A year after that, she won the Queen of ARSION Championship from Aja Kong herself, the founder of ARSION and one of Ayako Hamada's trainers, eventually dropping the title to the new Kong on the block, Amazing Kong. Hamada left ARSION in 2001 and would eventually go on to win AJW's WWWA World Single Championship in 2003, again dropping a title to Amazing Kong (nearly a year later), as the two competitors would cross paths many more times in their respective careers. But a week after that loss, she would win GAEA's AAAW Single Championship and hold it for a few months before losing it to Meiko Satomura.

Post-ARSION, most of Ayako Hamada's work in Japan came from the GAEA and HUSTLE wrestling promotions (with a match in New Japan Pro Wrestling, a promotion that doesn't focus on women's wrestling). Then in 2007, Ayako Hamada went back home to make her Mexican professional wrestling debut, eventually making AAA somewhat of her Mexican home promotion. The years 2007 and 2008 saw Hamada alternate between her work in Japan and her work in Mexico, though by November 2008, she was done with AAA; but that was because she had become a trainer at Martha Villalobos's wrestling school.

However, Ayako Hamada's story wasn't just going to end at becoming a trainer. Instead, after making a splash in both Japan and Mexico—just like her father had done before her—she signed with TNA (as just "Hamada"), a big coup for the promotion's Knockouts Division. She announced the news at a press conference in April 2009 and made her TNA debut August that year. She also made her debut in other American promotions, such as SHIMMER in the fall of 2009, Jersey All

Pro Wrestling (JAPW) in 2010, and CHIKARA (during its JoshiMania weekend) in 2011.

Hamada would have her first feud against Alissa Flash (Cheerleader Melissa's character in TNA at the time), a feud Hamada would very decisively win, culminating in a Falls Count Anywhere match. Hamada's early dominance would even lead to her getting a TNA Global Championship (the name of one of the company's secondary championships at the time) match at the end of 2009, with the then champion Eric Young defending his championship for the first time as something of an "initiation" to see if Hamada had what it takes to join his heel stable World Elite. The match sadly lasted less than two minutes, with Hamada dominating and even wowing the crowd until Young snuck away and was able to capitalize to pin her, with his legs on the middle rope for leverage. As for World Elite, it became clear immediately after Young won—as he celebrated like he'd just "won the Super Bowl"—that the actual reason he'd chosen Hamada as a challenger was to get an easy win. But this was clearly not an easy win.

After the failed Global Championship attempt, Hamada began teaming with Awesome Kong (Amazing Kong's character in TNA), with the pair winning the TNA Knockouts Tag Team Championship at the beginning of 2010. However, Kong was suspended from TNA the same month and then released two months later, and Hamada was stripped of the championship as a result. Hamada would be off TNA television for four months after this, eventually returning to win the TNA Knockouts Tag Team Championship again, this time with Taylor Wilde as her tag team partner. But Hamada would be stripped of the championship again, as she'd return to Japan that October and request her release—a request that would finally be granted in December.

When Hamada returned to Japan, she became a regular in the Pro Wrestling WAVE promotion, officially signing a contract with the company in 2012. In 2013, she and her tag team partner Yuu Yamagata (forming the team of Las Aventureras) won Pro Wrestling WAVE's Dual Shock Wave tag team tournament and then went on to win the WAVE Tag Team Championship (Hamada's first championship in WAVE) a few weeks later. At 270 days, Las Aventureras officially had the longest reign with that championship in that company's history, a record broken only by their third reign with the championship (which lasted 282 days). During their second tag team championship reign, Hamada became a double champion, winning the WAVE Single Championship (the top championship in the promotion) in February 2015—a title which she coincidentally lost to Yuu Yamagata, at the end of 2015.

In 2017, Ayako Hamada finally returned to Mexico and AAA—this time, paying homage to the inaugural AAA Reina de Reinas Champion (her sister Xóchitl) by winning the championship 18 years later. Unfortunately, this tribute was short-lived, as the reign (33 days) is currently the shortest in the history of the championship. Then in May 2018, Hamada was arrested for drug possession (methamphetamine), effectively ending her career in SENDAI Girls' Pro Wrestling—as she was the SENDAI Girls' World Champion at the time—and eventually, her professional wrestling career as a whole. She announced her official retirement from professional wrestling on July 18, 2018, the same day as her sentencing (18 months probation, which will become prison time if she violates said probation). Now faced with life after professional wrestling, Hamada seeks to use her fluency in both Japanese and Spanish to become an interpreter.

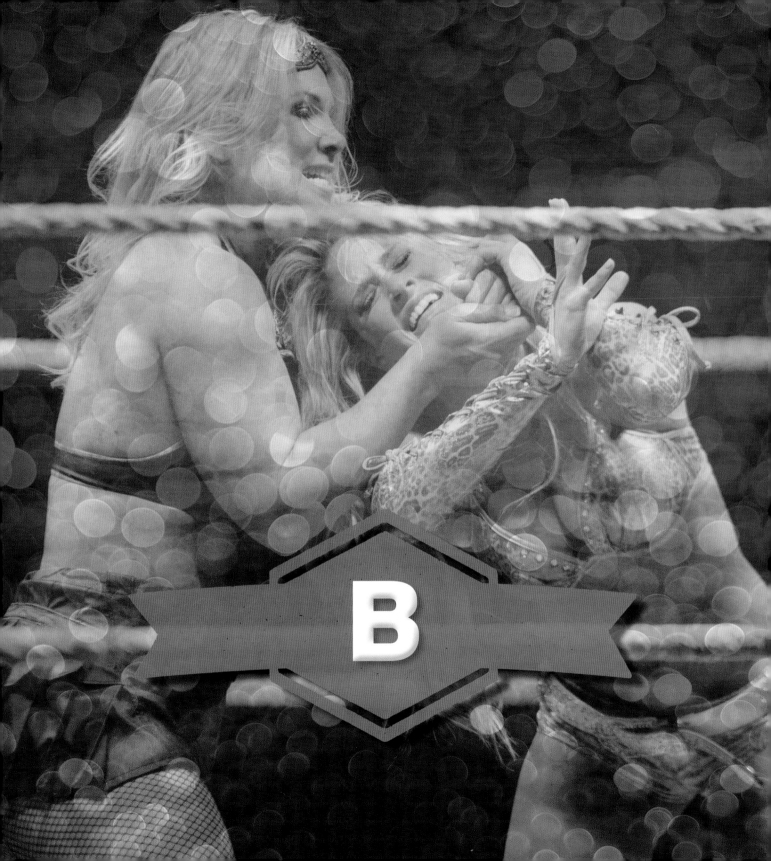

★ BAYLEY ★

YEARS ACTIVE: 2008–present

TRAINED BY: Jason Styles · Big Time Wrestling · WWE Performance Center

BILLED FROM: San Jose, California

ACCOMPLISHMENTS: 1x NXT Women's Champion · 1x WWE RAW Women's Champion · #5 in 2016 & 2017 PWI Female 50 · 2015 *Rolling Stone* NXT Match of the Year (vs. Sasha Banks, at NXT TakeOver: Brooklyn) · 2015 *Rolling Stone* Title Feud of the Year, NXT (vs. Sasha Banks, for the NXT Women's Championship) · 2015 PWI Most Inspirational Wrestler of the Year · 2016 PWI Most Inspirational Wrestler of the Year · 2015 PWI Match of the Year (vs. Sasha Banks, at NXT TakeOver: Respect) · 2015 Wrestling Observer Newsletter Most Improved · 2015 NXT Year-End Award for Female Competitor of the Year · 2015 NXT Year-End Award for Match of the Year (vs. Sasha Banks, at NXT TakeOver: Brooklyn)

AKA: Davina Rose · Pamela · 1/4 of The Four Horsewomen (WWE) · 1/2 of The Boss & Hug Connection · 1/2 of Team B'N'B

NOTABLE MATCHES: Davina Rose & Shazza McKenzie vs. Made In Sin (Allysin Kay & Taylor Made) at SHINE 4 (October 19, 2012) · Bayley vs. Charlotte (c) vs. Sasha Banks vs. Becky Lynch at NXT TakeOver: Rival, in a Fatal 4 Way match for the NXT Women's Championship (February 11, 2015) · Bayley vs. Sasha Banks (c) at NXT TakeOver: Brooklyn, for the NXT Women's Championship (August 22, 2015) · Bayley (c) vs. Sasha Banks at NXT TakeOver: Respect, in a 30-Minute Ironman match for the NXT Women's Championship (October 7, 2015) · Bayley vs. Asuka (c) at NXT TakeOver: Brooklyn II, for the NXT Women's Championship (August 20, 2016) · Bayley vs. Charlotte Flair (c) at WWE *Monday Night RAW*, for the WWE RAW Women's Championship (February 13, 2017) · Bayley vs. Alexa Bliss (c) vs. Emma vs. Nia Jax vs. Sasha Banks at WWE No Mercy 2017, for the WWE RAW Women's Championship (September 24, 2017)

Plenty of professional wrestlers have stories about how their fandom inspired them to get into the business. But for WWE's Bayley, she was able to translate how big of a wrestling fan she is into her actual character. In fact, her ring gear is influenced by one of those wrestlers she idolized: "Macho Man" Randy Savage, who Bayley credits as the first person she ever saw in professional wrestling and the one who hooked her when she was just eight years old. But it was the women wrestlers—like Ivory or Lita, with the Hardy Boyz—who inspired her to do the wrestling thing for a living.

Under the ring name "Davina Rose," the future WWE Superstar made her professional wrestling debut in 2008 at Big Time Wrestling in Northern California, her local promotion and one that she'd been going to since she was 11 years old. In fact, during her training at Big Time Wrestling, she was the only girl in her class. In October 2010, Davina Rose met former WWE Diva Serena Deeb when Deeb came to team with her at Big Time Wrestling's 14th Anniversary Show. Deeb would go on to take Rose under her wing, functioning as her mentor during her time on the independent scene. That same year, Davina Rose teamed with Awesome Kong on one occasion in Big Time Wrestling as well, an experience that Rose also found helpful in terms of her growth as a wrestler, crediting Kong with teaching her to slow down in the ring.

2011 was the year that Davina Rosa branched out from Big Time Wrestling, not just debuting in NWA Championship Wrestling From Hollywood (aka NWA Hollywood)—where she would both team with and wrestle against her longtime Big Time Wrestling rival Buggy—but also debuting in the SHIMMER women's wrestling promotion. Rose would debut at SHIMMER on Volume 41 in October 2011, against Mercedes Martinez, the woman Rose's mentor Serena considered her favorite opponent. But Rose wouldn't get a win until Volume 48 the next March, teaming with Mia Ying in a tag team match (after they'd previously lost their first tag team match, against The Canadian NINJAS, who Davina had a bit of a feud with upon arriving in SHIMMER). Then 2012 would see Rose make her SHINE Wrestling debut, as well as her ECCW debut, in a title match for KC Spinelli's ECCW Women's Championship. While Davina Rose fell short in both debut matches, the latter was something of a dream come true for her, as she'd made clear in more than one interview that she really wanted to wrestle in Canada and learn the Canadian style of wrestling.

The year 2012 would also see Davina Rose check off another goal on her wrestling bucket list: WWE. That December, it was announced that she'd signed with the company and would be reporting to WWE's developmental territory (NXT) in Orlando. Upon debuting in NXT—at an NXT house show the following January—Rose (billed under her real first name, Pamela) wrestled as a babyface and wore a mask. This choice was surprising but obviously just a test trial, as her next house show (the next day) had her work as a heel, without the mask. (Fun fact: The mask actually belonged to former wrestler/ current NXT trainer Sara Del Rey, as it was the mask she wore as the character "Nic Grimes" for MTV's short-lived wrestling series *Wrestling Society X*.) That February, she announced that her official NXT/WWE ring name would now be "Bayley" (which she also quipped would be pronounced "Bayleee!") and made her official NXT TV debut in an episode that March. Like most new NXT signees (especially at the time), Bayley's debut was with her character not yet fully formed, and it wasn't until an episode of *NXT* in June that she became the true Bayley character: an excited-to-be-there babyface superfan who wanted to hug every Diva and Superstar she met, even if she eventually had to face them in the ring. This of course was a big point in her one-off title match against AJ Lee, as the then WWE Divas Champion came down to NXT and faced and defeated Bayley, but it would also became a career-changing point as she started teaming with Charlotte (daughter of Ric Flair).

Bayley would team with Charlotte (who would help Bayley get her first win in NXT) and draw the attention of the Beautiful Fierce Females (The BFF)—Summer Rae and Sasha Banks—

who would try to recruit Bayley, essentially to the dark side. Instead, Charlotte ended up joining The BFFs and going on to win the NXT Women's Championship—leaving Bayley to feud with the evil trio and try to get back at Charlotte for her betrayal. (Though, The BFFs would implode on their own, as Summer Rae would head to the main roster and Charlotte would leave Sasha behind to face Bayley's wrath on her own.) Unfortunately, the story was that "nice girls finish last," and after beating Sasha Banks to become the #1 Contender to the NXT Women's Championship, Bayley still came up short when she challenged Charlotte at NXT TakeOver: Fatal 4-Way.

Then, history repeated itself for Bayley when she found an ally in Becky Lynch . . . who turned on her to join forces with Sasha Banks (to form Team B.A.E., Best At Everything). Only this time, Charlotte would turn face and join forces with Bayley to take on Team B.A.E.—but that wouldn't stop them from injuring Bayley (in storyline). Bayley would come for them again when she returned months later, coming up short in another NXT Women's Championship match, this time at Fatal 4-Way match at NXT TakeOver: Rival. After this loss, Bayley would have to start from the bottom again, feuding with Emma and Dana Brooke, who chastised Bayley for being too nice and unable to win the big one because of that. Once she took care of them, Bayley was back on her quest to earn the NXT Women's Championship, a quest that culminated at NXT TakeOver: Brooklyn on August 22, 2015, when she challenged then champion Sasha Banks.

This, simply put, was the turning point: Bayley vs. Sasha is considered arguably the greatest women's wrestling match in the history of WWE, as well as one of the greatest matches period in both WWE and its developmental branch of NXT. The match was named Match of the Year by Pro Wrestling Illustrated and NXT Match of the Year by *Rolling Stone* and WWE. At the same time, WWE named Bayley NXT's Female Competitor of the Year, and PWI ranked her at number five on its annual Top 50 singles female wrestlers that year. Bayley and Sasha

Banks—as well as Charlotte and Becky Lynch—would also be known collectively as The Four Horsewomen of the WWE, a callback to Charlotte's father's Hall of Fame faction The Four Horsemen, as well as a moniker that explains just how important these four were (and would continue to be) to women's wrestling in both NXT and main roster WWE. Triple H—who is an instrumental figure in the existence of NXT—called the match "one of the greatest I've ever seen."

The match's follow-up—a 30-minute Iron Man match, the first in the history of women's wrestling in WWE—would also gain high praise, and Bayley would become one of the faces of NXT as she retained and continued on as a fighting champion. However, Bayley's role as the face of the division slowly ground to a halt at NXT TakeOver: Dallas, when she lost the championship to Asuka, after holding it for over

200 days. After this, a somber Bayley resigned herself to the fact that Asuka was on a whole other playing field, but she went on to challenge Asuka to a rematch at NXT TakeOver: Brooklyn II—since the original TakeOver: Brooklyn meant so much to her career—and not only could she not get the job done, but it was her final match in NXT.

Two nights later, Bayley made her official WWE *Monday Night RAW* debut (after making a surprise debut as a mystery tag team partner for Sasha Banks the previous month at the Battleground pay-per-view). She'd immediately be thrust into a feud with one of her Four Horsewomen cohorts, Charlotte, who was at the time a heel and the RAW Women's Champion. Bayley would eventually beat Charlotte (who was using Dana Brooke as her sidekick) for the championship on an episode of *Monday Night RAW* in February 2017, even giving Charlotte her first pay-per-view loss when Charlotte challenged her to a rematch at Fastlane. Then, in Bayley's WrestleMania debut at WrestleMania 33, she retained the championship against Charlotte, Sasha Banks, and Nia Jax in a Fatal 4-Way Elimination match.

After WrestleMania, Bayley spent the rest of 2017 mostly feuding with Alexa Bliss (and Nia Jax, as an extension), dropping the championship to her after holding it for 76 days. Unfortunately, Bayley would completely come out on the losing side of her feud with Bliss, but in true Bayley fashion, her positivity has still shone through. And to think, according to Bayley, her trainer at Big Time Wrestling (Jason Styles) told her to stop smiling so much during training. Fast-forward to the present day, and Bayley and smiles are almost as synonymous as Bayley and hugs. As a child, Bayley, her brother, and her sister would stage their very own wrestling shows in their living room, called WFK (Wrestling For Kids). Today, Bayley is an inspiration to kids all around the world as the epitome of the happy-go-lucky babyface. One thing Styles did accept about her, however, was how genuine she was: "From the get-go, she always talked about how she was a wrestling fan since she was a kid, and that really came through, when she started training." In a WWE.com interview in 2013,

Bayley also explained her hugging mentality: "You know when you first meet someone and they shake your hand? Hugging is how I shake hands. . . . . I live hug life. So there isn't anyone I wouldn't hug."

★ BECKY LYNCH ★

YEARS ACTIVE: 2002–2008 · 2011 · 2013–present

TRAINED BY: Finn Balor · Gonzo De Mondo · Paul Tracey · NWA Ireland · NWA-UK Hammerlock

BILLED FROM: "The School of Hard Knox" · Dublin, Ireland

ACCOMPLISHMENTS: 1x World Queens of Chaos Champion · 1x SuperGirls Wrestling SuperGirls Champion · 2005 SuperGirls Championship Tournament · #4 in 2016 PWI Female 50 · 2x (and inaugural) WWE SmackDown Women's Champion

AKA: Rebecca Knox · K-Nox · Komeera · 1/4 of The Four Horsewomen (WWE) · 1/2 of Team B.A.E. (Best At Everything) · 1/3 of Team PCB · "The Lass Kicker" · "The Irish Lass Kicker" · La Luchadora · "Becky Balboa" · "Maiden Ireland" · "Straight Fire" · "The Man"

NOTABLE MATCHES: Rebecca Knox vs. Allison Danger at SHIMMER Volume 3 (February 12, 2006) · Rebecca Knox vs. Daizee Haze at SHIMMER Volume 4 (February 12, 2006) · Rebecca Knox vs. Daizee Haze at SHIMMER Volume 5, in a 2 Out of 3 Falls match (May 21, 2006) · Becky Lynch vs. Charlotte (c) vs. Bayley vs. Sasha Banks at NXT TakeOver: Rival, in a Fatal 4 Way match for the NXT Women's Championship (February 11, 2015) · Becky Lynch vs. Sasha Banks (c) at NXT TakeOver: Unstoppable, for the NXT Women's Championship (May 20, 2015) · Becky Lynch vs. Charlotte vs. Sasha Banks, in a Triple Threat for the vacant WWE Women's Championship at WrestleMania 32 (April 3, 2016) · Becky Lynch vs. Carmella vs. Alexa Bliss vs. Naomi vs. Nikki Bella at WWE Backlash 2016, in a 6-Pack Challenge for the inaugural WWE SmackDown Women's Championship (September 11, 2016) · Becky Lynch vs. Mickie James at WWE Elimination Chamber 2017 (February 12, 2017) · Becky Lynch vs. Carmella (with James Ellsworth) vs. Charlotte Flair vs. Natalya vs. Tamina Snuka at WWE Money in the Bank 2017, in a Money in the Bank Ladder match, for the inaugural Women's Money in the Bank contract (June 18, 2017) · Becky Lynch vs. Carmella vs. Charlotte Flair vs. Natalya vs. Tamina Snuka at WWE SmackDown LIVE, in a Money in the Bank Ladder match, for the Women's Money in the Bank contract (June 27, 2017) · Becky Lynch (c) vs. Charlotte Flair at WWE Evolution, in a Last Woman Standing match for the SmackDown Women's Championship (October 28, 2018)

★ In 2002, wrestler Fergal "Prince" Devitt (now known as WWE's Finn Balor) opened up a wrestling school in Ireland, about an hour and half away from where Rebecca Quin lived. She and her brother—who had aspirations of becoming a wrestler, while she just wanted to get in better shape for kickboxing—decided to train there that June. Five months later, Rebecca made her debut as "Rebecca Knox." (She'd also wrestle as "Komeera" in NWA Ireland for a time.) She was only 15 years old at the time—though she'd lied about her age to train—and had planned to become a lawyer when she grew up. Obviously, the plan didn't quite stick.

After spending her first few years wrestling up and down Europe—and deciding to drop out of college—in 2005, Rebecca moved to Canada and began wrestling in the North American wrestling scene. She'd become part of Canada's SuperGirls Wrestling promotion (ECCW's all-female offshoot), wrestling women like LuFisto and Cheerleader Melissa. She'd go on to become the inaugural SuperGirls Championship, as well as succeed in her first title defense (on the first SuperGirls DVD tapings) against LuFisto. She'd also do this while being a nefarious heel who took every possible shortcut she could to win her matches, which would lead to her holding the championship for just over 10 months—before dropping it to Lisa Moretti (WWF/WWE's Ivory). (Rebecca would also become known for being a wrestler without a set finisher, arguing instead that every wrestling match should end differently . . . instead of with the typical, expected move.) The same year, she'd also wrestle in the states at New England Championship Wrestling (NECW) and the All Pro Wrestling (APW) ChickFight tournament, before making her official debut in Japan. She'd team with joshi legends Aja Kong and Gran Hamada on her two-week tour of Japan, something which she considered a career highlight—especially as she was the youngest foreign woman to main event Korakuen Hall, at just 18.

Then in 2006, Rebecca Knox made her SHIMMER debut on SHIMMER Volume 3, wrestling (and proving herself still willing to do anything to win—like faking an injury) against Allison Danger. However, in Knox's appearance in SHIMMER Volume 4, she would lose to Daizee Haze, sparking a feud between the two (with Danger on the fringe). With regards to how Rebecca found her way on to the SHIMMER radar, promotion cofounder Dave Prazak recalled seeing one of her wrestling training tapes (courtesy of Lexie Fyfe), presenting her as a "19-year old wrestling prodigy out of Ireland." Rebecca Knox would go on to have quite the intense and well-regarded feud with Daizee Haze (and Allison Danger), but before they could have their scheduled 60-minute Iron Man match at SHIMMER Volume 7, Rebecca would be struck with a career-ending head injury while wrestling in Germany. Prior to this injury, Knox had suffered from broken ankles and stingers (injuries to the nerves in the neck), but those were the types of things that healed. But this injury—diagnosed as possible damage to her 8th cranial nerve at the time—led to headaches, as well as hearing and vision issues for her. Then, after being told not to wrestle for a few months, it looked like she was finally able to return to the ring—until she no-showed a SHIMMER event in 2008 and went on to back out of a ChickFight booking the following month. She would go on to say that wrestling no longer felt like the right choice for her, seemingly putting the sport behind her.

While retired, Rebecca would try her hand at many a career: flight attendant (which she would do for two and a half years, despite a fear of flying), actress, stunt woman, personal trainer. She even attended clown college. She returned to SHIMMER in 2011, temporarily, as manager to the mother-daughter team of Saraya and Britani Knight. For Rebecca, these jobs were attempts to fill the void left by professional wrestling, in one way or another; and in the case of her time as a flight attendant, she was also learning martial arts, surfing, and SCUBA diving. But while they could tick some boxes in similarity, they never ticked all of the boxes like wrestling did. So when a wrestler friend suggested Rebecca try out for WWE, she did.

"Having wrestling gone from my life for so long meant that I knew what it was like without it. Every day now I'll wake up and be told to do things, and put hard work in, but it seems effortless, because I know what the payoff to it all is. When I wasn't wrestling I was searching for something that I could feel strongly about as much as wrestling, and I never found that, so when I came back, and was able to make my living out of it, that was unbelievable."

Coming back from retirement for a second chance, her personal motto must have been ringing in her head: "Everything happens for a reason." And for whatever reason that was, it led to her getting signed to a developmental contract by WWE in April 2013, getting the new ring name of "Becky Lynch" that August (and eventually, the nickname of "The Lasskicker"), and then making her NXT TV in-ring debut in June 2014 (winning her debut match against BFFs member Summer Rae).

Despite her past work as a heel, Becky Lynch debuted on-screen as a face . . . and a stereotypical one at that. With a river dancing, Irish jig gimmick, something even Becky would rather not remember: "Let us never talk about that again. You know what, you can't get worse than that. Sometimes you've just gotta fricking make a fool out of yourself and then you become a little bit untouchable. . . . That was terrible, and we all know it was terrible. Let nobody else say anything different." The jig thankfully wouldn't last, and she would team with Bayley to take on the other BFFs members (Sasha Banks and then NXT Women's Champions Charlotte). However, after constant losses to both Sasha Banks and Charlotte (who would eventually break up, with Charlotte turning face) and some suggestion from Banks, Becky Lynch would turn heel. She and Banks would form the alliance Team B.A.E. (Best At Everything), a team Becky would constantly remind everyone was not a matter of friendship, just of convenience. Naturally, the team disintegrated, with Sasha Banks eventually winning the NXT Women's Championship and Becky chasing her for the championship. Becky would challenge Sasha at NXT TakeOver: Unstoppable, in May 2015, but she would unfortunately come up short.

However, in the ultimate show of respect from the fans—and signifier of a true babyface turn—the entire audience at Full Sail University (where the show took place) sang Becky Lynch's theme song to her as she made her exit. It became of the most memorable moments in NXT history, as well as another sign that women's wrestling truly meant something besides just a "bathroom break" in WWE. As was the case for Becky Lynch, Sasha Banks, Charlotte, and Bayley, as they were collectively known as The Four Horsewomen (in reference to Charlotte's father, Ric Flair, and his Hall of Fame faction) of the WWE. Becky stuck around NXT for a couple of months later (for tapings and house shows), but she (alongside Sasha and Charlotte) would make her WWE main roster debut in July 2015, on *Monday Night RAW*, as a part of the company's Divas Revolution. From that point on, Becky Lynch would be a face, joining forces with Charlotte and Paige to form the trio Team PCB. Team PCB would go on to feud with Team Bella (The Bella Twins and Alicia Fox) and Team B.A.D. (Naomi, Tamina, and Sasha Banks), with Team PCB coming out on top.

After Charlotte won the WWE Divas Championship, Paige would turn on her Team PCB members and go on to call Becky the "least relevant" member of the Divas Division, a statement that unfortunately felt like it had some truth to it—at least in the

form of her relevance compared to the other prominent Divas in the division. While both Becky and Charlotte individually got their revenge against Paige for her betrayal, Becky would experience another friendship turn right after, with Charlotte becoming heel during what was supposed to be a friendly rivalry. During this feud, Charlotte would have her father, Ric Flair, accompany her to the ring, working interference and even going as far as kissing Becky Lynch at the 2016 Royal Rumble pay-per-view to prevent her from defeating his daughter for the championship—a controversial moment that was removed from subsequent *Royal Rumble* showings on the WWE Network. The next month, Becky would realign with Sasha Banks—this time as faces—leading to the buildup of WrestleMania 32, in which Becky, Sasha, and Charlotte would all compete in a

Triple Threat for the WWE Divas Championship. Actually, the WWE Women's Championship, as the Divas Championship (that Charlotte was holding) would be retired, just like the term "Divas."

Becky did not win the WWE Women's Championship at WrestleMania 32, but any continued perception of irrelevance wouldn't be long for this world. That July, Becky Lynch would become the first woman drafted to SmackDown LIVE in the WWE 2016 brand split, as well as the inaugural SmackDown Women's Champion (her first championship in WWE). She'd then go on to feud with the conniving Alexa Bliss, who would defeat her for the championship in a Tables match that December and also bring Mickie James back into WWE as her backup against Becky. Spring of 2017 would see Charlotte move to SmackDown—as a face—and reuniting with Becky (alongside Naomi, as well), feuding with the heel team The Welcoming Committee. The Welcoming Committee would attempt to have Becky join them against Charlotte, but instead of giving in, Becky remained a face and hero. At the same time, Becky would get into a mini-feud—whether it was just character moments or even social media comments—with James Ellsworth, Carmella's manager and SmackDown's resident mansplainer. In November 2017, Becky faced James Ellsworth in what would turn out to be his last match and appearance in WWE as a contracted Superstar, beating him in a rare (for WWE) Intergender match dubbed as "Battle of the Sexes."

The end of 2017 also saw Becky Lynch take some time off from SmackDown LIVE to film the WWE film *The Marine 6: Close Quarters*, in which she was written off through an attack by the debuting heel trio known as The Riott Squad. Becky would return to get her revenge (and again help Charlotte and Naomi) against The Riott Squad to kick off 2018. What's next for The Lass Kicker? As long as it's with WWE, you can bet it'll be something that she loves.

★ THE BELLA TWINS ★

YEARS ACTIVE: Brie Bella: 2007–2016 · 2018, Nikki Bella: 2007–present

TRAINED BY: FCW · Dr. Tom Prichard · Natalya Neidhart

BILLED FROM: Scottsdale, Arizona · San Diego, California

ACCOMPLISHMENTS: 2013 Slammy Award for Diva of the Year · 2016 Teen Choice Awards Choice Female Athlete
Brie Bella: 1x WWE Divas Champion · 2013 Slammy Award for Couple of the Year (with Daniel Bryan) · 2014 Slammy Award for Couple of the Year (with Daniel Bryan) · #16 in 2014 PWI Female 50
Nikki Bella: 2x WWE Divas Champion · longest reigning WWE Divas Champion of all-time · 2015 Slammy Award for Diva of the Year · #1 in 2015 PWI Female 50 · 2015 *Rolling Stone* Diva of the Year

AKA: 2/3 of Team Bella
Brie Bella: "The Bella Dragon" · Brianna Bella
Nikki Bella: "Fearless Nikki" · Nicole Bella · "The Fearless One" · "The Fearless Superstar"

NOTABLE MATCHES: Brie Bella vs. AJ Lee (c) at WWE Hell in a Cell 2013, for the WWE Divas Championship (October 27, 2013) · Brie Bella vs. Stephanie McMahon at WWE SummerSlam 2014 (August 17, 2014) · Nikki Bella vs. Paige (c) vs. AJ Lee at WWE Night of Champions 2014, in a Triple Threat match for the WWE Divas Championship (September 21, 2014) · Brie Bella vs. Nikki Bella at WWE Hell in a Cell 2014 (October 26, 2014) · Brie Bella vs. AJ Lee at WWE SmackDown (March 5, 2015) · Nikki Bella vs. AJ Lee at WWE *Monday Night RAW* (March 16, 2015) · Nikki Bella (c) vs. Paige at WWE *Monday Night RAW*, for the WWE Divas Championship (March 23, 2015) · Brie Bella (with Nikki Bella & Alicia Fox) vs. Charlotte (with Becky Lynch & Paige) vs. Sasha Banks (with Naomi & Tamina) at WWE Battleground 2015 (July 19, 2015) · Team Bella (Brie Bella, Nikki Bella, & Alicia Fox) vs. Team PCB (Paige, Charlotte, & Becky Lynch) vs. Team B.A.D. (Sasha Banks, Naomi, & Tamina) at WWE SummerSlam 2015 (August 23, 2015) · Nikki Bella (c) vs. Charlotte at WWE Night of Champions 2015, for the WWE Divas Championship (September 20, 2015) · Nikki Bella vs. Charlotte (c) at WWE Hell in a Cell 2015, for the WWE Divas Championship (October 25, 2015) · Nikki Bella vs. Natalya at WWE SmackDown LIVE, in a Falls Count Anywhere match (February 21, 2017) · Nikki Bella vs. Carmella vs. Becky Lynch vs. Alexa Bliss vs. Naomi at WWE Backlash 2016, in a 6-Pack Challenge for the inaugural WWE SmackDown Women's Championship (September 11, 2016) · Nikki Bella & John Cena vs. Maryse & The Miz at WWE WrestleMania 33 (April 2, 2017) · Nikki Bella (with Brie Bella) vs. Ronda Rousey (c) at WWE Evolution, for the RAW Women's Champion (October 28, 2018)

⭐ "You can look but you can't touch." With these being the first lyrics of The Bella Twins' entrance theme (which eventually just became Nikki's theme), one might think they know what to expect when it comes to them. Especially as women on the WWE roster who were hired without any previous wrestling experience. However, despite all expectations, the Bellas perhaps are the ultimate bridging of the gap between the Divas Era of WWE and its Divas Revolution/Women's Evolution.

Growing up in Scottsdale, Arizona, Nicole Garcia-Colace (aka "Nikki") had always planned to be a professional soccer player. In fact, she was most likely going to get scouted for a soccer scholarship for college had she not broken her leg. Still, she was able to walk on to Grossmont College's (in San Diego) soccer team. But that didn't last long, as both she and her sister Brianna (aka "Brie") moved to Los Angeles within a year to look for an agent—marketing themselves as a package deal—and trying to get "discovered," while waitressing of course. Nikki even had to lose weight (as she'd had the more athletic build) and re-dye her hair back to dark brown (from blonde) to look more like her sister, something that would become very integral in their WWE careers. They'd appear in *Body Doubles: International Twins Search* in 2006, for the title of "The Most Beautiful Twins in the World," as well as a Budweiser campaign for the World Cup (as the "World Cup Twins"). Prior to this, the twins had appeared on the 2002–2003 NBC series *Meet My Folks*, which put them on WWE's radar in the first place. However, after attending a Diva casting and even being offered contracts, they turned it down, hesitant to relocate to Tampa (the base of WWE's then developmental territory, FCW). 2006 would see WWE reach their orbit once more, as they participated in that year's Diva Search, though they didn't make the cut for the top eight. Still, they would again be offered contracts from WWE, and after their mother talked to officials in the company to make sure everything was on the up-and-up, Brie and Nikki officially signed to a developmental contract with WWE in the summer of 2007.

In FCW, now known as The Bella Twins, Nikki and Brie would immediately feud with Nattie Neidhart (WWE's Natalya) and Victoria Crawford (WWE's Alicia Fox). It was during this feud that the Bellas introduced one of their signature moves—which would be known as "Twin Magic" on the main roster—with the fresher twin replacing the exhausted or hurt twin while the referee's back was turned. (In later years during their WWE careers, this would become more preposterous, especially after Nikki gained more muscle mass and got breast implants. Although it did once lead to the humorous moment of Brie removing tissue from her top to show the referee that she was not Nikki.)

The summer of next year, Brie made her main roster debut on *SmackDown*, entering into a feud with Victoria and Natalya. This feud would be integral to introducing Nikki (and Twin Magic), as it involved Brie regularly rolling out of and under the ring, only to come back out fresh and with the match won. Eventually, it would be revealed that there were "two of them," and The Bella Twins made their official WWE debut. (This would also be similar to how Nikki made her RAW debut after the twins had both been drafted there.) While the twins would wrestle, they'd also become known for their roles as valets (for wrestlers and even for WWE guests, especially in 2009) and their on-screen romances. First, they'd be romantically paired with The Colóns (Carlito and Primo), only to eventually split off into heel (Nikki) and face (Brie) dynamics with The Miz/John Morrison and The Colóns, respectively. This would be the first time the siblings feuded, with Brie technically getting a win over Nikki in a Six-Person Mixed Tag Team match and Nikki then beating her in a singles match (due to Miz and Morrison distraction).

The year 2010 saw the twins engage in a romantic storyline with Daniel Bryan, the WWE Superstar who would eventually become Brie's husband and father of her child. The story would have the two fight for his affection and accompany him to the ring, presumably with the purposes of . . . something possibly over the line of TV-PG, which is why the storyline didn't have a satisfying conclusion. The storyline itself ended in the beginning of 2011, as the Bellas witnessed Bryan kiss Gail Kim (his surprise on-screen girlfriend) backstage. The heel Bellas would momentarily feud with Gail Kim—and Brie and Bryan would eventually start dating off-screen—before moving on to bigger issues: like the Divas Championship.

Nikki and Brie would work together to help each other win the Divas Championship in 2011, but while Nikki would come up short in her attempt at winning the title from Eve Torres, she would help Brie accomplish that same goal the following month. This would be the first title win for either Bella Twin and Brie's only time holding the Divas Championship. Her reign lasted for over two months, but given the time period in WWE, she never had a title match longer than four minutes. Then by March 2012, the twins would split again (this time with heel Brie and face Nikki), reuniting only a month later after Nikki won her first Divas Championship. However, the reunion would be short-lived, as a failed attempt at Twin Magic cost Nikki the championship after a week-long reign, and the two were "fired" on-screen. Except they also really left the company.

Apparently, the Bellas left WWE because they were burnt out from the 300+ day road schedule and needed a break. Still, they returned almost a year later, again in the role of valet/love interest, this time to the heel team of Team Rhodes Scholars (Cody Rhodes and Damien Sandow). They would then feud with The Funkadactyls (as Team Rhodes Scholars feuded with "The Funkasaurus" Brodus Clay and Sweet T), leading up to an Eight-Person Mixed Tag Team match at WrestleMania 29, but the match was supposedly cancelled due to time constraints. "Supposedly" being the key word because it ended up also being an integral plot point in an episode of *Total Divas*, the E! reality series (focusing on the lives and behind-the-scenes of various Divas, especially the Bellas) that debuted that July. (Even Tom Casiello, who was a writer for WWE at the time and integral in providing actual storylines for the Divas, considered the very strong possibility that the match was just cut for *Total Divas* drama.)

The existence of *Total Divas* transformed certain storylines in WWE's Divas Division into storylines specifically created for the show. The Bellas would feud with their co-star Natalya in the summer of 2013 before turning face in a feud with the then Divas Champion AJ Lee, who cut a scathing promo on the entire *Total Divas* cast (calling them reality stars, not wrestlers). Eventually, this would lead to a traditional Survivor Series pay-per-view elimination tag team match, in which Team *Total Divas* won, but the words of AJ Lee would always somewhat hang over The Bella Twins in the eyes of many wrestling fans. In a way, it also didn't help that *Total Divas* acknowledged that Brie and Nikki were also in serious relationships with two of the WWE's biggest Superstars, Daniel Bryan and John Cena, respectively. However, in the case of Brie, her relationship allowed her to have her biggest storyline of her career, as she got involved in Bryan's feud with Stephanie McMahon at April 2014. This feud would lead to her "quitting" WWE and slapping Stephanie on her way out—as well as Nikki getting punished with unfair match stipulations as result. Brie would return in the RAW crowd to confront Stephanie, baiting Stephanie into slapping her in the face. This led to Brie threatening to have Stephanie arrested for assault—as Brie was simply an audience member at the time—unless Stephanie faced her in a match at that year's SummerSlam.

However, Brie's plans of SummerSlam vengeance were dashed by Nikki turning heel during the match and attacking her, securing Stephanie the win. This would lead to the most memorable Bella Twin feud (which would unfortunately fizzle out in a less than spectacular way), as Nikki was upset with Brie for being so selfish and allowing her sister to suffer because of her principles. Jerry Springer would even get involved during this literal blood feud, a feud in which Nikki Bella seriously got to utter the line "I wish you died in the womb," to her twin sister. Nikki would also join forces with Stephanie McMahon, being handed Divas Championship opportunities (though failing) and vengeance in the form of putting Brie in difficult matches as well. The feud would culminate in a match at the Hell in a Cell pay-per-view, in which the loser had to become the winner's personal assistant for 30 days. Nikki would go on to win this match and then the WWE Divas Championship from AJ Lee about a month later. However, after weeks of Nikki treating her sister like dirt, Brie helping her sister win the championship wasn't even due to the personal assistant plot; instead, they were just back to being happy heels together. And they would have Nikki follow-up her despicable behavior toward her sister by having her say, "I was brainwashed," an explanation even Nikki Bella went on the record of saying didn't make sense.

Still, this second championship reign of Nikki's would lead to her becoming the longest-reigning Divas Championship in company history at 301 days (breaking AJ Lee's record of 295 days). She would drop the championship at Hell in a Cell in October 2016 (to Charlotte) and then take another break from WWE, as she had apparently been working through a neck injury and needed surgery. While Nikki was away, Brie transitioned back into a face role, forming a feud with Lana, who would go on to say that people only "liked" her because of her now husband—especially as Bryan had just retired in February 2016 and Brie had been using his finishing submission and some of his signature moves as a tribute to him. This feud would lead into WrestleMania 32, in a 10-Diva Tag Team match in which Brie would tap Naomi

out. WrestleMania 32 would be Brie's final match in WWE (as a full-time wrestler) and Nikki—while still recovering from her neck injury—would even make a surprise appearance post-match to celebrate with her sister. Brie still works with the company in the form of being an ambassador for WWE. While Brie often talks about making a comeback to WWE in both *Total Divas* and *Total Bellas*, there hadn't really been any signs that she'd come out of in-ring retirement—at least not until the summer of 2018, as she and Nikki returned to team up with WWE newbie Ronda Rousey—and eventually feud with her (as heels). (Brie also entered into a feud on SmackDown just before the heel turn, alongside Byan, against The Miz and Maryse.)

But before that, Nikki would make her official return to WWE, after 10 months on the shelf, on the SmackDown brand and as a surprise tag team partner for Natalya and Alexa Bliss on

SummerSlam 2016. Despite teaming with heels for this match though, she'd be making her WWE return as a face, first feuding with Carmella, then feuding with a newly heel Natalya, both women who wanted to call Nikki out for only getting as far as she has in her career because of John Cena. Nikki would win her feud against Carmella, but she would lose the one against Natalya; the final match between the two (a Falls Count Anywhere match) would feature Maryse (The Miz's wife, *Total Divas* co-star, and known critic of the Bellas) attacking Nikki. This attack would lead to a feud between Nikki Bella/John Cena and Maryse/The Miz, culminating in a Mixed Tag Team match at WrestleMania 33. The Bella/Cena duo would of course win, and after the match, John Cena would propose to Nikki in the ring (which would also be the culmination of years of *Total Divas* and *Total Bellas* storylines about Cena not being down to remarry). After WrestleMania—having accepted the proposal, which would eventually be called off—Nikki Bella would take an indefinite hiatus from WWE, as she had aggravated her neck injury in the buildup to the match.

The Bella Twins made an appearance at the 25th Anniversary of *Monday Night RAW* in January 2018, but outside of *Total Divas* and their *Total Bellas* spin-off, they're not quite the fixture they once were in WWE. Still, the Bella Army runs strong.

★ BETH PHOENIX ★

YEARS ACTIVE: 2001–2012

TRAINED BY: AWF · Ron Hutchison · Joey Knight · Robin Knightwing · OVW · Danny Davis

BILLED FROM: Buffalo, New York

ACCOMPLISHMENTS: 1x Far North Wrestling Cruiserweight Champion · 1x GLORY Wrestling Champion · 1x OVW Women's Champion · #2 on 2008 PWI Female 50 · #2 on 2012 PWI Female 50 · 1x WWE Divas Championship · 3x WWE Women's Champion · 2008 Slammy Award for Diva of the Year · 2015 George Tragos/Lou Thesz International Wrestling Institute's Frank Gotch Award · WWE Hall of Fame Class of 2017

AKA: "Phoenix" · "Phoenix The Firebird" · "The Fabulous Firebird" · "The Total Package of Women's Wrestling" · "The Glamazon" · 1/2 of Glamarella · 1/2 of The Divas of Doom · "The Über Diva"

NOTABLE MATCHES: Beth Phoenix vs. Katie Lea (c) at OVW, in a Ladder match for the Undisputed OVW Women's Championship (December 23, 2006) · Beth Phoenix vs. Candice Michelle (c) at WWE No Mercy 2007, for the WWE Women's Championship (October 7, 2007) · Beth Phoenix vs. Mickie James (c) vs. Melina at WWE Judgment Day 2008, in a Triple Threat match for the WWE Women's Championship (May 18, 2008) · Beth Phoenix vs. Melina at WWE One Night Stand 2008, in an "I Quit" match (June 1, 2008) · WWE Royal Rumble 2010, in the Royal Rumble match (January 31, 2010) · Beth Phoenix & Natalya vs. LayCool (Layla & Michelle McCool) at WWE TLC 2010, in Divas Tag Team Tables match (December 19, 2010) · Eve Torres vs. Beth Phoenix (c) at Vengeance 2011, for the WWE Divas Championship (October 23, 2011) · Eve Torres & Beth Phoenix vs. Kelly Kelly & Maria Menounos at WWE WrestleMania XXVIII (April 1, 2012) · WWE Royal Rumble 2018, in the Women's Royal Rumble match (January 28, 2018)

★ Before she was "The Glamazon," the ultimate combination of beauty, strength, and power in the WWE, she was just an 11-year-old girl in New York. An 11-year-old girl who won a local newspaper's coloring contest and received tickets to a WWF television taping, officially sparking her interest in professional wrestling. It would be Bret Hart vs. Owen Hart at WrestleMania 10 that really inspired her and made her appreciate the pureness of professional wrestling. So in high school, she wrestled—in hopes that her amateur wrestling ability would help her stick out in the future—becoming the first female varsity wrestler in her school's history, as well as a member of USA Wrestling. After developing a championship-winning amateur wrestling background in high school, Beth decided it was time to get that professional wrestling career going (while also attending college).

Her training would begin in 2001 at Ron Hutchison's AWF (Apocalypse Wrestling Federation) Wrestling School, learning under Hutchison, as well as Joey Knight and Robin Knightwing (The All-Knighters). In AWF, Beth wrestled as "Phoenix," aka "Phoenix The Firebird," and her debut match was against Alexis Laree (Mickie James's indy moniker at the time), an opponent Beth Phoenix would cross paths with on more than just the independent circuit.

Beth has credited Nora Greenwald (aka Molly Holly) as one of the biggest reasons she eventually got signed by WWE, as Beth would meet the WWF/WWE Diva at a WrestleMania Fan Axxess event in Toronto and give her her wrestling match tape, which Greenwald would pass on to WWE trainer Dr. Tom Prichard. This tape would get Beth a tryout—though she didn't get signed—in May 2004, then due to Greenwald's urging, Beth would go to train at OVW (an independent wrestling school and promotion that also functioned as WWE developmental at the time) that July. She'd also get quite the surprise upon learning that Molly had ended up paying half of her OVW tuition, an action Greenwald considered her way of paying forward her past years of opportunities in the business. (She wouldn't even let Beth pay her back.) On OVW television, Beth would become "Beth Phoenix," working as the on-screen girlfriend/valet of Chris Masters before quickly being repackaged as manager to Aaron "The Idol" Stevens. Come fall of 2005, WWE would officially sign Beth to a developmental contract with them at OVW. By May 2006, Beth would be making her WWE main roster debut on *Monday Night RAW*, as an ally of Trish Stratus and someone from the heel Mickie James's mysterious past. She would go on to say that Mickie James "ruined her life," attacking her for weeks in a row. However, Beth and Mickie never got to complete their feud or even have a match against each other, as Beth would sustain a broken jaw during a match with Victoria

(which she continued and won, despite the injury) and then be sent back down to OVW (where she would return to action two months after the injury).

During her second stint in OVW, Beth eventually became the OVW Women's Champion and held it for 29 days. After she dropped the championship to Katie Lea, however, she would continue to come out with her own championship, claiming to still be the women's champion. (This would technically become part of her future main roster character, as even when she wasn't champion, she would always mime holding an invisible championship as one of her signature poses.) This led to a Ladder match—technically, the first-ever women's Ladder match in WWE—between Beth and Katie Lea to determine the Undisputed OVW Women's Champion, which Lea won. Beth would wrestle for a few more months in OVW before officially returning to the main roster, losing her final match to Katie Lea in a #1 Contender match.

BEFORE SHE WAS "THE GLAMAZON," THE ULTIMATE COMBINATION OF BEAUTY, STRENGTH, AND POWER IN THE WWE, BETH PHOENIX WAS JUST AN 11-YEAR-OLD GIRL IN NEW YORK.

Beth's return to the main roster in July 2007 would lead to the introduction of her heel persona, "The Glamazon," and she would soon get into a WWE Women's Championship feud with Candice Michelle. Phoenix would eventually capture the championship from Candice at No Mercy 2007 in October, later retaining in a 2 Out of 3 Falls rematch when Candice actually broke her clavicle. Eventually, Beth would be part of another WWE first: this time in her feud with Melina (after losing

a 25-Diva "Miss WrestleMania" match, where she would lose it all (after eliminating 12 other women) to Santino in drag (as his "twin sister" "Santina"). Glamarella would break up with Beth challenging "Santina" to a match for the "Miss WrestleMania" title, but she would lose.

After the Glamarella detour, 2010 would feature Beth becoming the second woman (after Chyna) in WWF/WWE history to participate in a Royal Rumble match. She eliminated the largest Superstar on the roster, The Great Khali—by kissing him—before being eliminated herself by CM Punk. To this day, Beth still looks back at this match and considers it her "WrestleMania moment," despite it not taking place at WrestleMania. She'd then become face, feuding with SmackDown authority figure Vickie Guerrero and LayCool, which led to her participation (with the help of Natalya) in the first-ever WWE Divas Tag Team Tables match.

However, by the summer of 2011, Beth Phoenix would be back on *RAW*—though the WWE brand split would completely end soon enough—but she'd also be a heel on a mission, teaming with Natalya (who'd also turned heel) to face off against the "Barbie Doll," models-turned-"wrestlers" in the Divas Division. Especially, in the form of Kelly Kelly, the Divas Champion and face of the division at the time. Together, they would form the "Pin-Up Strong" team of "The Divas of Doom." According to former WWE head writer Tom Casiello, at the time, Beth Phoenix—despite liking and respecting her colleagues behind the scenes—like a number of wrestling fans, didn't understand why she and Natalya had to play the heels simply because they were "wrestlers." After all, even though she preferred to play heel, it was wrestling. Still, during this feud, Beth would win the Divas Championship for the first and only time, from Kelly Kelly, holding onto it for 204 days before losing it to Nikki Bella. The Divas of Doom feuded with Kelly Kelly and Eve Torres on *RAW* while they also feuded with The Chickbusters (AJ Lee and Kaitlyn) on *SmackDown*, though the latter feud—which was dropped after it didn't go with the planned heel turn on Kaitlyn's

the championship to a new face Mickie James), in which the two of them would participate in the first-ever WWE women's I Quit match.

The second half of 2008 would see Beth Phoenix play a more comedic role, as the straight woman to WWE Superstar Santino Marella, forming the "power couple" of "Glamarella." At the time, Beth felt truly as though she needed to do something fresh, having wrestled all the women that were available at this time—so she pitched the *Norbit*-inspired Glamarella idea to Vince McMahon, and he greenlighted the idea the next week. During this time, Beth would win back the Women's Championship for the second time, with Santino winning the Intercontinental Championship. Perhaps as a result of this new, lighter role, she won that year's Slammy Award for Diva of the Year. However, at WrestleMania XXV, she competed in part—was less about the "Barbie Doll" issue (as neither AJ nor Kaitlyn truly fell under the Diva shtick Beth and Natalya were railing against) and more about Natalya's betrayal of her former on-screen protégés. After February 2012, The Divas of Doom seemed to quietly split, with Beth returning back to her face persona for a few months, without a story.

That fall, she would be the victim of a now heel Eve Torres's lies over who attacked Kaitlyn prior to a Divas Championship match; however, once she was cleared of those charges by SmackDown general manager Booker T, she wasn't able to get her revenge against Eve and lost their one-on-one match. She'd then soon return heel again—this time directing her attention at Kaitlyn, who believed Eve's lies at the time—again, losing in their match. Then on the October 29, 2012, edition of *Monday Night RAW*, after losing another match—this time, to AJ Lee—Beth's past enemy, and now RAW manager supervisor Vickie Guerrero would give Beth another chance to win, restarting the match. Beth would win, but later she'd still be "fired" (on a night where Vickie promised someone would be fired) by Vickie for her poor performance lately. Of course, in reality, Beth Phoenix had requested her release from WWE that September, eventually citing that, after a decade of putting her family second to the wrestling business, "it was time to come home to put family first." (Beth would go on to marry WWE Hall of Famer Edge, with whom she now has two daughters.)

In 2017, Beth Phoenix joined the same WWE Hall of Class as Kurt Angle, Diamond Dallas Page, and "Ravishing" Rick Rude, becoming the youngest in-ring performer to ever be inducted. Beth was inducted by her best friend and former Diva of Doom, Natalya. Beth would also eventually get into the announce booth for WWE, contributing commentary to both the company's inaugural events in 2017 and 2018: the Mae Young Classic (on the WWE Network) and the Mixed Match Challenge (on Facebook). She also made a surprise in-ring return in the first-ever WWE Women's Royal Rumble match, and considering just how young and still in shape she is, who

knows, maybe the Glamazon will get back into the ring full time with the new batch of female Superstars—as the women are no longer Divas—and see what they've got. She's already admitted to wanting to wrestle Charlotte Flair and Nia Jax, so they should probably watch out.

★ BILLIE KAY ★

YEARS ACTIVE: 2007–present

TRAINED BY: Pro Wrestling Alliance (PWA) Australia Training School · Madison Eagles · Ryan Eagles · WWE Performance Center

BILLED FROM: Sydney, Australia

ACCOMPLISHMENTS: 2x PWWA Champion · #34 in 2012 PWI Female Top 50 · 2016 NXT Year-End Award for Breakout Star(s) of the Year (with Peyton Royce)

AKA: Jessie McKay · Jessie · 1/2 of The Iconic Duo · 1/3 of The Pink Ladies · 1/2 of Team Australia · "Everybody's Favorite Girlfriend" · "The Femme Fatale" · 1/2 of The IIconics

NOTABLE MATCHES: Jessie McKay (c) vs. KC Cassidy at PWA Only The Strong 2010, for the PWWA Championship (March 5, 2010) · Jessie McKay vs. Sara Del Rey vs. Ayako Hamada SHIMMER Volume 34, in a 3-Way match (September 11, 2010) · Jessie McKay vs. Madison Eagles at SHIMMER Volume 35, for the SHIMMER Championship (September 12, 2010) · Jessie McKay vs. Nicole Matthews at SHIMMER Volume 39, in a 2 Out of 3 Falls match (March 27, 2011) · Jessie McKay vs. Madison Eagles (c) vs. Nicole Matthews at PWWA, in a 3-Way match for the SHIMMER Championship (September 3, 2011) · Jessie McKay vs. Athena vs. Mia Yim at SHIMMER Volume 42, in a 3-Way match (October 1, 2011) · Jessie McKay vs. Evie at PWA Call To Arms VI, in the Tournament Finals for the vacant PWWA Interim Championship (August 25, 2012) · Jessie McKay vs. Shazza McKenzie (c) at PWA Thin Red Line, for the PWWA Championship (August 23, 2014) · Billie Kay,

Peyton Royce, & Daria Berenato vs. Aliyah, Ember Moon, & Liv Morgan at NXT (November 23, 2016) · Billie Kay vs. Asuka (c) vs. Peyton Royce vs. Nikki Cross at NXT TakeOver: San Antonio, in a Fatal 4-Way match for the NXT Women's Championship (January 28, 2017) · The IIconics (Billy Kay & Peyton Royce) vs. Naomi & Asuka at WWE Super Show-Down (October 6, 2018)

⭐ On the independent scene, she was Jessie McKay (her actual name), the bubbly babyface known as "Everybody's Favorite Girlfriend"—a nickname she credits a friend for coming up with. In WWE's developmental program NXT, she became Billie Kay, "The Femme Fatale" and 1/2 of The Iconic Duo (now known as The IIconics, with Peyton Royce, who was KC Cassidy on the independents with Jessie). How did such a transformation occur?

McKay's brother introduced her to professional wrestling when she was 10 years old, and from the moment she saw The Rock work his magic, she knew that she wanted to become a wrestler. As she recounted in an interview with WWE.com: "I remember watching it once, because my brother forced me to sit down and watch it with him, and I fell in love with it." In looking for a wrestling school when she was 17 years old, it also just so happened that her brother was friends with Ryan Eagles, co-owner of PWA Australia Training School (alongside his then wife, Madison Eagles). Three months later, she was having her debut match—and winning, in a 3-Way against her trainer Madison Eagles and Aurora—on her 18th birthday. (This debut match is actually a point of contention, as she's also recorded as having a singles match against Madison Eagles on a PWA show 2 days earlier—and losing.) The match stipulation was to determine who would become the new PWA President, with the winner getting to appoint whoever they chose, and Jessie ended up choosing Madison Eagles anyway, due to their connection.

Unfortunately for Jessie, that would eventually come back to haunt her, as she would spend the next few months of 2007 on a losing streak all around Australia . . . until she beat Madison, Aurora, and Kellie Skater in a 4-Way match that

November. After the match, her friend and mentor would turn heel on her and attack her. This led to a feud that lasted all the way through May 2008—with Madison interfering in Jessie's matches, beating her down, and even powerbombing her onto chairs. The final match in the feud was a Tables match, and while Madison ended up winning, Jessie ended up getting the respect of the crowd—which is exactly the type of thing a good trainer would hope for their trainee to get out of this type of feud. After all of this brutality, Jessie also turned heel, joining forces with Madison Eagle to form The Pink Ladies (with Penni Lane eventually joining as their third). Then in August, with Madison at ringside, Jessie won her first professional wrestling championship, the Pro Wrestling Women's Alliance (PWWA) Championship, defeating Kellie Skater. Jessie would win the title twice during her time on the indies.

The year 2008 was also when Jessie made her presence known in the American independent wrestling scene, wrestling in CZW, ROH, and SHIMMER (with Madison). The Pink Ladies lost both matches they ever had in SHIMMER (at Volumes 21 and 22), but Madison would become the promotion's champion in 2010, and Jessie would eventually challenge her for that championship—both in a singles match and a 3-Way match—but would come up short. However, Jessie was more concerned with her ongoing feud with Nicole Matthews (and the Canadian NINJAS) in SHIMMER anyway, a feud that ended at Volume 39 with a 2 Out of 3 Falls match.

As WWE was always her end goal—The Rock was her childhood idol, after all—after getting the tip from her friend, fellow Australian WWE Superstar Emma, that WWE would be holding tryouts in Australia during a tour, Jessie decided to shoot her shot. After sending her information and wrestling clips to WWE, WWE gave her the okay to try out. Eight weeks later, she got another okay from them: this time, telling her they wanted to sign her. Then in April 2015, she was announced as one of WWE's class of 11 new signees to NXT and the WWE Performance Center in Orlando, Florida. She'd make her NXT

TV debut in a losing effort as "Jessie" that June, but she'd soon be given the name "Billie Kay." By the end of the year, she'd be a heel, but she wouldn't really get a storyline until the summer of 2016.

Billie would also appear on an episode of *WWE SmackDown* in June 2016, working a match (and losing) against Dana Brooke. Despite it only being a one-time deal—as it was only a matter of necessity in the first place, with a good portion of the WWE roster at the time being on an overseas tour—Billie would return to NXT TV, reminding General Manager William Regal that she is essentially a WWE Superstar and deserves to be treated as such. (She wouldn't even have her first win in NXT until July.) Then in October, she and Peyton Royce would form a tag team, eventually calling themselves "The Iconic Duo." Peyton Royce, aka KC Cassidy, was also part of the same NXT signee class as Billie. In fact, the two of them even went to the same high school together, though Billie (who was three years ahead of Peyton) has gone on the record saying they weren't friends, for one simple reason: "[W]e used to have a little silent competition as to who was the biggest WWE fan." They actually didn't become friends until they became wrestlers, as Peyton eventually trained at PWA as well.

IN OCTOBER 2016, BILLIE KAY AND PEYTON ROYCE WOULD FORM A TAG TEAM, EVENTUALLY CALLING THEMSELVES "THE ICONIC DUO."

As *the* mean girls of NXT, The Iconic Duo quickly became one of the highlights of the show—even when they were often being humiliated because of their hubris, especially by Ember Moon and Asuka. Still, despite their win-loss record and often writing checks their mouths couldn't cash—and all the Superstars they would pester backstage, from Johnny Gargano

to Hideo Itami—The Iconic Duo were voted Breakout Star(s) of the Year in the 2016 NXT Year-End Awards. Billie and Peyton even got to compete together in a Fatal 4-Way match for the NXT Women's Championship (against champion Asuka and Nikki Cross) at the start of 2017, where they both actively attempted to help the other win the match. Though they never did think to pin each other in the match—but no one ever said The Iconic Duo was the brightest duo. No one knows just what the rest of Billie Kay's professional wrestling career will bring, but if her pre-WWE work and even her work with Peyton Royce is any indication, it'll be quality. Their debut on the main roster—now as The IIconics, on SmackDown LIVE—right after WrestleMania 34 certainly promised as much.

★ BULL NAKANO ★

YEARS ACTIVE: 1983_1997

TRAINED BY: AJW Dojo

BILLED FROM: Kawaguchi, Japan

ACCOMPLISHMENTS: 1x AJW Champion · 1x AJW Junior Champion · 1x AJW All Pacific Champion · 1x WWWA World Single Champion · 3x WWWA World Tag Team Champion (1x with Dump Matsumoto, 1x with Condor Saito, 1x with Grizzly Iwamoto) · 1988 AJW Japan Grand Prix · 1985 AJW Tag League the Best (with Dump Matsumoto) · AJW Hall of Fame Class of 1998 · 1x Consejo Mundial de Lucha Libre (CMLL) World Women's Champion · Wrestling Observer Newsletter Hall of Fame Class of 2001 · 1x WWF Women's Champion · 1994 Slammy Award for Most Devastating

AKA: Keiko Nakano · member of Gokuaku Domei ("Atrocious Alliance") · 1/2 of the Japanese Devils/Devils of Japan · member of Gokumon-to

NOTABLE MATCHES: Gokumon-to (Bull Nakano & Grizzly Iwamoto) vs. Jungle Jack (Aja Kong & Bison Kimura) at AJW Survival Shot (August 19, 1990) · Bull Nakano (c) vs. Aja Kong at AJW Wrestlemarinepiad 1990, for the WWWA World Title in a Steel Cage match (November 14, 1990) · Gokumon-to (Bull Nakano & Kyoko Inoue) vs. Jungle Jack (Aja Kong & Bison Kimura) at AJW, in a Hair vs. Hair match (January 11, 1991) · Gokumon-to (Bull Nakano & Kyoko Inoue) vs. Jungle Jack (Aja Kong & Bison Kimura) vs. Manami Toyota & Esther Moreno at AJW (April 29, 1991) · Bull Nakano vs. Akira Hokuto at AJW (March 7, 1992) · Bull Nakano & Aja Kong vs. Akira Hokuto & Toshiyo Yamada at AJW Mid Summer Typhoon (August, 15, 1992) · Bull Nakano & Aja Kong vs. Eagle Sawai & Harley Saito at AJW Dream Slam 1 (April 2, 1993) · Bull Nakano & Aja Kong vs. Akira Hokuto & Kyoko Inoue at AJW (June 3, 1993) · Bull Nakano vs. Kaoru Ito at AJW (January 4, 1994) · Bull Nakano vs. Alundra Blayze (c) at WWF SummerSlam 1994, for the WWF Women's Championship (August 29, 1994) · Bull Nakano vs. Alundra Blayze (c) at AJW Doumu Super Woman Great War ~ Big Egg Wrestling Universe, for the WWF Women's Championship (November 20, 1994) · Bull Nakano (c) vs. Kyoko Inoue at AJW Wrestling Queendown 1995, for the WWF Women's Championship (Mach 26, 1995) · Bull Nakano & Akira Hokuto vs. Manami Toyota & Mariko Yoshida at WCW/NJPW Collision In Korea, Day 1 (April 29, 1995) · Bull Nakano vs. Kyoko Inoue at AJW Destiny (September 2, 1995) · Bull Nakano & Akira Hokuto vs. Cutie Suzuki & Mayumi Ozaki at WCW World War 3 1995 (November 26, 1995) · Bull Nakano & Akira Hokuto vs. Cutie Suzuki & Mayumi Ozaki at WCW Nitro (November 27, 1995)

★ Keiko Nakano was just 16 years old when she won the AJW Junior Championship, having only started her training at the AJW Dojo just the year before. Upon winning the championship, she would then become known as "Bull Nakano," a name meant to evoke thoughts of her in-ring presence and her size, like a "bulldozer." Standing at 5 foot 7 inches (and even taller with her hair) and billed at about 200 pounds (though that weight would increase over the years, until she lost it all post-retirement), Nakano's menacing presence, even at such a young age, made her a perfect heel. However, because she was so young, she wanted to remain Keiko and stay a face. Still, she'd go on to hold the Junior Championship until she vacated after eight months. Under the mentorship of fellow heel Dump Matsumoto—whose punk rock look transferred over to her mentee as they feuded with joshi icons like The Crush Gals—Nakano would then move on to the AJW Championship (a tertiary singles title in the company). That title she would win at the age of 17 and would go on to hold it for nearly three years (losing it to Yumi Ogura).

By 18, she'd be wrestling alongside Matsumoto in the WWF in the United States—a place she'd return to in her 20s, as the top contender to Alundra Blayze's WWF Women's Championship. In WWF (over the course of just three matches), Nakano and Matsumoto were known collectively as the "Japanese Devils" (or the "Devils of Japan") facing off against the likes of Dawn Marie and Velvet McIntyre.

As part of Matsumoto's heel faction Gokuaku Domei (aka "Atrocious Alliance"), Nakano would create an alliance with Aja Kong (then known as Erika Shishido), a partnership that would end after Matsumoto's retirement in 1988. 1990 then saw Nakano take over Gokuaku Domei as her own heel faction, Gokumon-to, and feud with Aja Kong and Bison Kimura (known as the team "Jungle Jack"). In the feud with Jungle Jack, Nakano and Kyoko Inoue would go on to win a Hair vs. Hair match against their rival tag team in 1991. And as leaders of their respective stables, Nakano and Kong also faced off in singles championship competition. In fact, Kong was the one to put an end to Nakano's (other) nearly three-year-long reign as AJW's WWWA World Single Champion. Still, Kong couldn't take away the fact that Bull Nakano had the longest WWWA World Single Championship reign in the company's history, at 1,057 days.

However, by the end of 1992—just after she'd lost the world title—AJW would phase Nakano out of the company, due to her own desire to wrestle more in North America. That June, she had started wrestling in CMLL in Mexico, becoming the promotion's first World Women's Champion that same month and holding the title for 282 days. After she dropped the championship to Xóchitl Hamada, she'd be done with CMLL. But Nakano would then sign with WWF in 1994, after Alundra Blayze (aka Madusa Miceli) was brought in to be the star of the company's Women's Division and pushed for them to sign her former AJW colleague. Blayze would retain the Women's Championship during their match at the SummerSlam 1994 pay-per-view; however, Nakano would get the win and the championship that November at the Tokyo Dome, in the historic AJW Big Egg Wrestling Universe show. Blayze would win the championship back on an episode of *Monday Night RAW* five months later. Still, WWF wanted to keep Nakano, and the plan was for her to feud with Bertha Faye next . . . until Nakano was allegedly found in possession of cocaine and arrested. That officially ended her stint in WWF, though she and Alundra Blayze (as Madusa) would feud again in 1996 at WCW, during its own attempt at a burgeoning women's division.

In fact, Madusa would be Nakano's final official wrestling opponent. By 1997, Bull Nakano was ready to step away from wrestling, officially retiring due to injuries accumulated from her bulldozing style at such a young age. Unlike most joshi stars, Nakano didn't have an official retirement match. Instead, she got out of the wrestling business completely, lost weight—even writing weight-loss cookbooks—became a professional golfer (though she didn't make it into the LPGA), and opened her own restaurant and bar in Japan called BullChan. However, in 2011, Nakano announced she would finally have her official retirement, in a self-produced wrestling show called Bull Nakano Produce Empress (or simply "Empress"). To do this, Nakano also broke her diet for a time, specifically to get back into "Bull" mode. Empress took place on her 44th birthday (January 8, 2012) and was a rare tribute show and retirement ceremony more about the future of the business than the past. In the

final segment—the ceremony itself—Nakano recreated spots from her most famous matches (including her 1990 Steel Cage match with Aja Kong), with video visuals to go along with the moments. After the re-creations, she also got married at the event, officially making it a show to remember.

While true in-ring action appears to be out of the question, as of 2012, Bull currently does commentary for STARDOM. At the end of 2017, she'd also bring back and manage a new version of Gokumon-to in the RISE Wrestling promotion—again focusing on the future of the business—consisting of Kris Wolf, "The Fallen Flower" Kikyo Nakamura, and "Dynamite" Didi Cruz.

★ CANDICE LERAE ★

YEARS ACTIVE: 2002–present

TRAINED BY: Bill Anderson · Jesse Hernandez · Mr. Excitement · TJ Perkins

BILLED FROM: Mr. Toad's Wild Ride · Anaheim, CA · Winnipeg, Manitoba, Canada

ACCOMPLISHMENTS: 1x Alternative Wrestling Show Women's Champion · 1x DDT Pro-Wrestling Ironman Heavymetalweight Champion · 1x Dreamwave Wrestling Tag Team Champion (with Joey Ryan) · 1x Family Wrestling Entertainment (FWE) Women's Champion · 1x Fighting Spirit Pro Wrestling Tag Team Champion (with Joey Ryan) · 1x Pro Wrestling Guerrilla (PWG) World Tag Team Champion (with Joey Ryan) · 2015 SMASH Wrestling Gold Tournament · #18 in 2016 PWI Female 50

AKA: "Candice Wrestling" · 1/2 of The World's Cutest Tag Team · Candice LaRae · Candice LaRea · Candice LaRoux · Sweet Candy · "The First Lady of PWG" · "The Canadian Goddess"

NOTABLE MATCHES: The World's Cutest Tag Team (Candice LeRae & Joey Ryan) & Drake Younger vs. Mount Rushmore (Kevin Steen, Matt Jackson, & Nick Jackson) at PWG All Star Weekend 10 Night 2 (December 21, 2013) · Candice LeRae vs. Adam Cole (c) at PWG Mystery Vortex 2, for the PWG World Championship (March 28, 2014) · The World's Cutest Tag Team (Candice LeRae & Joey Ryan) vs. The Young Bucks (Matt Jackson & Nick Jackson) (c) at PWG ELEVEN, in a Guerrilla Warfare match for the PWG World Tag Team Championship (July 26, 2014) · Candice LeRae vs. Ivelisse Vélez (c) at FWE ReFueled Night 2, for the FWE Women's Championship (October 4, 2014) · Candice LeRae vs. Kimber Lee at SMASH Wrestling Any Given Sunday 3 (March 15, 2015) · The World's Cutest Tag Team (Candice LeRae & Joey Ryan), Chris Hero, & Mike Bailey vs. Mount Rushmore 2.0 (Adam Cole, Matt Jackson, Nick Jackson, & Roderick Strong) at PWG All Star Weekend 11 Night 2, in a Guerrilla Warfare match (December 12, 2015) · Candice LeRae

vs. Nicole Savoy vs. Heidi Lovelace at SHIMMER Volume 80, in a Heart of SHIMMER Championship Tournament Finals 3-Way Elimination match for the inaugural Heart of SHIMMER Championship (April 2, 2016) · Team SHIMMER (Candice LeRae, "Crazy" Mary Dobson, & Solo Darling) vs. Team Original Divas Revolution (Jazz, Mickie James, & Victoria) at CHIKARA King of Trios 2016 - Night 1, in a King of Trios First Round match (September 2, 2016) · Candice LeRae vs. Sami Callihan (c) at AAW: Pro Wrestling Redefined (AAW) Don't Stop Believing, for the AAW Heavyweight Championship (January 20, 2017)

★ If there's one women's wrestler who could best be described as "one of the guys," it's probably Candice LeRae. And that's with the caveat that most of the guys probably don't appreciate that one of her signature wrestling moves is the Balls-Plex, a crotch clutch suplex. That's also including her husband, WWE fellow NXT

Superstar Johnny Gargano, who Candice has faced in singles competition on the independent circuit many times before.

Inspired by "Macho Man" Randy Savage, Shawn Michaels, and Chris Jericho—and her favorite women's wrestler of all time, Molly Holly—Candice got her start in the business in 2002 (when she was 17), training at Jesse Hernandez's School of Hard Knocks, which was about 30 minutes away from her hometown of Riverside, California. (Despite popular belief, she is not from Canada.) She'd make her official wrestling debut in August 2003, at Hernandez's independent wrestling promotion, EWE, under the ring name of "Sweet Candy." It was a dream she'd had since she was six years old.

Candice would wrestle all around California through 2006, making her debut in the Midwestern independent wrestling circuit in the summer of 2007. She'd also get a couple of dark matches in ROH (under the SHIMMER banner) against Sara Del Rey (in a title match for the SHIMMER Championship) and Daizee Haze. But PWG in Southern California is where Candice would make her name and consider her home promotion. She started there as a manager, before becoming one of the rare women to wrestle there at all. And then she'd eventually be the only woman to wrestle there, as well as one of the most beloved wrestlers to work at the promotion, period. Starting as a manager to the wrestler Human Tornado, she was involved in one of the promotion's rare serialized stories, as Human Tornado's physical and verbal abuse of Candice would come to a head at the 2007 Battle of Los Angeles tournament. There, she would intentionally cost him his match in the first round of the tournament, and Chris Hero would save her. She would go on to become Hero's manager in PWG then (and on his side in his feud with Human Tornado), while also wrestling in intergender matches and matches with the few other women's competitors in the promotion at the time.

But it wouldn't be until 2013 and 2014 that Candice became a legend in the hearts and minds of the PWG fans. (That's also when she would start wrestling in promotions like CZW, FWE,

WSU, SHIMMER, FIP, and even the more mainstream TNA.) A feud with Joey Ryan turned into the two of them eventually forming an alliance (against the PWG heel faction called Mount Rushmore) and then a tag team called The World's Cutest Tag Team. During this feud of Candice/Joey/PWG against Mount Rushmore, Candice even participated in a closely contested championship match against the then PWG Champion (and member of Mount Rushmore) Adam Cole. Then at PWG's 11th anniversary show, ELEVEN, in July 2014, The World's Cutest Tag Team faced Mount Rushmore members and PWG Tag Team Champions The Young Bucks in a match for the tag team championship. And it wasn't just a normal match: it was a Guerilla Warfare match, PWG's most brutal match concept, with anything goes rules. Not only would The World's Cutest Tag Team win the match and the championship, Candice would be the reason why they won. She'd also create a lasting image in professional wrestling history: a crimson red mask of blood on her face, after taking a superkick (from a shoe rigged with thumbtacks on the sole) from The Young Bucks' Matt Jackson.

Candice's involvement and success in PWG is honestly even more of an anomaly as Super Dragon, PWG cofounder and owner, had gone on the record in a Q&A in 2012 about how he hadn't "liked any women matches in PWG ever" and would "probably never fly anyone in for a womens [sic] match." According to him, that made it "hard" to find a place for Candice on the card. But The Young Bucks' own praise of Candice—Matt Jackson has called her "the best female wrestler in the world"—helped greatly in her becoming one of the most beloved faces in PWG history, and out of that came even more opportunities for her.

The Guerrilla Warfare match would get new eyes on Candice, and she'd go on to call it the "match [that] changed [her] career & life." In 2016, Candice would make her Japanese wrestling debut in both DDT Pro-Wrestling (alongside Joey Ryan) and its all-female sister promotion, Tokyo Joshi Pro.

Then in 2017, the still independent Candice would appear on WWE TV—in the form of its developmental series, *NXT*—

first in an NXT Women's Championship #1 Contendership Battle Royal, then in another battle royal (with the same goal). Then in the summer of 2017, she was announced as one of the 32 female competitors from all around the world to compete in the WWE's inaugural Mae Young Classic Tournament. She made it to the quarterfinals before being eliminated. For Candice, just competing in WWE (despite not being a contracted Superstar) was proof that all of her hard work had paid off:

> I used to think I got into wrestling at the wrong time and it was never going to happen for me because I was a little different than some of the other girls that I was around when I first started wrestling. I'm starting to realize everything happened as it was supposed to, and I got into it at exactly the right time, so I am very thankful.

In December 2017, Candice announced that her and Joey Ryan's merchandise would be sold in select Hot Topic stores across the United States. Then in January 2018, it was announced that Candice LeRae had signed a contract with WWE, making something that seemed like an inevitability finally become a reality.

★ CANDICE MICHELLE ★

YEARS ACTIVE: 2004–2009

TRAINED BY: Dave "Fit" Finlay · Arn Anderson · Trish Stratus

BILLED FROM: Milwaukee, Wisconsin

ACCOMPLISHMENTS: 2007 PWI Most Improved Wrestler of the Year · 2007 PWI Woman of the Year · 1x WWE Women's Champion · #10 in 2008 PWI Female 50

AKA: Candice · 1/3 of Ladies in Pink · 1/3 of Vince's Devils · "Go Daddy Girl" · "Miss GoDaddy.com"

NOTABLE MATCHES: Candice Michelle vs. Melina (c) at WWE Vengeance 2007, for the WWE Women's Championship (June 24, 2007) · Candice Michelle (c) vs. Melina at WWE The Great American Bash 2007, for the WWE Women's Championship (July 22, 2007) · Candice Michelle (c) vs. Beth Phoenix at WWE No Mercy 2007, for the WWE Women's Championship (October 7, 2007) · Candice Michelle vs. Beth Phoenix (c) at WWE *Monday Night RAW*, in a 2 Out of 3 Falls match for the WWE Women's Championship (October 22, 2007) · Candice Michelle vs. Lisa Marie Varon at House of Hardcore (HOH) 36: Blizzard Brawl 2017 (December 2, 2017)

★ In the early 2000s era of WWE Divas, Candice Michelle was notable for her desire to improve as a professional wrestler—even though all signs pointed to the fact that she didn't have to.

Coming from the modeling and acting world, Candice Michelle entered the world of WWE through the 2004 WWE Diva Search. While she didn't make it to the top 10 (and onto the weekly *RAW* show to officially compete), after making it to the semifinals, she was offered a three-year contract to the WWE. When she debuted on *RAW* in November 2004, she was given the gimmick of a makeup artist, and while that didn't exactly explain why she'd be part of in-ring competition, given the time period in WWE, "in-ring competition" in Candice Michelle's case often involved Divas Costume and Lingerie Pillow Fight contests. In 2005, she bounced back and forth between *RAW* and *SmackDown*, teaming up with Victoria and Torrie Wilson as a heel trio called Vince's Devils (originally Ladies in Pink)—until Candice announced that she'd be posing for *Playboy*, which caused tension between herself and Wilson (who became a babyface in the storyline). Soon after, all mentions to Vince's Devils were dropped, as was the relationship between the "remaining" two members, as Candice Michelle also eventually turned face. (Somewhere in all of that was an aspect where Candice Michelle was Vince McMahon's "sex slave.")

In addition to *Playboy*, Candice Michelle also found further mainstream success during her time in WWE as the "Go Daddy Girl" in GoDaddy.com commercials, notably commercials that aired during the Super Bowl.

The fall of 2006 was when the tide began to turn for Candice Michelle as an in-ring competitor, as fans began to notice (and were given the chance to notice) an improvement in her wrestling ability. The night after Lita lost her WWE Women's Championship at the Unforgiven pay-per-view, Candice beat her on *Monday Night RAW* in a singles match. The next week—in a first round match for the then vacated Women's Championship—she unfortunately couldn't create a repeat performance, as she was speared by Lita's significant other, Edge, who was also the special referee in the match. A couple of months later, Candice would have to take time off to repair her deviated septum, but she returned in January 2007 to feud with Melina. Again, the improvement in her wrestling ability was evident, as Candice even admitted that she would spend her days off training to improve her craft. To some, considering Candice Michelle's entrance into her company and all of the focus on her sex appeal, this would be surprising to learn; but for the girl whose childhood basement was covered in Hulk Hogan posters and who would go to wrestling shows whenever they'd come to Milwaukee, it was simply the drive of someone passionate about the business from a young age. Yes, she was still doing Bra & Panties matches and Pudding matches during her feud with Melina, but she'd also have competitive singles matches against Melina, Mickie James, and Victoria, who were all considered some of the top in-ring competitors in the division.

Then at the Vengeance: Night of Champions pay-per-view, Candice defeated Melina for the Women's Championship, making her the first woman from the WWE Diva Search competition to ever hold a championship WWE. She would even retain the championship in Melina's rematch against her. But unfortunately, Candice Michelle would next feud with "The Glamazon" Beth Phoenix, and she would lose the championship to her at No Mercy 2007. Even worse, the rematch a couple of weeks later—a 2 Out of 3 Falls match—would lead to Candice suffering a broken clavicle during the match, and she would be out of action for over three months. She'd return in February 2008 to get revenge on Beth Phoenix, only to be re-injured in her return match, this time breaking her clavicle in four different places. Ultimately, Candice would get the upper hand against Phoenix when she returned again, but she'd come up short when it came to winning the Women's Championship from Phoenix. Then, in the 2009 WWE draft after WrestleMania XXV, Candice Michelle was traded to SmackDown. Unfortunately, she never actually made her SmackDown debut and was released from the WWE that June.

In October 2017, Candice announced that she would have one last match—her first since 2009—in her home state of Wisconsin. The match would be at former ECW/WWE star Tommy Dreamer's independent wrestling promotion, House of Hardcore, and she'd be facing Lisa Marie Varon (known as Victoria during their time in WWE). After she won the match, she thanked Dreamer for allowing her to have an official retirement match, as well as Varon for helping her along the way when she was in WWE. While her time in WWE was short—and her time as a legitimate contender in WWE was even shorter—Candice Michelle showed an amount of improvement (and grit, considering her injuries) that should be looked back on fondly.

★ CARMELLA ★

YEARS ACTIVE: 2013–present

TRAINED BY: WWE Performance Center

BILLED FROM: Staten Island

ACCOMPLISHMENTS: 2x (and inaugural) SmackDown Women's Money in the Bank (2017) · #38 in 2017 PWI Female 50 · 1x WWE SmackDown Women's Champion

AKA: "The Princess of Staten Island" · "Ms. Money in the Bank" · "Hottest Chick In The Ring" · member of The Welcoming Committee · 1/2 of Fabulous Truth

NOTABLE MATCHES: Carmella, Enzo Amore, & Colin "Big Cass" Cassady vs. Alexa Bliss, Blake, & Murphy at NXT (June 17, 2015) · Carmella vs. Alexa Bliss vs. Nia Jax at NXT, for the #1 Contendership to the NXT Women's Championship (May 25, 2016) · Carmella vs. Becky Lynch vs. Alexa Bliss vs. Naomi vs. Nikki Bella at WWE Backlash 2016, in a 6-Pack Challenge for the inaugural WWE SmackDown Women's Championship (September 11, 2016) · Carmella (with James Ellsworth) vs. Becky Lynch vs. Charlotte Flair vs. Natalya vs. Tamina Snuka at WWE Money in the Bank 2017, in a Money in the Bank Ladder match, for the inaugural Women's Money in the Bank contract (June 18, 2017) · Carmella vs. Becky Lynch vs. Charlotte Flair vs. Natalya vs. Tamina Snuka at WWE SmackDown LIVE, in a Money in the Bank Ladder match, for the Women's Money in the Bank contract (June 27, 2017)

⭐ The fact that Carmella (or, Leah Van Dale) is a second-generation wrestler is a tidbit that might surprise most wrestling fans. The daughter of '90s WWF enhancement talent Paul Van Dale, Leah was "obsessed with Miss Elizabeth" growing up—her father would even carry her on his shoulder like Miss Elizabeth. Obviously, wrestling wasn't just her father's passion. "We would record *Monday Night Raw* every week so that I could watch it." But her road to WWE wasn't just a straight shot from childhood into wrestling. Instead, after graduating from college, she became a cheerleader for the New England Patriots and eventually a Los Angeles Laker Girl. However, wrestling was still in the back of her mind: When she'd moved to Los Angeles, she'd also submitted an audition to be part of the WWE reality competition series *Tough Enough* in 2010. While that didn't quite pan out, when the opportunity struck again for Van Dale to try out for WWE, she took it.

Signing with WWE in June 2013 and reporting to NXT and the WWE Performance Center to train that September, Van Dale (as Carmella) would debut about a year after she began training. Carmella got to debut in a way most wrestlers don't these days, with a pre-established career as part of her gimmick. Not exactly the same as being a wrestler whose profession is a gimmick though, as Carmella was introduced in a pre-taped segment as a hairdresser friend of Enzo Amore and Colin "Big Cass" Cassady. In the segment, Enzo and Cass went to Carmella's hair salon to test hair removal cream—as Enzo was preparing for a Hair vs. Hair match—and accidentally spilled the cream on her boss's dog. (Out of character, Carmella has since assured everyone that the dog is fine. In fact, there were actually two dogs—one with a lot of hair and one without for the shoot.) So to make things up for her losing her job as a result, they got her a job as a wrestler on NXT. It's certainly not one of the more far-fetched gimmick backstories in WWE history. While Enzo and Cass were face, however, Carmella (who also worked as their manager) was introduced as a heel.

Fans were frustrated that Carmella would ruin the dynamic between Enzo and Cass, both because she felt like a character siphoning off of the duo's established gimmick and because the story planted the seeds of the heel Carmella possibly manipulating the lovesick Enzo to do something reckless. (When she debuted, it was against an enhancement talent flippantly called "Blue Pants" by Cass, and the NXT crowd took to her much quicker than they did to Carmella.) However, once Carmella turned face—removing the natural antagonism between herself and Enzo—after the Blue Pants saga and during the trio's feud with Blake and Murphy (and eventually Alexa Bliss), fans became much more accepting of Carmella and what she brought to the table in NXT. It's a time Carmella still looks back on fondly:

> Working with them was so much fun. When I first got to NXT, they were the first two people who I made friends with. We all hung out all the time, and what you saw on-screen was kind of what it was like in real life.

We were just three friends who hung out. And of course, being able to manage them, they were such a popular tag team, I had so much fun with them. It was really such a blast, and it's really cool to see where they are now and how far they've come from their NXT days.

In the summer of 2016, after spending the first part of the year attempting to win the NXT Women's Championship from Bayley (her real-life best friend) and then Asuka, Carmella was the final person to be drafted in the 2016 WWE draft. Reporting to SmackDown LIVE, Carmella debuted as a face (feuding with Natalya), before turning heel again a month later and feuding with Nikki Bella. The end of the year then saw Carmella move on to James Ellsworth, a WWE enhancement talent-turned-Superstar (and the butt of many storyline jokes), giving him a makeover and essentially manipulating him into becoming her manager, manservant, and punching bag. Regarding the driving force behind the pairing, it was actually Carmella who came up with the idea—of her having this character to hang on to her every word and help her win her matches—and she pitched it directly to Vince McMahon himself. This relationship became even more beneficial to Carmella in the summer of 2017, when Ellsworth helped Carmella become the winner of the first-ever Women's Money in the Bank Ladder match by climbing the ladder himself and dropping the Money in the Bank briefcase (with a contract guaranteeing the holder an automatic title shot, any time, any place, for a year) right down to Carmella. That created a whirlwind of controversy, as the weeks of buildup to this match were all about the history being made with this match and the importance of it for the female Superstars . . . only for a man to "win" the match. Several days later, there would be a Money in the Bank Ladder match rematch on SmackDown LIVE, and Carmella would win again—this time climbing the ladder herself (with only minimal Ellsworth interference).

Alas, the relationship between Carmella and Ellsworth would not stay perfect. Eventually, Carmella would start keeping him on a dog collar. She'd also start scolding him more harshly for costing her matches and making mistakes. Then that November, after Ellsworth lost a match against Becky Lynch (who he'd been antagonizing nonstop during his association with Carmella), Carmella would superkick him, and that would be the end of their pairing. What that meant next for Carmella was still anyone's guess, but she still kept busy, both as Ms. Money in the Bank and as one of the newest cast members of WWE's E! reality series *Total Divas*, in its seventh season.

Two days after WrestleMania 34, Carmella cashed in her Money in the Bank contract on Charlotte Flair—after The IIconics had attacked her—to become the SmackDown Women's Champion for the first time, proving 'Mella really is money.

★ CHARLOTTE FLAIR ★

YEARS ACTIVE: 2012–present

TRAINED BY: Lodi · WWE Performance Center

BILLED FROM: "The Queen City"

ACCOMPLISHMENTS: 1x NXT Women's Champion · 2014 NXT Women's Championship Tournament · 1x WWE Divas Champion · 4x WWE (and inaugural) Women's/RAW Women's Champion · 2x WWE SmackDown Women's Champion · 2014 PWI Rookie of the Year · 2016 PWI Feud of the Year (vs. Sasha Banks) · 2016 PWI Woman of the Year · #1 in 2016 PWI Female 50

AKA: Ashley Flair · "Daddy's Little Girl" · "The Nature Girl" · "The Dirtiest Player In The Game" · "The Dirtiest Diva In The Game" · "The Queen" · "The Genetically Superior Athlete" · "The Flair of NXT" · 1/3 of The BFFs (Beautiful Fierce Females) · 1/3 of Team PCB · 1/4 of The Four Horsewomen (WWE)

NOTABLE MATCHES: Charlotte (with Ric Flair) vs. Natalya (with Bret Hart) at NXT TakeOver, for the vacant NXT Women's

Championship (May 29, 2014) · Charlotte (c) vs. Sasha Banks at NXT TakeOver: R Evolution, for the NXT Women's Championship (December 11, 2014) · Charlotte (c) vs. Bayley vs. Sasha Banks vs. Becky Lynch at NXT TakeOver: Rival, in a Fatal 4 Way match for the NXT Women's Championship (February 11, 2015) · Charlotte vs. Becky Lynch vs. Sasha Banks, in a Triple Threat for the vacant WWE Women's Championship at WrestleMania 32 (April 3, 2016) · Charlotte (c) vs. Sasha Banks, for the WWE RAW Women's Championship (October 3, 2016) · Charlotte Flair (c) vs. Sasha Banks at WWE *Monday Night RAW*, in a Falls Counts Anywhere match for the WWE RAW Women's Championship (November 28, 2016) · Charlotte Flair (c) vs. Bayley at WWE *Monday Night RAW*, for the WWE RAW Women's Championship (February 13, 2017) · Charlotte Flair vs. Carmella (with James Ellsworth) vs. Becky Lynch vs. Natalya vs. Tamina Snuka at WWE Money in the Bank 2017, in a Money in the Bank Ladder match, for the inaugural Women's Money in the Bank contract (June 18, 2017) · Charlotte Flair vs. Carmella vs. Becky Lynch vs. Natalya vs. Tamina Snuka at WWE SmackDown LIVE, in a Money in the Bank Ladder match, for the Women's Money in the Bank contract (June 27, 2017) · Charlotte Flair vs. Becky Lynch (c) at WWE Evolution, in a Last Woman Standing match for the SmackDown Women's Championship (October 28, 2018)

⭐ Charlotte Flair has won every possible Women's Championship she can in the WWE: the NXT Women's Championship, the now defunct WWE Divas Championship, the new WWE Women's Championship (which became the RAW Women's Championship after the 2016 brand split), and the SmackDown Women's Championship. Not bad for a woman who never planned to be a professional wrestler. That might be surprising, considering she's the daughter of wrestling legend and two-time WWE Hall of Famer Ric Flair, but before she was Charlotte Flair, Ashley Fliehr was a star high school and college volleyball player. Wrestling was the furthest thing from her mind, even though she, her mother, and her brother Reid had previously appeared on WCW television in a storyline between her dad and David Flair, her half-brother. She could also be seen in the crowd at WWE events during her father's big matches. Wrestling was

always just a part of Ashley's life, but unlike David or even Reid, it wasn't her life.

Yet in May 2012—after doing some preliminary wrestling training in her home state of North Carolina with the wrestler Lodi—she signed a developmental contract with the WWE. She's even admitted that she didn't really even watch wrestling or know anything about the intricacies of the sport pre-developmental. Debuting on NXT TV in the summer of 2013, Charlotte started off as a face and began teaming with NXT's resident fan girl, Bayley, who was in awe of Charlotte's existence as the daughter of Ric Flair. But by the fall of 2013, Charlotte would turn heel, joining NXT's villainous crew of Summer Rae and Sasha Banks, The BFFs (Beautiful Fierce Females). However soon after this turn, she would get injured for real and be on the shelf for two months. Charlotte has said that getting injured during her first real year as a wrestler was something of a wake-up call, as she was "forced to watch" Emma and Paige set the tone for women's wrestling in NXT—and set the stage for the eventual revolutionizing of the Divas Division on the main roster of WWE. That was when she noticed how it was more than just wrestling that mattered, as Emma and Paige were real characters who were connecting with the audience.

When she returned from her injury, she and The BFFs continued to feud with Bayley, as well as Bayley's backup in the form of Natalya (a member of the Hart wrestling family and the daughter of Jim "The Anvil" Neidhart). She would also feud with the then NXT Women's Champion, Paige, though she would never be able to win the title from Paige herself (as Paige would be called up to the main roster, vacating the championship). Charlotte, however, would make it to the finals of the vacant NXT Women's Championship Tournament at NXT TakeOver. As would Natalya, who had previously beaten her via disqualification during their earlier tag team feud. Charlotte credits her match with Natalya as being the true clicking point: "I needed that night. . . . That gave me everything I needed to know." That match would also have Ric Flair in Charlotte's corner and Natalya's uncle, Bret Hart, in hers.

Charlotte admits that her father didn't offer her any help or training until after she won the NXT Women's Championship. In her opinion, her father didn't really take women's wrestling seriously at that point in time, but these days, he's more than willing to tell anyone who will listen that he believes Charlotte is "the greatest, by far" when it comes to women's wrestling. (Once she turned heel on the main roster, Ric would be her manager. Until she turned on him too, that is.) By the summer of 2014, The BFFs would be broken up, and by that fall, Charlotte would be a face champion feuding with Sasha Banks. She'd also face Natalya one-on-one again—but not for the last time—during a special one-off appearance on the main roster, on the 2014 Slammy Awards episode of *Monday Night RAW*. While Charlotte initially retained her championship against Sasha Banks, she would drop it to her in a Fatal 4-Way match at NXT

TakeOver: Rival and would not get it back in rematches. The second rematch was Charlotte's last match as part of the NXT roster, and afterward she and Sasha would hug—a reminder of their past in NXT as well as their status as members of the group collectively known as The Four Horsewomen of the WWE. (The Four Horsewomen comprises Charlotte, Sasha, Bayley, and Becky Lynch, in a callback to Charlotte's father's Hall of Fame faction The Four Horsemen. Together and individually, these four women are considered integral players when it comes to women's wrestling in both NXT and main roster WWE.)

The summer of 2015 saw three quarters of The Four Horsewomen (Charlotte, Sasha, and Becky) be called up to the main roster, as Stephanie McMahon cut a promo calling for a "Divas revolution" on an episode of *Monday Night RAW*. With that, Charlotte and Becky would form a trio with Paige (as Team PCB), while Sasha Banks would join Naomi and Tamina (as Team B.A.D.), and both teams would feud with each other and Team Bella (The Bella Twins and Alicia Fox). While still part of Team PCB, Charlotte soon got into a Divas Championship feud with Team Bella's Nikki Bella, winning a main roster WWE title for the first time that September at Night of Champions. However, the following night, Paige turned on Charlotte and Becky—though she spent another month feigning contrition about this, so the team didn't immediately split—and she'd eventually fail to win the championship from Charlotte on multiple occasions for the rest of 2015.

It was toward the end of 2015 that Charlotte began her heel turn (with her father by her side) as Divas Champion, turning on Becky Lynch in the process. She also remained the Divas Champion during this time frame, and come WrestleMania 32—in a Triple Threat Championship match, which saw the Divas Championship replaced with the new WWE Women's Championship, as well as "Divas" now being referred to as "Superstars" like their male counterparts—she would become the inaugural WWE Women's Champion. Post-WrestleMania, she'd start feuding with Natalya in a main roster retread of sorts of their NXT feud—right down to them having a match with Ric Flair and Bret Hart in their respective corners. Charlotte would also get a new sidekick in the form of Dana Brooke, eventually dumping her father from the equation. (Yet despite her telling her father she didn't need him anymore, she would soon be referred to on WWE TV as "Charlotte Flair" instead of just "Charlotte." After the 2016 WWE draft—where Charlotte was drafted to RAW, and the title would be called the RAW Women's Championship—Charlotte would then spend the rest of 2016 feuding with Sasha Banks, with the two of them trading the RAW Women's Championship wins on pay-per-views and episodes of *Monday Night RAW.* This feud also led to the first-ever women's Hell in a Cell match, as well as the first time a women's match had ever main evented (as in, booked as the final match) a main roster WWE pay-per-view. Charlotte and Sasha would also participate in the first-ever women's 30-Minute Iron Man match on a main roster WWE pay-per-view; in both of these firsts (as well as every match they had on pay-per-view), Charlotte would win.

As it turned out, the woman who would have Charlotte's number was Bayley, who'd made her official main roster debut in the summer of 2016. In fact, the beginning of 2017 saw Charlotte drop the championship to Bayley and then fail to get it back in the rematch at Fastlane—a pay-per-view loss that would be Charlotte's first pay-per-view singles loss after going 16–0.

After WrestleMania 33, Charlotte would be traded to SmackDown LIVE, where she would soon turn face and also become the first woman ever to main event RAW, SmackDown, and a WWE pay-per-view. She'd take a break from WWE for a couple of months in the summer after her father had a medical emergency. Then in the fall of 2017—after starting a very familiar feud as soon as she returned from her break—she beat the then SmackDown Women's Champion Natalya to win that championship and officially win every possible women's championship she could have during her time in WWE. She'd also be surprised after the match by her father walking to the top on the entrance ramp to hug and celebrate with his daughter.

Charlotte Flair was obviously born into greatness, but it's clear she's cemented her own greatness all along the way. Since day 1, Charlotte has credited her decision to become a professional wrestler to wanting to fulfill her brother Reid's dreams—in March 2013, after a five-year wrestling career and a struggle with drugs, Reid passed away of an accidental heroin overdose. "Reid pushed me to pursue a WWE career, and now I'm living his dream. I sense his presence most when I'm performing—walking to the ring, feeling the canvas underneath my boots and the ropes across my hands. WrestleMania week is when I get the strongest sense that Reid is by my side. I think it will be that way for the rest of my life."

Living the dream, indeed.

★ CHEERLEADER MELISSA ★

YEARS ACTIVE: 1998–present

TRAINED BY: Christopher Daniels · Billy Anderson · Robert Thompson · APW Boot Camp · Daniel Bryan · Mariko Yoshida

BILLED FROM: Damascus, Syria · Los Angeles, California · San Francisco, California

ACCOMPLISHMENTS: 2007 Pro Wrestling Word-1 Queen's Cup · 2x All Pro Wrestling Future Legend Champion · 2011 nCw Amazones and Titans (with Jay Phenomenon) · 1x Pure Wrestling Association Elite Women's Champion · #1 in 2013 PWI Female 50 · 2014 Cauliflower Alley Club Future Legend Award · 2014 Cauliflower Alley Club Women's Wrestling (Active) Award · 1x ChickFight Transatlantic Champion · ChickFight V · ChickFight VII · 1x DDT Pro-Wrestling Ironman Heavymetalweight Champion · 1x GRPW Lady Luck Champion · 2015 GRPW Lady Luck Title Tournament · 2x Pro Wrestling Revolution Women's Champion · 1x River City Wrestling

Angels Division Champion · 1x River City Wrestling Champion · 1x River City Wrestling International Champion · 1x River City Wrestling Phoenix Champion · 1x River City Wrestling Tag Team Champion (with Darci Drake) · 2x SHIMMER Champion · 2015 SoCal Uncensored Southern California Match of the Year (vs. Hudson Envy, on May 30) · 2015 STARDOM 5☆STAR GP Technique Award

AKA: Melissa Anderson · Melissa · "The (Future) (Female) Legend Crash Terminator" · "Future Legend" · Malicia · Miss Spartan · Wildfire · Felony · Raisha Saeed · 1/3 of The Kongtourage · Alyssa Flash · Alissa Flash · Mariposa · 1/2 of MelisChif

NOTABLE MATCHES: Cheerleader Melissa vs. Nattie Neidhart at ECCW SuperGirls Volume 1 (September 23, 2005) · Cheerleader Melissa vs. MsChif at SHIMMER Volume 4, in a Falls Count Anywhere match (February 12, 2006) · Cheerleader Melissa vs. Sara Del Rey at SHIMMER Volume 9 (April 7, 2007) · Cheerleader Melissa (c) vs. Wesna at ChickFight VIII, in a Falls Count Anywhere match for the ChickFight TransAtlantic Championship (April 22, 2007) · Raisha Saeed & Awesome Kong vs. Gail Kim & ODB at TNA Lockdown 2008 (April 13, 2008) · Cheerleader Melissa & MsChif vs. Allison Danger & Sara Del Rey at SHIMMER Volume 17 (April 26, 2008) · Cheerleader Melissa vs. Sarah Stock at SHIMMER Volume 18 (April 26, 2008) · Cheerleader Melissa vs. Wesna Busic at SHIMMER Volume 23 (May 2, 2009) · Cheerleader Melissa vs. Saraya Knight (c) at SHIMMER Volume 48, for the SHIMMER Championship (March 18, 2012) · Cheerleader Melissa vs. Saraya Knight (c) at SHIMMER Volume 53, in a Steel Cage match for the SHIMMER Championship (April 6, 2013) · Cheerleader Melissa vs. Evie vs. Kay Lee Ray at SHIMMER Volume 71: The ChickFight Tournament, in a SHIMMER Championship #1 Contendership ChickFight Tournament Final 3-Way Elimination match (March 28, 2015) · Mariposa vs. Sexy Star at Lucha Underground, in a No Mas match (May 4, 2016) · Team USA (Cheerleader Melissa, Santana Garrett, & Sienna) vs. Team Canada (Allie, KC Spinelli, & Taya) at AAA Lucha Libre World Cup (Women's Division) - Night 2, in the Lucha Libre World Cup (Women's Division) Third Place match (June 5, 2016) · Cheerleader Melissa vs. Chelsea Green at SHIMMER Volume 97 (November 11, 2017) · Melissa, Mariko Yoshida, & Leon vs. Aja Kong, AKINO, & Mary Apache at Mariko Yoshida Retirement Produce "MARIKO FINAL" (November 19, 2017)

A second-generation wrestler, Melissa Anderson started her professional wrestling training in 1998, when she was just 15 years old. Trained by her father Doug Anderson's former tag team partner Billy Anderson (only related in kayfabe) at his wrestling school in San Bernardino—while also setting up the ring and selling merchandise—Melissa came into the business with past experience in amateur wrestling. In fact, she was one of four girls on her high school wrestling team. As for her in-ring inspiration, Melissa didn't aspire to be like the Divas on WWE—she wanted to move and wrestle like Rick Martel. Melissa would graduate high school early and move from Los Angeles to San Francisco to train under Robert Thompson at APW, which is the promotion she would get her start in.

This far into her career, some people might wonder where the "cheerleader" in Cheerleader Melissa comes from. It's not as though she ever comes out to wrestle in a cheerleader uniform, and "pep" isn't typically a word one associates with her character. As a matter of fact, it was the first gimmick she had when she started out in the business, managing the Ballard Brothers, a *Slap Shot*-inspired hockey-gimmicked duo. Cheerleader Melissa was the heel "evil bitch cheerleader" who interfered in all their matches. However, once she moved past that particular gimmick, the name still stuck—despite how much she wished it wouldn't—because just "Melissa" (which she tried her hand at wrestling as) wasn't exactly the catchiest wrestling name. At least not the catchiest wrestling name for someone who would wrestle in the United States, England, Germany, Japan, Canada, Mexico, India, and Taiwan.

Her first official match, however, took place on her 17th birthday, at a carnival show in Wyoming against Lexie Fyfe. She'd lose, but things were just getting started for her. Melissa was invited to the ARSION joshi promotion in Japan to tour and train when she was just 19 years old, after being seen during a training session. On her 20th birthday, she got to tag with joshi legend Lioness Asuka as a birthday present from the promotion. By age 21, Cheerleader Melissa would receive the Future Legends Award from the Cauliflower Alley Club—which would lead to her having the APW Above The Law Championship renamed the Future Legends Championship when she won it in July 2004—making her the first woman to do so. Ten years later, she would receive the Cauliflower Alley Club's Women's Wrestling (Active) Award.

After Melissa returned from Japan in 2004, she would become a mainstay in the ChickFight tournament and promotion, an all-female offshoot of APW. There, she would feud with the likes of Sweet Saraya and Wesna Busic, the latter of which transferred over to SHIMMER, a promotion Melissa would be a part of from the first show in November 2005 to the present. Melissa's feud with MsChif—which started at SHIMMER Volume 1—was the promotion's first major feud and a brutal one at that. Eventually the two would form mutual respect as well as a tag team—feuding with The Minnesota Home Wrecking Crew of Lacey and Rain—but the team would end once Melissa became focused on winning SHIMMER championship gold. Championship gold she would win from Madison Eagles (after previous encounters against her featuring Melissa on the losing end) at SHIMMER Volume 44 in 2011—the same day in which she won the #1 Contendership, at SHIMMER Volume 43, against Kana—and hold until Volume 48, when a familiar nemesis in the form of Saraya Knight (aka Sweet Saraya) defeated her for it. Cheerleader Melissa would eventually become a two-time SHIMMER Champion by winning it back from Saraya a little over a year later in a Steel Cage match at SHIMMER Volume 53. This second reign lasted 560 days, ending only when Nicole Matthews—the first challenger to Melissa's first champion reign—won it in a Four-Way Elimination match at SHIMMER Volume 68.

However, before her championship reigns in SHIMMER, Melissa had gotten a mainstream TV professional contract, signing with TNA Wrestling in 2008. Unfortunately for fans of Cheerleader Melissa, not only was her character "Raisha Saeed"—who was introduced as one of Awesome Kong's associates from Japan—more of a manager and assistant role than an actual wrestling role for her, the character required her to wear a *niqab* and speak in a "Syrian" accent. (Melissa had previously had a tryout match in WWE, which aired on an episode of *WWE Heat* in 2006, but even earlier than that and her time in TNA, she was coincidentally approached by WWE to play a similar character to Raisha Saaed.) Luckily, her affiliation with TNA at least allowed her to also wrestle in its Indian sister promotion, Ring Ka King. Eventually, she would get to play a new character in the form of Alissa Flash, but she rarely won a match in the character—and that was pretty much the character in a nutshell.

Following months of not being used, Melissa requested her release from TNA in the beginning of 2010. Changes behind the scenes at TNA caused her to leave the company, and she's gone on the record in saying there were no hard feelings on her end about how things went down. In fact, not only did she call it "the funniest time in [her] career" and say she "would do Raisha Saeed [again] in a heartbeat if [she] could," she actually did so at independent promotion Bar Wrestling's Christmas show in 2017. This was after it had been announced that TNA (now Impact Wrestling, under the ownership of Anthem Sports) would allow all past, present, and future employees to keep any previous gimmicks they'd had in the company.

A few months after leaving TNA, Melissa announced at the Cauliflower Alley Convention that she had a new project in the works called Female Fight League (FFL). Describing it as a "female version of the NWA," it began with ChickFight (California), Pro-Wrestling EVE (England), and nCw Femme Fatales (Canada) already in its stable of all-female wrestling promotions.

In 2015, it was announced that Melissa would be joining the roster of El Rey Network's *Lucha Underground* wrestling promotion/series. This time, she wasn't in a *niqab*, but she would be under a mask as Mariposa, the villainous sister of *Lucha Underground*'s psychotic Marty "The Moth" Martinez. While currently on *Lucha Underground*, Cheerleader Melissa still works in other independent wrestling promotions all around the world.

★ CHELSEA GREEN ★

YEARS ACTIVE: 2014–present

TRAINED BY: Lance Storm · Storm Wrestling Academy · Billy Gunn

BILLED FROM: Victoria, British Columbia · "Straight From The Wedding Chapel"

ACCOMPLISHMENTS: 1x All-Star Wrestling Women's Champion · 1x Impact Wrestling Knockouts Champion · #26 in 2017 PWI Female 50 · 1x Queens of Combat (QOC) Tag Team Champion (with Taeler Hendrix) · 2017 QOC Tag Team Championship Tournament (with Taeler Hendrix)

AKA: Jaida · Megan Miller · Chelsea · "LVN" · Laurel Van Ness · "Laurel Van Mess" · "The Lunatic Lush" · "Hot Mess" Laurel Van Ness · 1/2 of Dishonorable Impact · 1/2 of Fire and Nice · member of The Lady Squad · "Hot Mess" Chelsea Green

NOTABLE MATCHES: World Selection (Chelsea Green, Kellie Skater, Evie, Santana Garrett & Viper) (with Act Yasukawa) vs. STARDOM (Io Shirai, Jungle Kyona, Kairi Hojo, Mayu Iwatani, & Momo Watanabe), in an Elimination Ten Man Tag Team match at STARDOM 5th Anniversary – Night 3: STARDOM vs. The World (February 7, 2016) · Laurel Van Ness vs. Jade at TNA Xplosion (October 3, 2016) · Chelsea Green vs. Kairi Hojo (c) at STARDOM October Showdown, for the Wonder of Women Championship (October 30, 2016) · Laurel Van Ness vs. Gail Kim at TNA One Night Only: Against All Odds 2016 (November 4, 2016) · Dishonorable Impact (Chelsea Green & Taeler Hendrix) vs. The Lucha Sisters (Leva Bates & Mia Yim) at Queens of Combat QOC 18, in the QOC Tag Team Championship Tournament Final for the inaugural QOC Tag Team Championship (February 18, 2017) · Chelsea Green vs. Sexy Dulce vs. Rachael Ellering at WrestleCircus Taking Center Stage, in a 3-Way Elimination match for the vacant WrestleCircus Lady of the Ring Championship (February 19, 2017) · Chelsea Green vs. Allysin Kay at SHINE 42 (May 12, 2017) · Chelsea Green vs. Cheerleader Melissa at SHIMMER Volume 97 (November 11, 2017)

★ Despite her athletic (and Canadian) upbringing, Chelsea Green didn't grow up knowing she wanted to be a wrestler. Like most kids growing up during the Attitude Era in the mid-to-late-'90s, Green watched professional wrestling—in fact, Trish Stratus was her favorite—but it didn't go any deeper. It wasn't until 2013, while she was attending college in Calgary, Alberta, Canada—where wrestlers and wrestling talk were always around—that she even thought about it. She "wanted to try something crazy and new," and after stumbling upon a women's match on an episode of *Monday Night RAW*, she realized she could do what those women were doing. So after some thorough research on wrestling schools in the area, she called up Canadian pro wrestler and owner of the Storm Wrestling Academy, Lance Storm, and the rest was history.

In May of 2014 (after three months of training), Green debuted under the ring name "Jaida" at ECCW, the biggest independent promotion in Canada. She continued to wrestle solely in the Canadian independent scene—as Jaida, then eventually as Chelsea/Chelsea Green—until the fall of 2015, when she debuted at QOC 7 in North Carolina. By the end of 2015, she was becoming pretty much known *as* Chelsea Green.

"Lance basically taught me everything I know, from rolls to psychology. I credit Billy Gunn for supporting me and kicking my ass when I need it."

That ass-kicking would specifically come into play in the beginning of 2015, when Chelsea Green joined the cast of the latest edition of WWE's competitive reality series *Tough Enough*. (Billy Gunn was one of the coaches during the show.) After being cut in the *Tough Enough* Competition Special, Chelsea joined the cast as a replacement for Dianna Dahlgren, who had voluntarily left the show. This was actually Chelsea's second high-profile moment with WWE, as in August 2014—after only six months of wrestling experience—she would appear on WWE TV in the form of *Monday Night RAW*, playing Megan Miller, Daniel Bryan's physical therapist and alleged mistress. (To this day, some fans still call Chelsea "Megan Miller" when they meet her, despite it only being one segment.) This past WWE connection would even be mentioned as Chelsea competed in *Tough Enough*, but a career in WWE was not in the cards for Chelsea—at least not yet—and she'd be eliminated in week 7 of the 10-week competition, finishing fourth place out of the female competitors.

Despite not winning the competition and the WWE developmental contract that would come with it, Chelsea's newfound notoriety would allow her to get booked in more places. The year 2016 was a big one for her, momentum-wise, as she was invited to tour and train in Japan twice for joshi promotion STARDOM. A clip of her taking a stiff drop kick during a STARDOM match would even go viral during this time. She'd also travel to India to wrestle for The Great Khali's new Continental Wrestling Entertainment promotion, though she would injure her collarbone during her match—which she did wrestle to the end—and have to be airlifted to a hospital (while also cutting her first Japan tour short). She'd make appearances in 2016 as enhancement talent on TNA Impact Wrestling as "Chelsea" before officially signing a contract with the company that June. That fall, Chelsea Green would make her official TNA debut as "Laurel Van Ness," a character who started off as a spoiled, rich, daddy's girl and ally in Maria Kanellis-Bennett's Lady Squad (alongside Sienna).

CHELSEA GREEN MADE HER OFFICIAL TNA DEBUT AS "LAUREL VAN NESS," A CHARACTER WHO STARTED OFF AS A SPOILED, RICH, DADDY'S GIRL.

Laurel Van Ness would develop an antagonistic relationship with Maria's punching bag of an assistant, Allie, especially once she decided to engage in a relationship with a not-quite-willing Braxton Sutter (the object of Allie's affection). This story would all come to a head in February 2017, at the wrestling wedding between Laurel and Braxton, where Braxton would leave Laurel at the alter—professing his love for Allie—and Laurel would be left sobbing and drinking champagne in her wedding dress. What would follow from that was truly unexpected, as from that point on, Laurel would come out for matches (whether her own or Sienna's), still dressed in her (now much dirtier) wedding dress, with smudged make-up, no shoes, and a bottle of champagne always in hand. This mental breakdown would lead to Laurel now being called "The Lunatic Lush," as there was seemingly no rhyme or reason to her behavior. Sienna would try to help Laurel Van Ness by programming a monster (Kongo Kong) to help her get revenge on Allie and Braxton Sutter, but when that failed, Laurel remained this disheveled mess.

The "Laurel Van Mess" character would also have a brief face turn, as she'd eventually engage in a storyline with comedic wrestler Grado in his quest to marry in order to stay in the United States. For Laurel, the power of Grado's love would eventually knock her out of her stupor, and she'd be lucid again for the first time in months ... until Grado broke up with her, as he had finally realized she was Canadian and couldn't help him stay in America. Laurel would snap again, though her particular depiction would now be one of a (still manic) party girl on the rebound.

Despite the up and downs her character faced, Laurel Van Ness ended 2017 right: first, by becoming the second female wrestler (after Gail Kim) to join the Suplex Wrestling (SPLX) athletic clothing and lifestyle brand and, then, by winning the Impact Wrestling Knockouts Championship for the first time, defeating former champion Rosemary in the finals of a tournament for the vacant championship.

★ CHRISTY HEMME ★

YEARS ACTIVE: 2004–2009

TRAINED BY: Dave "Fit" Finlay · Arn Anderson · Ricky Steamboat · Dean Malenko · OVW · Scott D'Amore · Inoki Dojo

BILLED FROM: Los Angeles, California

ACCOMPLISHMENTS: #42 in 2008 PWI Female 50 · 2006 TNA Knockout of the Year · 2004 WWE Divas Search winner

AKA: Christy · Kristy Hemme · 1/3 of The Rock 'n Rave Infection

NOTABLE MATCHES: Christy Hemme vs. Trish Stratus (c) at WWE WrestleMania 21, for the WWE Women's Championship (April 3, 2005) · Christy Hemme vs. Victoria at WWE Vengeance 2005 (June 26, 2005) · Christy Hemme vs. Awesome Kong (c) at TNA Final Resolution, for the TNA Knockouts Championship (December 7, 2008)

★ Coming from a modeling background, Christy Hemme entered the wrestling business through the 2004 WWE Diva Search. She won the competition, which led to her getting a one-year contract with WWE and $250,000. Like most Diva Search competitors-turned-WWE Divas at the time, Hemme's early work in the company amounted to "non-traditional" wrestling matches. In fact, she won her debut feud (against her Diva Search runner-up, Carmella DeCesare) in a Lingerie Pillow Fight match. The match took place at the Taboo Tuesday pay-per-view, a semi-interactive concept where the fans could vote online for match stipulations; the other two options for Christy vs. Carmella were an Evening Gown match and an Aerobics Challenge. She next found herself in a feud with a heel Trish Stratus over the WWE Women's Championship, even challenging her for the title at WrestleMania 21. However, even with the aid of Trish's rival Lita (whose real-life injury made way for Hemme to be inserted into this feud) in her corner—and in story, having given her extra in-ring training—Hemme was defeated by Trish in a little more than four minutes.

Hemme's next feud—and final RAW feud before she was drafted to SmackDown—would be against Victoria, with Victoria coming after Hemme for the opportunities she'd gotten (the Diva Search, a *Playboy* cover, a WrestleMania match) barely a year on the roster. Again, Hemme was on the losing side of this feud, and that lack of momentum didn't change when she entered into a feud with Melina on SmackDown either. As soon as that feud ended in November of 2006, Christy Hemme was sent to WWE developmental at OVW in Louisville, Kentucky ... and was released from her WWE contract a few days later. According to WWE, the reason behind Hemme's release was a combination of budgets cuts and creative having nothing for her (the latter being a common occurrence in WWE). In 2008, Hemme would claim she actually left the company on her own terms. She wouldn't be seen on WWE TV again until she showed up to witness her fellow former WWE Diva Beth Phoenix be inducted into the company's 2017 Hall of Fame class.

In 2006, Hemme signed with TNA wrestling, joining their Knockouts Division in a host role, both on weekly TNA Impact shows and internet shows. That same year, she was actually even voted TNA Knockout of the Year. She also spent her time off getting more wrestling training—as she never quite got the chance back in WWE—both under the tutelage of Scott D'Amore and the Los Angeles Inoki Dojo. This would come in handy at the beginning of 2007, as she entered into a feud with the tag team the Voodoo Kin Mafia (VKM, a pointed play on Vince McMahon's initials), somehow becoming heel when she called the two men out for saying women didn't belong in wrestling. This particular storyline didn't lead to many pleasant memories—especially as VKM won, seemingly proving Hemme wrong about women wrestling, as this was before TNA would realize that their Knockouts were the promotion's secret weapon—but it did bring forth the introduction of The Rock 'n Rave Infection (Lance Hoyt and Jimmy Rave), a team/fake band that Hemme would manage and sing lead for.

Hemme eventually turned face at that aforementioned point when TNA realized its Knockouts were worth taking seriously, immediately feuding with the Knockouts Division's top heels, The Beautiful People (including their fashionist Cute Kip, who was previously a member of the VKM). After she moved past TBP, she found herself in contention for the TNA Knockouts Championship, facing the champion Awesome Kong at TNA's Final Resolution 2008, the last pay-per-view of the year. Hemme would technically win the match by disqualification—thanks to interference from Kong's sidekick, Raisha Saeed, who Hemme had beaten to become #1 Contender—but not the championship. While Hemme was all set to have a rematch at the next pay-per-view, her momentum was cut short by a neck injury she sustained while training and was out of action for seven months. Upon returning to in-ring action in TNA, she never quite regained her momentum—eventually admitting she felt tense about possibly aggravating her neck injury—and stepped away and

officially retired from wrestling at the end of 2009. But where one door closed, another opened: Hemme became a backstage interviewer with the company and eventually a ring announcer. Still, she'd find herself involved in storylines with wrestlers, like as the object of Jay Lethal's affection or the object of Samuel Shaw's obsession.

During her tenure in TNA, Christy Hemme would wear many hats—from host to wrestler to manager to backstage interviewer to ring announcer. And in 2014, she would also step behind the scenes to become a member of the promotion's creative team, something Hemme has said she considered her favorite thing she did in professional wrestling. However, in 2016, Hemme would officially step away from the company and professional wrestling—though, in this business, never say never.

★ CHYNA ★

YEARS ACTIVE: 1995–2011

TRAINED BY: Walter "Killer" Kowalski · Killer Kowalski Institute of Professional Wrestling

BILLED FROM: Londonberry, New Hampshire

ACCOMPLISHMENTS: 1x International Wrestling Federation (IWF) Women's Champion · 1996 Professional Girl Wrestling Association "Rookie of the Year" · 1998 Ladies International Wrestling Association Rookie of the Year · #106 in 2000 PWI 500 · 1x WWF Women's Champion · 2x WWF Intercontinental Champion

AKA: Joanie Laurer · Joanie Lee · Just Joanie · Chyna Doll · "The Ninth Wonder of the World" · member of D-Generation X (DX) · member of The Corporation · member of The Corporate Ministry · "Mamacita"

NOTABLE MATCHES: Chyna vs. Jeff Jarrett at WWF No Mercy 1999, in a Good Housekeeping match for the WWF Intercontinental Champion (October 17, 1999) · Chyna (c) vs. Chris Jericho at WWF Armageddon 1999, for the WWF Intercontinental Championship (December 12, 1999) · Chyna (c) vs. Chris Jericho vs. Hardcore Holly at WWF Royal Rumble 2000, in a Triple Threat match for the WWF Intercontinental Championship (January 23, 2000) · WWF Royal Rumble 2000, in the Royal Rumble match (January 23, 2000) · Chyna & Eddie Guerrero vs. Trish Stratus & Val Venis (c) at WWF SummerSlam 2000, for the WWF Intercontinental Championship (August 27, 2000) · Chyna vs. Ivory (c) at WrestleMania X-7, for the WWF Women's Championship (April 1, 2001) · Chyna (c) vs. Lita at WWF Judgment Day 2001, for the WWF Women's Championship (May 20, 2001)

> *"Don't treat me like a woman*
> *Don't treat me like a man*
> *Don't treat me like you know me*
> *Just treat me for who I am"*

⭐ Those lyrics to Chyna's entrance theme are perhaps the best ways to describe who Chyna was and the memory that wrestling fans have of her. Billed as "The Ninth Wonder of the World" (as André the Giant was "The Eighth Wonder of the World"), Chyna was something of an anomaly in the wrestling business. She was a woman of firsts and onlys: the first woman in the WWF to be an enforcer in a wrestling stable, the first and only woman to hold the WWF Intercontinental Championship, the first woman to participate in the Royal Rumble match, the first and only woman to participate in the King of the Ring tournament, the first and only woman to become #1 Contender to the WWF Championship.

Before getting into wrestling—and unfortunately, after—Joanie Laurer lived an extremely difficult and dysfunctional life. She was kicked out of her mother's house when she was 16, for being caught with marijuana, and had to move in with her alcoholic father. (She would not reconcile with her mother until 2015.) To Joanie, it wasn't as though she had a pick of female role models—women with whom she could relate or see herself in—to truly look up to.

"It was the age of the beauty queen and the aerobics queen and most of the very strong figures in our society were men unless they were very beautiful passive women. It was the age of Barbie. The irony is that I became this star in a male-dominated world where only a handful of men have succeeded. Could I have picked anything more difficult?"

Joanie spent a lot of her time in school studying other languages—becoming fluent in Spanish, German, and French—with plans of becoming a federal agent for either the FBI or the DEA. But after catching wrestling on television one night while channel surfing, Joanie realized that this was what she wanted to do. But she didn't want to be just a "Diva," she wanted to actually wrestle, just like the men. She wanted to wrestle *with* the men. Her body was already in the shape wrestling fans remember Chyna for, as she'd gotten into bodybuilding as a teenager and had started to enter fitness competitions after she graduated college. So she shouted "I can do that!" at the TV and went to train at Killer

Kowalski's wrestling school in Massachusetts. As "Joanie Lee," she'd wrestle her early matches in 1996 at International Wrestling Federation (IWF), Kowalski's wrestling promotion, with her first match actually being against a man dressed as a woman. In a way, Joanie was lucky to start wrestling when she did, because IWF would close that same year, and who knows what path she would have taken if she didn't have that outlet to wrestle.

1996 would also be the year that she got on the WWF's radar; after meeting Triple H (who had also been trained by Kowalski) and Shawn Michaels at a hotel bar after a wrestling show, the two would be so impressed by her physique, they'd asked to check out tapes of her matches. Upon seeing her work, they pushed for Vince McMahon to hire her as a sexy, intimidating, female bodyguard character—though Vince was hesitant at first that the audience would buy a woman beating up men. He was also worried that his male wrestlers wouldn't want to lose to or look weak compared to a woman. While the latter issue would sometimes come up when Chyna joined the company, little did Vince know the audience would buy Chyna's toughness against men for years to come. It just took about a year—and the looming possibility of WCW hiring her instead—to get Vince McMahon to get on board with Chyna.

Venus. Sheera. Phalan. Tigress. Teeva Gweeve. "Chyna" was the final choice out of all the names that were pitched for her character. She would make her WWF debut on RAW in February 1997, posing as a plant (a planted fan) who kept interfering in Triple H's matches against Goldust, attacking Goldust's manager Marlena each time. Soon, Triple H would reveal that she was his bodyguard, a role the silent-but-deadly Chyna—a name that would eventually be revealed as well—would continue as Triple H and Shawn Michaels (along with Rick Rude, as Michaels's bodyguard) formed the legendary heel stable D-Generation X (DX). As an original member of DX, Chyna was an integral part of the Attitude Era, the most popular (and sensationalized) era of professional wrestling. And she would only become more popular as DX eventually became faces.

Like she'd promised herself when she first saw wrestling, Chyna would stand toe-to-toe with the male wrestlers in WWF. At the Royal Rumble in 1999, she entered the 30-man Royal Rumble match at entrant #30, marking a first for a female member of the WWF/WWE roster. (And she'd be eliminated by "Stone Cold" Steve Austin, arguably the biggest star in the history of the company.) She'd also make it to the quarterfinals of the King of the Ring tournament (on pay-per-view), after becoming the first woman to even qualify for the tournament, that same year. Then she would feud with Jeff Jarrett that fall, for his WWF Intercontinental Championship. This feud led to the infamous Good Housekeeping gimmick match—a match featured "weapons" you could find in a kitchen, as on-the-nose as that was—in which Chyna became the first and only woman to win the Intercontinental Championship. This is where the concept of men not wanting to lose to Chyna would come into play, as the Good Housekeeping match was Jeff Jarrett's final match with the company, he allegedly only agreed to show up for the match and drop the title cleanly to Chyna if he was paid $300,000.

Chyna would then feud with Chris Jericho over the title. According to Jericho, Vince McMahon told him not to hold back on Chyna during the feud. However, once he accidentally gave her a black eye, Vince completely changed his tune. During this feud, Chyna and Jericho ended up as co-Intercontinental Champions— after a title match which finished with them both pinning each other at the same time—until Jericho won the championship decisively in a Triple Threat match at Royal Rumble 2000. Chyna would get some semblance of revenge during that year's Royal Rumble match though, as she would be the one to eliminate Jericho.

While Chyna obviously got her due as an intimidating force of nature in WWF, she'd also get the chance to be portrayed as a sex symbol—something she never quite expected when she planned to get into the business. After the Intercontinental Championship run, she would engage in a storyline with Eddie Guerrero as his girlfriend, the "Mamacita" to his "Latino Heat." She would also win the Intercontinental Championship again during their paring, though Eddie would soon after "accidentally" win it from her, and their storyline relationship would come to an end when she caught Eddie cheating on her. Chyna would also pose nude for *Playboy* around the same time—which, in storyline, Eddie was upset about—leading to a feud between herself and satirically conservative wrestler faction Right To Censor's Ivory. This feud would lead Chyna to quickly winning the WWF Women's Champion at WrestleMania X-Seven, her final championship in WWF. In May 2001, she'd defend the championship at Judgment Day against Lita and win, in what would end up being her last match in the company. For whatever reason, Chyna was then taken off TV for months before she finally left the company that November, causing the championship to be vacated.

Behind the scenes, Chyna had been in an actual relationship with Triple H since 1996, one that ended once she found out he was cheating on her with Vince McMahon's daughter, Stephanie McMahon. Chyna had stated in 2002 that the affair was not why she left the company and that she instead wanted to focus on her acting career; she had appeared in *Pacific Blue*, *The Martin Short Show*, *3rd Rock from the Sun*, and even *Mad TV* during her time in WWF. However, Chyna would later say that she wanted to stay in the company but had received a fax saying "You will not be needed anymore" while she was still under contract.

Joanie Laurer's/Chyna's life post-WWF, however, did not live up to the potential expected. She would make a few wrestling appearances in NJPW and TNA, but professional wrestling was no longer her world. In 2004, she made her porn debut with homemade sex tape *1 Night In China*, alongside her then boyfriend (and close friend of Triple H, as well as former DX partner) Sean Waltman. In 2005, she'd join the cast of the celebreality series *The Surreal Life*, where her issues with drinking and her relationship with Waltman (who she'd be arrested for beating that same year) were also on display. In 2007, Joanie Laurer legally changed her name to Chyna, calling out her former employer in the process. 2008 saw her appear on *Celebrity Rehab with Dr. Drew* for her alcohol and drug addiction, but she would still deny she had a problem. It wasn't until 2014—when she moved to Japan to teach English—that it looked like things might turn around for her and that she was finally in a good place mentally and physically.

On April 20, 2016, 46-year-old Chyna was found dead in her Redondo Beach, California, apartment. The cause of death was eventually ruled as a drug and alcohol overdose. Unfortunately, it took Chyna dying for her to be acknowledged again in a positive light by WWE, after Triple H had previously danced around the idea of her ever being in the WWE Hall of Fame (due to her porn career). In the official WWE statement on her passing, they wrote: "A physically striking and talented performer, Chyna was a true sports-entertainment pioneer." Like far too many wrestling stories, Chyna's story ended tragically, but she was still an inspiration to so many current (and surely, future) female wrestlers all over the globe.

★ DAIZEE HAZE ★

YEARS ACTIVE: 2002–2011

TRAINED BY: Kid Kash · Delirious · Gateway Championship Wrestling Training Center

BILLED FROM: Forest Park, Illinois · San Francisco, California

ACCOMPLISHMENTS: 1x APW Legend Champion · ChickFight VI · 2x NWA Midwest/IWA Mid-South (IWA-MS) Women's Champion · #15 in 2008 PWI Female 50 · 2009 Anarchy Championship Wrestling (ACW) American Joshi Queen of Queens · 1x SHIMMER Tag Team Champion (with Tomoka Nakagawa)

AKA: The Haze · "Miss Delirious" · Shelirious · member of The Embassy · member of BDK ("Brotherhood of the Cross") · Daisy Haze · Marley Sebastian · Marley · 1/2 of Team SHIMMER · 1/2 of HENTAI and the Haze

NOTABLE MATCHES: Daizee Haze, Mickie Knuckles, Sumie Sakai vs. Allison Danger, Rain, & Ranmaru at CHIKARA Tag World Grand Prix 2006 - Night 3 (February 26, 2006) · Daizee Haze vs. Lacey vs. Sara Del Rey at ROH Rising Above, in a 3-Way match (March 7, 2008) · BDK (Captain-Ares, Daizee Haze, Claudio Castagnoli, Delirious, Pinkie Sanchez, Sara Del Rey, Tim Donst, & Tursas) vs. Team CHIKARA (Captain-UltraMantis Black, Eddie Kingston, Hallowicked, Icarus, Jigsaw, Larry Sweeney, Mike Quackenbush, & STIGMA) at CHIKARA The Dark Cibernetico, in a Torneo Cibernetico 16-Person Elimination Tag Team match (October 23, 2010) · Daizee Haze & Amazing Kong vs. Sara Del Rey & Serena Deeb at ROH Final Battle 2010 (December 18, 2010) · Daizee Haze & Tomoka Nakagawa (c) vs. Ayumi Kurihara & Hiroyo Matsumoto at ROH Honor Takes Center Stage, Chapter 2, for the SHIMMER Tag Team Championship (April 2, 2011)

★ A hippie, stoner character in women's wrestling isn't exactly typical, at least not in any prominent way. And don't let her diminutive size fool you: dynamite comes in small packages.

Perhaps a definite sign of the times, "Daizee Haze" got the idea for her name from her sister, who—at the very specific time—wanted to legally change her own name to "Daisy Hayes," due to her crush on the Savage Garden front man Darren Hayes. As for the gimmick, as the daughter of a hippie father who passed away when she was 15, it was her tribute to him. Plus, it helped that she was actually a fan of marijuana. She also wasn't allowed to watch wrestling as a child—but in 2001, she started watching it, and that's when she was exposed to the technical marvel of wrestlers like Kurt Angle and Chris Benoit, as well as the toughness of women like Molly Holly. Then, after watching a friend attend wrestling school, Daizee got the itch to try the same thing. So she found herself being trained by Kid Kash and Delirious—the latter of which would become one of her closest allies and friends in this business—and would make her debut at the now defunct Gateway Championship Wrestling in Missouri. (And in addition to actually wrestling, she'd go on to design and make wrestling gear for herself, Delirious, Matt Sydal, and MsChif.) The hippie stoner gimmick was there from the beginning, as was the need to prove herself against any woman or man who stepped in her path.

She'd go on to be one of the most prolific and well-known names of the women's independent wrestling scene at this time, alongside women like Allison Danger, Sara Del Rey, Lacey, Mercedes Martinez, and MsChif.

In 2003, thanks to Kid Kash's connections, Daizee—as well as fellow Gateway Championship Wrestling alum Matt Sydal—started working on TNA shows during their weekly pay-per-view days in Nashville, specifically in matches on the promotion's supplemental program, *Xplosion*. While Daizee's time in TNA was relatively short—it was two years but not under contract and before the show got a national TV deal—it was there that she met Bill Behrens (NWA president; owner of NWA Wildside) and Dave Prazak (IWA-MS; co-founder of SHIMMER). With Behrens on her side, she was able to wrestle in Georgia, at NWA Wildside, and with Prazak, his championing of women's wrestling allowed Daizee to make her debuts in IWA-MS, ROH, and SHIMMER. If anything, it was her stint in TNA that made her more of a name on the independent scene.

Daizee would typically come with Matt Sydal to various independent promotions as a package deal, debuting in both IWA-MS (2003) and ROH (2004) as his manager, before branching out into both promotions' burgeoning women's divisions. In IWA-MS, she was a part of the tournament to crown the inaugural NWA Midwest/IWA-MS Women's Champion, making it to the finals in a 3-Way match against Lacey (the victor) and Mercedes Martinez. Daizee would win the championship in a Six-Pack Challenge, losing it to MsChif about three months later. After the championship was separated into two titles in the summer 2005 (with IWA-MS just having the IWA-MS Women's Championship), Daizee Haze would win the championship for a second and final time in a 3-Way match between herself, Sara Del Rey, and Mickie Knuckles in May 2008. The championship was deactivated at the end of 2008, making Daizee the final champion. As for ROH, Daizee Haze briefly feuded with a post-Prophecy Allison Danger (also in early 2005), when women's wrestling was still quite the rarity in the promotion, before moving on to manage the faction Generation Next once Matt Sydal joined. However, that November at ROH Vendetta, Daizee Haze—who's always considered herself a natural face because of her size —would turn heel on Generation Next and join The Embassy as one of its more aggressive and brutal members. After this version of The Embassy broke up in the fall of 2006, Daizee Haze returned to her roots as a face in the promotion, as the female counterpart to Lacey (who she also had encounters with in both IWA-MS and SHIMMER) in the Jimmy Jacobs feud against BJ Whitmer and Colt Cabana.

2005 really was a great year for Daizee Haze, as she would also debut in SHIMMER (main eventing its first four shows) and CHIKARA. Although, she wouldn't hit a major stride in CHIKARA until another heel turn, in 2009, when—after calling out CHIKARA in a promo, for patronizing her for being a woman —she joined the BDK stable (alongside familiar wrestlers such as Sara Del Rey and Delirious). Daizee would then go on to make a name for herself in SHIMMER with her feud against Rebecca Knox—beginning in SHIMMER Volume 4—which would lead to a 2 Out of 3 falls match and then a 60-minute Iron Man (or Iron Woman) match. However, the latter, blowoff match wouldn't happen, due to a career-ending injury sustained on Rebecca's part (*see* Becky Lynch). By the fall of 2008, Daizee was the head trainer at the SHIMMER Wrestling School, a female extension of the ROH Wrestling Academy at the time. While the SHIMMER Championship eluded Daizee Haze on multiple occasions, at SHIMMER Volume 40 in March 2011, she won the SHIMMER Tag team Championship with Tomoka Nakagawa, who she had formed a heel tag team with back at SHIMMER Volume 30. At SHIMMER Volume 41—after trying to weasel their way out of defending the championship—they would lose the championship. Later that night, Daizee would come out and rant about her loss and quit SHIMMER. Only the quitting part wasn't a joke, and on that night (October 1, 2011), Daizee Haze retired from professional wrestling.

Daizee did make an appearance the following year, accompanying MsChif at a Dynamo Pro Wrestling show and then came out of retirement for one night only on the SHIMMER 10th Anniversary Show (Volume 79), in a match that was also the retirement match of The Canadian NINJAS' Portia Perez. Naturally, her rival Lacey also came out of retirement to wrestle on the opposing side. For a time, Daizee, alongside Delirious, was a head trainer at the ROH Dojo (formerly known as the ROH Wrestling Academy), shaping the future of wrestling from behind-the-scenes.

★ DEONNA PURRAZZO ★

YEARS ACTIVE: 2012–present

TRAINED BY: D2W Pro Wrestling Academy · Team Adams Wrestling Academy · Damian Adams · Robbie E · Jersey Devil · Shawn Bennett · OVW · Rip Rogers

BILLED FROM: Hackettstown, New Jersey

ACCOMPLISHMENTS: 1x Dynamite Championship Wrestling Women's Champion · 1x East Coast Wrestling Association (ECWA) Women's Champion · ECWA 2nd Annual Super 8 ChickFight Tournament · ECWA 3rd Annual Super 8 ChickFight Tournament · 2016 ECWA Match of the Year (vs. Karen Q, on October 22) · 2016 ECWA Most Popular Wrestler · 2016 ECWA Most Shocking Moment (winning back-to-back ECWA Women's Super 8 Tournaments) · 2016 ECWA Wrestler of the Year · 1x Game Changer Wrestling Women's Champion · 1x MFPW Girls Champion · 1x NYWC Starlet Champion · 1x Paradise Alley Pro Wrestling Center Ring Divas Champion · #34 in 2017 PWI Female 50 · 2017 ROH Women of Honor Wrestler of the Year

AKA: Deonna · La Luchadora · 1/2 of Team Hottest Free Agents · "The Virtuosa"

NOTABLE MATCHES: Deonna Purrazzo vs. Tessa Blanchard at ECWA 2nd Annual Super 8 ChickFight Tournament, in a Super 8 ChickFight Tournament Finals match for the vacant ECWA Women's Championship (October 17, 2015) · Deonna Purrazzo vs. Santana Garrett at WWR Project XX (April 10, 2016) · Deonna Purrazzo vs. Kimber Lee at Women's Wrestling Revolution (WWR) Revolutionary (July 31, 2016) · Deonna Purrazzo vs. Karen Q at ECWA 3rd Annual Super 8 ChickFight Tournament, in a Super 8 ChickFight Tournament Finals match (October 22, 2016) · Deonna Purrazzo & Jinny vs. Dahlia Black & Dakota Kai at PROGRESS: New York City (August 12, 2017) · Deonna Purrazzo vs. Jinny vs. Dakota Kai at PROGRESS: Boston (August 13, 2017) · Deonna Purrazzo vs. Awesome Kong at WWR The Show Must Go On (August 20, 2017) · Deonna Purrazzo vs. Sumie Sakai at ROH/NJPW Global

Wars 2017, in a Women of Honor match (October 12, 2017) · Deonna Purrazzo vs. Karen Q at ROH, in a Women of Honor match (October 20, 2017) · Deonna Purrazzo (c) vs. Karen Q vs. Santana Garrett at ECWA 4th Annual Super 8 ChickFight Tournament, in a Super 8 ChickFight Tournament Finals 3-Way for the ECWA Women's Championship (October 21, 2017)

★ When it comes to true road warriors in the modern era of wrestling, Deonna Purrazzo's name has regularly been at the top of the list—and for good reason. In the span of less than a year (beginning in July 25, 2015), she managed to wrestle in every major North American professional wrestling company—WWE, Impact Wrestling, and ROH—without officially signing a contract to any company. In January 2017, she debuted in Japan's premiere joshi promotion, STARDOM. She's also the first wrestler—male or female—to win an ECWA Super 8 Tournament (in which she wrestled the ChickFight Tournament, specifically) in back-to-back years.

At nine years old—after seeing the work of Trish Stratus, Lita, and Victoria—Deonna told her parents wanted to be a professional wrestler. They thought she'd grow out of it, that it was just a phase; after all, she had other interests, as she was a competitive cheerleader for 12 years. However, as soon as she turned 18 years old, Deonna fulfilled her promise and began training at D2W Pro Wrestling Academy, under Damian Adams. She would train for a year before she would get her first match in December 2013, and then a few months later, she'd make her TNA debut—again, non-contracted—at the promotion's One Night Only: Knockouts Knockdown (an all-women's show) pay-per-view. Deonna would also continue to wrestle on D2W shows through the summer of 2015. By then, she had debuted in other independent promotions like FWE, OVW (where she trained additionally, under Rip Rogers), and ECWA, as well as ROH, where she would become an integral part of the building of the company's Women of Honor Division and brand.

On *NXT,* Deonna became temporarily infamous for her role as an enhancement talent who relatively new NXT talent Asuka quickly disposed of in less than three minutes (twice), to the point where that need for vengeance was part of her character's quest for championship gold. This led to her being the one non-contracted wrestler in a #1 Contender Battle Royal for the NXT Women's Championship on the January 13, 2016, episode of *NXT*. Obviously, Deonna didn't win, but her stock only went up from there. Not only would she work as enhancement talent on an episode of *SmackDown* that same year, she would play "La Luchadora"—until it was revealed to be Mickie James—in the Becky Lynch/Alexa Bliss SmackDown Women's Championship feud. She'd also be selected as an alternate for WWE's inaugural Mae Young Classic in 2017.

As for her work in ROH and Women of Honor, in 2017, Deonna would come to feud with the undefeated (500+ days) Kelly Klein, coming so close to beating her—even tapping Klein out with her patented Fujiwara armbar, though the referee was out cold and didn't see it—only for Klein to weasel her way out with a win. Deonna's friend and training partner Karen Q—for whom Deonna put in a good word with to the Women of Honor officials—however, would go on to beat Klein in her debut. It was via count-out, and Kelly Klein said it didn't count as truly defeating her, but it was a win in Karen's (and even Deonna's) book. This win would then lead to a 3-Way match between Deonna, Karen, and Kelly, in which Karen (in only her second Women of Honor match) pinned Deonna, gloating a lot more than you usually would if you'd just ruined your friend's chance of getting revenge. But when it finally looked like Deonna would truly beat Kelly Klein in a one-on-one match, said friend would come in and interfere—turning on Deonna in order to make sure she couldn't truly beat Klein (and in order to make her gloating that much worse). The two former friends would then face off in one-on-one competition themselves, with Karen getting the upper hand (again, Deonna would be screwed by a referee being too incapacitated to see her clearly win) and hitting Deonna with a chair. However, they'd have a No Disqualification rematch, and Deonna would finally come out on top.

So it's understandable why she was named ROH's Women of Honor Wrestler of the Year for 2017. Keep in mind, this ws all at the age of 23. There's a reason why they call her "The Virtuosa." And in 2018, they also called her an official ROH talent, as she finally signed a contract with a wrestling promotion—just after ROH announced a tournament (in which she would be a participant) to crown the inaugural Women of Honor Champion. While she surprisingly only made it to the quarterfinals—being knocked out of the competition by STARDOM star Mayu Iwatani—Purrazzo's luck was going to turn around eventually. And it did, sooner rather than later, as it was announced at the end of May 2018 that Purrazzo had finally been signed to a WWE developmental contract to NXT. As it turned out, patience was in fact a virtue for The Virtuosa.

★ EMBER MOON ★

YEARS ACTIVE: 2007–present

TRAINED BY: Skandor Akbar · Lance Hoyt · Booker T's Pro Wrestling Alliance · Booker T · Rodney Mack · Jazz · WWE Performance Center

BILLED FROM: Chicago, Illinois · St. Louis, Missouri · Dallas, Texas

ACCOMPLISHMENTS: 2x AIW Women's Champion · 3x ACW American Joshi Champion · 1x ACW Televised Champion · 2012 ACW Queen of Queens Tournament · 1x Pro Wrestling Alliance Women's Champion · #18 in 2017 PWI Female 50 · 2013 WSU/CZW Queen and King of the Ring (with AR Fox) · 1x NXT Women's Championship

AKA: Trouble · Athena · "The War Goddess" · "The Wrestling Goddess" · "The Hussy Buster" · Adrienne · Adrienne Reese · "The Shenom"

NOTABLE MATCHES: Athena vs. Rachel Summerlyn at ACW Guilty By Association 5, in a 10,000 Thumbtacks match (January 16, 2011) · Athena, ACH, & Tadarius Thomas vs. BJ Whitmer, Michael Elgin, & MsChif at ROH Night of Hoopla (July 11, 2011) · Athena vs. Mia Yim vs. Jessie McKay at SHIMMER Volume 42, in a 3-Way match (October 1, 2011) · Christina Von Eerie, MsChif, & Athena vs. Sara Del Rey & The Canadian NINJAS (Nicole Matthews & Portia Perez) at AAW Epic: The 8th Anniversary Show (March 16, 2012) · Athena vs. Mercedes Martinez at SHIMMER Volume 45 (March 17, 2012) · Athena vs. Kimber Lee at AIW Girls Night Out 8 (March 1, 2013) · Athena vs. Mia Yim at AIW Girls Night Out 11 (March 29, 2014) · Athena vs. Allysin Kay (c) at AIW Girls Night Out 12, in a No DQ Falls Count Anywhere match for the AIW Women's Championship (March 29, 2014) · Athena (c) vs. Nikki Storm at AIW Nuthin' But A G Thang, for the AIW Women's Championship (April 25, 2014) · Athena vs. Hania The Howling Huntress at WSU 8th Anniversary Show, in a Tables, Ladders, & Chairs match (February 21, 2015) · Athena vs. Mia Yim at SHIMMER Volume 71: The ChickFight Tournament, in a SHIMMER ChickFight Tournament First Round match (March 28, 2015) · Ember Moon vs. Asuka (c) at NXT TakeOver: Brooklyn III, for the NXT Women's Championship (August 19, 2017) · Ember Moon vs. Kairi Sane vs. Peyton Royce vs. Nikki Cross at NXT TakeOver: WarGames, in a Fatal 4-Way match for the vacant NXT Women's Champion (November 18, 2017)

★ "Three things that are very near and dear to my heart: . . . Skill. Honor. And heart. Keep them close to your head. Because these are the three things that drive me." Not only are these the three tenets of SHIMMER Women Athletes, these are the three things the woman now known as WWE Superstar Ember Moon keeps in the front of her mind at all times.

Now known for her smoothness in the ring, Texas-native Adrienne Reese was first exposed to professional wrestling by her grandfather, who was a huge fan. However, she didn't really care for it at the time; she would just do it to get out of doing chores. She only fell in love with it slightly after, during the Attitude Era and as a way to cope with bullying. From then on, she quickly became a huge fan of The Rock and Stone Cold—don't make her choose between the two—as well as women like Victoria, Trish Stratus, and Chyna, who were all bringing something different to the table. When she was in her senior year of high school, her grandfather had taken ill. The night before he died, they casually spoke about professional wrestling, with him telling her she could make it as one of those wrestlers if she really wanted to. About four months later, she decided to honor her grandfather's legacy by getting into the business. She began her training in April 2007, learning from Texas wrestling legend Skandor Akbar, who gave her the nickname "The Wrestling Goddess" as she was training against the men.

"I trained with Akbar Monday through Friday for about four to five hours each day. I learned the old-school way. I didn't even touch a ring until a month and a half later, when he felt I earned my way into it. Before that, I would have to run down the side of the freeway in 100-degree weather, hoping that it would be the day I was able to get into the ring. . . . When that day finally came, I was ecstatic, but before I could leap for joy, I had to learn to endure the brute force of landing and being thrown around on concrete. Akbar made me appreciate everything I did in the ring."

However, with Akbar's school on its way to shutting down, Reese would then be invited and go on to train under Lance Hoyt. This training was less intense, as it was only once a week (though she would train by herself two or three times a week), but Reese has since credited it for teaching her about striking and performing power moves. Continuing to become a well-rounded wrestler before ever having her first actual wrestling match, Reese would then move on to (after being called in for a tryout) learn under WWE Hall of Famer Booker T at his Pro Wrestling Alliance (now Reality of Wrestling, as of 2012) training school in Houston, Texas. Regarding Booker T's role as her trainer, Athena's gone on the record as saying he "gave [her] the confidence and motivation that [she] really needed to succeed in the wrestling world." This in turn allowed her to branch outside of Texas to go and get wrestling experience all over the world, something she couldn't have even imagined when she was younger; after all, while she eventually became a big fan of WWF/WWE in her youth, she didn't even realize its rival promotion WCW existed until 2001, when its final *Nitro* episode featured a simulcast with RAW.

At Pro Wrestling Alliance, Reese would be known as "Trouble," debuting as a valet for the twin brother tag team the "Samoan Soldiers"—better known now as the popular WWE tag team The Usos. But everywhere else—until she finally achieved her dream of being signed by WWE—she'd make herself known as "Athena." After making her in-ring debut against local independent wrestler J.T. LaMotta, Athena went on to make a name for herself in the Texas independent circuit, wrestling in places such as Pro Wrestling Alliance, Professional Championship Wrestling (where she began using the name "Athena"), and especially ACW. The latter promotion became one of Athena's home promotions during her time on the independents, as she feuded with the likes of Jessica James (who put in a good word for Athena at Pro Wrestling Alliance in the first place) and Rachel Summerlyn, the latter of whom she'd go on to call a "rival of epic proportions." Her breakout year was 2010, as she feuded with and eventually defeated Summerlyn for the ACW American Joshi Championship. She'd also drop the championship back to Summerlyn after holding it for 15 days, but she would win the title two more times during her time on the independent scene (holding it for 119 days and then 217 days, respectively). Athena's feud with Rachel Summerlyn would also lead to a brutal 10,000 Thumbtacks match, with Athena coming out on top—though they would continue to cross paths in ACW.

"THREE THINGS . . . ARE VERY NEAR AND DEAR TO MY HEART: SKILL. HONOR. AND HEART. . . . THESE ARE THE THREE THINGS THAT DRIVE ME."

The year 2010 was also when Athena debuted in SHIMMER, thanks to a match she'd had at ACW—at the 2nd Annual Queen of Queens Tournament—that June, against the former SHIMMER Champion MsChif. Athena would fall to MsChif in the first round of the tournament, but the next day, she'd get the call from SHIMMER, asking her to come and wrestle for the promotion. And she did, with her debuting a few months later at SHIMMER Volume 33, in a tag team match with "Bonesaw" Jessie Brooks against a couple of wrestlers Athena knew very well, Jessica James and Rachel Summerlyn. From 2010 to 2016, Athena would wrestle for SHIMMER for 36 volumes, failing to capture the SHIMMER Championship but compiling wins against women such as Jessie McKay (WWE's Billie Kay), Mia Yim, Mercedes Martinez, Kimber Lee (WWE NXT's Abbey Laith), and Candice LeRae.

In AIW—a promotion she debuted at in 2012—Athena was so in demand to wrestle for the company that fans helped raise money to cover the cost of her travel to Ohio. AIW also became something of Athena's home promotion away from home, after debuting at the promotion's annual Girls Night Out show in August 2012. She even has a "Best Of . . ." DVD compilation of her matches from the company, chronicling everything from her debut against Sassy Stephie to her first and second time winning the AIW Women's Championship.

While Athena progressively became more of a name in the independent wrestling scene, part of this was in response to her previous aspirations to become a name in the more mainstream scene. Originally, despite her talents—even just at an early age—WWE didn't think Athena had the "Diva look." So after three failed tryouts (at ages 18, 19, and 20), Athena was done trying to get into WWE and instead focused on making them want her—getting to do what she wanted to do, on her terms. She wouldn't try out again until seven years after her third tryout, and that was only at the urging of WWE Diva Paige (formerly known as Britani Knight, in SHIMMER), during a trip to Orlando. However, this fourth time, she knew it was going to be her last time—if she didn't get signed this time, she was going to hang up her boots and call it a day on her professional wrestling career.

By early September 2015, rumors were swirling that Athena had signed, especially as she was hinting about "bigger and better things" coming in the future: that same month, it was finally announced that WWE signed Athena to a developmental contract with WWE. After performing in dark matches and house shows under her real name, in June 2016, Adrienne officially became "Ember Moon." Also, "The Wrestling Goddess" became "The War Goddess," and her "O-Face" finishing maneuver would now be known as "The Eclipse." (Speaking of The Eclipse, during her initial NXT feud with Billie Kay and Peyton Royce, the two troublemakers would attempt to get the move banned for being far too dangerous.)

According to the woman herself, "Ember Moon" isn't just a cool-sounding wrestling name. Like Athena, it's a name that has a loaded meaning: "Ember is the last thing that comes with a flame. It's the part that is so hard to die down, that can combust at any moment. The moon is so cool. It changes faces all the time. So basically my name means something that is undying and ever changing."

After weeks of promotional vignettes—as well as house shows and dark matches—Ember Moon officially made her WWE debut at NXT TakeOver: Brooklyn II (in June 2016), facing off against 1/2 of The Iconic Duo, Billie Kay. After defeating Kay, Ember went on to have a winning streak in the NXT until April 2017, when she lost her championship match against NXT Women's Champion (and also undefeated) Asuka, at NXT TakeOver: Orlando. However, while she lost, Ember was certain she could beat Asuka if just given the chance (and if Asuka didn't try any cheap tactics to win this time). Unfortunately, Ember came up short yet again that August, at NXT TakeOver: Brooklyn III—though she's looked back on her ovation after the match as the first time she knew she had the respect of the WWE Universe. After this match, Asuka vacated the NXT Women's Championship and moved up to the main roster, leading to a Fatal 4-Way match to determine the new championship. Ember Moon would qualify to be one of the four participants in the match, and at NXT TakeOver: WarGames (in November 2017), Ember Moon finally won the NXT Women's Championship in her native state of Texas. During her feud with Asuka and even on the road to this championship match, Ember had refused to touch the championship until she won it. So this win was made even more poignant by Asuka being the one to award her the championship.

As Ember moon said after her NXT Women's Championship win, "This is only the beginning for me."

★ EMMA ★

YEARS ACTIVE: 2003–present

TRAINED BY: Lance Storm · Storm Wrestling Academy · FCW · WWE Performance Center

BILLED FROM: Melbourne, Australia

ACCOMPLISHMENTS: 2x ECCW Women's SuperGirls Champion · 2009 PWA Queensland Queen of the Warriors · #31 in 2015 PWI Female 50

AKA: Valentine · Tenille · Tenille Dashwood · Tenille Tayla · Tennille Williams · "The Dancing Queen" · Emmalina

NOTABLE MATCHES: Tenille Tayla vs. Nicole Matthews at ECCW Diva's Last Dance (May 7, 2011) · Emma vs. Paige at NXT, in the NXT Women's Championship Tournament Finals the inaugural NXT Women's Championship (July 24, 2013) · Emma vs. Summer Rae at NXT, in a Dance-Off (August 7, 2013) · Emma & Santino Marella vs. Summer Rae & Fandango, in a Mixed Tag Team match (October 2, 2013) · Emma vs. Paige (c) at NXT ArRival, for the NXT Women's Championship (February 27, 2014) · Emma vs. Asuka at NXT TakeOver: London (December 16, 2015) · Emma vs. Alexa Bliss (c) vs. Bayley vs. Nia Jax vs. Sasha Banks at WWE No Mercy 2017, for the WWE RAW Women's Championship (September 24, 2017)

★ Tenille Dashwood became a professional wrestler when she was just 13 years old. Yes, while she was idolizing "Stone Cold" Steve Austin, Trish Status, and Lita on WWE television—thanks to a brother who got her hooked on professional wrestling—she was already getting a leg-up in achieving that dream, training during her adolescence. After finding a local independent wrestling promotion with a school, Tenille began training there a couple of times a week, for a couple of hours. She'd even do shows once a month.

Unfortunately for young Tenille, she would also have her first major wrestling injury at a young age, suffering a dislocated shoulder (the beginning of shoulder issues for years to come). After that, she mostly stayed out of the ring for two years (from 16 to 18 years old), but she still remained part of the Australian independent wrestling scene, whether it was working ring crew, the merchandise table, or such. However, that was just a temporary setback, as at age 19 she moved out of Australia and to Canada for a few months in the summer of 2008 to train under Lance Storm at his wrestling school, the Storm Wrestling Academy. To Tenille, this was the perfect choice if she wanted to have a serious shot at a long career in professional wrestling. She returned to Australia in the fall of 2008, but it was only a few months before North American independent promotions were calling her name, thanks to a good word from Sara Del Rey. May

2009 saw her make both her SHIMMER debut in the United States and her ECCW debut in Canada, working as "Tenille Tayla" (which would become her primary independent name) in the former and "Tenille Dashwood" in the latter.

Tenille also returned to Storm Wrestling Academy in 2009, both for additional training and later to be one of the Academy trainees in the first season of professional wrestling reality series *World of Hurt*. (However, it was during filming where she suffered from another shoulder injury.) *World of Hurt* aired in 2011, and it technically wasn't Tenille's only contribution to the world of televised wrestling that year: After a tryout earlier that year, it would be announced that March that she had signed a developmental contract with WWE. However, she wouldn't report to FCW—WWE's then developmental territory—until June the following year, as she finally got shoulder surgery that she'd avoided all those years ago when she was just a teenage wrestler. A couple of months after she reported to FCW (and moved to Tampa, Florida), it was finally announced what Tenille's WWE name would be: "Emma." However, Emma wouldn't make her on-screen debut—after multiple house show appearances—until November 2012. It also wouldn't be until January 2013 that Emma's gimmick came into effect, as a woman who dances to the beat of her own oddly timed drum and has an affinity for bubbles and for puns based on her name (such as: "Emmalution" or "Emma-mite Sandwich").

After debuting this character as a delusional—but otherwise inoffensive—heel, Emma quickly became a fan favorite in NXT and had her first big opportunity when she made it to the finals of the inaugural NXT Women's Championship tournament. While she came out on the losing end, her performance throughout the tournament led her to feud with Summer Rae—who she beat in the semifinals—which led to a memorable dance-off between the two that only helped both women define their characters even more. Eventually, Emma would get another chance at the NXT Women's Championship, facing off against Paige (who beat her in the tournament) at NXT ArRival (the precursor to NXT's TakeOver events). This match would officially set the tone for the NXT Women's Division and its matches from then out, and it only got bigger from there.

IN JANUARY 2013 EMMA'S GIMMICK CAME INTO EFFECT, AS A WOMAN WHO DANCES TO THE BEAT OF HER OWN ODDLY TIMED DRUM AND HAS AN AFFINITY FOR BUBBLES AND FOR PUNS BASED ON HER NAME.

As 2014 rolled in, Emma would make her debut on the WWE main roster; she'd been in the audience of both *RAW* and *SmackDown* for weeks, with pun-based ("#EMMAlution," "#EMMAtaining") signs in tow. She would again feud with Summer Rae—this time on a bigger stage—as well as get into an on-screen relationship with comedy wrestler Santino Marella. As for her main roster pay-per-view debut, that just so happened to be at WrestleMania XXX, wrestling in the Vickie Guerrero Divas Invitational, a 14-Divas match for the Divas Championship. While she didn't win, the Santino/Emma relationship continued until Santino retired from WWE that July. That June, however, Emma had a bit of a misstep with the company, as news broke that she had been arrested for shoplifting. As a result, WWE immediately released her from the company. However, after pleading in court that she had merely accidentally forgot to pay for an iPad case at a self-checkout machine and performing a day of community service, the charge was dropped and WWE reinstated her a few hours after her release.

Emma would then return to NXT in the beginning of 2015, leading to the character having a change of heart—feeling as though the WWE Universe turned its back on her—and a new "All About Me" heel persona. NXT newcomer Dana Brooke became her sidekick, and together, the two would start trouble everywhere they went. This version of Emma would compete in a Fatal-4-Way between herself, Becky Lynch, Dana Brooke, and Charlotte and win. Except, Emma wasn't supposed to win—Charlotte was—and only did because Becky Lynch was reportedly momentarily knocked out (which prevented her from breaking up the pin). During her run with Dana, the duo would also enter into a somewhat one-sided feud with Asuka (with Asuka's side being the winning one). Emma would then close out the year in NXT in a well-received match (despite the loss) at NXT TakeOver: London against Asuka.

After the Asuka feud, Emma (with this current character) would make her return to the main roster in 2016. However, she would suffer a back injury—a ruptured disc—at a house show that May, one which required surgery. Her first match back would be in October that year, in a house show Six-Women Tag Team match. That same month would feature vignettes on *Monday Night RAW* highlighting a new gimmick for Emma, called "Emmalina" and promising to show the "makeover of Emma to Emmalina." After 17 weeks of vignettes—and after saying Emmalina would be "premiering" soon in December—Emmalina finally arrived on RAW in February 2017 . . . only to hype the transformation back to Emma ("the makeover from Emmalina to Emma") and simply head backstage. Emma remained off television for a couple of months, until returning back to the "All About Me" heel persona (also hyped in vignettes) that fans had wanted from her in the first place. To this day, the actual intent of the Emmalina character still isn't quite known. The vignettes for Emmalina emphasized her role as an Instagram model or a throwback to the stereotypical WWE Diva of the '90s, but considering her talent level and the company's Divas Revolution, it never quite seemed like the right fit. However, a month after she returned, Emma suffered another shoulder injury and was again off the shelf for another month.

That September saw Emma make her first WWE pay-per-view appearance since 2014, as part of the RAW Women's Championship Fatal 5-Way match. The next month, Emma was released from her contract by the WWE, right after putting on more solid in-ring performances against Asuka (in Asuka's main roster debut), both at the TLC pay-per-view and in a rematch on an episode of *RAW*. The next month, she announced her first independent wrestling dates, at WrestlePro and AIW the upcoming February, and eventually she would become a prominent part of ROH's Women of Honor division. With this return, she would once again wrestle under her real name, "Tenille Dashwood."

★ EVE TORRES ★

YEARS ACTIVE: 2007–2013

TRAINED BY: OVW · Dave "Fit" Finlay

BILLED FROM: Denver, Colorado · Los Angeles, California

ACCOMPLISHMENTS: 3x WWE Divas Champion · 2007 WWE Divas Search · #5 in 2010 PWI Female 50

AKA: Eve · "Hoeski" · "The Hellacious Heartbreaker"

NOTABLE MATCHES: Eve Torres vs. Maryse (c) at WWE *Monday Night RAW*, for the WWE Divas Championship (April 12, 2010) · Eve Torres vs. Beth Phoenix (c) at Vengeance 2011, for the WWE Divas Championship (October 23, 2011) · Eve Torres vs. Layla (c) at WWE Night of Champions 2012, for the WWE Divas Championship (September 16, 2012) · Eve Torres & Beth Phoenix vs. Kelly Kelly & Maria Menounos at WWE WrestleMania XXVIII (April 1, 2012) · Eve Torres (c) vs. Kaitlyn at WWE *Monday Night RAW*, for the WWE Divas Championship (January 14, 2013)

★ If there's one thing many people can agree about when it comes to Eve Torres, she left professional wrestling just when she'd truly hit her stride. Maybe it's a matter of not knowing what you've got 'til it's gone, but maybe it's really just a case of someone really knowing how to go out on a high note.

Like a lot of WWE Divas during her particular era, Eve Torres first entered the company as a contestant on the WWE's Diva Search (the 2007 edition). She won the competition that fall and then reported to WWE development at OVW before officially making her WWE main roster debut in the beginning of 2008. There would be vignettes promoting her debut on *SmackDown*, though her official debut was actually as one of the company's backstage interviewers (and as a face). During this time, SmackDown would also hold its own Diva Contest—in which Eve participated in a bikini contest, an obstacle course, and an arm wrestling competition—looking for the "top Diva" on the brand. However, Eve would not even get her first on-screen main roster match until November 2008, on *Monday Night RAW*'s 800th episode, in a 16-Diva Tag Team match. Her team would lose, but it would also feature women's wrestling legend Mae Young. The first part of 2009 would have her feuding with Michelle McCool and Layla, as well as managing and teaming with the male tag team Cryme Tyme, until she was traded to RAW in the fall.

On *RAW*, Eve had a temporary storyline with Chris Masters as his girlfriend/manager, before moving on to championship aspirations in 2010. She reached the semifinals of a tournament to capture the vacant WWE Divas Championship, losing to Maryse, who would go on to win the tournament. The night after WrestleMania XXVI, she'd pin Maryse in a 10-Divas Tag Team match but was not considered the #1 Contender until she won a match the following week. Again, given the era of WWE, Eve's #1 Contendership was earned in a "Dress To Impress" Battle Royal—but at least it was won in a match. The week after that, she would win her championship match against Maryse and win the Divas Championship for the first time. Eve Torres, the first Diva Search winner to hold the Divas Championship, would eventually be the first-ever three-time Divas Champion. During her first reign, Eve would hold the Divas Championship for 69 days, dropping it to Alicia Fox in a Fatal 4-Way match. It wouldn't be until Royal Rumble

2011 in January—in another Fatal 4-Way match—that she won the title for the second time, this time holding it for 71 days. After she dropped the championship for the second time, she formed a face alliance with Kelly Kelly, even accompanying Kelly to the ring once she won the Divas Championship. This pairing—which saw Eve essentially play Kelly's sidekick—seemed like it would have been the perfect way for Eve to turn heel, but that's a character choice that wouldn't happen until early 2012. And this turn would have nothing to do with the championship at all.

After Eve and Kelly feuded with The Divas of Doom—and that splintered into Eve vs. Beth Phoenix—Eve started a storyline with RAW Superstar Zack Ryder at the end of 2011. The two of them would team up in mixed tag team matches, with Eve eventually agreeing to go on a date with Ryder, one of the company's most beloved underdogs. At the same time, Zack Ryder was becoming involved in a feud between his friend John Cena and the monster heel Kane. As Kane used Ryder as a pawn in this feud, that also extended to him using Eve: Kane would attempt to kidnap Eve, only for John Cena to save her, and for Eve to kiss Cena as thanks (with Ryder sadly witnessing the moment). On *RAW* the week after that, Eve turned heel, as Cena overhead her tell The Bella Twins that she was just using Ryder, like she would do to Cena too. And in the case of the heel turn, according to former WWE head writer—and WWE Diva advocate—Tom Casiello mentioned that this was a decision made five minutes before *Monday Night RAW* even started. A nature of the beast that is WWE, it's actually known to be quite common for Vince McMahon to rewrite one of the shows before it starts, or even in the middle of the show. Prior to WrestleMania XXVIII, Eve convinced (some might say "seduced") Ryder to forgive her for her actions, only for her to intentionally distract him during the Team Johnny vs. Team Teddy (Ryder's team) match at WrestleMania and cause Team Teddy to lose. (Earlier that night, she had also lost a tag team match with Beth Phoenix, against her former friend Kelly Kelly and television personality Maria Menounos.) After the match, Eve hit Ryder with a low blow and was promoted by on-screen authority figure John Laurinaitis (the Johnny in "Team Johnny") to be his Executive Administrator of RAW and SmackDown (in addition to her in-ring duties).

The summer of 2012 saw Eve adding a new tactic to her in-ring arsenal, pretending to have turned over a new leaf and become sportsmanlike against her opponents like Kaitlyn and the Divas Champion at the time, Layla. Eve would soon participate in a Battle Royal to determine the #1 Contender to the Divas Championship, only to lose at the end when she legitimately eliminated herself by accident. Eve would then get into a 3-Way feud with Kaitlyn and Layla, as well as a third reign as the Divas Championship: with Kaitlyn being taken out by a masked attacker (eventually revealed as Aksana, a hired gun for Eve) at Night of Champions, Eve would get that championship opportunity instead and win. Kaitlyn would finally get her title shot a month later but fell short and almost fell victim to Eve's attempts to reinjure her. For the rest of 2012, Eve (with Aksana by her side) would feud with Kaitlyn, doing everything she could to keep Kaitlyn from capturing her Divas Championship.

But on January 14, 2013—the 20th Anniversary of RAW—Eve defended her WWE Divas Championship against Kaitlyn and lost. She then immediately "quit" WWE in a WWE App exclusive video after the match. ("I'm the victim here! I'm the victim! . . . I don't need WWE. I won a reality show." Let it never be said that Eve Torres wasn't a self-aware WWE Diva.) Only she technically really did quit WWE, as she had apparently requested her release from the company in December 2012 and it had been granted. A purple belt in Brazilian jiu-jitsu, Eve now works as one of the head instructors at the Gracie Academy's Women Empowered self-defense program. And considering she once actually put WWE Superstar Matt Hardy to sleep with a chokehold—back when she was still just a backstage interviewer in WWE—her students are in good hands. Eve still remains an ambassador to WWE and has even appeared in WWE Network original programming *Table For 3* in its "Divas Championship Club" episode (with Maryse and Kelly Kelly).

★ THE FABULOUS MOOLAH ★

YEARS ACTIVE: 1948–2004

TRAINED BY: Mildred Burke · Billy Wolfe · Mae Young · Johnny Long

BILLED FROM: Columbia, South Carolina

ACCOMPLISHMENTS: 1997 Cauliflower Alley Club Honoree · 2x NWA Women's World Tag Team Champion (with Toni Rose) · 5x NWA World Women's Champion · NWA Hall of Fame Class of 2012 · Professional Wrestling Hall of Fame and Museum Class of 2003 · 1991 PWI Stanley Weston Award · 4x WWF Women's Champion · WWF Hall of Fame Class of 1995

AKA: The Spider Lady · Slave Girl Moolah · Fabulous Moolah

NOTABLE MATCHES: The Fabulous Moolah & Kitty Adams vs. Joyce Grable & Vivian St. John at WWF on MSG Network, in a Best 2 Out of 3 Falls Tag Team match (July 30, 1970) · The Fabulous Moolah (c) vs. Wendi Richter at WWF The Brawl To End It All, for the WWF Women's Championship (July 23, 1984) · Spider Lady vs. Wendi Richter (c) at WWF on MSG Network, for the WWF Women's Championship (November 25, 1985) · The Fabulous Moolah, The Jumping Bomb Angels (Itsuki Yamazaki & Noriyo Tateno), Rockin' Robin, & Velvet McIntyre vs. Dawn Marie, Donna Christanello, The Glamour Girls (Judy Martin & Leilani Kai), & Sensational Sherri at WWF Survivor Series 1987, in a 5-on-5 Survivor Series Elimination match (November 26, 1987) · The Fabulous Moolah vs. Ivory (c) at WWF No Mercy 1999, for the WWF Women's Championship (October 17, 1999)

★ When it comes to the history of women's wrestling—both in terms of the good and the bad—you truly can't talk about the sport without talking about The Fabulous Moolah. Although, it's quite understandable that if you want to avoid the bad you choose not to mention her. It's just, unfortunately—and ultimately, allegedly— disingenuous. But for better or worse, in her heyday, there was absolutely no single female wrestler more dominant than Moolah. After all, that's why she was called "Moolah" in the first place: she was doing it all "for the moolah" (the money).

Born Mary Lillian Ellison (but known as Lillian to her friends) in 1923, the South Carolinian caught the wrestling bug from her father, who would take her to see local wrestling matches as a child. Seeing professional wrestling for the type of escapism that it is, Mr. Ellison hoped that these matches would cheer his daughter up, as she was still reeling from the death of her mother when she was eight years old. Eventually, this worked—specifically when she saw the matches of NWA World Women's Champion Mildred Burke. In fact, because of Burke, Ellison went to seek out her husband/trainer, NWA promoter Billy Wolfe, in 1948. With Wolfe's connections, Ellison was able to get a leg up in the competitive world of women's professional wrestling. However, also because of Wolfe, Ellison was exposed to the seedy part of that world as well, as Wolfe would try to pimp out his talent (suggesting his wrestlers offer up their service, sexually, in order to move up in the ranks and get bookings). While Ellison refused to prostitute herself out to other promoters, she allegedly didn't treat her own eventual trainees with the same respect she had for herself.

Eventually, Ellison left Wolfe's group to work for wrestling promoter Jack Pfefer, who gave her the name "Slave Girl Moolah." As Slave Girl Moolah, she served as a valet for "Nature Boy" Buddy Rogers in the early 1950s, until she allegedly ended the partnership because she rebuked Rogers's sexual advances. In 1955, thanks to a good word from Mae Young—as the two had become close friends when Young trained Moolah for Billy Wolfe—Moolah began wrestling for Vincent James McMahon's (aka Vince McMahon Sr.) Capitol Wrestling Corporation (pre-WWF). Then the following fall, Moolah won the vacant NWA World Women's Championship in a Battle Royal—with Vince Sr. proclaiming Moolah "The Fabulous Moolah." There was initially some conflict over Moolah's champion status, due to Billy Wolfe's power in the NWA and grudge with her for leaving his group and training her own female wrestlers. But this Battle Royal and Moolah's win proved that Wolfe's stranglehold in the business was no longer the norm: it was Moolah's world now.

In order for it to become Moolah's world, that also meant taking Billy Wolfe's ideas about monopolizing the world of women's professional wrestling and using them for herself. When it came to her trainees, allegedly, Moolah took a booking fee of anywhere from 25 to 50 percent from her girls—which was far from the worst allegations about her behavior as a promoter and trainer. As for in the ring, WWE history often mentions how Moolah held the Women's Championship for 28 years, but in reality, it was a matter of Moolah having the creative control to book the title however she saw fit—to the point of only losing the title a handful of very short times for nearly 30 years. Her initial run with the championship lasted over 10 years, and once June Byers (who was one of Wolfe's girls) officially retired 1964, Moolah was recognized

as the Undisputed Women's World Champion. In the late 1970s, she officially bought the legal rights to the championship. And from 1956 to 1983, Moolah held the championship for over 11,000 days. It wasn't until 1983, after signing an exclusive contract with Vince Sr. in WWF that the Women's Championship was finally no longer under Moolah's control.

IN HER HEYDAY, THERE WAS ABSOLUTELY NO SINGLE FEMALE WRESTLER MORE DOMINANT THAN MOOLAH. THAT'S WHY SHE WAS CALLED "MOOLAH": SHE WAS DOING IT ALL "FOR THE MOOLAH" (THE MONEY).

It was during her "28-year championship reign" that Vince McMahon ("Jr.") initiated the "Rock 'n' Wrestling Connection" Era, a cross-promotion between the WWF and the music industry (specifically, MTV). With Cyndi Lauper in Wendi Richter's corner and Captain Lou Albano in Moolah's, new, young eyes were on the wrestling product for The Brawl To End It All—a WWF Madison Square Garden show broadcast live on MTV on July 23, 1984. While The Brawl featured 11 matches, only this one actually aired on MTV. With Lauper's help, Richter won the match and the championship, ending Moolah's historic reign. And, due to the ratings success of The Brawl To End It All, the Rock 'n' Wrestling Connection Era officially began. (Moolah was, however, able to help her protégé Leilani Kai eventually win the championship from Richter.) While Richter was the young women's star of the era, the WWF/MTV relationship during the Rock 'n' Wrestling Connection did lead to Moolah (as well as Richter) being featured in the Cyndi Lauper music video for "Goonies R Good Enough," as well as (her likeness) in the eventual Saturday morning cartoon *Hulk Hogan's Rock 'n' Wrestling*.

However, none of this is to say Moolah was out of the spotlight. In fact, her hand in the ending of Richter's second reign with the WWF Women's Championship would make for a brand new form of spotlight: "The Original Screwjob." As Richter and McMahon came to an impasse over Richter's contract, McMahon decided to make sure WWF wouldn't get screwed out of getting the title back (had Richter decided to let her contract expire and leave). So a title match took place—at Madison Square Garden in November 1985—with Richter defending her championship against a masked opponent called "The Spider Lady." The Spider Lady won the championship thanks to a quick three-count from the referee (who was in on the Screwjob), and in her anger, Richter unmasked the new champion to reveal it was Moolah. While Richter quit WWF immediately as a result of this betrayal, Moolah was rewarded with more lengthy reigns, eventually losing the championship for the last time to Sherri Martel in the summer of 1987. From that point on, Moolah remained in a state of semi-retirement, returning to WWF post-Hall of Fame induction as a veteran comedic form (alongside Mae Young) during the Attitude Era—when she was 76 years old. Still, at 76 and beyond, Moolah had no problem taking guitar shots from Jeff Jarrett or RKOs from Randy Orton. And at 76, she was able to win the WWF Women's Championship one more time—making her the oldest WWF Women's Champion in history—from Ivory before losing it back to her the following week. Moolah continued to make appearances in WWE up until SummerSlam 2007. A few months later, in the fall of 2007, Moolah passed away at the age of 84, after a shoulder replacement surgery.

In the spring of 2018, the WWE announced the inaugural "Fabulous Moolah Memorial Battle Royal," a female counterpart Battle Royal to the annual (as of 2014) "Andre The Giant Memorial Battle Royal." However, soon after the announcement, a combination outcry and backlash on social media (directed both at WWE and WrestleMania's primary sponsor, Snickers) and write-ups in mainstream news publications called out the hypocrisy of WWE's continued refusal to acknowledge the allegations against Moolah—this time in more public, self-congratulatory way. Attention was shone on a 2006 article about the original Sweet Georgia Brown (Susie Mae McCoy)—Moolah's first black student—and how she was allegedly robbed of her earnings and prostituted out by Moolah (and Moolah's husband at the time, Buddy Lee).

Mad Maxine, another Moolah trainee, also put out a statement in reaction to the WWE decision to celebrate Moolah with the Battle Royal: "The Fabulous Moolah was a real-life heel. A lot of women paid to train at her school and then went out on the road. They risked life and limb in their matches, and she repaid them with the worst kinds of abuses. She skimmed their money, she ignored women who were badly hurt, she pimped women out to creepy men, and on and on. She was not a mother figure. She was more like Kali, the Indian Goddess of Destruction. I met her in my early 20s, and I had never met such a monstrous person." Maxine also added that while she understood how Moolah's "dirt poor" upbringing turned her into the type of person who never wanted to live that life again, that was still not an excuse for "her dog-eat-dog behavior." She ended the statement with this: "May she be the last of her kind."

Eventually, Snickers issued a statement addressing the controversy surrounding the Battle Royal, calling the entire situation "unacceptable" and saying that they would contact the WWE to settle it. Almost immediately, WWE issued a follow-up statement of their own and changed the match name to the "WrestleMania Women's Battle Royal" instead.

With more than 50 years of wrestling under her belt, Moolah was naturally eulogized as the person whose name was most synonymous with women's wrestling. But despite Moolah's importance to women's professional wrestling, in terms of name value, her legacy has certainly not been without its critics. Solely from an in-ring standpoint, wrestling journalists like Dave Meltzer and David Bixenspan have pointed out how Moolah's style was that of the "hair-pulling," catfight variety, which didn't necessarily help women's wrestling evolve. But still, the Moolah name has endured.

★ GAIL KIM ★

YEARS ACTIVE: 2000–2018

TRAINED BY: Ron Hutchison · Rob "El Fuego" Etcheverria · Squared Circle Training · OVW · Dave "Fit" Finlay

BILLED FROM: Korea · Tampa, Florida · Toronto, Ontario, Canada

ACCOMPLISHMENTS: 2001 Apocalypse Wrestling Federation Diva of the Year · 1x ABC Women's Champion · 1x Funkin' Conservatory (FC) Women's Champion · 1x Imperial Wrestling Revolution Diamond Champion · #1 in 2012 PWI Female 50 · 7x (and inaugural) TNA/Impact Wrestling Knockouts Champion · 1x TNA Knockouts Tag Team Champion (with Madison Rayne) · 2007 TNA Knockout of the Year · 2007 TNA Knockouts Gauntlet for the Gold · 2016 TNA Knockouts Gauntlet for the Gold · 2015 TNA World Cup (with Jeff Hardy, Gunner, Rockstar Spud, Davey Richards, & Crazzy Steve) · TNA Hall of Fame Class of 2016 · 1x WWE Women's Champion

AKA: "The Queen of the Cats" · La Felina · 1/3 of America's Most Wanted (AMW)

NOTABLE MATCHES: Gail Kim vs. Jazz (c) vs. Ivory vs. Jacqueline vs. Trish Stratus vs. Victoria vs. Molly Holly at WWE *Monday Night RAW*, in a Battle Royal for the WWE Women's Championship (June 30, 2003) · Gail Kim & Molly Holly vs. Lita & Trish Stratus at WWE Unforgiven 2003 (September 21, 2003) · Gail Kim (c) vs. Awesome Kong at TNA Turning Point 2007, for the TNA Knockouts Championship (December 2, 2007) · Gail Kim (c) vs. Awesome Kong at TNA Final Resolution 2008, in a No Disqualification match for the TNA Knockouts Championship (December 2, 2007) · Gail Kim (c) vs. Awesome Kong at TNA Final Resolution 2008, in a No Disqualification match for the TNA Knockouts Championship (January 6, 2008) · Gail Kim vs. Awesome Kong (c) vs. ODB at TNA Destination X 2008, in a 3-Way Dance match for the TNA Knockouts Championship (March 9, 2008) · Gail Kim vs. Taryn Terrell at TNA Slammiversary XI, in a Last Knockout Standing match (June 2, 2013) · Gail Kim vs. Taryn Terrell at TNA Impact Wrestling, in a Ladder match for the #1 Contendership to the TNA Knockouts Championship (July 11, 2013) · Gail Kim vs. Taryn Terrell (c) vs. Awesome Kong at TNA Impact Wrestling, in a 3-Way Dance match for the TNA Knockouts Championship (March 20, 2015) · Gail Kim (CANADA) vs. Allie (USA) at SMASH Wrestling CANUSA Classic 2017 (December 3, 2017)

★ Just before she became a professional wrestler, Gail Kim majored in kinesiology and then nutrition in college. So health and fitness was always at the top of her mind. It was also during college that she became "obsessed" with professional wrestling—though she'd fallen in love with the sport as a child, a fan of Tito Santana, The British Bulldog, and Ricky "The Dragon" Steamboat—and especially with the athleticism of the women at the time. The self-admittedly "spontaneous" Kim then told herself, "I want to do that," and the rest was squared circle history. She didn't tell her family at first, as her choice in career didn't exactly jibe with her traditional Korean upbringing—nor did putting her tuition money toward her wrestling school training.

Like plenty of accomplished Canadian wrestlers before her, Gail Kim was trained by Ron Hutchison in Toronto. She then moved on to Rob Etcheverria's wrestling school (also in Toronto) before making her official in-ring debut in December 2000 at Hutchison's Apocalypse Wrestling Federation (AWF, again, in Toronto). But she did not debut as "Gail Kim;" instead, she debuted with a masked wrestler gimmick, as "The Queen of the Cats" La Felina. Regarding the reason Kim started under a mask, she was allegedly told she was "too pretty" of a wrestler. She would wrestle as La Felina from 2001 to 2002 in Canadian independent promotions like AWF and nCw and Border City Wrestling (BCW), as well as American independent promotions like IWF and WXW. Along the way, she'd cross paths with Phoenix (WWE Hall of Famer Beth Phoenix's independent persona), Angel (fellow TNA Impact alumni Angelina Love), and Nikki Roxx. As La Felina, she feuded with "Miss Tracy" (Tracy Brooks, who would eventually become a TNA Impact alum just like Gail Kim), culminating in a Hair vs. Mask match which Kim would lose. While she would no longer be a masked persona, Kim wouldn't fully drop the La Felina persona until the fall of 2002. Regarding the entire La Felina persona, Kim has gone on the record in saying she doesn't miss the gimmick at all: "I don't miss that mask at all. I was paying my dues as part of my wrestling days. I never came up with that idea. . . . I want to forget about those days."

Two years into her wrestling career, then WWF Diva Molly Holly—who Kim had met in 2001, thanks to an introduction from wrestler Jason Sensation—encouraged Gail Kim to send in her wrestling tapes to WWF officials at the time, leading to a tryout. This tryout also included (another Molly Holly–supported wrestler) Beth Phoenix, but this time, Gail was the one to walk away with a contract. She'd officially sign with the company (now WWE) in October 2002, reporting to developmental at OVW. That December, she'd also technically debut on the main roster at a WWE house show, against Dawn Marie . . . in a Bra & Panties match.

Gail Kim would eventually make her official, on-screen main roster debut on WWE *Monday Night RAW* in June 2003—after weeks of *Matrix*-inspired (as her gimmick was supposed to be) promotional vignettes for her character—participating in and winning a Battle Royal match for the WWE Women's Championship. After holding the championship for a month as a babyface, upon losing the championship to Trish Stratus on another edition of *RAW*, Kim would turn heel and team with her real life ally Molly Holly in order to feud with WWE's perennial female duo, Trish and Lita. This led to Kim appearing in her first WWE pay-per-view, Unforgiven 2003, in a tag team match between the feuding pairs that the heel team lost. While the feud would continue after this, that November, Kim would suffer an injury in the form of a broken right collarbone during a *Sunday Night Heat* match against Trish and ended up sidelined from action for five months. (She'd also miss another two weeks due to a ruptured breast implant, something that ended up happening to Kim at least five times in her in-ring wrestling career.) When Kim returned to *RAW*, she did so as a heel, picking up where

she and Molly Holly left off. However, despite remaining in contention for the Women's Championship, Kim would not win it for a second time. And by November 2004, she was released by WWE, reportedly because the company wanted to take the Divas Division in another direction—a direction which ultimately continued the devolution of women's wrestling in WWE.

Following her WWE release, Kim made a few indie appearances, wrestling in South Korea, Australia, Japan, and Mexico (as well as the United States) before officially arriving in the wrestling promotion (after her 90-day no-compete clause from WWE completed) she would become synonymous with: TNA, which eventually became known as just Impact Wrestling. Kim signed her TNA contract in September 2005, debuting on-screen the following month as the manager to Jeff Jarrett and (more notably) the tag team of America's Most Wanted (AMW, with

"Wildcat" Chris Harris and "The Cowboy" James Storm). While Kim's role as manager often involved her getting physical—as an interfering heel—it wouldn't be until July the following year that she actually made her in-ring debut for the promotion, at the Victory Road pay-per-view. There, she teamed with AMW in a Six-Person Mixed Tag Team match against the Phenomenal Angels ("The Phenomenal" A.J. Styles and "The Fallen Angel" Christopher Daniels) and their female answer to Kim and her constant interference, Sirelda. While AMW and Kim lost the Victory Road match, Kim would at least go on to beat Sirelda the following month at the Hard Justice pay-per-view, in her first singles match with the company. After AMW became faces in the fall of 2006 and then disintegrated that winter (with Storm turning heel), Gail had a brief feud (with Chris Harris by her side) with Storm and his new manager, Jackie Moore (former WWF/WWE Diva Jacqueline), before moving on to a feud with Bobby Roode (then going by Robert Roode) and Ms. Brooks (Traci Brooks).

But 2007 in TNA was an important year for Gail Kim and not just because she won TNA Knockout of the Year. It was the year TNA decided to expand their Knockouts Division—their women's division—moving forward. That October, TNA introduced its Knockouts Championship with a 10-Women Gauntlet match for the title, a match that Kim won to become the inaugural champion. During her tenure in TNA/Impact Wrestling, Gail Kim would go on to win the championship a recording-setting seven times. But the road to Knockouts greatness was not without its own hurdles. Her first championship feud was a David vs. Goliath situation against the monster known as Awesome Kong, and together, Kim and Kong defined the Knockouts Division. During this time, the Knockouts Division was easily the company's biggest draw, with segments that were regularly the highest rated on weekly episodes of *TNA Impact*. However, by the summer of 2008, Kim was out of TNA and WWE-bound once more to end the year.

Officially re-debuting in March 2009, Kim fought her way toward the newly introduced Divas Championship during her second life in WWE, but championship gold eluded her. While she would finally make her WrestleMania debut (at WrestleMania XXV, a month after her re-debut), she'd do so in a 25-Diva Battle Royal match (not even for a championship and featuring a male wrestler dressed in drag winning) instead of a one-on-one competition, and her WrestleMania appearance the following year would see her on the losing side of a 10-Diva Tag Team match. In 2011, she wouldn't even be a part of WrestleMania, and by that summer, Kim was done with WWE. However, that was before she even told WWE she was done. During a Divas Battle Royal on the August 1, 2011, episode of *Monday Night RAW*, Gail Kim eliminated herself—rolling out underneath the bottom rope, as that was considered a legal elimination during Divas battle royals at the time, as opposed to standard over-the-top rope eliminations—from the match. According to Kim on Slam.Canoe.com, it was a long time coming:

> I don't regret what I did at all. It was a respect thing. I was told to get eliminated as soon as possible, so that's what I did. I saw my decision as a case of either continuing to take their lack of respect or doing something about it. . . . While a lot of fans watching *Raw* noticed what I did, nobody from WWE noticed, that just shows how much they didn't care. I went up to [John Laurinaitis] after and spoke about the Battle Royal and his reaction towards the match was, 'Yeah, I heard it was pretty shit.' I was amazed, and I then told him how I eliminated myself and he just laughed. . . . How can fans take the division seriously if the people working for the company aren't? If it had been one of the men who had eliminated themselves they would have been punished, but because it was the women nobody cared, not even after I had told them.

Four days after the battle royal, she requested her release from the company, but she wouldn't be granted it—despite the battle royal being her final match in the company—until her contract expired at the end of September. After leaving the world of WWE for a second (and final, as she has often vowed) time on somewhat of her own terms, Kim acknowledged that at least one person in a position of authority cared when she left. According to her, Triple H told her, "You're talented, and don't let anyone else tell you any different." And that's something she continued to let drive her in her professional wrestling career.

KIM STARTED WRESTLING UNDER A MASK, AS SHE WAS ALLEGEDLY TOLD SHE WAS "TOO PRETTY" OF A WRESTLER.

That October, she returned to TNA Impact Wrestling—as a heel—and almost immediately became the TNA Knockouts Tag Team Champion (with Madison Rayne), also becoming the Knockouts Champion (her second reign) the following month. By the spring of 2012, Kim and Rayne would lose their tag team championship and split up, and that summer, she'd lose her title to Brooke Tessmacher (after achieving a record-setting—at the time—210 day reign). 2013 would see Gail Kim back in title contention, this time in a feud—arguably her most historic feud outside of her time against Awesome Kong—against new Knockout Taryn Terrell, who began in-story as a referee for the division, one who kept poorly officiating during and interfering in Kim's matches. During their feud, Kim and Terrell both took the division to the next level with their Last Knockout Standing match (which Terrell won) at Slammiversary and then their Ladder match (which Kim won) for the Knockouts Championship #1 Contendership.

The two rivals wouldn't face each other again until the summer of 2014, in which Kim defended her Knockouts Championship—during her fourth reign—against Terrell and renewed their feud. This feud would also eventually include the new Impact Wrestling monster on the block at the time, Havok,

to whom Kim would lose the championship that September. After selling a kayfabe injury at Havok's hands, Kim challenged Havok for the Knockouts Champion in November, only to come up short in her attempt to retrieve the championship. Early 2015 would then see Kim team up with longtime rival Awesome Kong against the new faction of The Dollhouse (led by Taryn Terrell).

Kim would win the Knockouts Championship for the fifth time that September, successfully defending the championship—and reigniting the feud—against Kong at the company's biggest show of the year, the Bound For Glory pay-per-view, the following month. She wouldn't lose the championship until the spring of 2016, a couple of months before becoming the first (and only) female inductee into the TNA Hall of Fame. At Bound For Glory 2016, she would win the title for the sixth time, only to vacate it days later due to a back injury. Upon returning to the company (in the form of Global Force Wrestling) the following July, Gail Kim announced her plans to retire at the end of 2017.

That year at Bound For Glory (with the company officially known as Impact Wrestling), Kim won the Knockouts Championship for a record-setting seventh time in a 3-Way Dance against the then champion Sienna and Kim's on-screen protégé, Allie. (The match was originally supposed to be a Four-Way with a returning heel Taryn Terrell, but she had to pull out of the match and company.) She vacated the title and officially retired on Impact Wrestling's weekly television show in the episode that aired two weeks after her win. However, despite wrestling her last match for the company, Kim did not forget all that the company had done for and given her—which is why she transitioned into a backstage role, as an agent, trainer, and producer for the Knockouts, as well as a member of the creative department. She also spent some time in the fall of 2017 working with the actresses of Netflix's *GLOW* for its second season.

Gail Kim's last official wrestling match took place on February 3, 2018—defeating Kasey Owens at Southside Wrestling's Raw Deal 7 show, in England. As Kim later wrote in an Instagram post, retiring in the United Kingdom was her dream.

★ IO SHIRAI ★

YEARS ACTIVE: 2007–present

TRAINED BY: Takashi Sasaki · Tomohiko Hashimoto

BILLED FROM: Kamakura, Kanagawa · Tokyo, Japan

ACCOMPLISHMENTS: 2007 JWP Joshi Puroresu 5th Junior All Star Photogenic Award (with Mio Shirai) · 1x Pro Wrestling WAVE TLW World Young Women's Tag Team Champion (with Mio Shirai) · 2009 Pro Wrestling WAVE Captain's Fall Six Person Tag Team Tournament (with Mio Shirai & Gami) · 2009 Pro Wrestling WAVE TLW World Young Women's Tag Team Tournament (with Mio Shirai) · #6 in 2017 PWI Female 50 · 2015 Tokyo Sports Joshi Puroresu Grand Prize · 2016 Tokyo Sports Joshi Puroresu Grand Prize · 1x Americas World Mixed Tag Team Champion (with NOSAWA) · 6x Artist of STARDOM Champion (1x with Mayu Iwatani & Takumi Iroha, 1x with Kairi Hojo & Mayu Iwatani, 1x with HZK & Momo Watanabe, 2x with AZM & HZK, 1x with HZK & Viper) · 1x Goddess of STARDOM Champion (with Mayu Iwatani) · 1x High Speed Champion · 1x SWA World Champion · 2x Wonder of STARDOM Champion · 2x World of STARDOM Champion · 2013 STARDOM MVP Award · 2014 STARDOM MVP Award · 2014 STARDOM 5☆STAR GP · 2015 Goddesses of STARDOM Tag Tournament (with Mayu Iwatani) · 2013 Red Belt Challenge STARDOM Tournament · 2016 SWA World Championship Tournament · STARDOM's first Grand Slam Champion · 2015 STARDOM 5☆STAR GP Best Match Award (vs. Mayu Iwatani, on August 23) · 2013 STARDOM 5☆STAR GP Technique Award · 2015 STARDOM Best Match Award (vs. Meiko Satomura, on December 23) · 2016 STARDOM Best Match Award (vs. Mayu Iwatani, on December 22) · 2015 STARDOM Best Tag Team Award (with Mayu Iwatani) · 2016 STARDOM MVP Award · 2017 Artist of STARDOM Championship Tournament (with Mayu Iwatani) · 2017 STARDOM 5☆STAR GP Technique Award

AKA: 1/3 of Triple Tails · Hitokiri · Oyuki · Biba Kasai · Iotica · Midnight Angel · Oyuki · T-2 Mask · Tenkū Shōjo Lusca · "Tenku no Genius" ("Genius Of The Sky") · "Woman In The Sky" · "Darkside Itsujo" · 1/2 of The Purple Thunder Sisters · member of Planet · 1/2 of Thunder Rock · 1/2 of Heisei Star · 1/2 of Heisei-gun ("Heisei Army") · member of Queen's Quest

NOTABLE MATCHES: Io Shirai vs. Mio Shirai at Team Vader Time 5 ~ Return Of The Emperor, in a Pinfall of Submission Only match (April 29, 2010) · Io Shirai vs. Mio Shirai at WAVE/Ice Ribbon/Union Pro Mio Shirai Produce M.I.O. (February 14, 2015) · Io Shirai & Mio Shirai vs. Hiroyo Matsumoto & Mayu Iwatani at STARDOM X STARDOM 2015 - Night 1 (July 26, 2015) · Io Shirai vs. Mayu Iwatani at STARDOM 5☆STAR Grand Prix 2015 - Night 1, in a Block B match (August 23, 2015) · Io Shirai vs. Meiko Satomura (c) at STARDOM Year-End Climax 2015, for the World of STARDOM Championship (December 23, 2015) · STARDOM (Io Shirai, Jungle Kyona, Kairi Hojo, Mayu Iwatani, & Momo Watanabe) vs. World Selection (Kellie Skater, Evie, Chelsea Green, Santana Garrett, & Viper) (with Act Yasukawa), in an Elimination Ten Man Tag Team match at STARDOM 5th Anniversary – Night 3: STARDOM vs. The World (February 7, 2016) · Io Shirai (c) vs. Mayu Iwatani at STARDOM Gold May 2016, for the World of STARDOM Championship (May 15, 2016) · Io Shirai vs. Meiko Satomura (c) at SENDAI Girls' 10th Anniversary Show ~ Women's Wrestling Big Show in Niigata, for the SENDAI Girls' World Championship (July 2, 2016) · Hitokiri vs. Pentagon Dark at Lucha Underground (November 30, 2016) · Io Shirai (c) vs. Mayu Iwatani at STARDOM Year-End Climax 2016, for the World of STARDOM Championship (December 22, 2016) · Io Shirai (c) vs. Viper at STARDOM 6th Anniversary, for the World of STARDOM Championship (January 15, 2017) · Io Shirai (c) vs. Shayna Baszler at STARDOM of Champions, for the World of STARDOM Championship (February 23, 2017) · Io Shirai (c) vs. Kairi Hojo at STARDOM The Highest 2017, for the World of STARDOM Championship (March 20, 2017) · Io Shirai (c) vs. Mayu Iwatani at STARDOM Galaxy Stars 2017, for the World of STARDOM Championship (June 21, 2017) · Io Shirai vs. Toni Storm at WWE Evolution, in a Mae Young Classic Finals match (October 28, 2018)

★ When you look at the list of all of Io Shirai's accolades, you know one thing's for sure: she's a badass. As one of the most highly decorated members of the STARDOM promotion roster—if not the outright "ace"—by 10 years into her career, there were only a few things left in her career for Io Shirai to achieve. Making her wrestling debut at age 16 (she was still a high school student), she teamed with her older sister Mio Shirai (who was 19 at the time) on the Japanese independent wrestling circuit.

Pro Wrestling WAVE, SENDAI Girls', All Japan, ZERO1, Ice Ribbon, Osaka Pro, and more—from 2007 to 2011, the Shirai sisters wrestled anywhere they possibly could. It was in the summer of 2010 when Io formed the heel faction Triple Tails with Mio and Kana (now known as WWE's Asuka). And it was a little over a year later that Io decided to leave the faction—transforming Mio and Kana into Triple.Tails.S—choosing instead to focus on her own singles career. The following month, Io debuted in STARDOM. From there, she got the nickname "Sky Genius" or "Genius Of The Sky" for her high-flying style. Then in March the following year, on her wrestling career's fifth anniversary, she announced she was done working as a freelance wrestler and was now officially a full-time STARDOM roster member.

But proving that the truth is sometimes stranger than fiction, in May 2012, Io and her boyfriend, wrestler NOSAWA Rongai, were arrested at an airport after returning home from a tour in Mexico—for suspicion of drug possession and smuggling into the country. Despite denying any wrongdoing, after a search, 75 grams of marijuana were found hidden within paintings they'd received from fans in Mexico. (They then assumed that the fans themselves had planted them.) Given Japan's harsh sentencing and perception on marijuana, there was a fear that—even without jail time—Io would become blackballed and lose her job in STARDOM. The following month, Io held a press conference to issue a formal public apology—still denying any wrongdoing. By the end of the month, the charges were surprisingly dropped, although the damage had already been done: not only had Io and NOSAWA broken up, but Io's name had been dragged through the mud. (Prior to the scandal, Io Shirai's real name—Masami Odate—was not publicly known. She and Mio had chosen the ring surname "Shirai," meaning "Purple Thunder.") Mio even chimed in on the matter through a blog post, revealing that the sisters had had a falling out—which, in hindsight, made her feel guilty about how things had turned out—and she had learned about the drug scandal through the media, just like everyone else. If nothing else came out of this, the two sisters eventually reconciled. Then at the beginning of July, SUGI (a Mexico-based Japanese wrestler) confessed in a press conference of his own that he had planted the drugs on Io and NOSAWA, as part of a conspiracy with AAA representative Masahiro Hayashi (who held a grudge against NOSAWA), in exchange for a full-time contract.

Io returned to in-ring action in STARDOM that July, and by April the following year, she defeated Alpha Female to win the World of STARDOM Championship. During her first reign as the World of STARDOM Champion, Io also won the High Speed Championship (the company's championship for the speedier high-flyers), as well as the 2013 MVP Award and 2014 STARDOM 5☆STAR GP Best tournament. As if her 2014 wasn't enough to prove she was the ace of STARDOM, by the end of 2015, Io had become the only Grand Slam Champion (having held every championship in the company) in STARDOM history. And while she didn't beat Nanae Takahashi's historic 602-day World of STARDOM Championship reign—as she had promised to do—she did break her successful championship defense streak—with 10 successful defenses in her 468-day reign to Takahashi's original record of seven. (Io's second World of STARDOM Championship reign ended up being 546 days long, with a new record: 14 successful defenses.) And while Mio retired in 2015 due to injuries—eventually becoming a referee and trainer for Ice Ribbon—she did make her debut in STARDOM that July in order to give the Japanese audience the final Shirai sisters tag team match. (Unlike most wrestling sibling duos, Io and Mio rarely faced off in singles competition against each other—while they'd been on opposite sides in tag team scenarios, they'd only faced each other one-on-one twice before Mio's retirement.)

Io's 2016 began with the formation of a stable called "Threedom" ("Three" + "STARDOM"), comprised of herself and two of her biggest STARDOM rivals, Kairi Hojo and Mayu Iwatani. As three of the top stars in STARDOM and women's wrestlers in the world, Threedom quickly won the Artist of STARDOM Championship. And in April of that year, the trio filmed a storyline in the United States (that would air that November) for *Lucha Underground* season three. As members of the Black Lotus Triad, Io (as Hitokiri), Kairi (Doku), and Mayu (Yurei) wrestled as mercenaries on behalf of Black Lotus's vendetta against Pentagon Dark, leading to an entire *Lucha Underground* episode featuring Pentagon's in-ring battle against the team. By the time this *Lucha Underground* episode had aired though, Threedom (as well as Thunder Rock) had officially broken up . . . and Io had moved on to her newest stable, Queen's Quest.

That same fall, it was reported that Io Shirai would be signing with WWE and reporting to their developmental territory at the WWE Performance Center in Orlando—along with Kairi Hojo. Unfortunately, after she'd taken her physical in the spring, WWE rescinded the offer. Reports eventually came out that WWE's decision not to sign Io stemmed from issues with her neck, though it was later reported (but never confirmed by Io herself) that the issue was with her heart. As a result, Io returned to STARDOM, as Japanese doctors had considered her fit to wrestle. However, Io made clear that WWE was still her ultimate goal. In May 2018, it was reported once more that Io would officially be leaving STARDOM for WWE—this time having a clean bill of health—with her final STARDOM match scheduled for June 17th at Korakuen Hall.

★ IVELISSE VÉLEZ ★

YEARS ACTIVE: 2004–present

TRAINED BY: Carlos Colón Sr. · Quique Cruz · Savio Vega · FCW · Bill DeMott

BILLED FROM: Chicago, Illinois · Puerto Rico · San Juan, Puerto Rico

ACCOMPLISHMENTS: 1x FWE Women's Champion · 2x Lucha Underground Trios Champion (with Angelico & Son of Havoc) · 2015 Lucha Underground Trios Championship Tournament (with Angelico & Son of Havoc) · 2x Pro Championship Wrestling Women's Champion · #7 in 2014 PWI Female 50 · 1x Pro Wrestling Revolution (PWR) World Women's Champion · 2x SHINE

Champion · 1x SHINE Tag Team Champion (with Mercedes Martinez) · 1x World Wrestling League (WWL) Goddess Champion · 1x Wrestling Superstar Women's Champion · 3x Vanguard Wrestling All-Star Alliance (VWAA) Women's Champion

AKA: Sexy Juliette · Juliet · Juliette The Huntress · "The Huntress" · "The Baddest Bitch in The Building" · "Anti-Diva" · Ivelisse · 1/2 of the Anti-Diva Army/The Anti-Divas · member of Los Perros del Mal · member of Valkyrie · member of Las Sicarias

NOTABLE MATCHES: Ivelisse vs. Athena at SHINE 5 (November 16, 2012) · Ivelisse vs. Kimber Lee at SHIMMER Volume 62 (April 5, 2014) · Ivelisse (Aces & Eights) vs. Mickie James (Team USA) at TNA One Night Only: World Cup 2013, in a World Cup match (December 6, 2013) · Ivelisse Vélez (c) vs. Candice LeRae at FWE ReFueled Night 2, for the FWE Women's Championship (October 4, 2014) · Ivelisse, Angélico, & Son of Havoc vs. The Crew (Bael, Cortez Castro, & Mr. Cisco) at Lucha Underground, in a Lucha Underground Trios Championship Tournament Final No DQ match for the inaugural Lucha Underground Trios Championship (April 22, 2015) · Ivelisse, Angélico, & Son of Havoc (c) vs. The Crew (Bael, Cortez Castro, & Mr. Cisco) at Lucha Underground, in a Ladder match for the Lucha Underground Trios Championship (May 20, 2015) · Ivelisse vs. Fenix vs. Johnny Mundo vs. King Cuerno vs. Pentagon Jr. vs. Taya at Lucha Underground, for the Lucha Underground Championship #1 Contendership (June 15, 2016) · Ivelisse (with Amanda Carolina Rodriguez) vs. Madison Eagles (c) (SHIMMER) vs. Taylor Made (c) (SHINE) vs. Allysin Kay (TNA) at SHINE 35, in a 4 Way match for the SHINE Championship/SHIMMER Championship/TNA Knockouts Championship (June 17, 2016) · Ivelisse Vélez vs. Rachael Ellering vs. Jessicka Havok at AAW Legacy, in an AAW Women's Championship Tournament Finals Elimination 3-Way match (December 2, 2017)

⭐ "The Baddest Bitch in The Building" is quite the moniker to live up to, but for Ivelisse Vélez, it's simply a fact of life. Having started her wrestling career when she was only about 15 years old in Puerto Rico—idolizing "Stone Cold" Steve Austin—she trained underneath Puerto Rican wrestling legend and WWE Hall of Famer Carlos Colón Sr. before debuting at his World Wrestling Council (WWC) promotion, Puerto Rico's premier wrestling promotion. She was still in high school when she made her TV wrestling debut in Puerto Rico, after about a year of training. At WWC and eventually in IWA Puerto Rico, Ivelisse wrestled as "Sexy Juliette," aka "Juliette The Huntress." But in 2008, Ivelisse finally made it to the States proper, debuting in the Midwest at AAW's One Twisted Christmas show (in a tag match as Juliet).

After spending the next couple of years wrestling in Illinois and Indiana, 2011 was considered a breakout year of sorts for Ivelisse, at least in terms of notoriety: she was accepted as a contestant on the fifth season revival of WWE's *Tough Enough* reality show competition. However, during the competition, she suffered a knee injury, which led to her elimination from the competition and series. Still, she was on WWE's radar, and as a result, Ivelisse was offered a developmental contract at FCW that same year. She technically made her FCW debut at an episode taping that November—under her real name—but it wouldn't be until the taping in the first week of January 2012 that she would make her official debut as a character on FCW TV as "Sofia Cortez." Sofia Cortez teamed with then fellow developmental talent Paige as The Anti-Divas, a heel faction opposed to the cookie-cutter Divas image in the WWE's women's division at the time. This only lasted until the FCW rebrand into NXT in the summer of 2012, in which all three Divas went their separate ways. A heel Cortez only made three in-ring appearances (with her only loss being in her debut match, against second-generation wrestler Tamina Snuka) in NXT before her release was announced that August.

It's well known that around that time in WWE, the Divas were often told not to "wrestle like the men," which Ivelisse has since said that she had pushed back against that during her tenure in the company. Especially when officials themselves would refer to the Diva matches as "bathroom breaks." (It also didn't help that WWE had enforced a policy of no intergender wrestling, despite Ivelisse having more experience—and continuing to thrive in such a realm, post-WWE—wrestling against men than against women.) Based on reports, Ivelisse was reportedly released because of her "attitude," however it eventually came out that Ivelisse was one of the first WWE development wrestlers around that time to report then developmental head trainer Bill DeMott for misconduct (including sexual harassment, as well as physical and verbal abuse). As Ivelisse herself had tweeted, she allegedly "lost everything for speaking up," being the first to do so, and ended up as an example to others who had dared to do the same.

> I was very outspoken about what I believed in. I wasn't being disrespectful; I just knew we deserved respect like the guys. That's what I wanted to bring to the table. . . . I guess I was there at the wrong place, wrong time. It just didn't work out. Maybe my strong character rubbed off the wrong way because they weren't used to that, I don't know. I always tried to respectfully state my case. If it's not received in a respectful way, then obviously they're going to take whatever I'm saying as something negative because it's not what they want to hear. . . . If it's not what they want to hear, it's a bad attitude.

Regarding DeMott specifically, during a Reddit AMA in 2017, Ivelisse spoke more specifically about his role in her release for WWE:

> I've been pretty vocal, never 100 percent on the record, but he had a big part to play in it. . . . I'll never know if it was intentional or if he was just trying to secure his position. . . . Before I'm released, I'm told, 'they're thinking of bringing me up,' and I'm about to film a video package to . . . debut. And I'm training the girls in the beginner's class and all these other things are happening with that particular person, and I tried to

stand my ground. All of the sudden I am let go, there could be no other explanation. After I am gone, they literally had a meeting telling talent I wasn't let go for speaking up. These were things that only DeMott would have brought up. I tried to not let it bring me down. I had so much more to offer, but I have no time to waste on being screwed over, because I'm not the first, and I won't be the last.

After a group of former WWE wrestlers went public with their complaints and allegations regarding DeMott in 2015 (after initially making the complaints in-house with WWE from 2012 to 2015), various media outlets and social media (with the trending hashtag #FireDeMott) picked up the story; and in March, despite public denial of the allegations of harassment and other misconduct, DeMott resigned from WWE.

"THE BADDEST BITCH IN THE BUILDING" IS QUITE THE MONIKER TO LIVE UP TO, BUT FOR IVELISSE VÉLEZ, IT'S SIMPLY A FACT OF LIFE.

After getting released from WWE, Ivelisse returned to the indies under her real name, mostly wrestling in the newly formed all-women independent promotion SHINE. And in 2016, she became the first/only woman in SHINE history to have the SHINE Championship multiple times. She also held the record for longest reigning SHINE Champion, holding it for 296 days—from January 2014 to December 2014—in that first reign, a record broken by LuFisto's historic 529-day reign (which began after Ivelisse had to vacate the title during her second reign, due to injury). She held the title in her second reign for 210 days, just 86 days shy of tying that record. It was also in SHINE that Ivelisse gained more of an appreciation for wrestling other women:

> Then I went to SHINE, where it's all women, and I had the longest SHINE title reign—that's where I learned to do that dynamic even more. I love learning. I still love to wrestle everybody. Any character is a puzzle to learn, an art. I love trying to figure out what would be the best possible story to bring out. 'How would this character react to my character?' 'What story could that provide?' Whether female or male, it's that puzzle I like to crack.

Post-WWE, Ivelisse also made a few appearances in TNA in dark matches, as well as the promotion's One Night Only pay-per-view specials, eventually becoming a competitor in the promotion's Gut Check competition (for a shot at a TNA contract) in 2013. Despite defeating fellow Gut Check competitor Lei'D Tapa in their Gut Check singles match, the three Gut Check judges voted to sign the more inexperienced Tapa instead of Vélez. While working SHINE, EVOLVE, and some other smaller independent shows at the time, without steady employment as a wrestler, Ivelisse eventually ended up carless. However, she was fortunate enough to have the help of Sal Hamaoui (owner of WWN, the World Wrestling Network, of which SHINE and EVOLVE are also part) in getting to wrestle at Dragon Gate USA and essentially getting her back on track in her professional wrestling career.

After rebuilding her name on the independent scene, Ivelisse became known as "The Baddest Bitch in The Building" when the Robert Rodriguez/Mark Burnett-produced *Lucha Underground* rolled around onto the El Rey Network in the fall of 2014. The first season of *Lucha Underground* (a serialized wrestling show featuring fantastical elements and a rich mythology) featured a storyline in which Ivelisse entered into an unlikely alliance with Son of Havoc (her character's boyfriend, played by Matt Cross, one of Ivelisse's fellow *Tough Enough* season competitors) and Angélico, with the three becoming the underdog story of the season as well as the

inaugural Lucha Underground Trios Champions. This also made Ivelisse the first woman in Lucha Underground—which follows intergender wrestling rules—to win a championship. Interestingly enough, during this storyline and the first season of the show, Ivelisse actually injured her ankle . . . yet she didn't miss any TV time and continued to factor into title defenses with a cast and crutches. (In fact, she had broken her ankle in practice, right before the finals of the Lucha Underground Trios Championship.) It wasn't until Ultima Lucha (the season finale of *Lucha Underground*) that Ivelisse's team lost their trios championship, and it was only as a result of interference from Catrina (the manager of the team challenging them, The Disciples of Death). Catrina would then factor into Ivelisse's subsequent Ultima Lucha matches in Lucha Underground: interfering in and costing Ivelisse's singles match against Taya at Ultima Lucha Dos, then losing to Ivelisse in a singles match at Ultima Lucha Tres.

At the end of 2017, Ivelisse made it to the Finals of AAW's inaugural AAW Women's Championship tournament, only to lose to Jessicka Havok in a 3-Way Elimination match. However, as she continues to work in Lucha Underground, AAW, SHINE, SHIMMER, and has even made her way to wrestling promotions in the United Kingdom (WCPW) and Australia, Ivelisse shows no signs of letting up.

★ IVORY ★

YEARS ACTIVE: 1986–2006

TRAINED BY: Mando Guerrero

BILLED FROM: Seattle, Washington

ACCOMPLISHMENTS: 1x Carolina Championship Wrestling Women's Tag Team Champion (with Bambi) · 1x Gorgeous Ladies of Wrestling (GLOW) Champion · 1x GLOW Tag Team Champion (with Ashley Cartier) · 1x Ladies Sports Club (LSC) Champion · 2x Powerful Women of Wrestling (POWW) Champion · Pro Wrestling This Week Wrestler of the Week (March 13–19, 1988) · 1x SuperGirls Wrestling Champion · WSU Hall of Fame Class of 2011 · 3x WWF Women's Champion · 2012 Cauliflower Alley Club Women's Wrestling Award · WWE Hall of Fame Class of 2018

AKA: Lisa Moretti · Tina Ferrari · 1/2 of T & A · 1/2 of The Beverly Hills Girls · Tina Moretti · Nina · member of Right to Censor · member of The Alliance

NOTABLE MATCHES: Tina Ferrari vs. Ninotchka at GLOW, for the GLOW Crown (May 15, 1987) · Ivory vs. Debra (c) (with Jeff Jarrett) at WWF *Monday Night RAW*, for the WWF Women's Championship (June 14, 1999) · Ivory vs. Lita (c) vs. Jacqueline vs. Trish Stratus at WWF SmackDown, in a Four Corners match for the WWF Women's Championship (November 2, 2000) · Ivory (Alliance) vs. Trish Stratus (WWF) vs. Jacqueline (WWF) vs. Jazz (Alliance) vs. Mighty Molly (Alliance) at WWF Survivor Series 2001, in a 6-Pack Challenge for the vacant WWF Women's Championship (November 18, 2001) · Ivory & Jacqueline vs. Jazz & Molly Holly at WWE *Sunday Night Heat* (May 25, 2003)

⭐ Few women can say they were part of wrestling history twice over. But as the only member of the Gorgeous Ladies of Wrestling (GLOW) roster to make it to the bright lights of the WWF, Lisa Moretti certainly can. And it all happened because in 1985, her actress friend Nadine Kadmiri (who would become known as her GLOW tag team partner, Ashley Cartier) had her audition for GLOW with her, even though Moretti herself had absolutely no interest in professional wrestling. In fact, according to Moretti, "I didn't get at first that people have an extreme passion for wrestling and the wrestlers. The fans are really intimately connected with each wrestler." And it wasn't even GLOW that gave her this understanding but her eventual work in the big leagues, in WWF. At the time, Moretti was just a student at USC (and eventually graduated with degrees in photojournalism and public relations) and had also been a squad director/cheerleader for the L.A. Express (part of the United States Football League) for a year; the only real exposure she had had to professional wrestling were her older brothers, as they would roughhouse with her and her older sister because of the sport.

Trained for six weeks under Mando Guerrero from the legendary Guerrero wrestling family, Moretti and the rest of the GLOW girls were taught the in-ring basics of professional wrestling and were given the training ground rules to always pay attention, not to laugh, and not to hang on the ring ropes. That last part about not hanging on the ropes resulted in a moment where Mando Guerrero put a trainee who broke that rule in a hold and made her cry . . . which is what officially hooked Moretti into wanting to learn more about wrestling and got her to come back to training, despite wanting nothing to do with it originally.

After six weeks of wrestling training and a move to Las Vegas, Nevada, for 10 to 12 of the women, Lisa Moretti was now known to GLOW and the world as "Tina Ferrari," one half of the tag team T & A (aka The Beverly Hills Girls) with Ashley Cartier. The two became the inaugural (and first of only two) GLOW Tag Team Champions, though there was no physical championship for the title. During her time as Tina Ferrari, she went on to win the GLOW Championship (a crown) in 1986, holding it for over a year before she dropped it to Colonel Ninotchka (whom she had defeated to win the championship in the first place). GLOW became something of an overnight sensation, airing for four seasons (104 episodes, from 1986 to 1990) on syndicated television. It differed from WWE not just because of its all-female roster but because of character beats like personalized raps from each GLOW Girl, comedy sketches, and bright, vivid, neon imagery that even the most flamboyant WWF wrestler would balk at. To provide context for just how popular GLOW was, in 2018, "Stone Cold" Steve Austin revealed on his podcast that he had a crush on Tina Ferrari at the time. As for an excerpt from Tina Ferrari's personalized rap:

> *When I wrestle, you'll want to cheer*
> *'Cause I'm a winner and I make that clear*
> *All my opponents know I'm a stud.*
> *What can I say? It's the Italian blood.*

According to Moretti, on the legacy of GLOW:

> One thing we did right was character. I thought
> at that time, there was a definite foofing up in the
> WWF. There were a lot more colorful characters, and
> it really started glitzing up. . . . That's about the time

they came out to say it's an entertainment show and choreographed. They put much more entertainment into it, and that led to the confession.

The confession was of wrestling's existence as "sports entertainment" instead of as a legitimate sport. After the GLOW series ended, Moretti wrestled in both Powerful Women of Wrestling (PWOW)—an all-women's promotion from GLOW founder David McClane—and Ladies Professional Wrestling Association (LPWA)—which was considered a more serious evolution of GLOW, as it hired established women's wrestlers for its shows. In the former, which featured plenty of other former GLOW Girls, she wrestled as Nina; she wrestled as Tina Moretti in the latter.

As Nina and Tina Moretti in other promotions, Moretti made wrestling appearances in the AWA in 1988 and United Wrestling Federation in 1994, but she would essentially be done with wrestling. In fact, she had started working as a makeup artist at Revlon toward the end of her GLOW run. Moretti, however, would enter a whole new world—still in the familiar world of professional wrestling but one far afield from the old custom raps and neon outfits—as she signed a contract with the WWF in January 1999.

Prior to officially debuting in the company, she appeared as an extra of sorts, as one of the "hos" of The Godfather (as he was a pimp character). WWF had actually called her and flown her out for the appearance, providing travel back for the next day—as she had Revlon training to attend—since "they needed a girl who could look good in a dress and take a bump." That same day, after the appearance, Ivory was called by WWF commentator and then Vice President of Talent Relations Jim Ross, who told her to get together a demo tape so he could show it to Vince McMahon. The rest was history—and in a way, a whirlwind—as Moretti (now Ivory) would become WWF Women's Champion a few months later. As for how she was officially introduced to the WWF audience as Ivory, she became "Sexual Chocolate" Mark Henry's solution to his and his tag team partner D'Lo Brown's problem with their rival team's, Jeff Jarrett and Owen Hart, female companions (Debra, Terri Runnels, and Jacqueline). Unfortunately, due to the numbers game, Ivory ended up being bested by her female foes—and eventually splitting from Henry and Brown—but got the last laugh by beating Debra for the WWF Women's Champion that June. And in doing so, she returned some honor and credibility to the title; after all, Debra was only a valet, despite carrying the championship for about a month.

FEW WOMEN CAN SAY THEY WERE PART OF WRESTLING HISTORY TWICE OVER. BUT AS THE ONLY MEMBER OF THE GORGEOUS LADIES OF WRESTLING (GLOW) ROSTER TO MAKE IT TO THE WWF, IVORY CAN.

Ivory's character was a heel and a shrill one (of course) who ranted about the Attitude Era's form of objectification in the women's (or Divas) division, from *Playboy* spreads to salacious gimmick matches. (In theory, that should have made her a babyface, but the combination of that particular era of WWF and the way in which she came about her message prevented that.) Unfortunately, Ivory was faced with putting over talents in the division who truly embodied the era at that time, despite her veteran experience in comparison. In fact, Ivory's second (out of three, total) WWF Women's Championship reign ended with an Evening Gown Pool match, in which she lost her title to the untrained wrestler Miss Kitty. And her initial championship reign ended during a comical feud with The

Fabulous Moolah and Mae Young (both 76 years old at the time), in which Moolah won the championship from her. (Ivory won the title back the following week.)

Eventually, Ivory's self-righteous gimmick became even more conservative, and she joined the newly formed Right to Censor (RTC) stable in the summer of 2000. The RTC was Vince McMahon's personal answer to the Parents Television Council (PTC) and their criticism of the WWF, as it was an over-the-top anti–Attitude Era gimmick that even turned some of the more controversial characters in WWF (like The Godfather and Val Venis, whose gimmick was that of a porn star) into ones who opposed the more objectionable parts of WWF. As the sole woman of the group, Ivory wore the standard uniform—white button up shirt, black slacks, and in her case, a bowtie, which she credited Terri Runnels with suggesting behind-the-scenes—and adopted the censorship, "no fun" gimmick of the RTC. Since her days in the RTC, Ivory has called the gimmick her favorite of her career: "It was something I really could sink my teeth into. It was good to have an identity, and it really helped the matches. The women don't always have that. . . . [I] think I was the most hated woman in wrestling for a while."

The RTC Era of Ivory's career also surprisingly allowed for more genuine in-ring competition—presumably in order to allow the gimmick to work as a threat of sorts—especially in her feud with fan favorite Lita (and matches against Lita, Trish Stratus, Jacqueline, and Molly Holly as a result, all considered the workhorses of the time in their own rights). During this feud, she won the Women's Championship for the third and final time and went on to feud with Chyna—the impetus being Chyna posing for *Playboy*—from the end of 2000 to April 2001, defending the title in a match at WrestleMania X-Seven. The following month, the RTC was over. According to Ivory, the gimmick and faction ended abruptly because "the guy who was writing for us wasn't going to do it anymore and none of the other writers wanted to pick it up." If there was one regret or lasting frustration Lisa Moretti had with her WWF/WWE career, it was the swift and sudden ending to the Right To Censor gimmick, seemingly just because.

The rest of Ivory's WWF (and eventually WWE) career found her out of the spotlight, in smaller stories and other pursuits within the company. The rest of 2001 saw Ivory as a member of the WCW/ECW Alliance side of the WWF vs. The Alliance Invasion storyline, while 2002 featured her as a trainer on *Tough Enough's* second season. Despite her portrayal as a relatively fair and positive trainer, Ivory returned to WWE television after the season as a heel, feuding with the season's co-winners, Jackie Gayda (who then turned heel and joined Ivory) and Linda Miles. Ivory would then go on to feud with Trish Stratus, before finally turning face again in 2003 and then returning to *Tough Enough* (for its third season) as a trainer once more. Ivory spent her last few years in WWE transitioning more into a host and trainer position, with her last official match on the main roster being on an episode of *Sunday Night Heat* in December 2003. (In OVW, WWE's developmental territory at the time—which she'd worked at as a trainer for two months—she'd wrestled Jillian Hall in a singles match in March 2004.) She'd wrestled a couple of independent shows in Southern California during this time and eventually leave the company—opting not to renew her contract—in July 2005.

Ivory (back to Lisa Moretti) wrestled some more independent dates in 2005, but it was her work in 2006—in the then newly formed ECCW (at the time known as Extreme Canadian Championship Wrestling) and its women's division—that really made a splash on the independent scene for women's wrestling at the time. As the second NWA/ECCW SuperGirls Champion, Moretti feuded with the inaugural champion, Rebecca Knox (now better known as WWE's Becky Lynch). She would eventually lose the title to Nattie Neidhart (now known as WWE's Natalya), but in her 170-day reign as champion, she established some credibility and put some eyes on the burgeoning division before officially hanging up her wrestling boots.

After retiring, Moretti opened a cat and dog grooming service, tapping into her love of animals. But her contributions to the wrestling world have not been forgotten, even with her being out of the world herself. She was inducted into independent promotion Women Superstars Uncensored's (WSU) Hall of Fame in 2011, and in 2012, she received the Cauliflower Alley Club's Women's Wrestling Award. Then 2018 saw Ivory inducted into that year's WWE Hall of Fame class, alongside legends such as Goldberg, Jeff Jarrett, and The Dudley Boyz. At the ceremony, she was inducted by her Attitude Era contemporary Molly Holly and gave a speech about how proud she was of how things have "come a long way" for the women in WWE. She acknowledged her pre-WWE past in GLOW, toasting to the GLOW Girls and fellow female WWF legends who had since passed away and thanked her "sisters" during the Attitude Era (Trish Stratus, Lita, Jacqueline, Molly Holly, Victoria, Terri Runnels, Gail Kim, Jazz, and Stephanie McMahon) who put in the work with her even when the division didn't get as much respect or attention at the time. Thankfully, this induction proved it was all worth it, in some way.

★ JACQUELINE ★

YEARS ACTIVE: 1988–present

TRAINED BY: Skandor Akbar

BILLED FROM: Dallas, Texas · Memphis, Tennessee

ACCOMPLISHMENTS: 1x Independent Association of Wrestling Women's Champion · #249 in 1993 PWI 500 · #17 in 2008 PWI Female 500 · 14x United States Wrestling Association (USWA) Women's Champion · 1x Universal Wrestling Federation Champion · 2x WWF Women's Champion · 1x WWE Cruiserweight Champion · WWE Hall of Fame Class of 2016

AKA: Sweet Georgia Brown · Jackie · Miss Jacqueline · Jackie Moore · Miss Texas · Miss Tennessee · "The Pride of Tennessee" · Queen Moesha · Sgt. Rock · member of Militia · 1/3 of the Pretty Mean Sisters (P.M.S.) · Wynonna

NOTABLE MATCHES: Jacqueline (with Marc Mero) vs. Sable at WWF *Monday Night RAW*, for the vacant WWF Women's Championship (September 21, 1998) · Jacqueline (WWF) vs. Ivory (Alliance) vs. Trish Stratus (WWF) vs. Jazz (Alliance) vs. Mighty Molly (Alliance) at WWF Survivor Series 2001, in a 6-Pack Challenge for the vacant WWF Women's Championship (November 18, 2001) · Jacqueline & Ivory vs. Jazz & Molly Holly at WWE *Sunday Night Heat* (May 25, 2003) · Jacqueline vs. Chavo Guerrero (with Chavo Classic) at *WWE SmackDown*, for the WWE Cruiserweight Championship (May 6, 2004) · Ms. Jackie Moore vs. Gail Kim at TNA Lockdown 2007, in a Cage match (April 15, 2007)

★ A Texas native, Jacqueline Moore loved the Von Erich wrestling family and was inspired by their work to become a professional wrestler herself. As the only female student (and standing at 5 foot 3 inches, at that) at Skandor Akbar's professional wrestling school in Dallas, Texas, back in 1988, a then 24-year-old Jacqueline Moore trained for eight months before she had her first wrestling match. And it just so happened to be on live television. No pressure, right?

Moore made her debut as "Sweet Georgia Brown"—as a tribute to the original "Sweet Georgia Brown" Susie Mae McCoy, Texas's original women's wrestling champion of African American descent, who died in 1989—and spent the first couple of years of her career under this persona. Moore wrestled as Sweet Georgia Brown in World Class Championship Wrestling, the promotion where she debuted, which was at the time owned by Kerry and Kevin Von Erich (making her Von Erich–based dreams come true) and Jerry Jarrett (whose son Jeff Jarrett would be an integral part of Moore's entire career, on multiple levels). She also took the Sweet Georgia Brown name to LPWA, Women's Pro Wrestling, and Frontier Martial-Arts Wrestling (FMW), a hardcore wrestling promotion that took her all the way to Japan and the legendary Korakuen Hall.

It was her work in both Texas (the first two years of her career) and Tennessee (Memphis, specifically) that first got her noticed in the wrestling world, especially her work in Memphis's United States Wrestling Association (USWA) in 1990. There, she was quickly no longer "Sweet Georgia Brown": she was "Miss Texas," a competitor who would take on all comers, be they male or female.

> When I first started out in the wrestling business, I was wrestling more men than I was women. The guys gave me more of a challenge, they challenged me more. That's where I got my toughness from. . . . A lot of the women didn't like to wrestle me back then because they said I wrestle too much like a guy. That's how I developed more in the ring, from wrestling guys, and they didn't take it easy on me either. They wrestled me just like I was another guy.

In USWA, Miss Texas's official introduction was as the valet to "Team Texas" (Tom Prichard and Eric Embry) in a Texas vs. Tennessee (with wrestlers like Dirty White Boy, Dirty White Girl, and Jeff Jarrett) feud. While in USWA, Miss Texas competed in Hair vs. Hair, Street Fight, and Loser Leaves Town matches; she became the inaugural USWA Women's Champion and held said championship 14 times; she feuded (and eventually became allies) with the new Sweet Georgia Brown; in 1993, she became the first woman to make Pro Wrestling Illustrated's (PWI) 500 list (of the top 500 wrestlers in the world). Moore's work in USWA—while often ignored in favor of her WWE or even TNA Impact Wrestling work—was somewhat the stuff of legend. And by the end of 1993, that same year that she made the PWI 500, it appeared that she'd be WWF-bound, joining Jeff Jarrett as he performed under his "Double J," country music singer gimmick. Moore would debut as "Wynonna," Double J's manager and part of his entourage, and WWF even filmed and aired vignettes with Wynonna alongside her client. However, due to an injury, Moore's WWF career ended before it even began. (Although, on an episode of *RAW* in 1999, Jacqueline would eventually take a patented Jeff Jarrett guitar shot to the head.)

After the injury and missed connection with WWF, Jacqueline Moore barely wrestled again until four years later, when she eventually pursued WCW and was offered a contract in 1997. (She had temporarily—literally just a month—worked for Smoky Mountain Wrestling (SMW) in 1995 as a wrestler called "Sgt. Rock" before the promotion shut down. She had three matches.) Like in her USWA days, Moore (who performed under her real name) feuded with both men and women, quickly becoming known for her ability to body slam male competitors around the same time Chyna had come onto the scene and done the same in WWF. (Though it was slightly more impressive on Moore's end, given her diminutive stature.) She got her start as Kevin Sullivan's manager (and feuding with Chris Benoit and Benoit's wife, Woman, as a result) before moving on to manage the Harlem Heat and then feuding with (and defeating, on pay-per-view) Disco Inferno before she ended her year-long stint in WCW and moved on to WWF—for real this time.

Debuting as Marc Mero's new on-screen girlfriend and manager, Moore's debut immediately thrust her into a high-profile (and what Moore recalls as her best) feud with Mero's on-screen ex (but off-screen wife at the time) and WWF Attitude Era fan favorite, Sable. A sign of the times, Moore's feud with Sable included a Bikini Contest (which Moore actually won, due to a technicality), but it also allowed the WWF to bring back the WWF Women's Championship, which had been defunct since 1995, when Alundra Blayze quit the company as champion and dumped the belt into the trash can on rival promotion WCW's *Monday Nitro* (one of the most infamous moments of the WWF/WCW Monday Night Wars). While Sable ultimately won the feud, Jacqueline Moore was able to win the Women's Championship first—becoming the first African American WWF Women's Champion—before dropping the title to her rival just two months later. (In terms of landmark moments with titles in WWE, Jacqueline would also eventually become the first and only woman to win the WWE Cruiserweight Championship. She would also challenge Dean Malenko for the WWF Light Heavyweight Championship in 2000 but come up short.)

Moving on from Sable, Jacqueline joined forces with Terri Runnels (and eventually Ryan Shamrock) to form P.M.S.—aka the Pretty Mean Sisters. As P.M.S. got involved with ruining the Mark Henry/D'Lo Brown tag team, this led to the debut of Ivory to feud with them—specifically Jacqueline, as they became rivals. As the name of the stable suggested, P.M.S. was pretty much one of the more bottom of the barrel Attitude Era storylines to come from the mind of then WWF head writer Vince Russo, as the story featured the introduction of wrestler Shawn Stasiak as "Meat"... for the very literal reason that P.M.S. used him as "piece of meat" (aka their "love slave"). Also like a lot of Attitude Era gimmicks, eventually this one just ran its course, with Jacqueline simply leaving the team (due to Terri exhausting Meat, despite that being his very purpose) on an episode of *Sunday Night Heat* in August 1999.

Jacqueline's second Women's Championship reign would come after defeating WWF referee Harvey Wippleman in drag (going by the name of "Harvina"), and she would only hold the title for a month in 2000—even having a brief feud with

Luna Vachon, which Jacqueline looks back on fondly—before dropping it to Stephanie McMahon. The rest of Jacqueline's 2000–2001 would also consist of mini-feuds against the likes of Lita and Trish Stratus, as well as a role (in 2001) as one of the trainers on the first season of WWF's reality show (for a WWF contract) *Tough Enough*, her first time training other wrestlers. In 2002 she then begin splitting her time between wrestling and refereeing for women's matches, and as tough as Jacqueline was in the ring, she also got to show her toughness as an official. In fact, if a competitor would get rough with referee Jacqueline, referee Jacqueline would just give it right back. However, the referee spot wasn't a permanent position, and while she'd go on to win the WWE Cruiserweight Championship from Chavo Guerrero in May 2004 (and get to defend it on pay-per-view, even though she'd lose that match), there wasn't much she'd gotten to do between all of that. So, as the saying goes, "Creative has nothing for you"—meaning she'd reached the end of the road in WWE in terms of stories and her character—and Jacqueline was released from her WWE contract. "It wasn't my decision to leave. I was told by the WWE that the writers couldn't come up with any storyline for me at this time."

Just a few months later, a face Jacqueline would make her appearance in TNA Wrestling (a company created and owned by her longtime friend, Jeff Jarrett), first as a competitor and then as a referee in her second appearance (in a match that saw her reunited with her former on-screen beau Marc Mero—as "Johnny B. Badd"—as well as her former foe Disco Inferno—as Glenn Gilberti), at TNA's Turning Point pay-per-view that December. She'd also wrestle on a couple of TNA house shows in 2006. However, it wasn't until 2007 that she made her official debut as a heel. Attacking Gail Kim—James Storm's manager—at the Final Resolution pay-per-view that January, Moore then became Storm's manager. She continued to feud with Kim, leading to TNA's first female Steel Cage match, as well as a Street Fight (in which Moore lost her two front teeth but continued to wrestle through the match). Eventually, Moore would go on to manage James Storm's team

with Bobby Roode (known as Beer Money), but by the summer of 2009, she would have already been moved to a backstage producer role and ended her tenure with TNA. Moore was instrumental in the start and success of TNA's Knockouts Division—both on-screen and eventually off-screen, as a road agent behind-the-scenes—especially as an alternative to WWE's Divas Division, which was still following the "bathroom break," "don't fight like the men" mentality. She'd temporarily return in 2011 for a heel duo with ODB—in a storyline in which they attempted to take over the Knockouts Division, as outside, unsigned wrestlers—but after the storyline culminated in the two women getting their contracts, Moore made no further appearances, and her actual TNA contract ended that November. So while Moore's last official match as a member of the TNA Impact Wrestling roster was in August 2011—in a winning Six-Woman Tag Team effort of herself, ODB, and Velvet Sky against Angelina Love, Sarita, and Rosita—she would make a few more appearances in 2013 (in TNA's One Night Only pay-per-views).

In 2016, Jacqueline Moore was officially inducted into the WWE Hall of Fame. And not only was she honored, she got to be honored in her hometown of Dallas. Making history once more, Moore was also the first African American woman to be inducted into the Hall, and as Triple H wrote in a tweet about the induction announcement, "Jacqueline was a fierce, barrier-breaking female competitor." She'd later make an appearance at WWE *Monday Night RAW*'s 25th Anniversary show, during a moment of acknowledgment of the past of WWE's women's division—and then appear later that week as a surprise entrant in the inaugural Women's Royal Rumble match at that year's Royal Rumble pay-per-view. Jacqueline may have technically finished off her in-ring career in Impact Wrestling—she's denied that she's retired—but even if she never laces up her boots in a full match ever again, she'll be known for a list of accomplishments that may never be replicated by any other woman—African American or otherwise—ever again. Even WWE's online biography of Jacqueline calls her "the toughest woman to ever step foot in the ring."

★ JAZZ ★

YEARS ACTIVE: 1998-present

TRAINED BY: Rod Price · Junkyard Dog · Rodney Mack

BILLED FROM: New Orleans, Louisiana

ACCOMPLISHMENTS: 1x Downsouth Championship Wrestling Louisiana State Champion · 1x NWA Cyberspace Women's Champion · 1x NWA World Women's Champion · WSU Hall of Fame Class of 2010 · #13 in 2012 PWI Female 50 · Texas Wrestling Hall of Fame Class of 2012 · 1x WSU Tag Team Champion (with Marti Belle) · 1x Women's Extreme Wrestling (WEW) World Champion · 2x WWF/WWE Women's Champion

AKA: Jazzmyn · Jazzmine · "The Female Fighting Phenom" · member of the Impact Players · "The Baddest Bitch" · "The Bad-ass Bitch" · member of The Alliance · 1/3 of Team Original Divas Revolution

NOTABLE MATCHES: Jazz (Alliance) vs. Ivory (Alliance) vs. Trish Stratus (WWF) vs. Jacqueline (WWF) vs. Mighty Molly (Alliance) at WWF Survivor Series 2001, in a 6-Pack Challenge for the vacant WWF Women's Championship (November 18, 2001) · Jazz (c) vs. Trish Stratus at WWF Backlash 2002, for the WWF Women's Championship (April 21, 2002) · Jazz vs. Victoria (c) (with Steven Richards) vs. Trish Stratus at WWE WrestleMania XIX, in a Triple Threat match for the WWE Women's Championship (March 30, 2003) · Jazz & Molly Holly vs. Jacqueline & Ivory at WWE *Sunday Night Heat* (May 25, 2003) · Jazz vs. Sara Del Rey at SHINE 1 (July 21, 2012) · Jazz vs. Ivelisse (with April Hunter) at SHINE 9, in a SHINE Championship Tournament Qualifying match (April 19, 2013) · Team Original Divas Revolution (Jazz, Mickie James, & Victoria) vs. Team SHIMMER (Candice LeRae, "Crazy" Mary Dobson, & Solo Darling) at CHIKARA King of Trios 2016 - Night 1, in a King of Trios First Round match (September 2, 2016)

★ Carlene Moore was certainly inspired by Jacqueline Moore's (no relation) work in WWF; honestly, she probably didn't expect to eventually, essentially replace her hero in the eyes of the company and its fans. But after dropping out of college (and giving up on her basketball scholarship) due to a knee injury, Carlene decided to train under Junkyard Dog at his wrestling school in Lafayette, Louisiana. Junkyard Dog passed away soon after Carlene began her training, but she was able to train under Rod Price. And Carlene was pretty much on as much of a fast track as a woman could be in professional wrestling at the time (without being a bikini or fitness model prior). After a quick six [to eight] months learning her craft under Rod Price, Carlene made her in-ring debut: against none other than Jacqueline Moore.

In theory, that could have been the end of her professional wrestling story, as she got to face her in-ring hero on her first go around in the squared circle. But instead, she continued with her in-ring career, soon joining ECW in February 1999 as Jazzmine

(Jazz, for short), the female muscle of the heel stable the Impact Players. Pretty quickly, however, Jazz went on to feud with her Impact Players stablemate Jason (aka Jason Knight), as Jason and Justin Credible made Jazz's time in the group a living hell. While the rest of the Impact Players allowed her to continually do their bidding and interfere in their matches, they also refused to allow her name to be announced, with Jason calling the tactic a way to keep her angry and have her anger be channeled into protecting Impact Players' leader Justin Credible. Eventually Jazz stood up to Jason, which led to her debut pay-per-view match to settle the score with Jason. Not only did she win (as she had in all her matches against Jason in live events leading up to the pay-per-view), but she gained the support of the rowdy ECW crowd as a result, and she continued to work as a face for the rest of her time in the company. However, that was also definitely her peak storyline in the company, especially as ECW soon shut down in 2000.

JAZZ HOLDS A VERY SPECIFIC DISTINCTION OF BEING THE LAST WWF WOMEN'S CHAMPION AND THE INAUGURAL WWE WOMEN'S CHAMPION.

But Jazz wouldn't be out of the wrestling game for long, as WWF signed her to a contract in 2001—after a tryout match with Ivory—and had her wrestle in the developmental territory at OVW for six weeks until they were ready to officially debut her on the main roster. Debuting as a heel, Jazz played the role of the powerhouse (and "The Baddest Bitch," by her estimation) of the division, somewhat filling the void of Chyna, who had recently left the company and vacated the WWF Women's Championship. Particularly, she was someone who could tussle with either the women or the men, although Jazz's focus was more on fighting the women during her time in WWF/WWE.

Jazz immediately entered into a high-profile feud against Trish Stratus for the WWF Women's Championship, defeating Stratus for the title (after defeating Jacqueline for the #1 Contendership) in February 2002. She'd then also retain the championship in a Triple Threat match against Trish Stratus and Lita, arguably the two most popular WWF/WWE Divas to ever enter the squared circle, even back then. Due to the changing of the company name from World Wrestling Federation (WWF) to World Wrestling Entertainment (WWE) in May 2002—meaning the changing of the names of the company's championships—Jazz holds a very specific distinction of being the last WWF Women's Champion and technically the inaugural WWE Women's Champion. But her championship reign was cut short that May as the result of a legitimate injury (a torn ligament in her knee). Jazz would then return in January 2003 to pick up where she left off in her feud with Stratus, as well as against Victoria, leading to a Triple Threat title match between the three at WrestleMania XIX. While Stratus retained at WrestleMania, after getting a one-on-one match—and now with Teddy Long as her manager—Jazz won the title back from Stratus and began her second reign as champ. However, yet again, injury cut her reign short, this time in the form of a dislocated shoulder.

After returning from the second injury in 2004, Jazz's push as the top heel of the Divas Division was essentially over, and WWE transitioned her into the manger/valet for Rodney Mack (her real life husband and fellow former Teddy Long client). Unfortunately, just like her wrestling inspiration Jacqueline, Jazz got the "Creative has nothing for you" treatment and was released from her WWE contract that fall.

Post-WWE, Jazz worked on the independent scene—even opening an independent promotion with Rodney Mack in Louisiana called Downsouth Championship Wrestling—and won championships in Women's Extreme Wrestling (WEW) and the Cyberspace Wrestling Federation, as it was known at the time. In addition to her and her husband's independent promotion (with their wrestling school, The Dog Pound, in honor of Junkyard Dog), Jazz also opened up a fitness gym to help keep Louisiana kids off the streets and give back to the community. Jazz also participated in an ECW reunion show called Hardcore Homecoming, which was somewhat of a precursor to her temporary return to WWE in 2006, as one of the roster members of WWE's new, rebooted version of ECW. Even two years later, however, WWE still had nothing story-wise for Jazz, and after a title match against WWE Women's Champion Mickie James and a couple of ECW house show performances, she was again released by WWE (as was Rodney Mack). Returning to the independent scene, Jazz became even more of a force with her work in Women Superstars Uncensored (WSU), CHIKARA (alongside her former WWE colleagues, Mickie James and Victoria), and especially SHINE in 2012–2013, where she main evented in the all-women's promotion's first five shows, showing that "SHE'S STILL GOT IT."

However, despite the general consensus of Jazz's importance to WWF/WWE during a time when the women weren't taken as seriously—and as someone who made audiences take them more seriously, whether they wanted to or not—it may be a a while before Jazz gets the recognition from WWE she deserves or even a third possible shot at making any new WWE dream matches come true. In July 2016, Jazz joined a class action lawsuit against the WWE regarding traumatic brain injuries and the belief that WWE knew and covered up information about the effects of these repeated injuries and chronic traumatic encephalopathy (CTE).

★ JAZZY GABERT ★

YEARS ACTIVE: 2001–present

TRAINED BY: Joe E. Legend · Murat Bosporus · GWF Training School

BILLED FROM: Berlin, Germany

ACCOMPLISHMENTS: 2013 ABC Women's Championship #1 Contendership Tournament · 1x cOw Ladies Champion · 1x Deutsche Wrestling Allianz Women's Champion · 1x Empresa de Wrestling Europea (EWE) Women's Champion · 1x Extreme American Wrestling Tag Team Champion (with Ultra Mark Massa) · 1x Pro Evolution Wrestling Women's Champion · 1x Pro-Wrestling: EVE Champion ·1x Swiss Wrestling Entertainment Ladies Champion · 1x Turkish Power Wrestling Ladies Crown · 2016 Westside Xtreme Wrestling (wXw) Femme Fatales · #48 in 2017 PWI Female 50 · 1x Artist of STARDOM Champion (with The Female Predator "Amazon" & Kyoko Kimura) · 1x Goddess of STARDOM Champion (with Kyoko Kimura) · 1x World of STARDOM Champion

AKA: The Alpha Female · Jazzy Bi · member of Kimura Monster-gun

NOTABLE MATCHES: Nikki Storm vs. The Alpha Female (c) at Pro-Wrestling: EVE Wrestle-Fever, for the Pro-Wrestling: EVE Championship (November 10, 2012) · Alpha Female vs. Nanae Takahashi (c) at STARDOM The Highest 2013, for the World of STARDOM Championship (March 17, 2013) · Alpha Female vs. Io Shirai at STARDOM Ryogoku Cinderella Champions Fiesta, for the World of STARDOM Championship (April 29, 2013) · Alpha Female & Marius van Beethoven vs. Alpha Lovers (Melanie Gray & Alpha Kevin) at wXw Dead End XVI, in a Tag Team Street Fight match (February 24, 2017) · Alpha Female vs. Melanie Gray at wXw We Love Wrestling Tour 2017: Stuttgart (April 28, 2017) · Jazzy Gabert vs. Abbey Laith at the WWE Mae Young Classic, in a Mae Young Classic First Round match (August 28, 2017) · Jazzy Gabert, Kay Lee Ray, & Tessa Blanchard vs. Marti Belle, Santana Garrett, & Sarah Logan at the WWE Mae Young Classic – Road To The Finals (September 11, 2017) · Alpha Female & Wesna vs. Martina & Shanna at GWF Women's Wrestling Revolution 4 (June 3, 2017)

★ The road to professional wrestling has certainly not been an easy one for Jazzy "The Alpha Female" Gabert. Born in Berlin, East Germany, Jazzy spent her time in a foster home until she was six years old. When she was adopted, it was to a family with three sons and that desperately wanted a daughter. Unfortunately for Jazzy, as she wasn't a "typical" girl, her adoptive parents soon tried

to conceive another child and gave birth to another daughter. After that, she and her adoptive brothers (who already weren't fans of Jazzy because she had been the sole focus of their parents when she was the only daughter) became afterthoughts. In 1989, when the Berlin Wall fell, her parents decided to move the family. It was during the process of packing that she saw one of her brothers had a wrestling book—full of pictures of people like Hulk Hogan and Randy Savage—to which Jazzy was instantly drawn. As Jazzy tells the story, after that, wrestling became her family since she didn't feel she belonged in the "real world"—she was bullied in school, her brothers and parents didn't care for her. Every night she would sneak to the living room to watch wrestling on the local TV sports channel at 3 a.m.

Jazzy says that, "without wrestling, I swear I wouldn't be here," and considering the additional strife she went through, that sentiment is understandable. She would dream that her real parents were professional wrestlers, especially as her brothers went down bad paths of drugs, alcohol, and jail. When her parents divorced, Jazzy eventually moved back to Berlin with her mother and sister, but at age 16, she was jumped and raped by a gang. By 17, she was homeless, and by 18, she was in the hospital for a suicide attempt.

Then in 2001, at the age of 19, she started training at the German Wrestling Federation (GWF) Training School to become a professional wrestler—after knocking on one of the trainer's doors every day for three months asking to be allowed to train there. She'd originally wanted to become a referee; it wasn't until she was 17 years old that she'd learned about local wrestling shows, with women actually wrestling (instead of Bra & Panties matches), that she decided that wrestling itself would be for her. Standing at 6 foot 1 inch, Jazzy obviously had a leg up sizewise against the women she'd be competing against. But happy days weren't quite on the horizon in her personal life, not just yet. By age 22, she was severely in debt for—according to her—"trusting the wrong person."

Also, according to Jazzy, the school she trained at was all about deciding what she should do in the ring, what she should wear, and what her name and gimmick would be. And because she was a woman—even an imposing one—the choice they made for her was based on the central concept that "sex sells." This is why she went by the ring name "Jazzy Bi" at the time, as in "Jazzy Bisexual." Having felt like a victim and that she was being held back during that time, under that character, and at the school—she left after five years, becoming "The Alpha Female" in the process. While Jazzy got plenty of experience wrestling in Germany against Wesna and Blue Nikita (with additional tag team partners, on rare occasions)—the two women she wrestled in her in-ring debut—it was now time for her to branch out. By the end of 2006, she was debuting under the Alpha Female moniker in Paris, France's Queens of Chaos wrestling promotion, wrestling the likes of April Hunter, Allison Danger, and Jetta. In 2008, she won her first championship ever, this time at EWE in Spain, a championship she even got to defend against her longtime GWF rival Wesna.

In 2010, The Alpha Female moved to England and made her debut in the British women's wrestling promotion Pro-Wrestling: EVE—and in 2012, she became the Pro-Wrestling: EVE Champion, a reign that would last 223 days. In fact, she would lose the title to Nikki Storm, the woman who beat her in the semifinals of the inaugural championship tournament the previous year. Alpha Female's 2012 would also see her make her joshi debut in Japan at the STARDOM promotion—thanks to a talent scout from Japan seeing her at Pro-Wrestling: EVE—with her moving to Japan in 2013 to wrestle there more regularly. When she returned to STARDOM in 2013, she won the main championship—the World of STARDOM Championship—from the seemingly unbeatable inaugural champion Nanae Takahashi in her first match back. After ending Takahashi's 602 day reign, The Alpha Female would hold the title for a little over a month. During her time in Japan, Jazzy also came under the mentorship of Japanese wrestling legend Masahiro Chono, to the point where she was essentially adopted by him and his German wife into his family—so after all this time, she really did find her family in wrestling. According to Jazzy, with her time in Japan, she finally "found peace."

In June 2017, it was announced that Jazzy Gabert would compete in WWE's inaugural Mae Young Classic, representing Germany. In the first round, she faced NXT Superstar Abbey Laith, and while she didn't win, she certainly made quite the impression. She later got to show more of herself in a six-women's tag team match on the tournament's Road to the Finals special, and the entire match, the Full Sail (the venue) crowd couldn't help but chant for Jazzy, whether she was in the ring or not. This was even more surprising because Jazzy came into the tournament as a monster heel and even played the same role in the tag team match—to a point where she was visibly moved by the vocal show of adoration. But that didn't stop the crowd from chanting "PLEASE SIGN JAZZY" after Jazzy got the win for the team in the match. (Triple H would later come out as a response to the chants, joking that the crowd always costs him money when

they do that; a similar chant occurred for Cedric Alexander's final performance in WWE's Cruiserweight Classic tournament.) Before the tournament even aired, in an interview with NBC Sports, Triple H pointed Jazzy out as "a real standout performer" in the Mae Young Classic.

At the end of 2017, Jazzy appeared as a guest on E&C's Pod of Awesomeness podcast, explaining her status with WWE, or lack thereof. According to her, she was in fact offered a contract after the Mae Young Classic, only for it to be rescinded after her physical revealed she had three herniated discs in her neck. She also explained that she'd be getting surgery to fix the issue the following spring, but given the ever-changing nature of the wrestling business, it's not quite 100 percent certain if a WWE contract will still be waiting for her when she recovers. However, the memory of those "PLEASE SIGN JAZZY" chants won't be forgotten any time soon.

★ JESSICKA HAVOK ★

YEARS ACTIVE: 2004–present

TRAINED BY: Shasta · Justin Diaz · Lones Oaks

BILLED FROM: Massillon, Ohio · Defiance, Ohio · Munich, Germany

ACCOMPLISHMENTS: 1x AIW Women's Champion · 1x Main Event World League (MEWL) Cruiserweight Champion · #4 in 2013 PWI Female 50 · 1x Ring Divas Fight Girl Champion · 1x TNA Knockouts Champion · 2x WSU Champion · 1x WSU Spirit Champion · 1x WSU Tag Team Champion (with Hailey Hatred) · 1x Rockstar Pro Trios Champion · 1x (and inaugural) AAW Women's Champion

AKA: Havok · "The Havok Death Machine" · 1/3 of The Midwest Militia · 1/2 of The Killer Death Machines · 1/2 of Team Be Jealous · member of Rain's Army · member of Flexor Industries · member of the Killer Kult

NOTABLE MATCHES: Jessicka Havok vs. Luna Vachon at CAPW A Night of Legends, in a Hardcore match (August 5, 2007) · Jessicka Havok vs. Rain at WSU 4th Anniversary Show (March 5, 2011) · Jessicka Havok vs. Rain (c) at SHINE 12, for the SHINE Championship (August 23, 2013) · Jessicka Havok vs. Mia Yim at WSU United, in an Uncensored Rules match (July 12, 2014) · Havok (c) vs. Gail Kim vs. Taryn Terrell at TNA Impact Wrestling, in a 3-Way match for the TNA Knockouts Championship (November 19, 2014) · Havok vs. Awesome Kong at TNA Lockdown 2015, in a Six Sides of Steel Cage match (February 6, 2015) · Jessicka Havok vs. Heidi Lovelace at AAW Windy City XII, in an I Quit match (November 26, 2016) · Jessicka Havok & Tessa Blanchard vs. Hiroyo Matsumoto & Jungle Kyona (c) at STARDOM Gold May 2017 - Night 1, in a Goddess of STARDOM Championship match (May 14, 2017) · Jessicka Havok vs. Rachael Ellering vs. Ivelisse Vélez at AAW Legacy, in an AAW Women's Championship Tournament Finals Elimination 3-Way match (December 2, 2017)

⭐ A native of Ohio and a product of WWF Attitude Era fandom—she fell in love with wrestling the first time she saw "Stone Cold" Steve Austin and Triple H on the TV—Jessica Cricks became a wrestler almost as soon as she decided to become a wrestler. Having been introduced to wrestling at age nine, by the time she was 16 years old, she'd made up her mind: she was going to be a professional wrestler. So in 2004, at age 17, Jessica began training under Shasta (aka Kevin Ballew) at The Stomping Grounds, a training school in Massillon, Ohio.

The 6-foot-tall wrestling lover made her professional wrestling debut in 2004, making her name (now known as "Jessicka Havok") in independent promotions around the state, such as Mega Championship Wrestling, Ohio Championship Wrestling, MEWL (where she eventually won the MEWL Cruiserweight Championship in an intergender match), and Main Event Championship Wrestling (owned by Shasta). But Cleveland All Pro Wrestling (CAPW) was especially important to her progression as a wrestler, as that is where she found a mentor in J.T. Lightning, a big name in Ohio independent wrestling before

he passed away in 2011 due to cancer. It was also where she got the chance to face wrestling legend Luna Vachon in a Hardcore match, an experience Havok at one point called the "worst ass beating of my life."

However, 2009 was when Havok became more of a name on the independent wrestling scene, as she participated in Ohio promotion AIW's inaugural Girls Night Out tournament event show (eventually winning the AIW Women's Championship in 2011) and debuted in New Jersey's Women Superstars Uncensored (WSU) a month later. In WSU, teamed up with fellow Ohio native Hailey Hatred, and in their debut, they challenged for the WSU Tag Team Championship. While they didn't win, they did win their rematch and the titles a couple of months later. They also participated in a 3-Way Dance for the WSU World Championship around that time, clearly destined for great things in WSU. Eventually, Havok and Hatred would part ways—having a kayfabe falling out after eventually losing the tag titles—but Havok would certainly continue to be a fixture in WSU. And in 2010, she joined the heel faction Rain's Army as their enforcer, only to eventually turn on Rain (after Rain showed respect to her opponent, Mercedes Martinez, prompting Havok to call Rain "soft"). Havok and Rain would meet in a one-on-one competition at the WSU 4th Anniversary Show, with Havok defeating Rain and moving on up in the card. (Rain would get some semblance of revenge in the SHINE promotion, however, as Havok failed to defeat her at both SHINE 11—in the tournament to crown the inaugural SHINE Champion—and SHINE 12—where Rain defended the SHINE Championship against Havok.)

Later that year, Havok again beat Rain, this time for the WSU Spirit Championship (the company's secondary title) . . . the same day that Rain won it in the first place. Then, in March 2012 at the WSU 5th Anniversary Show, Jessicka Havok defeated Mercedes Martinez in a Title vs. Title match to win the WSU World Championship as well. Martinez would win the title back a month later . . . only for Havok to win it back—for her second title reign—later that same day. This feud culminated in the summer of 2012, as Havok defended the WSU World Championship (and retained) against Martinez in a Casket match. (As for the Spirit Championship, Havok had dropped it to Marti Belle earlier on that same show.)

In the summer of 2014, Jessicka Havok—after competing against Madison Rayne in a One Night Only pay-per-view—joined the TNA Impact Wrestling roster as just "Havok," the new heel monster on the block. That October—after debuting and attacking Knockouts Champion Gail Kim and Kim's longtime rival, Taryn Terrell—Havok would win the Knockouts Championship from Gail Kim and put Kim on the shelf (with a kayfabe injury, to sell Havok's dominance) until November. She would then retain the championship in Kim's rematch attempt, although failing to do so in a 3-Way match between Kim and Terrell (who came out on top in that instance). The beginning of 2015 saw Havok feud with a returning Awesome Kong, but after losing their one match, Havok was nowhere to be found on Impact Wrestling for months—and eventually confirmed she was no longer with the company. According to Havok, however, she was never officially under contract in her nine months with the company—and when TNA decided to bring Awesome Kong back, they were allegedly done having plans for Havok. "The one positive is that I got to hold the Knockout(s) Championship for five weeks on national television. No one can take that from me. I got to wrestle in Tokyo, Japan, on Bound for Glory. No one can take that from me. I just wish I was given a bigger chance to shine." In 2014, Havok also featured in a WSU storyline (though, at the time, fans weren't sure if it was a work or shoot) where she was stripped of the WSU World Championship and "banned for life" from the company, ending a two-year title reign. However, she was able to revoke that ban by winning an Uncensored Rules match (a Hardcore match) against Mia Yim two months later.

In 2015, Jessicka Havok was literally at a WWE tryout when controversial old tweets (circa 2010–2012) of hers resurfaced,

featuring both racist and homophobic rhetoric, as well as tweets insulting the Divas of WWE at the time. Once they came out—and people on Twitter directed the tweets to the Twitter accounts of WWE and TNA—according to Havok, she did "not remember tweeting half of it" and that she "had an ex that used to play on her phone" who wrote the tweets. In a later tweet apology—which she also eventually deleted and only even tweeted because Dave Lagana, a then producer from TNA, encouraged her to—she still remained stalwart in her argument that she didn't remember tweeting half of the stuff, but she did instead call the tweets "inside jokes" that she had "said things to make my friends laugh at the time." Havok has since gone on the record saying that these tweets were the one thing that killed her chances with WWE: "I busted my ass, and I killed it. I nailed my promo. The coaches seemed to love me. I have every right and reason to believe I was getting signed." Based on various behind-the-scenes reports, NXT officials were in fact impressed with Havok's work at the tryout, but these tweets put an end to all of that.

Despite this setback, Havok has remained a fixture in the independent scene, wrestling in ROH's Women of Honor Division, Japan's STARDOM promotion, CZW, Rockstar Pro Wrestling, SHIMMER, and more. In December 2017, she defeated Rachael Ellering and Ivelisse in a Triple Threat Elimination match in order to become the inaugural AAW Women's Champion, the culmination of a months-long tournament.

★ THE JUMPING BOMB ANGELS ★

YEARS ACTIVE: 1981-1991
Itsuki Yamazaki: 1981-1991
Noriyo Tateno: 1981-2010

TRAINED BY: AJW Dojo

BILLED FROM: Japan

ACCOMPLISHMENTS: 1x WWWA World Tag Team Champions · 1x WWF Women's Tag Team Champions
Itsuki Yamazaki: 1x AJW Champion
Noriyo Tateno: 1x AJW Junior Champion · 1x AJW All Pacific Champion · 1x Ladies Legend Pro-Wrestling (LLPW) Singles Champion · 2x LLPW Six-Woman Tag Team Champion (1x with Rumi Kazama & Yasha Kurenai, 1x with Keiko Aono & Harley Saito) · 1x LLPW Tag Team Champion (with Eagle Sawai) · 1x LPWA Tag Team Champion (with Eagle Sawai)

AKA: The Angels
Itsuki Yamazaki: Itzuki Yamazaki · "Red Angel"
Noriyo Tateno: "Pink Angel"

NOTABLE MATCHES: The Angels (Itsuki Yamazaki & Noriyo Tateno) vs. Crush Gals (Lioness Asuka & Chigusa Nagayo) at AJW, for the WWWA Tag Team Championship (March 20, 1986) · The Jumping Bomb Angels (Itsuki Yamazaki & Noriyo Tateno), The Fabulous Moolah, Rockin' Robin, & Velvet McIntyre vs. The Glamour Girls (Judy Martin & Leilani Kai), Dawn Marie, Donna Christanello, & Sensational Sherri at WWF Survivor Series 1987, in a 5-on-5 Survivor Series Elimination match (November 26, 1987) · The Jumping Bomb Angels (Itsuki Yamazaki & Noriyo Tateno) vs. The Glamour Girls (Judy Martin & Leilani Kai) (c) (with Jimmy Hart) at WWF Royal Rumble 1988, in a 2 Out of 3 Falls match for the WWF Women's Tag Team Championship (January 24, 1988) · The Jumping Bomb Angels (Itsuki Yamazaki & Noriyo Tateno) vs. Devil Masami & Jaguar Yokota at Ladies Legend Pro Wrestling (LLPW) Revolution 16th (August 10, 2008)

★ As products of the AJW Dojo in the early 1980s, Itsuki Yamazaki and Noriyo Tateno were both individually and collectively a part of a very interesting time in women's professional wrestling. After Lioness Asuka vacated the AJW Championship in January 1984, Itsuki and Noriyo ended up competing against each other for it, with Itsuki coming out on top (and vacating it about a year later). Around this time, joshi was selling out arenas and bringing ratings success in Japan, and Itsuki and Noriyo would capitalize on that when AJW put them together as "The Angels."

In early 1986, The Angels defeated Bull Nakano and Condor Saito to win the vacant WWWA World Tag Team Championship (the women's tag title of AJW), only to lose them to the Crush Gals (Lioness Asuka and Chigusa Nagayo) a couple of months later. While the Crush Gals were easily the more popular and well-known team at the time (attributing greatly to the ratings success), Itsuki and Noriyo were popular in their own right—which is what got them a feud with the Crush Gals in the first place.

The Angels got even more mainstream attention, however, when they feuded against The Glamour Girls (Judy Martin and Leilani Kai, two of The Fabulous Moolah's students) in WWF. It was actually thanks to the Girls putting in a good word for them—and Vince McMahon's desire at the time to have a solid women's tag team division—that The Angels got that chance to wrestle for WWF. These two teams spent most of the summer of 1987 facing off against each other in house shows and eventually got to have their own marquee match on WWF pay-per-view: The Jumping Bomb Angels (as they became known in WWF) versus The Glamour Girls, in a 2 Out of 3 Falls match for the WWF Women's Tag Team Championship, at the inaugural Royal Rumble pay-per-view (in 1988). This was also the first women's match in WWF/WWE history to achieve a 3 Star (out of 5) rating from renowned wrestling journalist Dave Meltzer. And despite the language barrier and the fact that the "bomb angels" weren't necessarily bombshells, the duo became a very popular pair in WWF because of their athleticism. Because of this, the Bomb Angels' success boded well for the future of women's wrestling in the WWF.

However, reportedly, The Fabulous Moolah wasn't a fan of them or their matches with The Glamour Girls, as that type of athleticism was the complete opposite of Moolah's brand of wrestling—meaning, the audience was getting excited for a wrestling style that was the antithesis of her style, which could only spell disaster for her own popularity. (Their match at Survivor Series in 1987 was essentially an omen for Moolah, as the Angels and Girls spent the whole match showing off a previously unseen to WWF audiences version of athleticism, and the Angels ended up being the "sole survivors" in the Elimination match.) Months after winning the tag championship, the feud led to The Glamour Girls challenging The Jumping Bomb Angels in their native Japan, with the Angels's WWF Women's Tag Team Championship on the line. The plan was apparently for the Angels to retain the title on their home turf, only for the Girls to win them back in the States. According to Leilani Kai, The Fabulous Moolah (pretending to represent WWF) called the Japan office to tell them there had been a change of plans—

and for there to be a title switch—and the Girls won the titles back. Because of that, WWF fired The Glamour Girls for ruining the storyline. Partially as a result of what appeared like a failed experiment to the WWF, their Women's Division entered into a dark age, with nary an attempt at reviving it until 1993 (which only lasted a couple of years before another dark age of women's wrestling, during WWF's sexed-up Attitude Era).

THE "BOMB ANGELS" BECAME VERY POPULAR IN WWF BECAUSE OF THEIR ATHLETICISM. THEIR SUCCESS BODED WELL FOR THE FUTURE OF WOMEN'S WRESTLING IN THE WWF.

In 1991, Itsuki retired from in-ring competition, presumably due to AJW's concept of forced retirement at age 25/26 rule. This was a policy that did more harm than good to AJW and its popularity, as popular talent would have to quit at their hottest. For example, the Crush Gals retired in 1989, despite their popularity. This rule was eliminated by the mid-1990s—alowing the Crush Gals to return, yet also creating a problem where established, top stars would no longer make way for the younger stars. However, in Noriyo Tateno's case, she got around the retirement "rule" by going to work for LLPW instead, where she predominantly wrestled until her retirement in 2010.

In 2008, at LLPW's 16th anniversary show, The Jumping Bomb Angels reunited for one last time. Itsuki only came out of retirement for two more matches after that, Manami Toyota's 25th anniversary celebration and Manami Toyota's 30th anniversary/retirement celebration.

★ KAIRI SANE ★

YEARS ACTIVE: 2011–present

TRAINED BY: Fuka Kakimoto

BILLED FROM: Yamaguchi, Japan

ACCOMPLISHMENTS: #10 in 2017 PWI Female 50 · 4x Artist of STARDOM Champion (1x with Kaori Yoneyama & Yuhi, 1x with Chelsea & Koguma, 1x Io Shirai & Mayu Iwatani, 1x with Hiromi Mimura & Konami) · 3x Goddess of STARDOM Champion (1x with Natsumi Showzuki, 1x with Nanae Takahashi, 1x with Yoko Bito) · 1x NXT Women's Champion · 1x Wonder of STARDOM Champion · 1x World of STARDOM Champion · 2013 STARDOM Outstanding Performance Award · 2014 STARDOM 5☆STAR GP Best Match Award (vs. Nanae Takahashi, on August 24) · 2014 STARDOM Best Match Award (with Nanae Takahashi vs. Risa Sera & Takumi Iroha, on December 23) · 2014 STARDOM Best Tag Team Award (with Nanae Takahashi) · 2015 STARDOM MVP Award · 2015 STARDOM 5☆STAR GP · 2016 Goddesses of STARDOM Tag League (with Yoko Bito) · 2016 STARDOM Best Tag Team Award (with Yoko Bito) · 2016 STARDOM Technique Award · WWE Mae Young Classic

AKA: Kairi Hojo · Doku · "Mystery Hunter" · "People's Champ" · "Onna Kaizoku" ("Female Pirate") · 1/2 of Candy Crush · 1/2 of Ho-Show Tennyo · 1/2 of 7Kairi · "The Pirate Princess" · member of Zenryoku Joshi · 1/3 of Threedom

NOTABLE MATCHES: Kairi Hojo vs. Act Yasukawa (c) at STARDOM 3rd Anniversary Show, for the Wonder of STARDOM Title (January 26, 2014) · Kairi Hojo (c) vs. Meiko Satomura at STARDOM Galaxy Stars 2015 - Night 1, for the World of STARDOM Championship (June 14, 2015) · Kairi Hojo (c) vs. Meiko Satomura at STARDOM X STARDOM 2015 - Night 1, for the World of STARDOM Championship (July 26, 2015) · Kairi Hojo vs. Act Yasukawa at STARDOM Appeal The Heat, for the #1 Contendership to the World of STARDOM Title (October 11, 2015) · Kairi Hojo & Yoko Bito (c) vs. Kay Lee Ray & Nixon Newell at STARDOM 6th Anniversary, for the Goddess of STARDOM Championship (January 15, 2017) · Kairi Hojo vs. Io Shirai (c) at STARDOM The Highest 2017, for the World of STARDOM Championship (March 20, 2017) · Kairi Sane vs. Tessa Blanchard at the WWE Mae Young Classic, in a Mae Young Classic First Round match (August 28, 2017) · Kairi Sane vs. Bianca Belair at the WWE Mae Young Classic, in a Mae Young Classic Second Round match (September 6, 2017) · Kairi Sane vs. Toni Storm at the WWE Mae Young Classic, in a Mae Young Classic Semifinals match (September 6, 2017) · Kairi Sane vs. Shayna Baszler the WWE Mae Young Classic, in a Mae Young Classic Finals match (September 12, 2017) · Kairi Sane vs. Shayna Baszler (c) at NXT TakeOver: Brooklyn IV, for the NXT Women's Championship (August 18, 2018) · Kairi Sane (c) vs. Shayna Baszler at WWE Evolution, for the NXT Women's Championship (October 28, 2018) · Kairi Sane vs. Shayna Baszler (c) at NXT TakeOver: War Games 2018, in a 2 Out of 3 Falls match for the NXT Women's Championship (November 17, 2018)

★ After college, Kairi Housako had aspirations of being a professional actress. In a way, those aspirations came true in the form of becoming a professional wrestler. After STARDOM General Manager Fuka Kakimoto saw Kairi act as a wrestling heel in a live theater performance, she invited Kairi to watch a STARDOM show (in hopes of getting her to join the roster). The invitation worked, as Kairi was drawn to the combination of acting and sport inherent in professional wrestling. So in 2011, she began training under Fuka, making her debut in January 2012 as "Kairi Hojo" and eventually becoming one of the most popular babyfaces in the entire company and known for (arguably) the best elbow drop in the entire wrestling business. Children would even come to chant "Ganbare!"—meaning "Give it your best!"—to Kairi during her matches.

Kairi's real-life background in competitive yachting (with ambitions of making it to the Olympics) became a part of her gimmick. She became known as the "Female Pirate" and "The Pirate Princess" once she joined up with Yuzuki Aikawa's (the woman she lost to in her debut match) Zenryoku Joshi stable a month after debuting. Nearly a year later, the stable would be dissolved once Kairi challenged and faced off with Aikawa for the Wonder of

STARDOM Championship (the secondary title in the company). While Kairi didn't win, she went on to win her first championship in STARDOM—the Goddess of STARDOM Championship, the company's tag titles—a few months later with Natsumi Showzuki. This reign only lasted a month; a career-ending injury for Showzuki led to their team, Ho-Show Tennyo, being stripped of the titles. Two months later Kairi won another STARDOM championship, this time in form of the company's trios championship (the Artist of STARDOM Championship) with Kaori Yoneyama and Yuhi, for the first time. At the STARDOM year-end awards, she was awarded the Outstanding Performance Award for 2013.

After just a couple of years of wrestling, Kairi was already seen as one of the best women's wrestlers in the world. In May 2014, she made her Mexican debut as a representative of STARDOM, and a few months later, she was Goddess of STARDOM Champion again (this time with Nanae Takahashi). However, partner injury struck again—after around eight months instead of just one—and she was once more stripped of the title. Following the "Ghastly Match" between Act Yasukawa and Yoshiko, the World of STARDOM Championship was vacated, leading to a tournament in March 2015 to decide the new champion. Kairi won the tournament, becoming the World of STARDOM Champion for the first time. By the end of the year—despite eventually losing the championship to Meiko Satomura—she was named STARDOM's MVP during the year-end awards.

As 2016 began, Kairi formed a stable called "Threedom" ("Three" + "STARDOM") with Io Shirai and Mayu Iwatani, two of her biggest rivals in STARDOM—and as wrestling journalist Dave Meltzer put it, these were "three of the best wrestlers in the world." A month later, the team won the Artist of STARDOM Championship; and a few months after that, Kairi finally won the Wonder of STARDOM Championship. At the end of November 2016 (though filmed back in April of that year), Kairi Hojo—along with her Threedom partners—made her United States wrestling debut as part of Lucha Underground's third season. As members of the Black Lotus Triad, Kairi (as Doku,

meaning "Poison"), Io (Hitokiri, aka "Assassin"), and Mayu (Yurei, meaning "Ghost") wrestled as mercenaries on behalf of Black Lotus's vendetta against Pentagon Dark, and Lucha Underground dedicated an entire episode to Pentagon's in-ring war with the Triad and Black Lotus. The episode was eye-opening to a lot of wrestling fans who weren't as familiar with the joshi stars as they were other wrestlers. Around the same time as their stint on Lucha Underground aired, Threedom officially broke up, after losing the Artist of STARDOM Championship and Io turning on Mayu.

In the spring of 2017, the rumor mill was buzzing that Kairi would be leaving STARDOM for WWE. While she didn't confirm at the time that she was WWE-bound, she did acknowledge that she was leaving STARDOM, and there were then more rumors of possible retirement. After all, in her few years in STARDOM, Kairi had won every championship there was for her to win in the company (winning the Artist of STARDOM and Goddess of STARDOM Championships multiple times). That June, Kairi officially left STARDOM for WWE and its developmental territory of NXT, immediately taking part in—and winning—the inaugural Mae Young Classic tournament under her new ring name, "Kairi Sane." (Her patented elbow drop—which, according to rumors, WWE had told her to lose as her finisher—became the "InSane Elbow" as a result.) After the Mae Young Classic, Kairi officially debuted on the NXT roster and ended up challenging for the vacant NXT Women's Championship at NXT TakeOver: WarGames that November. The following January, she appeared on a main roster pay-per-view as an entrant in the inaugural Women's Royal Rumble match and did so again for the inaugural WrestleMania Women's Battle Royal that April. Despite fears that WWE would change Kairi, she's still known as "The Pirate Princess" and has yet to change from that lovable, fiery babyface she was known as in STARDOM. After all, her original video package for the Mae Young Classic featured her making this earnest request: "Please cheer for me."

In 2017, women's wrestling-centric Squared Circle Sirens named Kairi Sane one of their Wrestlers of the Year. Given her accomplishments—both receiving a WWE contract and winning the inaugural Mae Young Classic, on top of everything else she had done in her career up to that point—it's easy to see why.

★ KAITLYN ★

YEARS ACTIVE: 2010–2014, 2017–present

TRAINED BY: FCW

BILLED FROM: Houston, Texas

ACCOMPLISHMENTS: *WWE NXT* Season 3 · #5 in 2013 PWI Female 50 · 1x WWE Divas Champion

AKA: Celeste Bonin · Ricki Vaughn · "The Girl Next Door" · "The Hybrid Diva" · "The Powerhouse Diva" · 1/2 of The Chickbusters · 1/2 of Kait-Man

NOTABLE MATCHES: Kaitlyn vs. Eve Torres (c) at WWE *Monday Night RAW*, for the WWE Divas Championship (January 14, 2013) · Kaitlyn (c) vs. AJ Lee at WWE Payback 2013, for the WWE Divas Championship (June 16, 2013) · Kaitlyn & Dolph Ziggler vs. AJ Lee & Big E Langston at WWE SummerSlam 2013 (August 18, 2013) · Kaitlyn vs. AJ Lee (with Tamina) at *WWE Main Event* (January 8, 2014)

★ In one of the many examples of professional wrestlers with real names far more interesting than their ring names, Celeste Bonin is better known as the WWE's Kaitlyn. Originally a competitive body fitness model, Bonin was signed to a WWE developmental contract (to FCW) in July 2010. Despite debuting in FCW that same month—in a Bikini Contest, under her real name—Kaitlyn had actually only wrestled one match (a Mixed Tag Team match) before she technically got the call up to the main roster. This "call up" involved Kaitlyn being added as a very last-minute replacement

(a few days before the show started, despite all of the video packages promoting the original contestant) for a contestant in WWE's *NXT* season three, the Diva edition of WWE's game show version of *NXT*. In FCW, she was originally known as "Ricki Vaughn"—it wasn't until the day she was set to debut on *NXT* that she learned from John Laurinaitis, the head of Talent Relations at the time, that her new name would be "Kaitlyn."

While in NXT, babyface Kaitlyn was under the advisement of heel Vickie Guerrero as her pro. In the storyline, Vickie had replaced her original rookie with Kaitlyn because she didn't want to be overshadowed; however, what followed instead was Kaitlyn entering into a romantic entanglement with Dolph Ziggler, Vickie's on-screen boyfriend. Upon realizing something was going on between the two, Vickie would treat Kaitlyn cruelly—and in a way, Kaitlyn gave back just as good as she got, like when she dressed as Vickie for a NXT Diva Halloween Costume contest. Kaitlyn would feud with Vickie both on *NXT* and *SmackDown*—while also still training in FCW—and despite the obstacles in her path, she would also go on to win her season of *NXT*, as her feud with Vickie Guerrero (and her friendship formed with fellow *NXT* contestant AJ Lee both on- and off-screen) easily made her a sympathetic character.

After *NXT*, Kaitlyn officially joined the *SmackDown* roster at the end of 2010. In May 2011, she and AJ Lee would form the Divas tag team known as (at least, to them and their fans) "The Chickbusters," under the mentorship of Natalya. Kaitlyn and Lee would also return to *NXT* to pull duty in season five, *NXT Redemption*, a 67-week version of the show that became less of a competition and more of a WWE cult favorite. Kaitlyn would eventually enter into a feud with Maxine, forming a love triangle between the two and Maxine's wounded puppy of a love interest (and Kaitlyn's "bro" friend), Derrick Bateman. The love triangle would culminate in an intervention, with Kaitlyn professing her love for Bateman and the two getting the celebrity couple portmanteau of "Kait-Man." On *SmackDown*, The Chickbusters ended up feuding with Natalya, as she turned heel and formed The Divas of Doom with Beth Phoenix in August. The Chickbusters feuded with The Divas of Doom for a couple of months and lost, effectively splitting up the team—but their relationship would always remain a key facet of their characters. The original plan was actually for Kaitlyn to turn heel on AJ and join forces with the Divas of Doom—to the point where the segment was actually taped—but the choice ended up being scrapped and the taped segment never aired.

In the summer of 2012, Kaitlyn became the #1 Contender to Layla's Divas Championship in a "very unexpected" fashion when Eve accidentally eliminated herself from a Battle Royal for the championship. (The elimination occurred as a result of Eve attempting to have Kaitlyn redo a clothesline spot harder, however, Eve lost her balance on the redone spot and ending up getting eliminated as a result.) Kaitlyn credits the moment and her subsequent feud with Eve—who she technically retired—

with officially "starting" her career and making her a more relevant part of the WWE and Divas roster. Kaitlyn pushed behind the scenes for WWE Creative to let her continue to be part of the championship storyline—instead of just being written out because of the botched finish—and as a result, she entered into a 3-Way feud with Eve and Layla. At Night of Champions 2012, Kaitlyn lost her championship opportunity due to a masked attacker (who would eventually be revealed to be Aksana, as a hired gun for Eve) jumping her backstage, leading to Eve getting the title shot and beating Layla. A month later on *Monday Night RAW*, Kaitlyn finally got her title shot, but fell short and almost fell victim to Eve's attempts to reinjure her. For the rest of 2012, Kaitlyn would feud with Eve and Aksana, struggling to win the Divas Championship in the process. But then on the 20th Anniversary of *RAW*, Kaitlyn would finally win the championship from Eve, in her hometown of Houston, despite hometown wins being a rarity in WWE.

Earlier in 2012, prior to Kaitlyn's road to the Divas Championship, Kaitlyn and AJ Lee's friendship would officially be broken for the first time in the WWE storyline when AJ physically lashed out at Kaitlyn (as well as Natalya) for voicing her concern about AJ's unhealthy relationship with Daniel Bryan. Flash forward to March 2013, and Kaitlyn would officially enter into a championship feud with AJ (who was backed up by her on-screen boyfriend at the time, Dolph Ziggler, and her muscle, Big E Langston). Kaitlyn would receive gifts from a secret admirer during this time, one who would turn out to be Big E. But Big E's feelings were not to be trusted, as the entire secret admirer situation was actually the act of cruel mind games from AJ Lee (with Big E as her loyal co-conspirator). Upon facing off at the Payback pay-per-view, Kaitlyn lost her championship to AJ, but that wasn't the end of the feud. In fact, their feud even created WWE history, with the two of them participating in the first-ever Divas in-ring contract signing segment for their championship rematch at Money in the Bank. The two former friends would continue to feud through the summer of 2013, with Kaitlyn coming out on top (though not regaining the Divas Championship). When looking back at her WWE career, Celeste Bonin would regularly credit AJ Lee as the one who helped her perform her best in-ring work on the main roster, from her first match (at NXT) to her best match (at Payback) to her last match (at *WWE Main Event*).

On an episode of *The Agenda Podcast*, former WWE head writer—and notably the head writer of *NXT Redemption*—Tom Casiello brought up an idea for a storyline that had originally been discussed for the Kaitlyn character.

> We had discussed, and she was down with this, we had discussed Kaitlyn being the first female member of The Wyatt Family.... The idea was that after the Big E thing, the AJ thing, and all of that. She's left with nothing. She has no title, she has no best friend, and she has no boyfriend. She's got nothing and she's outside alone the arena one night. You see someone behind her like "hello, Kaitlyn," then a scream, and you have the black[out]. Two months later, she shows up as zombie Kaitlyn Wyatt.

The storyline, however, never came to fruition, for fear that the story could be misconstrued (especially in the sense of a woman being abducted). And unfortunately, according to Casiello, Vince McMahon didn't see Kaitlyn as a draw the same way he saw AJ Lee—and Kaitlyn herself has said Triple H would usually go to bat for her against Vince. It also didn't help that, despite endearing herself to a certain subsection of the WWE Universe with her quirky personality and sense of humor (which she's said was inspired primarily by *The Simpsons*), none of that ever quite translated into the broad comedy of WWE and what the higher-ups wanted. Ultimately, this led to Kaitlyn requesting her release from the company on January 8, 2014, the same day her final match with the company aired.

In October 2017, Celeste Bonin revealed her struggles with drug and alcohol addiction post-WWE, as well as how her marriage contributed to her mental and physical problems at the time. Soon after, Bonin began hinting at a return to professional wrestling, posting photos of her training in a wrestling ring for the first time in nearly four years—though she had shown up backstage at a taping of *Monday Night RAW* in 2016, even appearing in videos and photos with Big E and several of her former colleagues—and rekindling a love of the sport she appeared to have lost when she requested her release from WWE. Around the same time, rumors surfaced of WWE being interested in bringing her back as Kaitlyn. Then, at the end of 2017, it was finally announced that she'd be making her return to wrestling—and her official in-ring debut outside of the WWE banner—at Coastal Championship Wrestling (in Florida) on February 10, 2018.

★ KATARINA LEIGH ★

YEARS ACTIVE: 2000–present

TRAINED BY: Jon Ryan · NWA-UK Hammerlock · Mark Sloan · FWA Academy · Alex Shane · OVW

BILLED FROM: Chelsea, England

ACCOMPLISHMENTS: 1x British Empire Wrestling (BEW) Woman's Champion · 3x British Independent Circuit Women's Champion · 1x FWE Women's Champion · 2x OVW Women's Champion · 2010 TNA Knockouts Tag Team Championship Tournament (with Angelina Love) · #18 in 2012 PWI Female 50 · 1x World Queens Of Chaos Champion · 2x TNA Knockouts Champion · 1x TNA Knockouts Tag Team Champion (with Angelina Love)

AKA: Katie Lea · Katrina Lea · Katie Lea Burchill · Nikita · member of Team Players · Winter · Kat La Noir · Kat Waters · Katarina Waters · Temptress · "Queen of Chaos" · "The Queen of England" · Kat · Katarina · "The Scarlet Witch" · "The Beautiful Nightmare" · "The British Vixen"

NOTABLE MATCHES: Nikita, Alex Shane, & Ulf Herman vs. The Family (Brandon Thomas, Paul Travell, & Scott Parker) at

ROH/FWA Frontiers of Honor, in a Six Man Tag Team Hardcore match (May 17, 2003) · Nikita vs. Erin Angel vs. Jersey vs. Rebecca Knox vs. Skye vs. Sumie Sakai vs. Sweet Saraya vs. Trinity at Queens of Chaos Queen's Crowning, in a Royal Rumble match for the inaugural World Queens of Chaos Championship (May 13, 2005) · Katie Lea (c) vs. Beth Phoenix at OVW, in a Ladder match for the Undisputed OVW Women's Championship (December 23, 2006) · Katie Lea (with Paul Burchill) vs. Mickie James (c) at WWE Night of Champions, for the WWE Women's Championship (June 29, 2008) · Winter vs. Mickie James (c) at TNA No Surrender 2011, for the TNA Knockouts Championship (September 11, 2011)

★ Like a lot of kids growing up, there was a time Katarina Leigh Waters thought professional wrestling was real. She was taken by the over-the-top characters, the action, and the larger-than-life feel of everything and watched both WWF and WCW religiously, with hopes that she could one day be part of this world. But also like a lot of kids growing up, she had no idea how to make that dream a reality—she had no idea there were schools for wrestling, and she certainly had no idea wrestling existed outside of the United States, outside of WWF and WCW. Born and raised in Germany to British parents, Waters finally moved to England for school when she was 18 years old; but it wasn't until three years into her studies that she learned about British independent wrestling promotions. Upon seeing her first live wrestling show, Waters knew she could make her dream a reality, but she also knew that the wrestling she saw wasn't the kind of sports entertainment she'd fallen in love with. According to her, "[The indy wrestlers] put me in touch with a few people, but the training school was too far away, and the show I saw was in the old school British style, whereas I preferred the more American showbiz stuff." So again, she kept her wrestling dream as just that, a dream.

Surprisingly, the person who convinced Katarina to bite the bullet and finally go to wrestling school was a personality whose work can sort of be compared to sports entertainment: Jerry Springer. The way Waters tells it, "One day I was watching Jerry's UK show, and Alex Shane and Dominator were on it in their wrestling gimmick outfits and looking larger than life. It was at that point I decided I wanted to be like them." So after that, Katarina Waters finally looked up training schools and got to work at NWA-UK Hammerlock in Kent, England.

Waters began her wrestling career in 2000 as "Nikita," inspired by her favorite television series at the time, *La Femme Nikita* (which often aired after episodes of *WWF RAW* on the USA Network). Plus, she had to give up on her original preferred ring name—Kat—due to the existence of WWF Diva The Kat. Nikita debuted in February of 2000 as part of ITV Meridian's TransAtlantic Wrestling Challenge, a 16-man tournament (eight wrestlers from the United Kingdom, another eight from the United States) and six-episode series; on the final episode, Nikita beat Riptide (aka The Prodigette, an ECW alumnus) and won the TWC Ladies trophy. Still early in her career, Nikita eventually got to wrestle in her native Germany, against wrestling legend Sherri Martel and German independent women's wrestling star Wesna. She also continued her wrestling training at FWA Academy, studying under the person who finally inspired her to start wrestling in the first place, Alex Shane. Nikita became instrumental in making FWA a fixture on the independent scene, and as such, she entered into a major intergender feud with Paul Travell and his heel faction The Family. It was a feud that essentially made her famous in the independent scene, as it led to a moment in a 2003 FWA/ROH co-event with the American independent promotion ROH (while still being a young organization, the relationship put more eyes on FWA). That moment, in which Nikita made a death-defying dive from the balcony of York Hall onto The Family, was all anyone could talk about despite The Family winning the match.

While Nikita remained a fixture in FWA, she also debuted in France (for Queens of Chaos), Japan, and the United States (at SHIMMER) over the next few years. Back in the United Kingdom, she also developed a feud with Sweet Saraya, considering her the one wrestler who prevented her from being "the undisputed Queen of British Wrestling." While Nikita won every non-title match against Sweet Saraya in various promotions, she just couldn't seem to beat her when it came to winning the WAWW World Championship (the women's championship at World Association of Wrestling, an independent promotion owned by Sweet Saraya and her husband Ricky Knight), a win that could have added insult to injury had she achieved it. Nikita did, however, win gold in the form of becoming the inaugural Queens of Chaos Champion in France, during a Royal Rumble match featuring Sweet Saraya and Rebecca Knox (aka WWE's Becky Lynch), among others. Nikita held the title for over 387 days before announcing that she'd be vacating it due to signing a developmental contract with WWE (at OVW). Nikita's last order of business on the independent scene was a match in Germany against Blue Nikita (who came up in the independent German wrestling scene around the same time as Nikita had in the United Kingdom), for the rights to the Nikita name. Blue Nikita won, and from that point on (in OVW and on the WWE main roster), Katarina was known as "Katie Lea."

Reporting to OVW in August 2006, Katie Lea quickly found herself in the OVW Women's Championship scene against women such as Serena Deeb, Beth Phoenix, Kelly Kelly, and ODB. By November of that year, she won the championship from Beth Phoenix in a Gauntlet match. The following month, she defended and retained the championship in a one-on-one rematch with Beth Phoenix, in the first-ever women's Ladder match in OVW (and technically in WWE). Katie Lea held the championship for 211 days, the longest OVW Women's Championship reign during its time as a WWE developmental territory. And it was a reign that featured one of the best Divas feuds of the era, despite only being in developmental, ending with Katie Lea eventually earning Beth Phoenix's respect, after months of Phoenix refusing to accept her championship loss in the first place. After losing the championship, Katie Lea remained in developmental, wrestling on a few WWE main roster house shows (during tours in the United Kingdom), and wouldn't make her official main roster debut (on *RAW*) until February 2008 . . . alongside Paul Burchill, who would play her kayfabe brother. Now as "Katie Lea Burchill," the storyline originally teased a *Cruel Intentions*-esque, incestuous relationship between the brother-sister duo; but those implications ended as soon as WWE transitioned all of its weekly programming to TV-PG, effectively turning Katie Lea into more of a spoiled brat character. (The pair's catchphrase of "What Katie wants . . . Katie gets" from the original iteration of their characters then worked in a different way to fit the gimmick.) Despite technically debuting in February—and even technically being a part of WrestleMania XXIV, as a LumberJill in a Divas match—Katie Lea didn't make her in-ring debut until the end of April that year.

Unlike her time in OVW, Katie Lea's run on the main roster wasn't a dominant one. After dropping the incest tones of the Burchill family dynamic, Katie Lea challenged Mickie James for the WWE Women's Championship in the summer of 2008 but came up short multiple times. By the end of the year, Katie Lea and Paul Burchill were drafted to the WWE's rebooted ECW brand, but the change of scenery didn't exactly lead to an upswing for the duo. At the beginning of 2010, Katie Lea was moved back to *RAW*—without Paul—still without a major push or story and ended up being released by WWE at the end of that April. (Paul was released by WWE that previous February.)

After her release from WWE, Katarina debuted in TNA in the fall of 2010, in what is now remembered as quite a bizarre storyline. Debuting as Winter, Angelina Love's biggest fan, she appeared for a month in backstage vignettes, seemingly as a figment of Love's imagination—until she appeared during a backstage brawl to help Love out. Winter and Love would win the TNA Knockouts Tag Team Championship a month later, but Love's The Beautiful People stablemate Velvet Sky would accuse Winter of trying to break up their team. And after Velvet Sky accidentally cost Love and Winter the tag belts, a new facet of the storyline was revealed: mind control. Specifically in the form of a drink she'd keep having Angelina Love drink, which she called "medicine." Turning a mind-controlled Love heel, she was able to force Love to attack anyone whom Winter possibly saw as a threat. Eventually, Angelina Love chose to do Winter's bidding without the "medicine," but the story essentially stopped progressing after that reveal, with no firm conclusion or feud between the two as a result of this mind control. What made matters so frustrating was that the storyline unfortunately was incomplete. That's really a simplified version of the Winter character as well, as the entire storyline with Winter and Angelina Love was both bizarre and, unfortunately, incomplete.

The storyline did, however, eventually lead to Winter winning the Knockouts Championship from Mickie James and becoming the first (and only) British Knockouts Champion (and the sixth Knockout to have won both it and the Knockouts Tag Team Championship). Winter and Mickie James traded Knockouts Championship wins—leading to both of them becoming two-time Knockouts Champions in the process—but Winter didn't get a long reign at either win. (The combined length of her two reigns was 53 days.) After Velvet Sky ended Winter's second reign at the Bound For Glory pay-per-view in October 2011, Winter spent the rest of the year (both on-screen and at house shows) on a losing streak. The streak continued into 2012, and by 2012—with nary a mention of the Winter/Angelina Love storyline at all that year—Katarina (as well as Angelina Love) had been released from the company. Regarding her release, Waters later said, "I never found out why they let me go, and I know that's how the cookie crumbles sometimes." However, she did leave the door open to return if they wanted her back.

Post-TNA, Waters continued to wrestle on the independent scene under the name Winter, as well as Kat Waters, and Katrina Lea, and Katarina Leigh. However, she eventually settled on the last one, Katarina Leigh, while continuing to wrestle in the United Kingdom, Germany, and the United States (mostly in Southern California). And outside of wrestling, Katarina focused on acting and screenwriting. In April 2018, it was reported that Katarina had made her return to Impact Wrestling—as Katarina, with no acknowledgment of her past as Winter or a former Knockout—alongside comedy character Grado, as his new girlfriend. Like before, mystery surrounds Katarina, only this time, the story is far less fantasy genre and more a question of, "Is she really going out with him?"

★ KAY LEE RAY ★

YEARS ACTIVE: 2009–present

TRAINED BY: Kid Fite · Premier British Wrestling Academy · Colin McKay

BILLED FROM: Glasgow, Scotland

ACCOMPLISHMENTS: 2x Insane Championship Wrestling (ICW) Women's Champion · 1x ICW Fierce Females Champion · 1x Defiant (formerly known as WCPW) Women's Champion · #36 in

2015 PWI Female 50 · #28 in 2016 PWI Female 50 · 3x Southside Wrestling Entertainment (SWE) Queen of Southside Champion · 1x SWE Speed King Champion

AKA: Cuntstable Kay Lee Ray · 1/2 of Fly High WDSS · "Hardcore Daredevil" · "The KLR in Killer" · "KLR" · "The Queen of Hardcore" · 1/2 of Lucha Lee Ray · 1/2 of Team FTW · member of Black Label · member of The Filthy Generation · member of New Age Kliq · member of Righteous Army · "The First Lady of Chaos" · "The Duchess of Destruction" · "The Matriarch of The Filthy Generation" · "The First Lady of The Filthy Generation"

NOTABLE MATCHES: Kay Lee Ray vs. Carmel at ICW: Fierce Females, in a Last Woman Standing match (September 30, 2012) · Kay Lee Ray vs. Carmel at ICW Fear & Loathing 4, in a Deathmatch (October 10, 2011) · Kay Lee Ray vs. Nikki Storm at SHIMMER Volume 71: The ChickFight Tournament, in a SHIMMER ChickFight Tournament First Round match (March 28, 2015) · Kay Lee Ray vs. Evie vs. Cheerleader Melissa at SHIMMER Volume 71: The ChickFight Tournament, in a SHIMMER Championship #1 Contendership ChickFight Tournament Final 3-Way Elimination match (March 28, 2015) · Fly High WDSS (Kay Lee Ray & Mia Yim) vs. The Kimber Bombs (Kimber Lee & Cherry Bomb) (c) vs. Team Slap Happy (Heidi Lovelace & Evie) vs. BaleSpin (KC Spinelli & Xandra Bale) at SHIMMER Volume 84, in a Four Corners Elimination match for the SHIMMER Tag Team Championship (June 26, 2016) · Kay Lee Ray vs. Toni Storm at STARDOM 5☆STAR Grand Prix 2016 - Night 4, in a Block A match (September 3, 2016) · Kay Lee Ray vs. Princesa Sugehit at the WWE Mae Young Classic, in a Mae Young Classic First Round match (August 28, 2017) · Kay Lee Ray, Jazzy Gabert, & Tessa Blanchard vs. Marti Belle, Santana Garrett, & Sarah Logan at the WWE Mae Young Classic – Road To The Finals (September 11, 2017) · Kay Lee Ray vs. Viper (c) at WCPW Built To Destroy 2017, in a WCPW Women's Championship match (June 16, 2017) · Kay Lee Ray vs. Toni Storm (c) at PROGRESS Chapter 50: I Give It Six Months, for the PROGRESS Women's Championship (June 25, 2017) · Kay Lee Ray (c) vs. Kasey vs. Viper at ICW Fear & Loathing X, in a 3-Way Steel Cage match for the ICW Women's Championship (November 19, 2017)

⭐ As far as wrestling names go, Kayleigh Rae went with a pretty easy choice in hers: "Kay Lee Ray." Simple enough, right? Less simple was her wrestling debut (at the age of 17), as it was a #1 Contendership match for the NWA Scottish Heavyweight Championship. Of course, it was also an intergender Battle Royal with 29 other competitors, but it was certainly one way to make an entry into the world of professional wrestling.

Two years prior, Ray's boyfriend (ICW's Stevie Boy) was training to become a wrestler himself, and his love of wrestling soon became her love of wrestling as well. As for wrestlers outside of her boyfriend who inspired her, one of the first female wrestlers she was drawn to was WWE's Lita. According to Ray, Lita's attitude and style eventually would influence her own as a wrestler and a character—which you can probably tell from Ray's flaming red hair and punk rock demeanor. But it was her boyfriend showing Ray her first-ever WWE match (Shawn Michaels vs. British Bulldog from WWF King of the Ring 1996) that fully got her hooked. So at age 16, Ray started training to become a wrestler too, and after one day of training, she knew it was the life for her.

It wasn't until 2011 though when things started to pick up for Kay Lee Ray on the independent scene, as 2011 was the year she began wrestling for Pro-Wrestling: EVE (a women's promotion, which dubs its roster as the "Riot Grrrls of Pro Wrestling") and ICW (arguably Scotland's premier independent wrestling promotion, as well as one known for its hardcore wrestling and edgier sports entertainment content). ICW especially became a big deal for Kay Lee Ray, as she became known as "The Queen of Hardcore" (among many other nicknames) because of her work there, competing in and winning "Scotland's 1st ever Women's Deathmatch!" (as it was promoted) in the fall of 2011, at ICW Fear & Loathing 4. (She eventually became the first woman to main event an ICW show, as well as the first and only woman to technically—as she was filling in for another wrestler—hold ICW tag titles.) As Fear & Loathing is ICW's biggest show of the year, this was perhaps the biggest match of her career at the time. This match was part of a feud against Carmel Jacob that spanned years in Scotland, through a number of promotions, but it was in ICW (and its all-women's offshoot, Fierce Females) that Ray and Carmel went to their most extreme, facing off in multiple Last Woman Standing matches as well as another Deathmatch (in tag team form). So in 2013, it was a no-brainer that Kay Lee Ray became the inaugural Fierce Females Champion, eventually holding the title for 755 days. It was also a no-brainer that Kay Lee Ray would end up being one of ICW's cockiest heels, given all her achievements.

In 2014, Kay Lee Ray competed in the second season of TNA Impact Wrestling's reality show (similar to WWE's *Tough Enough*) *TNA British Boot Camp*, alongside a list of names who would eventually end up becoming big names in the British independent scene, as well as in TNA and WWE. In retrospect, Kay Lee Ray was certainly in good company, competing against wrestlers such as Nikki Storm (now known in WWE and NXT as Nikki Cross), Viper, El Ligero, Grado, Noam Dar, and more. Ray made it to the final three competitors, along with Rampage Brown and Mark Andrews (the winner, who received a TNA contract and is now signed to WWE) and wrestled a couple of matches on TNA's supplemental show *Xplosion* during a United Kingdom tour, but she wasn't offered an official contract from the company.

That same year, Kay Lee Ray spent a few weeks making herself known outside of the United Kingdom, as she officially made her debut in three different promotions in the United States. First, she wrestled at Ohio independent promotion AIW for its Girls Night Out event (Girls Night Out 11 and 12), falling to Veda Scott in her first match but beating Kimber Lee in her next. She also debuted in SHIMMER and wrestled in Volumes 62 through 66. Volume 62 was a big show for the company, as it was a pay-per-view in New Orleans, Louisiana, during WrestleMania Weekend, the biggest (and most concentrated) week of the year for professional wrestling. The rest of the shows were in SHIMMER's home of Berwyn, Illinois, and as far making an impression goes, Kay Lee Ray was able to win both in her debut and on her last

show of her mini-US tour. Then it was on to Florida, to make her SHINE debut before returning to the United Kingdom. Kay Lee Ray would return to SHIMMER later in 2014, but in the meantime, she continued to make the most of her time on her home turf, winning the SWE Speed King Championship in an intergender singles match.

In 2015, Ray continued to collect gold and entered uncharted territory, winning SWE's Queen of Southside Championship, debuting in wXw (Germany's top independent promotion), winning SHIMMER's ChickFight Tournament, and losing a Loser Leaves Southside match (though she returned a few months later). And that year, it also became apparent that Ray was at least somewhat on WWE's radar, as she was hired as enhancement talent (for a match against Nia Jax) on an episode of *WWE NXT*. The following year, she made her Japanese wrestling debut, in 2016's STARDOM 5☆STAR Grand Prix tournament, as well as her debut in PROGRESS Wrestling back in the United Kingdom. She'd also win the ICW Women's Championship for the first time toward the end of the year. If it sounds like she was busy, that's because she most certainly was: that year, she had over 80 wrestling matches, all over the world. And she only got busier in 2017, with more than 100 matches. For comparison, in her debut year in 2009, she only had two matches. And unlike in 2017, neither one of those matches were in WWE.

But yes, after popping up for a quick moment in *NXT* in 2015, Kay Lee Ray returned to the WWE spotlight in a bigger way as one of the 32 female competitors from around the world to compete in the inaugural Mae Young Classic tournament. While Ray didn't make it past the first round, it was certainly the biggest audience Ray would have in her eight years in the business. Post-tournament, Ray took another tour in Japan for STARDOM and also won the Defiant (formerly known as WCPW) Women's Championship and continued her habit of never stopping or slowing down in her career.

★ KELLY KELLY ★

YEARS ACTIVE: 2006–2012

TRAINED BY: OVW

BILLED FROM: Jacksonville, Florida

ACCOMPLISHMENTS: 1x WWE Divas Champion · 2011 Slammy Award for Divalicious Moment of the Year (winning the Divas Championship) · #15 in 2012 PWI Female 50

AKA: Barbie Blank · 1/2 of The Blondetourage · 1/3 of Extreme Exposé · "Smelly Kelly" · K2

NOTABLE MATCHES: Kelly Kelly (with Tiffany) vs. Layla (c) (with Michelle McCool) at WWE Money in the Bank 2010, for the WWE Women's Championship (July 18, 2010) · Kelly Kelly vs. Brie Bella (c) at WWE *Monday Night RAW*, for the WWE Divas Championship (June 20, 2011) · Kelly Kelly (c) vs. Beth Phoenix at WWE Night of Champions 2011, for the WWE Divas Championship (September 18, 2011) · Kelly Kelly vs. Beth Phoenix (c) at WWE Hell in a Cell 2011, for the WWE Divas Championship (October 2, 2011) · Kelly Kelly & Maria Menounos vs. Eve Torres & Beth Phoenix at WWE WrestleMania XXVIII (April 1, 2012)

★ As the story goes, back in 2006, WWE's then Head of Talent Relations, John Laurinaitis, "discovered" a 19-year-old Barbie Blank, picking both her and Victoria Crawford (known to WWE fans as "Alicia Fox") out of a fashion catalog, contacting their agents, and signing them to WWE after the fact. According to Crawford, that hiring decision was something of an "experiment" on WWE's end to see if they could even teach models how to wrestle. The experiment led to both women eventually becoming WWE Divas Champions, so perhaps it was a success.

Despite no prior wrestling experience, WWE offered Blank a development tryout (she was in college studying broadcast journalism at the time) and then contract in May 2006. While she was still training at OVW, she debuted on the main roster—on the rebooted ECW brand—the following month, as "Kelly Kelly" (despite her actual name being quite perfect for professional wrestling). Kelly's debut wasn't as a wrestler though: it was as a self-proclaimed "exhibitionist," one who performed a striptease called Kelly's Exposé every week. One of the most memorable stories to come out about the inception of Kelly's Exposé was Kelly Kelly's later recounting of how the gimmick was explained to her . . . by Vince McMahon himself: "My first day, Vince was like, 'Okay, this is what you're gonna do.' . . . Then he had this like chair set up and he was like, 'Okay, you're gonna use this chair,' and he kinda like showed me the dance. And he like took his jacket off and kind of swung it around, and I'm standing there, like 19 years old: 'Yeah, I used to watch this man when I was like 12.' . . . He was good. He was really good!" (There was no chair during the actual segment though, so Kelly instead had to wing it.) In fact, McMahon was reportedly quite hands on with her gimmick's creation, as it was his idea for her name to be "Kelly Kelly" and not just "Kelly."

However, the striptease would remain just a tease, as this led to a story in which her kayfabe boyfriend, Mike Knox, would put an end to the exposé and reveal himself to be a controlling boyfriend. Knox would force Kelly to be his valet to the ring, so he could keep an eye on her. Mike Knox's controlling boyfriend gimmick would lead to feuds with ECW Originals like Tommy Dreamer and The Sandman—in which part of the story featured Knox using Kelly as a human shield, causing Kelly to take a hit from The Sandman's signature Singapore cane—as well as the new ECW's biggest face, CM Punk. Kelly made her main roster in-ring debut during the first feud, in a Six-Person Mixed Tag Team match, but it was in the CM Punk storyline that Kelly got to show off more character, as she had developed a crush on Punk. (Knox lost both feuds.) Eventually, Knox and Kelly broke up, with Knox hitting his finisher and kayfabe injuring her.

Post-Knox, Kelly's Exposé returned at the beginning of January in a rebooted form as Extreme Exposé, featuring Kelly, Layla, and Brooke. This went on for months—until Brooke was released from her contract in November—even though, since the show was TV-14, it's not as though there was ever any actual nudity. However, outside of the segment itself, there was a storyline brewing with the trio, as they became infatuated with The Miz (whose gimmick at the time was pick-up-artist–inspired, calling himself "The Chick Magnet"). However, Kelly Kelly developed a crush on ECW Original Balls Mahoney instead, leading to a feud between Miz and Mahoney, as well as clarification that Kelly was the face to root for in the trio, as opposed to Layla and Brooke. The storyline was cut short when Brooke was released, but it did lead to a feud between Kelly and Layla (still supported by The Miz) and more in-ring action from both women for once. From this point on, Kelly remained a face in her WWE career and eventually became the top face of the division.

By May 2009, Kelly Kelly had gone from model with no wrestling experience whatsoever to #1 Contender to the WWE Divas Championship (now on the RAW roster). While she didn't win the title from then champion Maryse, Kelly remained in the title hunt from that point on. After being drafted to *SmackDown* in 2010, Kelly entered into another feud with Layla—only this time, Layla had backup in the form of her tag team partner Michelle McCool, forming the heel mean girl team known as LayCool. During this feud, LayCool would try to distract Kelly and interfere during her matches, as well as insult her in promos and backstage segments (calling her "Smelly Kelly," as LayCool were never exactly known for their wit when it came to their heel personas). While LayCool both individually got their comeuppance, with Kelly Kelly defeating them both in singles competition, when it came time to challenge one of them for the WWE Women's Championship (as LayCool considered themselves co-champions), Kelly fell short yet again. (This was also the last pay-per-view title match for the original WWE Women's title.) Eventually, Kelly's feud with LayCool crossed over into a feud with the Acting General Manager of SmackDown, Vickie Guerrero, as LayCool had Guerrero on their side—leading to Guerrero abusing her power and firing Kelly when she started teaming with Guerrero's kayfabe ex-husband, Edge. However, Kelly was rehired by returning General Manager Teddy Long, and she and Edge were able to defeat Guerrero and Drew McIntyre (who had developed a romantic obsession with Kelly), leading to Guerrero's on-screen firing instead.

The year 2011 saw Kelly Kelly return to RAW and a new version of K2: champion. After unsuccessfully challenging the Divas Champion at the time, Brie Bella, Kelly got a second chance the next month when a fan vote on *Monday Night RAW* decided that she (with 53 percent of the vote, beating Beth Phoenix and Eve Torres) would get a title shot that night. And this time, she won. She also retained in her rematch and went on to hold the Divas Championship for 104 days. Kelly's first feud as champion, however, wasn't an easy one, as she had to go up against a Diva who was probably her polar opposite, "The Glamazon" Beth

Phoenix. (Phoenix was also one of the first people Kelly feuded with when she first arrived to RAW in 2008.) While able to defeat Phoenix in two consecutive pay-per-views—which Phoenix essentially considered fluke wins from a "Barbie doll" like Kelly—Kelly couldn't slay The Glamazon for long and lost the title on their third encounter. However, the match was over eight minutes long, which was absolutely unheard of for Divas matches at the time (Kelly's original title win was three minutes long, and her first defense on pay-per-view was less than five).

Also at the time, Kelly Kelly's run on top felt much longer, even though she lost her championship to the first and only person she ever defended it against. Really, it was a symptom of the Divas Division at the time: at a certain point in her final year with the company, Kelly Kelly was seemingly only having matches against Eve Torres, Beth Phoenix, or Natalya. Of course, all three are very talented women, but it's still quite monotonous when you consider the amount of talent on the roster and just in women's wrestling in general. However, surprisingly, at the end of September 2012, it was announced that Barbie Blank had been released from her contract, Kelly Kelly no more. In an interview months later, Blank revealed that she had needed the time off to rest—she had taken off some time from WWE in June that year as well—and to recover from developing neck issues.

Since leaving WWE, she became a reality star on the E! series *WAGS LA* (about the wives and girlfriends of sports stars), the world of the squared circle seemingly completely behind her. However, early 2017 saw "Kelly Kelly" make her return to WWE TV, appearing in backstage interviews visiting *Monday Night RAW*, WrestleMania Weekend (both at WrestleMania Axxess and at the Hall of Fame ceremony) and ushering in rumors that she would be making her return to WWE sooner, rather than later. She was even featured in an episode of the WWE Network original series *Table For 3*, a "Divas Champions Club" of herself, Eve, and Maryse (who had since come back to WWE after originally departing in 2011). When asked about a possible return, Kelly simply answered: "I would love to do one more run . . . in the future. You never know."

Her return to the fold wasn't exactly in the form of a full-blown comeback though: while she made an appearance at *RAW*'s 25th anniversary show in January 2018 (as WWE honored some of its historic women), the extent of her in-ring return was as a surprise entrant in the inaugural Women's Royal Rumble match.

★ KIMBER LEE ★

YEARS ACTIVE: 2011–present

TRAINED BY: CZW Academy · Drew Gulak · WWE Performance Center

BILLED FROM: Seattle, Washington

ACCOMPLISHMENTS: 1x AAW Women's Champion · 1x CHIKARA Grand Champion · 2015 CHIKARA Challenge of the Immortals (with El Hijo del Ice Cream, Ice Cream Jr., & Jervis Cottonbelly) · 1x Dynamite Championship Wrestling Women's Champion · 1x JAPW Women's Champion · 1x (and inaugural) Legacy Wrestling Women's Champion · 1x Maryland Championship Wrestling (MCW) Women's Champion (with Cherry Bomb) · #17 in 2016 PWI Female 50 · 1x SHIMMER Tag Team Champion · 1x SHINE Tag Team Champion (with Cherry Bomb) · 2x WSU Tag Team Champion (with Annie Social)

AKA: Kimber Lee · Princess KimberLee · 1/2 of The Kimber Bombs · Kimberly Frankele · "Bombshell" · "Princess Palmstrike" · 1/2 of Chicks Using Nasty Tactics · "The Crown Jewel of NXT"

NOTABLE MATCHES: The Kimber Bombs (Cherry Bomb & Kimber Lee) vs. Courtney Rush & Vanessa Kraven at SMASH Wrestling Super Showdown III (August 23, 2015) · Kimber Lee vs. Mickie James (c) at MCW Autumn Armageddon Tour 2015 - Night 5, for the MCW Women's Championship (November 13, 2015) · Princess KimberLee vs. Hallowicked (c) at CHIKARA Top Banana, for the CHIKARA Grand Championship (December 5, 2015) · Kimber Lee (with Cherry Bomb) vs. Courtney Rush at SMASH Wrestling

SMASH vs. CZW (January 16, 2016) · Princess KimberLee vs. Mickie James at CHIKARA National Pro Wrestling Day (February 6, 2016) · Kimber Lee vs. LuFisto at WWR Project XX (April 10, 2016) · The Kimber Bombs (Kimber Lee & Cherry Bomb) (c) vs. Team Slap Happy (Heidi Lovelace & Evie) vs. BaleSpin (KC Spinelli & Xandra Bale) vs. Fly High WDSS (Kay Lee Ray & Mia Yim) at SHIMMER Volume 84, in a Four Corners Elimination match for the SHIMMER Tag Team Championship (June 26, 2016) · Abbey Laith vs. Jazzy Gabert at the WWE Mae Young Classic, in a Mae Young Classic First Round match (August 28, 2017)

⭐ Despite the old saying that professional wrestling "ain't ballet," for Kimberly Frankele, bridging the gap between the two sports made perfect sense. A classically trained ballerina with a degree in dance education, Laith first fell in love with professional wrestling as a teenager, drawn to the world and inspired to join it by the sheer force of will that was WWF Diva Chyna. It was while attending college in Pennsylvania that she chose to achieve that dream and began training at the CZW Academy, becoming the first woman to graduate from the school and beginning her professional wrestling career under the ring name Kimber Lee.

It was during this time as Kimber Lee that she became known not just for her skills against her fellow female wrestlers but also against male competitors. Her first wrestling match was at CZW, winning an intergender match against Austin Uzzie, and eventually she teamed up with her CZW Academy trainer, Drew Gulak, in his faction, A Campaign for a Better Impact Zone. Kimber Lee wrestled for CZW from 2011 to 2014, facing both men and women and becoming a top name in intergender wrestling.

In 2013, Kimber Lee debuted in top American women's wrestling promotions SHIMMER and SHINE, the latter promotion in which she formed a tag team with fellow heel Cherry Bomb called The Kimber Bombs (formerly known as Team Combat Zone). While failing to make it past the first round of the tournament to crown the inaugural SHINE Tag Team Champions at SHINE 17, The Kimber Bombs eventually won the titles at SHINE 25. A month later, they won the SHIMMER Tag Team titles at SHIMMER Volume 72, dropping them over a year later at SHIMMER Volume 84 (in a Four-Way match where Kimber accidentally hit Cherry with the championship titles).

Despite her notorious heel behavior both with CZW and as 1/2 of The Kimber Bombs, the version of Kimber Lee that debuted at CHIKARA in 2014 was true blue babyface in Princess KimberLee. As KimberLee, the grace of her ballerina past was able to exist in her professional wrestling work. Princess KimberLee was a benevolent and courageous monarch, leading a band of underdogs from losers (collectively known as Crown & Court) to the surprise winners of CHIKARA's 2015 Challenge of the Immortals double round-robin tournament. Upon winning the Challenge of the Immortals in the CHIKARA season finale Top Banana, Princess KimberLee cashed in her Golden Opportunity (from the Challenge of the Immortals) that same night to achieve another first, becoming to the first woman to win the CHIKARA Grand Championship.

In January 2017, it was announced that Kimber Lee had signed with the WWE and would be reporting to the WWE Performance Center to work for WWE's developmental brand, NXT. Then in June that year, she became Abbey Laith. Under this ring name, Laith was then announced that same month as one of the 32 participants in WWE's inaugural Mae Young Classic. As Laith stated during the tournament, this was quite the honor, as her finishing maneuver—the inescapable Alligator Clutch pin—was passed down from Mae Young to her CZW trainers, who in turn passed it down to her. While Laith was eliminated from the Mae Young Classic in the quarterfinals by Mercedes Martinez, her performance certainly paid proper respect to Mae Young and promised more quality wrestling in her future as a NXT Superstar. However, early in March 2018, it was reported that Abbey Laith was released from her NXT contract. She returned to independent (as well as intergender) action as Kimber Lee the following month (working predominantly in Beyond Wrestling) and won the AAW Women's Championship from inaugural champion Jessicka Havok that May.

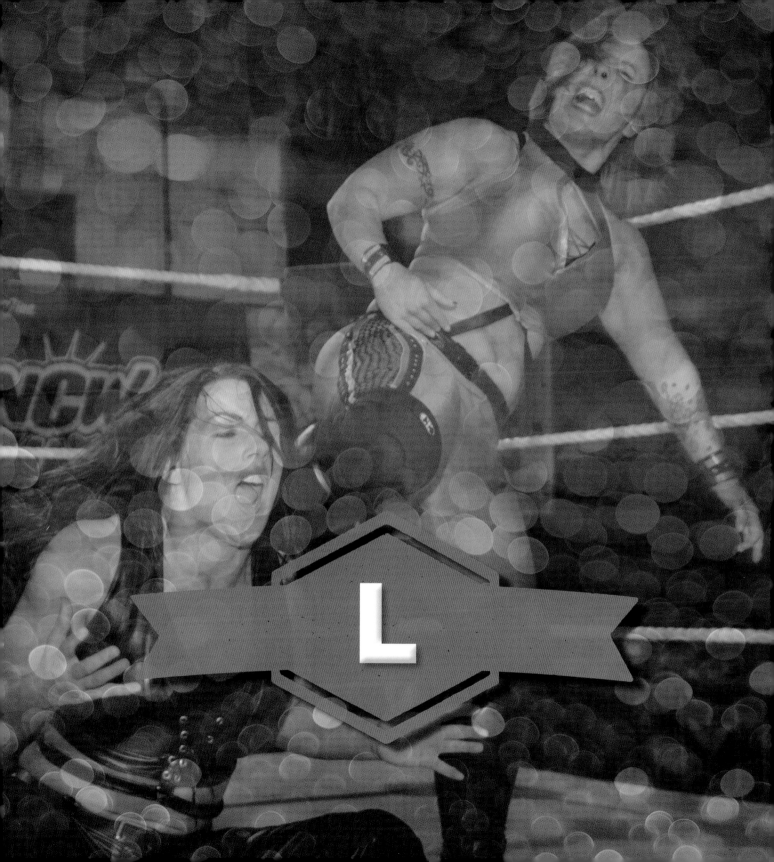

★ LAYLA ★

YEARS ACTIVE: 2006–2015

TRAINED BY: Dave "Fit" Finlay · Jesse Hernandez · Booker T

BILLED FROM: Miami, Florida

ACCOMPLISHMENTS: 2006 WWE Divas Search · 1x WWE Women's Champion · 1x WWE Divas Champion · 2010 Slammy Award for Knucklehead Moment of the Year (LayCool loses to Mae Young, with Michelle McCool)

AKA: Layla El · 1/3 of Extreme Exposé · 1/2 of LayCool · 1/2 of The Slayers

NOTABLE MATCHES: Layla (c) (with Michelle McCool) vs. Kelly Kelly (with Tiffany) at WWE Money in the Bank 2010, for the WWE Women's Championship (July 18, 2010) · LayCool (Layla & Michelle McCool) vs. The Divas of Doom (Beth Phoenix & Natalya) at WWE TLC 2010, in Divas Tag Team Tables match (December 19, 2010) · LayCool (Layla & Michelle McCool) & Dolph Ziggler vs. Trish Stratus, Nicole "Snooki" Polizzi, & John Morrison at WWE WrestleMania XXVII (April 3, 2011) · Layla vs. Michelle McCool at WWE Extreme Rules 2011, in a No Count-out No Disqualification Loser Leaves WWE match (May 1, 2011) · Layla (c) vs. Eve Torres at WWE Night of Champions 2012, for the WWE Divas Championship (September 16, 2012)

★ Before WWE, Layla El was a professional dancer, not professional wrestler; she'd danced for the Miami Heat, P. Diddy, Kanye West, and John Legend. But when her trainer suggested that she audition for the 2006 WWE Diva Search—with a prize of a $250,000 WWE one-year contract—Layla went for it. And she won it, officially debuting at that year's SummerSlam pay-per-view in a backstage "initiation" skit. Layla originally debuted as a face on *SmackDown* post-SummerSlam, but by January 2007, she was on the rebooted ECW brand and part of the brand's Extreme Exposé

segment/stable (featuring Kelly Kelly and Brooke). Outside of the segment, the trio had a storyline where they became infatuated with The Miz during his pick-up artist–inspired "The Chick Magnet" gimmick. However, once Kelly Kelly developed a crush on ECW Original Balls Mahoney instead, Layla and Brooke officially turned heel against their stablemate. The full storyline was cut short when Brooke was released, but the feud between Layla (still supported by The Miz) and Kelly Kelly continued, providing more in-ring action from both inexperienced women's wrestlers. In the summer of 2008, Layla moved to RAW, where she eventually became William Regal's valet during his Intercontinental Championship push. At the 2008 year-end Slammy Awards, Regal and Layla were even nominated for the "Best Couple" award. However, the most important partnership in Layla's wrestling career was yet to come.

The spring of 2009 saw Layla get separated from Regal, as she was drafted to SmackDown. It was also a big year as a competitor for Layla, as it was the year she and Michelle McCool formed the—what they would call "flawless"—heel duo known as LayCool. First, they would feud with Mickie James in the infamous "Piggy James" storyline, which bled into early 2010. During this time, Michelle McCool was the WWE Women's Champion, and Layla would interfere in matches to help her retain the championship, until it eventually backfired and McCool lost the championship to James. LayCool would also befriend SmackDown consultant (and sometimes Acting General Manager) Vickie Guerrero, making her feel like she was part of their mean girls clique—even allowing her to manage them—in order for her to place the odds in their favor. This led to Guerrero functioning as the Special Referee in McCool's championship rematch against James, allowing McCool to win the championship back. Following the LayCool/Mickie James feud, the duo turned their sights on Beth Phoenix, again using schoolyard mean girl tactics (and Vickie Guerrero) to get the upper hand . . . and again with McCool losing the championship to her opponent, despite Layla and Guerrero's help. However, this rematch ended up being a Handicap match (LayCool vs. Beth Phoenix), and Layla pinned Phoenix to become the new WWE Women's Champion—winning the title for the first time. (Layla was the first British woman and Diva Search winner to hold the WWE Women's Championship, as well as the final woman to hold the original championship before it was deactivated—merged/replaced with the Divas Championship—in 2010.) From that point on, LayCool referred to themselves as co-champions (basically utilizing Freebird rules with the title), each with their own personalized Women's Championship.

When SmackDown General Manager Teddy Long tried to tell them there could only be one champion—during their feud with Kelly Kelly, in which they called her "Smelly Kelly"—LayCool ignored that directive, instead opting to split one championship belt in half. And upon Michelle McCool beating WWE Divas Champion Melina in a unification match, LayCool considered themselves co-Divas Champions. At the same time, LayCool were tasked with working as Pro mentors on the second season of the original competition game show version of *NXT*, with their Rookie being Kaval (better known outside of WWE as "Low-Ki"). The contrast of their superficial, self-absorbed behavior to Kaval's dour, self-serious demeanor made for quite the entertaining combination. At the end of 2010, LayCool faced off against the team of Natalya and Beth Phoenix (aka The Divas of Doom) in the first ever Divas Tag Team Tables match, which was the beginning of the end for LayCool. The following month at the 2011 Royal Rumble, LayCool lost the Divas Championship to Eve Torres. While LayCool tried to get over their miscommunications and losing streak through couples therapy (as shown in various vignettes), eventually, McCool turned on Layla, attacking her during one of the therapy sessions. The two former friends eventually had a one-on-one match to settle their differences, but it ended in a double count-out; so at Extreme Rules, they had a No Count-out No Disqualification Loser Leaves WWE match, which Layla won. (Michelle McCool's loss signaled the legitimate end of her WWE career, as she was retiring, which explained the quickness with which the LayCool breakup proceeded.)

However, while Layla won the match, she'd also suffered a real injury during the match—tearing both of her ACLs and MCLs—and had to be written off—through an attack by WWE monster at the time, Kharma—to get surgery and recover. Layla would return to the main roster in April 2012 after almost a year off—as a face—facing Nikki Bella for the Divas Championship (as a replacement for the now-injured Beth Phoenix) and winning. Again, Layla made history, as the first Diva Search winner to win both the Women's and Divas Championships. Layla's reign lasted 140 days, eventually functioning as a buffer for heel Eve's title run and face Kaitlyn's rise to defeat Eve.

At the end of 2013, Layla took a hiatus from WWE, returning in the spring of 2014, just in time for WrestleMania XXX (participating in the Divas Invitational Match for AJ Lee's Divas

Championship). Layla soon entered into a bizarre love triangle feud with Summer Rae over Fandango . . . which turned into an even more bizarre girl power story with Layla and Summer Rae dancing with each other (and eventually calling themselves "The SLayers"). It was Layla's last storyline in the company before she took time off for another surgery (at the beginning of 2015), as well as her last storyline in the company whatsoever. She returned that April, but this time around there was no team-up or championship storyline. On July 29, 2015, Layla officially retired from WWE—and was, at the time, the longest-tenured Diva on the roster —with WWE.com even featuring a non-gimmick, non-story-line farewell interview from the former champion. As she told WWE.com, after nine years of being on the road, it was "just time to start the next chapter of [her] life."

★ LITA ★

YEARS ACTIVE: 1997–2006

TRAINED BY: The Funkin' Conservatory · Dory Funk Jr. · Ricky Santana · Kevin Quinn · David Sierra · Ace Steel · Steel Domain · Danny Dominion · Matt Hardy · Jeff Hardy · Bones Breakers · Dan McDevitt · Memphis Championship Wrestling

BILLED FROM: Sanford, North Carolina · Atlanta, Georgia

ACCOMPLISHMENTS: 4x WWF/WWE Women's Champion · 2006 WWE Women's Championship Tournament · WWE Hall of Fame Class of 2014 · 2005 PWI Feud of the Year (with Edge vs. Matt Hardy) · 2001 PWI Woman of the Year

AKA: Angelica · Miss Congeniality · 1/3 of Team Xtreme · 1/3 of Rated RKO · Amy Dumas · 1/2 of Team Bestie

NOTABLE MATCHES: Lita vs. Stephanie McMahon (c) at WWF *Monday Night RAW*, for the WWF Women's Championship

(August 21, 2000) · Lita & Trish Stratus vs. Molly Holly & Gail Kim at WWE Unforgiven 2003 (September 21, 2003) · Lita & Trish Stratus vs. Chris Jericho & Christian at WWE Armageddon 2003, in a Battle of the Sexes match (December 14, 2003) · Lita vs. Trish Stratus (c) at WWE *Monday Night RAW*, for the WWE Women's Championship (December 6, 2004) · Lita & Edge vs. Trish Stratus & Carlito at WWE *Monday Night RAW* (August 7, 2006) · Lita (c) vs. Trish Stratus at WWE Unforgiven 2006, for the WWE Women's Championship (September 17, 2006) · Lita (c) vs. Mickie James at WWE Survivor Series 2006, for the WWE Women's Championship (November 26, 2006)

★ For a good number of girls growing up during the Attitude and Ruthless Aggression Eras of WWF/WWE, this particular question strikes a chord: Are you a Lita or a Trish? As two of the most influential Divas to come out of the company at this time, few hardcore WWE fans can claim to have no preference either way. But for those who always considered themselves a bit more "alternative," chances are, they were Team Lita. Matt Hardy once described her as "the girl who's cool enough to hang with anybody."

But before there was even a Lita, there was Amy Dumas, a woman in her early 20s who was awestruck and inspired by the lucha libre style of WCW's Rey Mysterio Jr. In fact, she hadn't even considered professional wrestling a career path (or a source of entertainment) until that exposure, as the image of wrestling she had in mind was that of graceless brutes. The opposite of Mysterio in every way, basically, but—inspired by Mysterio's originality and high-flying style—Dumas became obsessed with wrestling, watching *WCW Nitro* every week to get her fix of luchadors, only to get even more invested in the rest of the world of sports entertainment. The summer of 1997, she attended her first WCW show and got the chance to go backstage, and eventually Dumas earned enough money to go down to Mexico and learn a thing or two about lucha libre. While in Mexico, she met some of her future WWF colleagues at CMLL (back when it was Empresa Mexicana de la Lucha Libre, aka EMLL), such as Steele (who would eventually be known as Val Venis) and Mr. Águila (whom she would eventually manage in WWF, when he became Essa Rios). While Dumas got a chance to model and appear in vignettes in CMLL—peeking behind the curtain, as well—she wasn't given the chance to learn how to become a wrestler. When she returned to the United States (to Richmond, Virginia), she saved up money again for another stay in Mexico—this time a shorter stay in which she was determined to get the most out of lucha libre. It was during this three-week trip in the fall of 1997 that Amy Dumas finally got some wrestling training, as Ricky Santana and Kevin Quinn taught her the basics.

She also got to be part of CMLL's 65th anniversary show, accompanying Los Boricuas to the ring.

Having made quite a few connections while in Mexico, Dumas returned to the United States and took Kevin Quinn's advice to train more with him, this time in Chicago (at Ace Steel and Danny Dominion's Steel Domain wrestling school). After a week of intensive training, she felt that she'd had enough to start actually wrestling, and she got in touch with a contact who had an in at NWA Mid-Atlantic (in North Carolina). So on January 9, 1999, Amy Dumas finally had her first wrestling match as "Angelica" (inspired by the fact that she was also valeting for "The Fallen Angel" Christopher Daniels). And at her third NWA Mid-Atlantic show, she met Matt and Jeff Hardy, hitting it off with them fairly quickly and soon training under them as well (developing her high-flying style). The Hardys eventually invited Dumas to join them at a show for MCW, and she would add the promotion's affiliated wrestling school (Bone Breakers) in Baltimore to the ever-growing curriculum of her wrestling education. Fairly soon into Dumas's non-stop wrestling lifestyle in 1999, she was contacted by the ECW owner, who wanted to hire her. And so "Angelica" eventually became "Miss Congeniality," the valet for the ECW tag team Danny Doring and Roadkill, debuting in July 1999 on pay-per-view.

(She'd "technically" debuted in WWF a week before, though, as an extra. Like Ivory before her and Victoria after her, she first got her start in WWF as one of The Godfather's "hos.")

Early into her run in ECW, she got a chance to train at Dory Funk Jr.'s Funkin' Conservatory for a week, which led to Dory sending in a tape of her work to WWF. That September, she got into talks with WWF (to sign to a developmental contract), and by October, she was finishing her obligations (though she wasn't contracted) with ECW.

MATT HARDY ONCE DESCRIBED LITA AS "THE GIRL WHO'S COOL ENOUGH TO HANG WITH ANYBODY."

Debuting in February 2000, as "Lita," she was originally paired with Essa Rios as both his valet and girlfriend. Lita's hook, as it were, was her ability to hit the moonsault and hurricanrana, which would come in even more handy post-breakup, when she joined the Hardy Boyz (as Matt and Jeff's team was called) to form the face trio "Team X-Treme." This was where the "alternative" concept came in with regards to Lita. As the Hardy Boyz, Edge & Christian, and the Dudley Boyz were all sticking out in the WWF's tag team division because of their inventiveness and originality during their gimmick-based tag team matches, Lita also stuck out because of her willingness to get down and dirty with the guys, even if it led to dire (tables, ladders, and chairs-based) consequences. And she often did so with her thong sticking out from her baggy pants, which certainly seemed cool at the time. (This also got her into a feud with Right to Censor stable member Ivory at one point.) Even better for Lita's popularity was the love story brewing between herself and Matt Hardy, both on and off-screen—though the latter's conclusion would one day affect the former's status. By June 2000, Lita was in title contention for the WWF Women's Championship, which was held by the boss's daughter, Stephanie McMahon-Helmsley, at the time. She eventually won the championship for the first time in one of the biggest ways possible: in the main event of *RAW*, with The Rock as the Special Guest Referee. She would, however, eventually lose the championship because of that aforementioned willingness to get down and dirty, as Edge and Christian cost her the championship for interfering in their matches against the Hardy Boyz.

Despite being known for her high-risk in-ring style compared to the other Divas of the era, Lita suffered her most significant injury—a broken neck—while filming a guest spot on the FOX series *Dark Angel* in April 2002. Lita wouldn't return to in-ring action until September 2003, although she spent some of her time on the shelf as a commentator for *Sunday Night Heat*.

The counterpoint to Lita was, of course, Trish Stratus, the platinum blonde bombshell who supposedly wouldn't know "extreme" if it put her through the table. (Of course, during the Attitude Era, Stratus would end up going through the table, courtesy of the Dudley Boyz.) They would first become intertwined in the Hardy Boyz vs. T & A (Test and Albert) feud, before Lita won the Women's Championship for the first time. However, come the WCW/ECW invasion storyline in the summer of 2001, Lita and her rival would eventually have to learn how to co-exist—and co-exist they did. While it was always a joy to see Lita and Trish as allies, as the years went on, it was even better to see them as foes. Especially as the harder-edged babyface fire of Lita made the sleazy, anything's fair game heel approach of Trish hit more; where Lita could back up her side of things in the ring, Trish was able to run her mouth in a way that made the audience want to see Lita back up right into her. (In both women's final runs, the roles were reversed—with Lita as the heel and Trish as the face—which really mostly worked because the general excitement was just in the idea of both women facing off again.)

And another thing that seemingly completed Lita's character was her on-screen romantic relationship with Matt Hardy, perhaps because the audience realized it was art imitating life. During the spring of 2004, Lita was put into a storyline with Matt and Kane, in which Kane became obsessed with Lita and set out to destroy Matt to get him out of the way. This culminated in a "Till Death Do Us Part" match at SummerSlam 2004, with the stipulation being that Lita—who had become pregnant with Kane's baby after he'd kidnapped her earlier in the storyline—had to marry the winner. Kane won, leading to a marriage segment (aka "The Wedding From Hell") where Lita wore all black in protest—as opposed to heel Trish, who wedding crashed as the self-proclaimed "maid of honor" in white lingerie, to add insult to injury—and Matt Hardy tried (and failed) again to save his beloved. Continuing the way only a wrestling storyline could continue, Lita eventually suffered from a miscarriage . . . and joined forces with Kane in order to get revenge on the wrestler responsible for it. With Lita now on good terms with her husband/rapist, she also set her sights on Trish—who naturally mocked her for the miscarriage as well—resulting in Lita defeating her to win the Women's Championship for the second time . . . but nearly reinjuring her neck in one of their matches and tearing her left ACL in the rematch.

A couple of months after returning in the spring of 2005, a still betrothed (and seemingly happy) Lita turned heel for the first time in her WWE career, joining forces with Edge (and divorcing Kane, in order to storyline marry Edge). Around the same time, news of the real-life breakup between Lita and Matt Hardy had come out, with the reveal that Lita had cheated on him (though eventually it was revealed it was an emotional affair, not physical) with Edge (who was married at the time, as well as one of Matt's best friends). Even before the heel turn, while Lita was at ringside—or even in a segment with the heel Trish, who broke character at one point to defend her—fans who were aware started chanting "WE WANT MATT" and "YOU SCREWED MATT." What followed was a storyline that blurred the lines of reality and kayfabe, as Matt Hardy went from actually being fired from the company—for his unprofessional handling of the personal situation—to being rehired months later to continue the feud. As Matt would come after Lita and Edge both online and at WWE shows, referring to them both by their real names ("Amy" and "Adam"), it became difficult to tell what was and wasn't real. But one thing that was real was just how hated Lita became as a character by the WWE audience at the time.

After the Matt Hardy feud—and for the rest of her full-time WWE career—Lita remained with Edge, as the two flaunted their decadent, debaucherous relationship as main event heels, while Edge engaged in a WWE Championship feud with John Cena. After years of being an "alternative" Diva and fan favorite, Lita was now considered a sexpot and a jezebel (as commentary Jim Ross would call her), which made her retirement match in 2006, a few months after Trish's, arguably one of the most upsetting ways for someone as influential as Lita to go out. (Two words: "Ho Sale.") However, Lita has since dispelled rumors that she retired because of fan response and the constant slut-shaming (both on-screen and off-screen), instead admitting that she had felt like she'd done all she possibly could have done in WWE.

After about a year of retirement, Lita began making guest appearances on WWE TV, returning as a face (and friends once more with Trish Stratus), with barely a reminder of the hostility of the last couple of years she had in her full-time career there. Then in 2014, Lita was announced as one of the latest inductees in the WWE Hall of Fame, inducted of course by her real life "bestie," Trish Stratus. The following year, she worked as a trainer on the latest season of WWE's *Tough Enough*, eventually transitioning into a behind-the-scenes role as a writer and producer for WWE. After being such an influential part of the Divas Division during her own time on the roster, Lita got to be part of a new wave of influence in 2016, as she presented the new WWE Women's Championship at WrestleMania 32 (along with the dissolution of the "Divas" brand, in general). By the end of 2016, Lita no longer worked backstage full-time, but since then, she's served as a commentator for the inaugural WWE Mae Young Classic tournament, as well as a surprise entrant in the inaugural Women's Royal Rumble match.

Surprisingly, despite Lita's obvious popularity, the four times she held the WWF/WWE Women's Championship only added up to a 160-day combined reign. Her first run in 2000 lasted the longest—at 71 days—while her next two reigns both lasted 34 days, and her final reign was barely a short month (21 days). No one can say Lita's run in WWF/WWE was without memorable moments outside of the gold, as a championship reign said nothing about the fact that she was in the first-ever Divas main event of *RAW* (the title match against Stephanie) or the first-ever Divas Cage match (with Victoria) or her work with Trish Stratus, of course.

★ LUFISTO ★

YEARS ACTIVE: 1997–present

TRAINED BY: Eric Larochee · Patrick Lewis · Yves Millette · ARSION Dojo · Mariko Yoshida · AKINO

BILLED FROM: Montreal, Quebec · Tokyo, Japan · Benton, Ohio

ACCOMPLISHMENTS: 1x All-Star Wrestling Canadian Champion · 1x Alpha Omega Wrestling Women's Champion · 1x Association de Lutte Feminine (ALF) Champion · 2007 ALF Sherri Memorial Cup Tournament (with El Generico) · ALF Quebec Female Wrestling Hall of Fame · 1x Atomic Championship Wrestling Heavyweight Champion · 2008 CZW Best of the Best People's Choice · 1x CZW Iron Man Champion · 2005 Evolution of Wrestling Super 8 Women's Tournament Championship · 2007 IWA-MS Queen of the Deathmatch Tournament · 1x Inter-Championship Wrestling Olympic Champion · 2x ICW Provincial Champion · 2x ICW Tag Team Champion (1x with Sexy Julie, 1x with Mr. Saturday Night) · 2007 ICW Queen of the Deathmatches Tournament · 1x International Wrestling Cartel (IWC) Women's Champion · 1x JAPW Women's Champion · 1x Lucha Libre Feminil (LLF) Extreme Champion · 1x Lucha Promotion Original Pro-Lucha (POP) Women's Champion · 2010 nCw Femmes Fatales Championship Tournament · 2x (and inaugural) nCw International Femmes Fatales Champion · 1x North Shore Pro Wrestling Champion · #5 in 2014 PWI Female 50 · 1x Slam Angels Wrestling World Champion · 2006 Stranglehold Wrestling King of the Deathmatches · 1x SHINE Wrestling Champion · 1x Ultimate Wrestling Alliance Cruiserweight Champion · 1x WSU World Champion

AKA: Lucifer · Lucy Fer · Luscious Lucy · Precious Lucy · "First Lady of Hardcore" · "Super Hardcore Anime" · "Wounded Owl Ronin" · 1/2 of Les Femmes Fatales · 1/2 of Missionaries of Violence · 1/2 of Partners in Crime · 1/2 of Team PAWG (Perfect Athletes With Glutes) · member of C4 · member of Electric Avenue · 1/3 of Team Sailor Moon

NOTABLE MATCHES: The Canadians (LuFisto, Kevin Steen (c), El Generico, & Franky The Mobster) vs. The Forefathers of CZW (Eddie Kingston, Justice Pain, & Nick Gage) vs. BLKOUT (Joker, Robby Mireno, Ruckus, & Sabian) at CZW Trapped, in an All Out War Barbed Wire Cage Elimination match for the CZW Iron Man Championship (August 12, 2006) · LuFisto vs. Cheerleader Melissa at SHIMMER Volume 20 (July 5, 2008) · LuFisto vs. Amazing Kong at SHIMMER Volume 27, in a SHIMMER Championship #1 Contendership match (November 8, 2009) · LuFisto vs. Sara Del Rey (c) at JAPW 13th Anniversary Show - Night 2, for the JAPW Women's Championship (December 11, 2010) · LuFisto vs. MsChif (c) vs. Amazing Kong at SHIMMER Volume 28, in a 3-Way Elimination match for the SHIMMER Championship (November 8, 2009) · LuFisto vs. Mercedes Martinez at nCwnCw Femmes Fatales IX (July 7, 2012) · LuFisto vs. Ivelisse at SHINE 7 (February 22, 2013) · LuFisto vs. Kimber Lee at WWR Project XX (April 10, 2016)

★ If there's a "badass" requirement necessary in order to truly make it as a professional wrestler, well then LuFisto has fulfilled said requirement about 100 times over. Overcoming back problems, a knee injury, a stroke, ovarian cancer, and even the Ontario Athletics Commission (OAC), the 20-plus year veteran of women's professional wrestling—and even tougher, given the lack of stability in women's independent professional wrestling—has become synonymous with success in the face of adversity.

A Quebec native, she was just a 17-year-old girl named Genevieve Goulet when she began training to become a professional wrestler. Goulet originally watched professional wrestling when she was younger—in the Hulk Hogan/Ultimate Warrior Era—but eventually checked out of it when she was around eight years old. But four years later, a friend's suggestion—

during the slightly-edgier-but-still-not-full-tilt era of characters like Yokozuna and Undertaker—brought her back to the fold. And that's when she really saw women's wrestling for the first time, in the form of Alundra Blayze versus Bull Nakano (who became her favorite female wrestler, as The Undertaker had become her favorite male), which soon transformed into Goulet getting hooked on *joshi puroresu*, Japanese women's wrestling. The strength and intensity of the Japanese ladies stayed in Goulet's mind, becoming the calling card of her own style and character.

Goulet went through multiple ring name changes in her early career before settling on "LuFisto." As a valet for Steve Ramsey, she was "Precious Lucy." Then as a wrestler, she made her in-ring debut as "Lucifer" (her take on an Undertaker-esque character), changing it to "Lucy Fer" (an even more flamboyant version of the character) in 1998 during her first wrestling tour in the United States . . . and then to "Luscious Lucy" by the end of that year. (Also, in 2008, the indy wrestler better known as "Daffney" went by "Lucy Furr" for a time, speaking to the originality of the name's concept.) The following year, "Luscious Lucy" returned to "Precious Lucy," a name change decided by Quebec wrestling legend Jacques Rougeau Jr. (aka The Mountie), a mentor of Goulet's. She made her debut as Precious Lucy on Rougeau's first Lutte Internationale (International Wrestling) 2000 show—in February 1999, despite the "2000" in the promotion's name. However, "Precious Lucy" she was not: "He wanted me to be his 'Miss Elizabeth,' and I tried very hard but couldn't."

Of course, the reason she couldn't be that is because LuFisto has been credited with bringing her "hardcore," deathmatch style to places in professional wrestling where women weren't exactly doing that. The deathmatch style of wrestling is already a pretty niche one, but in the case of LuFisto, deathmatches and women wasn't just niche—it was a specialty. When she wrestled in Mexico in the summer of 2003 during her Precious Lucy days—after an aborted attempt in the summer of 2002, due to the wrestling company canceling shows—the promotion surrounding Lucy's debut was specifically surrounding her ability to bring her particular style of wrestling to Mexico. It was also the first time that Lucy had wrestled a hardcore/deathmatch against another female wrestler, typically only wrestling male wrestlers in this type of environment. In fact, she was doing intergender deathmatches long before most independent promotions were considering intergender matches of any type.

In the spring of 2002, Goulet was scheduled to participate in a Hardcore, Intergender Tag Team match (which was also the main event) in Ontario independent promotion Blood Sweat and Ears (aka BSE Pro Wrestling) when she suddenly got an email from the promoter informing her that he would no longer book her. Apparently a rival promoter had tipped the OAC off and filed a complaint that this match would be happening, breaking the regulation that banned intergender wrestling in the province. With BSE refusing to book her, that essentially prevented her from getting work anywhere else in Ontario. At first, Goulet admitted that she thought it was a joke, considering how long she had already been wrestling against men in Canada. After filing a complaint of her own with the Ontario Human Rights Commission (OHRC)—for the regulation being a form of gender discrimination—in 2006, LuFisto not only won her fight over their stance on intergender wrestling, she won a fight against the OAC's bureaucratic red tape when it came to professional wrestling in Ontario in general, allowing independent wrestling to thrive much more in the province.

And naturally, given her original inspiration to get into the professional wrestling game, it was in Japan in 2003 that Goulet finally chose and stuck with "LuFisto" as her ring name. Training at AtoZ (formerly ARSION) for two months under Mariko Yoshida and AKINO, LuFisto finally got to live her joshi dream. However, during the tour, LuFisto injured her left knee while training that September, bending it the opposite way. As it turns out, her left ACL had been destroyed over time—finally tearing pretty much a year after she'd already injured and lost her right ACL and meniscus. Upon returning to Canada in 2004, there was no more Lucy, only LuFisto there, too.

After her OAC defeat in 2006, LuFisto continued to make waves in the independent scene with her intergender wrestling. That summer, she debuted in CZW and defeated fellow Quebec native Kevin Steen (now known as Kevin Owens in WWE) for the CZW Iron Man Championship two months later, officially becoming the only woman to win a CZW championship. She also won the first deathmatch tournament in Canada—as if there was anyone more deserving—that fall (the Stranglehold Wrestling King of the Deathmatches tournament), defeating deathmatch legend Necro Butcher in the final round. At the end of the year, she also became the first woman to wrestle in CZW's infamous Cage of Death match.

Despite her intergender leanings, LuFisto still maintained her status as an equal opportunity asskicker, debuting in SHIMMER as well in 2006. And after an early possible retirement scare (due to back issues), 2007 eventually saw LuFisto win IWA-MS's Queen of the Deathmatch Tournament. She also had a hand in bringing forth nCw Femmes Fatales in 2009, an all-female offshoot of Quebec's nCw independent promotion. A little over a year later though, post-match, a 30-year-old LuFisto suffered a stroke. (In a statement to fans, LuFisto explained how her family had a very bad history of heart disease.) While that might have been enough to get any other wrestler to retire, LuFisto was back in action two months later and went on to become the inaugural nCw International Femmes Fatales Champion by the end of the year.

However, for all of her accomplishments and coming back from the other side of adversity, LuFisto isn't afraid to admit the mental wear and tear that goes into this line of work. In an editorial, she wrote about an intergender wrestling match (between Kimber Lee and Chris Dickinson) that went viral and became a topic of controversy in 2015 and got honest about her thought process behind wrestling men. "A lot of female wrestlers, including myself, feel that they need to push the limits to be accepted in this men's world. We want to be taken seriously, and we want people to see us as equals to our male colleagues. We will do crazy things only to prove that we are worth as much and that we are not the weaker sex. All this in the hope to be seen as a wrestler/worker . . . Not someone who's 'good for a girl.'" LuFisto went on to admit that she personally believed her own 18 years of hard work, however, got her absolutely "nowhere" and that the crazy things she became known for are most likely to blame for not getting signed by WWE. In fact, LuFisto even compared herself to Mickey Rourke's tragic Randy the Ram character from *The Wrestler*.

While LuFisto never actually mentioned WWE by name in the editorial, it was clear that was what she was referring to, as a run there is the one thing that's truly eluded her in her professional wrestling career. In 2015, LuFisto auditioned for a season of WWE's *Tough Enough*, but she didn't end up making it on the show—with the implication being that she was too "experienced," as she was 35 at the time. As a vocal critic of WWF/WWE's women's division during the lowest points of its Divas Division, LuFisto has been around long enough to see the transformation on-screen of the Divas Revolution to the Women's Evolution in WWE (with women now being referred to as "Superstars" like their male counterparts, getting to main event shows, and with more focus being put on in-ring ability). While she admitted in the editorial that she was happy for her colleagues and peers who did get a chance at making it to WWE, she was honest enough to also admit that she still felt like a failure in comparison and like someone who—as an indy wrestler—would end up not being remembered.

On her 38th birthday, LuFisto announced that she had been diagnosed with cervical cancer, just one more thing in an apparent string of bad luck in her life. But after a successful surgery a couple months later, she was able to be cleared of the cancer. During all of this, she still maintained a healthy wrestling schedule, in SHINE, SHIMMER, wXw (in Germany), Beyond Wrestling, and more. While LuFisto might think she won't be remembered when all is said and done, her work and ability to come back from real-life issues says otherwise.

★ LUNA VACHON ★

YEARS ACTIVE: 1985–2007

TRAINED BY: Vivian Vachon · Paul Vachon · The Fabulous Moolah

BILLED FROM: Montreal, Quebec, Canada · "The Other Side of Darkness"

ACCOMPLISHMENTS: 1x American Wrestling Federation Women's Champion · 2009 Cauliflower Alley Club Women's Wrestling Award · 1x Great Lakes Championship Wrestling (GLCW) Ladies Champion · 1x Ladies Major League Wrestling (LMLW) World Champion · 2x POWW Tag Team Champion (with Hot Rod Andie) · 1x Sunshine Wrestling Federation (SWF) Ladies' Champion · #306 on 1995 PWI

500 · 1x USWA Women's Champion · 1x Wild Women of Wrestling (WWOW) Television Champion · WSU Hall of Fame Class of 2011

AKA: Trudy Herd · Luna · Princess Luna · Angelle Vachon · Angel Baby · member of The Oddities · member of the Army of Darkness · 1/2 of the Daughters of Darkness · member of the Satanists · member Raven's Nest · "Tick" · "Luna-tic"

NOTABLE MATCHES: Luna Vachon vs. Madusa Miceli at TWA Summer Sizzler II (August 3, 1991) · Luna Vachon & Cactus Jack vs. Madusa Miceli & Eddie Gilbert at TWA Autumn Armageddon II, in a Hair vs. Hair Mixed Tag Team match (September 21, 1991) · Luna Vachon & Tommy Dreamer vs. Raven & Stevie Richards (c) (with Beulah McGillicutty) at ECW Hardcore Heaven 1995, in an ECW World Tag Team Championship match (July 1, 1995) · Luna & Goldust vs. Sable & Marc Mero at WrestleMania XIV, in an Intergender Tag Team match (March 29, 1998) · Luna Vachon vs. Jessicka Havok at CAPW A Night of Legends, in a Hardcore match (August 5, 2007)

⭐ Growing up in a wrestling family—the adopted daughter of Paul "Butcher" Vachon and niece of "Mad Dog" Vachon—Gertrude "Luna Vachon" Wilkerson (her birth father's surname) wanted nothing more than to carry on her family's legacy. Of course, as a woman, her family tried to dissuade her from joining the lifestyle, both because of the mistreatment of women in the industry and the lack of respect. They did everything they could to talk her out of it—even enlisting her godfather, Andre the Giant, to try and scare her straight when she was 12—but she was set in her way. As she told Andre, when he tried to explain that wrestling wasn't good for women: "I'm going to make it different for women."

While she began training at age 16 (under her aunt, Vivian Vachon, and The Fabulous Moolah), it wasn't until she was in her early 20s that she officially began her wrestling career (after getting away from Moolah's 25 percent cut of her pay). The introduction of "Luna Vachon" was an interesting one, especially for that time period in wrestling. Debuting in NWA Championship Wrestling from Florida (CWF) as "Trudy Herd," a mild-mannered interviewer, her Luna-ness was awoken by the evil Kevin Sullivan and

his abuse toward her. As a result of Sullivan's influence, Trudy became the more familiar Luna, with half of her head shaved (the rest eventually shaved early on in her long-lasting feud with Madusa Miceli), body paint, and a sneer that could frighten a small child. Simply put, Luna Vachon was heavy metal personified.

After all that time of her father trying to stop her from being a wrestler, he'd eventually act as her manager when she wrestled in Japan. In the early years of her career, Luna went just about everywhere, both as a wrestler and a manager—from CWF to AWA to TWA and more. By 1992, there was seemingly only one place she had left to go: WWF.

In 1993, Luna made it to the bright lights of the WWF—debuting at WrestleMania IX—replacing Sensational Sherri as Shawn Michaels's manager during his feud with Tatanka.

This in turn began a Luna/Sherri feud, which ended that same summer when Sherri was released from the WWF. Luna then began an on-screen romance with Bam Bam Bigelow—which eventually led to a bizarre love triangle, once Bastion Booger joined the storyline. But toward the end of 1993, Luna had her sights set on championship gold, with Alundra Blayze (aka Luna's longtime rival, Madusa Miceli) leading the charge of the WWF's newly revitalized women's division as the WWF Women's Championship. Luna came up short in her many attempts to defeat Blayze for the championship in 1994, but she was able to send in a ringer—in the form of Japanese wrestler Bull Nakano—to get the job done. However, soon after Nakano became champion, Luna left WWF for the independent scene and WWF's competition in the form of ECW and WCW. (For the latter—WCW—in 1997, Luna was basically plagued with a case of déjà vu, as she continued to lose every match she had with Madusa.)

> LUNA TOLD ANDRE THE GIANT, WHEN HE TRIED TO EXPLAIN THAT WRESTLING WASN'T GOOD FOR WOMEN: "I'M GOING TO MAKE IT DIFFERENT FOR WOMEN."

Upon returning to WWF in 1997, Luna managed Goldust, eventually leading to a feud between Goldust/Luna and Marc Mero/Sable—one which extended outside the ring in the case of the women. The fact that Luna didn't look like Sable or the other WWF Divas (or even women in WCW) was part of her appeal, part of what made her stand out. In her own words: "I was in *Playboy* because I was a weirdo and *Hustler* because I was a nutcase." However, with the rise of the Attitude Era, WWF was going with Sable, who was in *Playboy* because she was the blonde

bombshell. And while Luna had worked so hard to prove herself as tough and someone who belongs in the wrestling business, she was tasked with making someone who didn't have to do any of that look good. As they prepared for their WrestleMania XIV Tag Team match, Luna was reportedly told not to hurt Sable (who was about to shoot her *Playboy* spread), an essentially untrained wrestler that wouldn't take bumps in the ring. According to Luna back in 2008, it was the only time in her entire career that she had to choreograph a wrestling match.

It's hard to believe, but Luna Vachon was never the WWF Women's Champion. And it was something that, unfortunately, ate at her. While it's easy to call professional wrestling "fake"—it is predetermined 99 percent of the time, after all—Luna had arguably done everything she was supposed to in order to at least get one run with the championship. Especially in the case of her work with Sable: "I was scheduled to win the title three times. Once I was caught smoking a cigarette in front of the fans, and the other two occasions Sable forgot the belt in her hotel room. She did it on purpose, I'm positive about that."

This was something that weighed heavily on Luna, and she eventually missed out on another title shot—though it wouldn't have guaranteed a win—as she got suspended in early 1999 for a backstage fight with Sable. She wouldn't return until six months later, but even after returning, the Women's Championship eluded her—and the women's division only got more and more sexualized. The next year, after another backstage situation, Luna was released from the WWF for good.

Luna wrestled and managed on the independent scene for a few more years, retiring in 2007. Two years later, she was honored by the Cauliflower Alley Club with their Ladies Wrestling Award for lifetime achievement. However, Luna Vachon's story is a wrestling story with an unhappy end. While Luna had gone to WWE-sponsored rehab on multiple occasions, in August 2010, she was found in her Florida home dead from a drug overdose. Her ashes were scattered at Andre the Giant's North Carolina ranch, the same place his ashes were scattered.

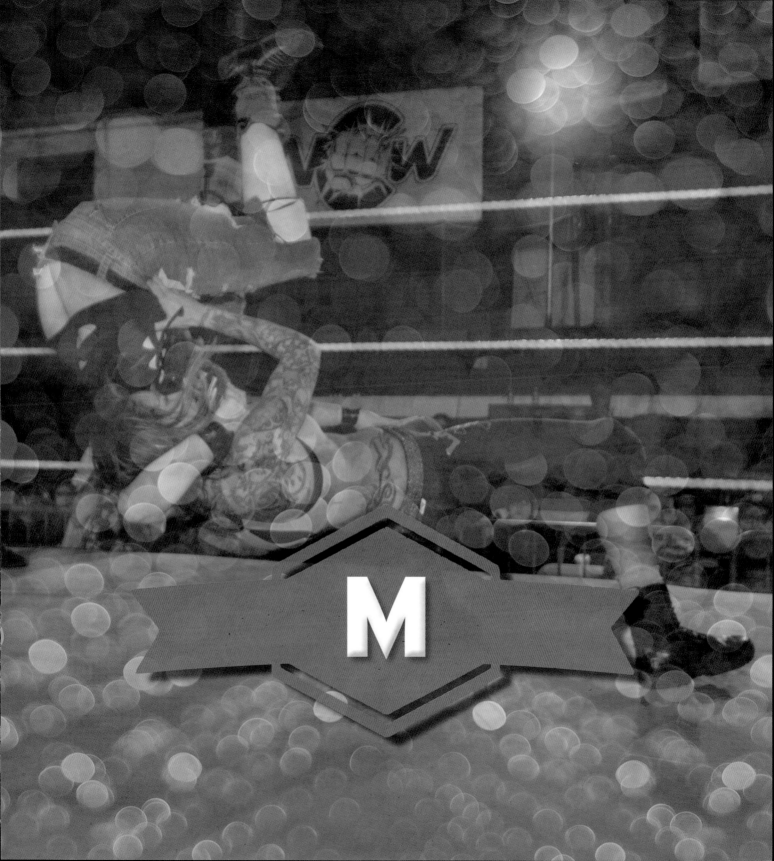

★ MAE YOUNG ★

YEARS ACTIVE: 1939–2010

TRAINED BY: Mildred Burke

BILLED FROM: Sand Springs, Oklahoma

ACCOMPLISHMENTS: 1x Championship Wrestling From Florida NWA Florida Women's Champion · 1x (and inaugural) NWA United States Women's Champion · 1x NWA Women's World Tag Team Champion (with Ella Waldek) · Professional Wrestling Hall of Fame Class of 2004 · 1x WWE Miss Royal Rumble · WWE Hall of Fame Class of 2008 · 2010 Slammy Award for Knucklehead Moment of the Year

AKA: Marie Young · Johnnie Mae Young · "The Queen" · "The Matriarch of the Mat" · "The Original Diva" · Miss May Young · "Queen of the Canvas" · "The First Diva" · The Great Mae Young · Mae the Queen · Madame X · Mrs. Stasiak

NOTABLE MATCHES: Mae Young vs. The Fabulous Moolah (c) at WWF *SmackDown*, for the WWF Women's Championship (October 21, 1999) · Mae Young vs. LayCool (Layla & Michelle McCool) at WWE *Monday Night RAW* "Old School," in a Falls Count Anywhere Two-On-One Handicap match (November 15, 2010)

★ In a world where it's easy to find a wrestler (especially a female wrestler) who had a problem with The Fabulous Moolah, the same can't be said about Mae Young, her trainer and oldest friend. A legitimate pioneer of women's professional wrestling—alongside her trainer, Mildred Burke—Mae Young was instrumental in bringing popularity to the sport during and after World War II (when they wrestled in post-war Japan). Prior to becoming a professional wrestler, Mae Young was the type of person who wrestled amateur style first, getting her start on the boys' high school wrestling team. While attending a wrestling show in Tulsa, 15-year-old Mae Young attempted to challenge the Women's

Champion, Mildred Burke . . . and ended up beating up Burke's opponent instead (as a tryout of sorts), drawing the attention of Billy Wolfe, Burke's husband/manager. Two years later, Mae was off to become a professional wrestler. (There's been some discrepancy about just when Mae actually began wrestling and how old she was, though it was most likely 1941 and age 18, respectively.)

Mae Young spent most of her early career wrestling against Burke, before moving on to other competition in the form of June Byers and Mae Weston. Together with Burke, though, Mae Young made wrestling more accessible for women in and outside of the United States. Unfortunately, most of the footage of Mae Young's contribution to professional wrestling—outside of her twilight years in WWF/WWE, as the comedic old woman—is only left in the form of newsreel footage and clips, no full matches.

Which is part of the reason why it's so difficult to piece together the full picture of her life as a wrestling pioneer—though the 2004 documentary *Lipstick and Dynamite, Piss and Vinegar: The First Ladies of Wrestling* helped bring more understanding to the struggles at the time. However, one aspect of her career that's fully documented is her late-in-life run in the WWF/WWE.

At the age of 76, Mae Young debuted in WWF alongside the returning Fabulous Moolah (who Mae had helped get hired by WWF in the first place, during the Vince Sr. days) at the height of the Attitude Era. During the appearance, Moolah was hit by Jeff Jarrett with a guitar shot to the head—and when Mae tried to help, she ended up being put into a figure-four leg lock. From that point on, Mae and Moolah appeared as a comedic tandem, taking bumps (at 77 years old, Mae took multiple powerbombs through tables, courtesy of Bubba Ray Dudley), and being sexually suggestive—honestly, they were a couple of dirty old women. In 2000, Mae Young explained the method to her madness, at least in terms of the crazy bumps she and Moolah would take during this time: "I have never thought of my age as any barrier, because I feel I can do anything these 15- and 16-year-old kids can do." The peak of this insanity was Mae Young's storyline with "Sexual Chocolate" Mark Henry, a romantic storyline which resulted in Henry impregnating the experienced Mae Young. The story culminated in Mae Young giving birth to their child . . . a rubber hand. As for the explanation, strangely enough, the Mae Young/birth-to-a-hand storyline could have been so much more. . . . Well, it could have been different, but not necessarily better. According to Jerry "The King" Lawler:

At the production meeting that morning, Vince was going over that part of the show, but he said Mae Young was going to give birth to a douche bag, and all the women in the room were offended. They said he was going to turn off all the women watching. They talked him out of it, even though no one was going to say "douche bag" on the air. They sat there and wondered what she could give birth to. Somehow, someone came up with an idea that I think was one of the worst they've ever had and just didn't make any sense. So on the air, she gave birth to a hand, a big old rubber hand.

And despite no expectations for a follow-up to the storyline, WWE eventually provided one 12 years later on the 1000th episode of *RAW*, as Mae Young introduced the hand (a man in a hand costume), all grown up.

While Mae Young made most of her WWE appearances with Moolah, the last time they appeared together was at SummerSlam 2007, just a couple of months before Moolah's passing. The following year, Mae was inducted into the WWE Hall of Fame and made a handful more appearances up until the spring of 2013. On January 14, 2014, Mae Young passed away in the South Carolina home she had once shared with Moolah (from 1991 all the way to Moolah's passing). Still, her memory and influence lives on. In the summer of 2017, WWE aired the Mae Young Classic, a tournament for 32 female wrestlers from all around the world, serving as a reminder of what Mae Young fought for in her prime.

★ MADISON EAGLES ★

YEARS ACTIVE: 2001–present

TRAINED BY: International Wrestling Australia (IWA) · OVW · CHIKARA Wrestle Factory · Claudio Castagnoli · Mike Quackenbush · ROH Wrestling Academy

BILLED FROM: Sydney, Australia

ACCOMPLISHMENTS: #1 in 2011 PWI Female 50 · 4x International Wrestling Australia Women's Champion · 1x New Horizons Pro Wrestling (NHPW) IndyGurlz Australia Champion · 2016 NHPW Global Conflict Shield Tournament · 2018 NHPW Global Conflict Shield Tournament · 1x (and inaugural) Pacific Pro Wrestling Pacific

Women's Champion · 1x PWA Tag Team Champion (with Mick Moretti) · 1x PWWA Champion · 2x SHIMMER Champion

AKA: 1/2 of Green Nation · 1/3 of The Pink Ladies · 1/2 of The Worst Best Friends · member of 5 Star Mafia · member of The Four Nations · "The Punisher" · "The Master of Wrestling"

NOTABLE MATCHES: Madison Eagles vs. MsChif (c) at SHIMMER Volume 31, for the SHIMMER Championship (April 11, 2010) · Madison Eagles vs. Kellie Skater at PWA Ladies Show Last Woman Standing, in a Last Woman Standing Tournament Finals No Disqualification match (July 3, 2010) · Madison Eagles vs. Sara Del Rey at CHIKARA Clutch of Doom (February 20, 2011) · Madison Eagles (c) vs. Mercedes Martinez at SHIMMER Volume 37, for the SHIMMER Championship (March 26, 2011) · Madison Eagles (c) vs. Jessie McKay vs. Nicole Matthews at PWWA, in a 3-Way match for the SHIMMER Championship (September 3, 2011) · Madison Eagles vs. Nicole Matthews at SHIMMER Volume 58 (October 19, 2013) · Madison Eagles vs. Ivelisse (c) at SHINE 22, for the SHINE Championship (October 10, 2014) · Madison Eagles (c) (SHIMMER) vs. Taylor Made (c) (SHINE) vs. Allysin Kay (TNA) vs. Ivelisse (with Amanda Carolina Rodriguez) at SHINE 35, in a 4-Way match for the SHINE Championship/SHIMMER Championship/TNA Knockouts Championship (June 17, 2016)

⭐ Despite growing up a dancer, gymnast, diver, and surfer, when Aussie Alex Ford saw her first wrestling match on TV, she knew it was the sport she wanted to make her life—contact and all. She had just turned 17 years old, and the combination of acting and sports hooked her right away. So she immediately signed up for wrestling school. Standing at 6 foot, 1 inch (meaning "definitely taller than Nicole Matthews"), Ford's original role was as a "bodyguard" for A.J. Freely, but she made her in-ring debut as "Madison Eagles" in November that same year. By early 2003, she'd already had a United States wrestling tour under her belt, competing for CAPW, USA Pro Wrestling, and Heartland Wrestling Association (HWA). During this tour, she attended an OVW training camp—when OVW was still WWE developmental—impressing enough that she was

invited to try out later that year, when WWE came to Australia. However, she wasn't signed.

Madison Eagles is also a star maker, having a hand in the training of WWE Superstars Billie Kay and Peyton Royce (aka The IIconics), as well as indy standouts like Shazza McKenzie. In 2007, she and her then-husband (known as "Ryan Eagles") founded the independent promotion/wrestling school that would become known as PWA Australia, as well as the all-women's offshoot PWWA. Upon beginning wrestling in SHIMMER in 2008, Eagles brought along PWA trainee Jessie McKay (aka WWE's Billie Kay) as her tag team partner, but Eagles was clearly destined for singles success. In April 2010, Madison became the third-ever SHIMMER Champion, defeating MsChif at Volume 31 and holding the championship for 539 days. She was also the first SHIMMER Champion to defend the championship outside of the United States, taking it to PWWA, in a match against Jessie McKay and Nicole Matthews. The year 2011 saw Eagles be named #1 on the PWI Female 50, the first time an

independent wrestler (or anyone outside of the "major leagues" of WWE or TNA) had topped the list. Unfortunately, Eagles didn't get to follow up that momentum going into 2012, as she suffered a career-threatening knee injury that October after jumping off the ropes. Despite fears of possible retirement, Eagles returned to the ring in January 2013, ready to get back to the top.

It was during this return that Madison Eagles developed a friendship-turned-bitter rivalry with Nicole Matthews (of the Canadian NINJAs—National International Nation of Jalpeño Awesomeness—tag team) in SHIMMER. What began as a friendly competition—with Matthews answering an open challenge from the former champ, leading to a 20-minute time limit draw at SHIMMER Volume 58—turned into one of determination to prove which one of the so-called Worst Best Friends was the better woman (and better friend). Eventually, for Matthews, it became even less about that and more about winning (with the help of her Canadian NINJAs partner, Portia Perez), leading to her burning Eagles with a fireball to the face at Volume 67, during a Four-Way Elimination match for the championship. The Worst Best Friends were officially friends no more. Then in 2015, Eagles became a two-time SHIMMER Champion—at Volume 77, during SHIMMER's 10th anniversary weekend—finally ending her rival Nicole Matthews's reign for a 260-day reign of her own. (To prove just how much the two women wanted to hurt each other, at one point early on during the match, Madison Eagles retrieved Kay Lee Ray from the backstage area . . . and threw her at Matthews, like a makeshift weapon.)

In her 17-year career, Madison Eagles has wrestled all over the world, in many of the top independent promotions—ROH, CHIKARA, CZW, nCw Femme Fatales, SHINE, STARDOM—proving her dominance everywhere she goes. Back in 2012 (when she was on the shelf with her knee that was "pretty much shot"), when asked what her goals in professional wrestling were, Eagles had this to say: "I am going to be selfish and say I want everything. I want to be an even better performer and in better shape as an athlete, as well as a lot more international travel."

★ MANAMI TOYOTA ★

YEARS ACTIVE: 1987–2017

TRAINED BY: AJW Dojo · Jaguar Yokota

BILLED FROM: Masuda, Japan

ACCOMPLISHMENTS: 1x AJW Champion · 2x AJW All Pacific Champion · 1x IWA World Women's Champion · 4x WWWA World Single Champion · 3x WWWA World Tag Team Champion (2x with Toshiyo Yamada, 1x with Mima Shomida) · 1990 AJW Japan Grand Prix · 1995 AJW Japan Grand Prix winner · 1998 AJW Japan Grand Prix · 1999 AJW Japan Grand Prix · 1993 AJW Tag League the Best (with Akira Hokuto) · 1994 AJW Tag League the Best (with Takako Inoue) · 1996 AJW Tag League the Best (with Rie Tamada) · 1999 AJW Tag League the Best (with Miho Wakizawa) · 2001 AJW Tag League the Best (with Yumiko Hotta) · 1x AAAW Single Champion · 1x AAAW Tag Team Champion (with Carlos Amano) · 1x Ice Ribbon Triangle Ribbon Champion · 1x JWP Openweight Champion · 1x JWP Tag Team Champion (with Kaoru Ito) · 1x OZ Academy Openweight Champion · 2x OZ Academy Tag Team Champion (with Carlos Amano) · 1x Universal Wrestling Association (UWA) World Women's Tag Team Champion (with Toshiyo Yamada) · 1x World Woman Pro-Wrestling Diana (WWWD) World Single Champion · 1993 Wrestling Observer Newsletter Match of the Year (with Toshiyo Yamada vs. Dynamite Kansai & Mayumi Ozaki, on April 1) · 1995 Wrestling Observer Newsletter Match of the Year (vs. Kyoko Inoue, on May 7) · 1995 Wrestling Observer Newsletter Most Outstanding Wrestler · 1995 Wrestling Observer Newsletter Readers' Favorite Wrestler · Wrestling Observer Newsletter Hall of Fame Class of 2002

AKA: "Manamana" · "The Flying Angel" · 1/2 of the Tokyo Sweethearts

NOTABLE MATCHES: Manami Toyota & Esther Moreno vs. Jungle Jack (Aja Kong & Bison Kimura) at AJW (April 29, 1991) · Manami Toyota (c) vs. Toshiyo Yamada at AJW Mid Summer Typhoon, in a Hair vs. Hair match for the IWA World Championship (August 15, 1992) · Manami Toyota & Toshiyo Yamada (c) vs. Dynamite

Kansai & Mayumi Ozaki at AJW Dream Slam 2, in a 2 Out of 3 Falls match for the WWWA Tag Team Championship (April 11, 1993) · Manami Toyota & Toshiyo Yamada vs. Dynamite Kansai & Mayumi Ozaki (c) at AJW St. Battle Final 1993, for the WWWA Tag Team Championship (December 6, 1993) · Manami Toyota & Akira Hokuto vs. Kyokoo Inoue & Toshiyo Yamada at AJW Tag League the Best 1993 – Night 28, in a Tag League the Best match (December 10, 1993) · Manami Toyota & Akira Hokuto vs. Kyokoo Inoue & Toshiyo Yamada at AJW Tag League the Best 1993 – Night 28, in a Tag League the Best Finals match (December 10, 1993) · Manami Toyota vs. Aja Kong at AJW Doumu Super Woman Great War ~ Big Egg Wrestling Universe, in a V*TOP Five Star Tournament First Round match (November 20, 1994) · Manami Toyota (c) vs. Kyoko Inoue at AJW G*Top 2nd, for the WWWA World Championship (May 7, 1995) · Manami Toyota (c) vs. Aja Kong at AJW, for the WWWA World Championship (June 27, 1995) · Manami Toyota & Sakie Hasegawa vs. Double Inoue (Kyoko Inoue & Takako Inoue) (c) at AJW WWWA Champions Night, in a 2 Out of 3 Falls match for the WWWA Tag Team Championship (August 30, 1995) · Manami Toyota vs. Akira Hokuto at AJW Destiny (September 2, 1995) · Manami Toyota vs. Chigusa Nagayo (c) at AJW 30th Anniversary Show, for the AAAW Championship (November 29, 1998) · Manami Toyota & Mike Quackenbush vs. BDK (Sara Del Rey & Claudio Castagnoli) at CHIKARA Through Savage Progress Cuts The Jungle Line (September 19, 2010) · Manami Toyota, Jigsaw, & Mike Quackenbush vs. Team SENDAI Girls' (Meiko Satomura, DASH Chisako, & Sendai Sachiko) at CHIKARA King of Trios 2012 – Night 2, in a King of Trios Quarterfinals match (September 15, 2012)

⭐ Breaking out into wrestling during the Japanese joshi boom of the '80s, Manami Toyota naturally debuted as a professional wrestler when she was just 16 years old. A graduate of the AJW Dojo, that also meant she most likely had 10 more years to go before she was forced to retire. However, there was no way anyone was going to tell Manami Toyota to retire; and if they did, they'd surely regret preventing the world from witnessing someone who is arguably the greatest female wrestler of all time.

(There's also been plenty of argument that she's the greatest wrestler of all time, period. But in 2009, there was at least a Wrestling Observer Newsletter vote that agreed on the "female wrestler" part.)

While it's difficult to determine just which year was Manami's peak year, she certainly had a breakout year as early as her second year in the business. Her big break came in that year, wrestling a preliminary tag team match on AJW's first annual Wrestlemarinpiad show with Mima Shimoda (they were the Tokyo Sweethearts) that stole the show . . . despite not even officially being on the show. A few months later, Manami would

be the AJW Champion, vacating it a month before she won the AJW All Pacific Championship for the first time.

From 1991 to 1995, Manami Toyota received at least one 5 Star match a year (generally the highest of his ranking) from Dave Meltzer and his Wrestling Observer Newsletter, achieving 175 Star matches in total. That's the most of any female wrestler and fourth of all wrestlers Meltzer has had the chance to grade. With feuds against Toshiyo Yamada (perhaps both her greatest rival and ally, sharing a good amount of those 5 Star matches), Kyoko Inoue, Aja Kong, Akira Hokuto (also in the greatest rival/greatest ally conversation)—and this doesn't even begin to scratch the surface on her "one-time-only" match against Chigusa Nagayo in 1998—Manami Toyota's career is so epic that it requires its own book, not just a profile here.

Already with such an impressive wrestling career under her belt, Toyota made her United States wrestling debut in 2010, for CHIKARA. In fact, after that September, the only promotion Toyota wrestled for in the States was CHIKARA. Her last U.S. match was in September 2012, at the final night of that year's CHIKARA's King of Trios tournament. And when she finally returned to Japan, it was time to celebrate her 25th anniversary as a wrestler.

Five years later, on November 3, 2017, Manami Toyota officially called her wrestling career quits after 30 years, with her retirement ceremony ("Retirement To The Universe") being produced by joshi promotion OZ Academy. The ceremony featured a gauntlet of matches (singles, Handicap, and even intergender), set to a one-minute time limit, between Toyota and various challengers (50 matches in total . . . which is less traditional). To complete the 50 one-minute matches, she competed in a three-match series with her protégé, Tsukasa Fujimoto; Toyota won the first two matches, but Fujimoto was successful in the third, signaling the official passing of the torch.

★ MARIA KANELLIS ★

YEARS ACTIVE: 2004–present

TRAINED BY: Dave "Fit" Finlay · OVW

BILLED FROM: Chicago, Illinois

ACCOMPLISHMENTS: #21 in 2008 PWI Female 50 · 2009 Slammy Award for Diva of the Year · 2x FWE Women's Champion · 1x TNA Knockouts Champion

AKA: Maria · "The First Lady of ROH" · "The First Lady of Professional Wrestling" · member of The Kingdom · member of The Lady Squad · Maria Kanellis-Bennett

NOTABLE MATCHES: Maria vs. Santino Marella at WWE *Monday Night RAW*, in a No Disqualification match (March 31, 2008) · The Kingdom (Maria Kanellis-Bennett, Mike Bennett, & Matt Taven) vs. Bullet Club (Doc Gallows & Karl Anderson, & Amber Gallows) at NJPW Wrestling Dontaku 2015, in a Six-Person Intergender Tag Team match (May 3, 2015) · Maria Kanellis-Bennett vs. Gail Kim vs. Jade vs. Marti Bell vs. Rebel vs. Velvet Sky at TNA Impact Wrestling, in a Ladder match for Leader of the Knockouts (April 19, 2016) · Maria Kanellis-Bennett vs. Allie (c) at TNA Impact Wrestling, for the TNA Knockouts Championship (September 1, 2016) · Maria Kanellis-Bennett (c) vs. Gail Kim at TNA Bound For Glory 2016, for the TNA Knockouts Championship (October 2, 2016)

★ Prior to her wrestling career, Maria Kanellis competed in beauty pageants. So it perhaps came as no surprise when she entered the 2004 WWE Diva Search, especially as she'd been a fan of professional wrestling growing up. In fact, Maria learned about the Diva Search in the first place while watching *WWE RAW*, though the Diva Search certainly didn't bank as much on class as beauty pageants. (It was during this particular Search where the infamous—and never again replicated—"Diss The Diva" segment occurred.) While Maria only placed fifth in the competition, WWE eventually signed her to a contract . . . after a bit of persistence:

"I've been told no so many times in life that it's one of my favorite words, because I like to prove people wrong. Being eliminated was just great motivation for me; I was told, 'No, [you'll] never model,' 'No, you'll never do something on TV.' No this, no that. And when they eliminated me, I called every single week to the WWE and said, "Let me try and do this." . . . I got a call back from Talent Relations and they said, 'What do you think about going to [OVW] and learning how to wrestle?' And I responded, 'I'll start driving now!'"

"I LIKE TO PROVE PEOPLE WRONG. BEING ELIMINATED WAS JUST GREAT MOTIVATION FOR ME."

Post-Diva Search, Maria became known to WWE audiences as RAW's ditzy, but well-meaning, backstage interviewer. As WWE would describe her, she "wasn't afraid to ask any question, from the hard-hitting to the quirkily obvious." Her interviewer job would be something she held in conjunction with her in-ring career; though because of her "innocent" gimmick, when she wasn't just part of a multi-woman gimmick match, Maria was mostly used as fodder to get heels over. For example, after upsetting Eric Bischoff during an interview (asking him if he thought he would be fired), Bischoff retaliated by putting her into a match against Kurt Angle. In the summer of 2007, Maria had a romantic storyline with comedic wrestler Santino Marella, and again, Maria's gimmick as an innocent character came into play: The relationship became abusive, with Marella criticizing Maria for posing in *Playboy* (she was actually the last active Diva to pose for the magazine), and Maria eventually breaking up with (and wrestling) him.

In 2008, Maria was drafted to SmackDown from RAW, where she ended up actually having a championship feud against Divas Champion Michelle McCool (and eventually, McCool's tag team parter Layla). After losing the feud, Maria began another on-screen romance—this time with Dolph Ziggler—again factoring in the naïve face character of Maria with a heel (this time, an unfaithful one). Following this storyline, Maria took a hiatus from WWE to film a season of NBC's *The Celebrity Apprentice*. Then, upon returning—despite arguably not being a top Diva star—Maria won the 2009 Slammy Award for Diva of the Year. Yet despite her popularity among WWE fans, a couple of months later, Maria was released from her WWE contract. Maria made sure to let her fans know on social media that she had not requested said release, and in later interviews she admitted she was "caught off guard" by the decision. However, she also admitted that WWE might have thought she wasn't as committed to wrestling, especially as she had publicized wanting to do more outside of the company (like a music career).

After almost two years away from the spotlight, Maria's post-WWE career became a proper reinvention. Returning to wrestling at ROH's Final Battle pay-per-view in December 2011, she accompanied her real-life boyfriend, Mike Bennett, to the ring for his Television Championship title match. There, the woman who was once known for playing a lovable airhead was now known as a devilish mastermind, one who could get heat just by uttering a few words. As Maria helped Mike win the championship, she became a fixture in ROH and part of his act, officially proclaiming that she was "The First Lady of ROH." While plenty of other female wrestlers tried to neutralize Maria during Mike's feuds—women like Sara Del Rey, Lisa Maria Varon, and ODB—somehow, she would only get brasher. And it reached an all-time high when in 2014 she and Mike joined ROH Champion Adam Cole's stable The Kingdom (alongside Matt Hardy and, eventually, Matt Taven). The following year, she, Mike, and Taven debuted in New Japan Pro Wrestling (NJPW), as the guys became the IWGP Tag Team Champions. (And surprisingly, they were cheered in Japan, despite being huge heels in the States.) Maria of course interfered in their matches, but it was The Kingdom's tag team matches against Bullet Club members Doc Gallows and Karl Anderson where she was especially integral, as Maria's presence at ringside literally mesmerized Anderson every time he saw her.

At the end of 2015, Maria and Mike—who had gotten married in the fall of 2014—left ROH for Impact Wrestling. As Mike became "The Miracle" Mike Bennett, Maria (as Maria Kanellis-Bennett) proclaimed herself "The First Lady of Professional Wrestling" and the new leader of the Knockouts Division. This led to a feud with Gail Kim—arguably the definitive Knockout—in which Maria did everything she could to achieve power without actually wrestling (especially wrestling Gail Kim). However, Maria eventually won a Ladder match to become the new Knockouts Commissioner—giving her actual power, in storyline—and she soon hired new Knockout Allie to be her personal assistant. As Maria created her cabinet as Commissioner—The Lady Squad, including muscle Sienna and spoiled rich girl Laurel Van Ness—she continued to abuse Allie, interfering in Allie's burgeoning relationship with Braxton Sutter, and even forcing Allie to lie down in order for Maria to win the Knockouts Championship from her. But Maria essentially signed her own death warrant, as winning the Knockouts Championship put the target from Gail Kim on her back once more, and Gail defeated Maria in the fall of 2016 at the Bound For Glory pay-per-view to win the Knockouts Championship and remove Maria from her position of power.

In March 2017, it was announced that Maria and Mike were now done with Impact Wrestling, and this time rumors were abuzz that they had signed a contract with WWE—marking Maria's return and Mike's debut in a company he'd always wanted to wrestle in. That June, they debuted as "Maria and Mike Kanellis" at WWE's Money in the Bank pay-per-view, two lovebirds (heels, of course—this is wrestling) who would shove their love in everyone's face, whether they were interested in said love or not. Then that September, Maria took time off from WWE: she and Mike were expecting their first child.

★ MARYSE ★

YEARS ACTIVE: 2006–present

TRAINED BY: OVW · FCW · Al Snow · Dave "Fit" Finlay · Steve Keirn · Dr. Tom Prichard · Ricky Steamboat

BILLED FROM: Montreal, Quebec, Canada

ACCOMPLISHMENTS: #9 in 2009 PWI Female 50 · 2x WWE Divas Champion · 2010 Divas Championship Tournament

AKA: Maryse Ouellet · Maryse Ouellet-Mizanin · Maryse Mizanin · "The French Phenom" · "The French-Canadian Beauty" · "The Sexiest of Sexy" · "The Sultry Diva" · "The Ultra-Dangerous Superstar" · 1/2 of the "It" Couple

NOTABLE MATCHES: Maryse vs. Michelle McCool (c) at WWE Unforgiven 2008, for the WWE Divas Championship (September 7, 2008) · Maryse vs. Michelle McCool (c) at *WWE SmackDown*, for the WWE Divas Championship (December 26, 2008) · Maryse vs. Mickie James (c) at WWE Night of Champions 2009, for the WWE Divas Championship (July 26, 2009) · Maryse & The Miz vs. Nikki Bella & John Cena at WWE WrestleMania 33 (April 2, 2017)

★ When the French-Canadian Maryse Ouellet auditioned for the 2006 edition of the WWE Divas Search, she admittedly couldn't speak more than 10 words of English. While WWE's a global company, it is United States and English-speaking based, so she had to learn English quickly. However, her natural charisma and presentation in her native French impressed WWE officials at the time, and not only did she make it to the top eight finalists (ending up in seventh place) of the Diva Search, a month after her elimination, WWE signed her to a developmental contract at OVW.

A month into her time training and wrestling at OVW (and eventually FCW), Maryse simultaneously made her soft main roster debut. Said "soft" debut was in the form of a collection of pre-taped "Welcome Back" vignettes, with Maryse living a life of French leisure (in the tub, on a bed, etc.).

These played upon *SmackDown* returning from commercial break, which aired intermittently from September 2006 to April 2007. After that, Maryse remained in OVW/FCW full-time, save for a *RAW* appearance in May 2007 to introduce the national debut for Timbaland music video "Throw It On Me" (featuring a number of WWE Divas, including Maryse). But after working a couple of main roster house shows and dark matches toward the end of 2007, Maryse officially joined the SmackDown roster in early 2008. Debuting as a heel, Maryse

seduced SmackDown Assistant General Manager Teddy Long into giving her a job, despite the fact that—in theory— she was already employed by SmackDown (because of the aforementioned "Welcome Back" vignettes).

While Maryse had gotten much better at English during her first two years in WWE, in a way the language barrier was the best thing that could have existed for her as a wrestler and a character:

> [It was hard] because I couldn't understand anybody,
> but I learned so much. I learned how to listen carefully
> to everything, every detail, and I think that I needed a
> character that people could relate to, without speaking,
> which is very hard. I developed a heel persona and
> everything about Maryse was presentation, facials,
> gestures. . . . Over the years, I learned how to work a
> live crowd and perfect my craft.

Maryse may have had the French seductress gimmick down, but it was her role as a devious, vindictive snob that made her stand out. By the summer of 2008, Maryse found herself in title contention for the newly introduced WWE Divas Championship, feuding with Natalya for #1 Contendership and then Michelle McCool for a chance at the gold. Then, becoming the #1 Contender to Michelle McCool's championship at the end of 2008, Maryse finally defeated McCool, winning the Divas Championship for the first time and becoming the second person ever to hold it. After being drafted to RAW with the Divas Championship in the spring of 2009, Maryse entered into a feud with Mickie James, doing everything she could—like spraying her patented hairspray into James's eyes—to keep the veteran Diva from being #1 Contender. Of course, Maryse was right to worry, as she lost the Divas Championship in her first title defense against James. And Maryse wouldn't even have the chance to challenge James to a rematch, as she had to undergo knee surgery following her loss.

Returning to RAW four months later, Maryse still had the Divas Championship on her mind, only there was a new champion to challenge: Melina. However, as luck would have it, Melina ended up with a legitimate injury of her own—tearing her ACL—leading to the Divas Championship being vacated and Maryse competing in (and winning) a tournament for the title. A couple months later, Maryse ended up dropping the championship to Eve Torres, thus ending Maryse's time as a champion for the rest of her WWE career. Though Maryse continued to wrestle, her storyline became more focused on her role as a valet for Ted DiBiase (son of "Million Dollar Man" Ted DiBiase), as—naturally—a character as shallow as Maryse would of course gravitate to the son of the "Million Dollar Man" and holder of the Million Dollar Championship. Alongside DiBiase, Maryse was a Pro mentor in the fourth season of the game show version of *NXT*, with Brodus Clay as their Rookie . . . until he traded them for Alberto Del Rio's mentorship. The following season (*NXT Redemption*) saw Maryse as a co-host this time, as well as the eye of many *NXT* competitors' affections—especially Lucky Cannon, who tried to woo Maryse with knockoff designer accessories. However, Maryse eventually left her hosting (and storyline) duties in *NXT Redemption* that August.

"EVERYTHING ABOUT MARYSE WAS PRESENTATION, FACIALS, GESTURES. . . . OVER THE YEARS, I LEARNED HOW TO WORK A LIVE CROWD AND PERFECT MY CRAFT."

Maryse was then released from WWE on October 28, 2010, while recovering from abdominal hernia surgery (the reason for her original absence in August). But having been a two-time Divas Champion and the longest-reigning Divas Champion in WWE history (216 days) at the time, she felt like she'd achieved all that she could achieve in WWE and considered the release a mutual situation. Post-WWE, Maryse started a career in acting, as well as real estate. She also married longtime boyfriend WWE Superstar Mike "The Miz" Mizanin, who had proposed to her in the same convention room they'd first met in during the Diva Search (he was the host at the time). But while she had left the in-ring competition behind, she spent some time in independent wrestling promotion FWE as a commentator for women's matches. And besides, Maryse's WWE career ended up not being as finished as it seemed. . . .

In 2016, on *RAW* after WrestleMania 32, Maryse made her official WWE return by distracting Zack Ryder—by slapping Ryder's dad, in the front row—in order for Miz to win back the WWE Intercontinental Championship. From that point on, Maryse was back full-time, as the missing piece to her husband's act as a Hollywood A-lister. After all, what good is an A-lister without the other half of their power couple? And this wasn't just some valet situation—in the span of over a year, Maryse was portrayed as an integral part of Miz's entire gimmick and story; and, while she wasn't wrestling again, she was cutting promos right alongside him and causing trouble herself. This eventually led to a feud between Miz and longtime rival John Cena, as well as Maryse and Cena's girlfriend Nikki Bella, leading into a Mixed Tag Team match (Maryse's first match in over six years) at WrestleMania 33. (Upon returning to WWE, Maryse also joined the cast of *Total Divas*, where her real-life past issues with The Bella Twins were also brought up prior to the feud). While Maryse and Miz lost the match, the build-up to the match—with their constant parodying of their rivals—was generally considered the most entertaining part of it all.

In the fall of 2017, Maryse and Miz announced on *RAW* that they'd be entering the next stage of their lives: parenthood. Maryse then took time off from WWE TV again, this time for maternity leave. And a couple of months prior to the birth of their new daughter, it was announced that USA Network had greenlit a docu-series about their new family life, titled *Miz & Mrs.* Considering how Maryse thought she had done it all the first time she was in WWE, it'll be interesting to see what happens next.

★ MAYU IWATANI ★

YEARS ACTIVE: 2011–present

TRAINED BY: Fuka Kakimoto · Nanae Takahashi

BILLED FROM: Mine, Yamaguchi, Japan

ACCOMPLISHMENTS: #15 in 2017 PWI Female 50 · 4x Artist of STARDOM Champion (1x with Hiroyo Matsumoto & Miho Wakizawa, 1x with Io Shirai & Takumi Iroha, 1x with Io Shirai & Kairi Hojo, 1x with Saki Kashima & Tam Nakano) · 2x Goddess of STARDOM Champion (1x with Io Shirai, 1x with Saki Kashima) · 1x High Speed Champion · 2x Wonder of STARDOM Champion · 1x World of STARDOM Champion · 2015 STARDOM Cinderella Tournament · 2016 STARDOM Cinderella Tournament · 2015 Goddess of STARDOM Championship Tournament (with Io Shirai) · 2015 Goddesses of STARDOM Tag Tournament (with Io Shirai) · 2015 STARDOM 5☆STAR GP Best Match Award (vs. Io Shirai, on August 23) · 2017 STARDOM 5☆STAR GP Best Match Award (vs. Kagetsu, on September 18) · 2014 STARDOM 5☆STAR GP Outstanding Performance Award · 2016 STARDOM Best Match Award (vs. Io Shirai, on December 22) · 2015 STARDOM Best Tag Team Award (with Io Shirai) · 2014 STARDOM Technique Award · 2015 STARDOM Technique Award

AKA: Yurei · "STARDOM no Icon" ("Icon Of STARDOM") · "Sky Blue no STARDOM Future" · Mayuchica · Mayuchika · Mayucica · "Hyper Technician" · "The Gift" · 1/2 of Thunder Rock ·1/2 of AMA ·1/3 of Tawashis · member of Planet

NOTABLE MATCHES: Mayu Iwatani vs. Io Shirai at STARDOM 5☆STAR Grand Prix 2015 - Night 1, in a Block B match (August 23, 2015) · STARDOM (Mayu Iwatani, Io Shirai, Jungle Kyona, Kairi Hojo, & Momo Watanabe) vs. World Selection (Kellie Skater, Evie, Chelsea Green, Santana Garrett, & Viper) (with Act Yasukawa), in an Elimination Ten Man Tag Team match at STARDOM 5th Anniversary – Night 3: STARDOM vs. The World (February 7, 2016) · Mayu Iwatani (c) vs. Evie at STARDOM 5th Anniversary – Night 5: STARDOM vs. The World II, for the High Speed Championship (February 27, 2016) · Mayu Iwatani vs. Io Shirai (c) at STARDOM Gold May 2016, for the World of STARDOM Championship (May 15, 2016) · Mayu Iwatani vs. Io Shirai (c) at STARDOM Year-End Climax 2016, for the World of STARDOM Championship (December 22, 2016) · Mayu Iwatani vs. Mayu Iwatani at STARDOM Galaxy Stars 2017, for the World of STARDOM Championship (June 21, 2017)

★ Considering how good she is—especially at such a young age—it's amazing Mayu Iwatani didn't realize she wanted to be a professional wrestler until just about the time she decided to become a professional wrestler. After seeing her first Dragon Gate wrestling show, Mayu supposedly got in contact with Fuka Kakimoto and let her know she was interested in becoming a wrestler for her new promotion, STARDOM. After that, Mayu moved to Tokyo to take part in STARDOM's first class of trainees, making her in-ring debut in January 2011.

Also, considering how good she is, it's amazing Mayu Iwatani didn't even win a one-on-one match until December 2011. Clearly, her incomparable suplex technique hadn't yet been perfected.

Mayu eventually won her first championship in STARDOM (Artist of STARDOM) at the end of 2013, with her Tawashis stablemates (Hiroyo Matsumoto and Miho Wakizawa), and then the following July won her first singles championship (the vacant Wonder of STARDOM Championship). It was clear that Mayu could no longer be seen as the weakest wrestler in the company, but she was just getting started. After losing both the Artist of STARDOM and Wonder of STARDOM Championships, Mayu began to focus more on the company's top Championship, the World of STARDOM Championship. In April 2015, Mayu won the first ever STARDOM Cinderella Tournament—and would win the second one, in 2016—but came up empty after challenging Kairi Hojo for the World of STARDOM Championship. So she continued to keep herself busy, with Thunder Rock and with the High Speed Championship. For example, at the beginning of 2016, Io Shirai formed a stable called "Threedom" ("Three" +

to Storm that year. After winning the Wonder of STARDOM Championship for the second time (beating Kairi), Mayu challenged Io for the World of STARDOM Championship again, this time winning (and becoming the first wrestler to hold both titles simultaneously). That September, Mayu dropped the Wonder of STARDOM Championship, but controversy occurred during her World of STARDOM Championship defense against Toni Storm. In that anticipated title defense—because of the past Cinderella Tournament face-off—before Mayu could expectedly suplex the life out of Toni, the match had to be stopped just a couple of minutes in, due to a dislocation of Mayu's elbow. As a result, Toni Storm became the brand-new World of STARDOM Champion, despite clearly not being happy with how it happened—and having quite the uphill battle to prove that she was deserving of the championship.

Returning from injury in December 2017, Mayu returned to the States to debut in ROH, as part of the tournament to crown the inaugural Women of Honor Champion. And within STARDOM, she essentially had to start back at the bottom until she could challenge Toni Storm to a rematch. However, upon getting that rematch, Toni proved she was ready for a 100% Mayu and retained the World of STARDOM Championship. But Mayu remains patient enough to know her time will come again.

"STARDOM"), comprised of herself, Kairi Hojo, and Mayu. Threedom quickly won the Artist of STARDOM Championship, and that April the trio filmed a storyline in the United States (which would air that November) for *Lucha Underground* season three. As members of the Black Lotus Triad, Io (as Hitokiri), Kairi (Doku), and Mayu (Yurei) wrestled as mercenaries on behalf of Black Lotus's vendetta against Pentagon Dark, leading to an entire *Lucha Underground* episode featuring Pentagon's in-ring battle against the team. By the time this *Lucha Underground* episode had aired, though, Threedom (as well as Thunder Rock) had officially broken up . . . and Io was the World of STARDOM Champion that Mayu just couldn't beat.

Mayu Iwatani was prepared to win the Cinderella Tournament for the third time in a row in 2017, but she ended up losing in the finals to Toni Storm—and it wouldn't be the last time she lost

★ MEIKO SATOMURA ★

YEARS ACTIVE: 1995–present

TRAINED BY: Chigusa Nagayo · GAEA Dojo

BILLED FROM: Sendai, Japan

ACCOMPLISHMENTS: 2016 CHIKARA King of Trios (with DASH Chisako & Cassandra Miyagi) · 2x AAAW Single Champion · 3x (and inaugural) AAAW Junior Heavyweight Tag Team Champion/

AAAW Tag Team Champion (1x with Sonoko Kato, 1x with Ayako Hamada, 1x with Chikayo Nagashima) · 1996 GAEA Japan Hustling Cup · 1998 GAEA Japan High Spurt 600 · 2001 GAEA Japan High Spurt 600 · 1995 GAEA Japan Splash J & Running G (with Kaoru & Tomoko Kuzumi) · 1x SENDAI Girls' World Champion · 2011 SENDAI Girls' Pro Wrestling Joshi Puroresu Dantai Taikou Flash Tournament (with DASH Chisako, Hiren, Kagetsu, Miyako Morino, Ryo Mizunami, Sendai Sachiko) · 2013 Tokyo Sports Joshi Puroresu Grand Prize · 1x World of STARDOM Champion · 2015 STARDOM Best Match Award (vs. Io Shirai, on December 23) · 1x Fight Club: PRO (FCP) Champion

AKA: Meiko Satomura Deluxe · Meiko Satomura DX · Mei · "Big Match Meiko"

NOTABLE MATCHES: Meiko Satomura vs. Aja Kong (c) at GAEA Yokohama Double Destiny ~ Battle Of The Crush Gals, for the AAAW Championship (September 15, 1999) · Meiko Satomura vs. Chigusa Nagayo at GAEA Eternal Last Gong (April 10, 2005) · Team SENDAI Girls' (Meiko Satomura, DASH Chisako, & Sendai Sachiko) vs. Manami Toyota, Jigsaw, & Mike Quackenbush at CHIKARA King of Trios 2012 – Night 2, in a King of Trios Quarterfinals match (September 15, 2012) · Meiko Satomura vs. Kairi Hojo (c) at STARDOM Galaxy Stars 2015 – Night 1, for the World of STARDOM Championship (June 14, 2015) · Meiko Satomura (c) vs. Io Shirai at STARDOM Year-End Climax 2015, for the World of STARDOM Championship (December 23, 2015) · Meiko Satomura (c) vs. Io Shirai at SENDAI Girls' 10th Anniversary Show ~ Women's Wrestling Big Show in Niigata, for the SENDAI Girls' World Championship (July 2, 2016) · House SENDAI Girls' (Meiko Satomura, DASH Chisako, & Cassandra Miyagi) vs. House Strong Style (Pete Dunne, Tyler Bate, & Trent Seven) at CHIKARA King of Trios 2017 – Night 3, in a King of Trios finals match (September 3, 2017) · Meiko Satomura vs. Chris Brookes (c) at FCP Dream Tag Team Invitational 2018: Night 1, for the FCP Championship (March 30, 2018) · Meiko Satomura vs. Mercedes Martinez at the WWE Mae Young Classic II, in a Mae Young Classic Second Round match (October 3, 2018 · Meiko Satomura vs. Toni Storm at the WWE Mae Young Classic II, in a Mae Young Classic Semifinals match (October 24, 2018)

At just 15 years old, Meiko Satomura began her professional wrestling career in joshi promotion GAEA Japan, debuting on its debut show. A year later, she was wrestling for WCW in the United States. Trained by GAEA Japan founder and 1/2 of the Crush Gals, Chigusa Nagayo, Satomura even dropped out of school to get an early jump on her professional wrestling career. These days, there's a reason why people call her "Big Match Meiko," and her ability to perform under pressure and at the highest level was something that was seen early on. Going on to win the AAAW Tag Team Championship and AAAW Single Championship multiple times, Meiko Satomura was going to be the new ace of GAEA Japan once Nagayo retired. However, as soon as Nagayo retired, GAEA Japan closed. Meiko did get to defeat her mentor, though, in the main event of the final GAEA Japan show—a retirement ceremony for Nagayo.

Post-GAEA Japan closure, Meiko joined forces with Michinoku Pro Wrestling's Jinsei Shinzaki to create joshi promotion SENDAI Girls' Pro Wrestling. (She continues to wrestle in other wrestling

promotions in Japan and around the world, but SENDAI Girls' is her baby.) The debut show saw Meiko defeat Aja Kong in the main event, continuing a feud that first began in GAEA Japan, where Meiko had ended Aja's second AAAW Single Champion reign and Aja did the same to Meiko. When Meiko missed the majority of 2008 out on injury—a fractured orbital socket—her return match that October also saw her face off against Aja Kong (with Aja winning that one). But come the spring of 2009, Meiko had to take more time off, dealing this time with a back injury and surgery. After all these years, Meiko Satomura's injuries appeared to be catching up to her, but she remained "Big Match Meiko."

In 2012, SENDAI Girls' got big attention in the US independent wrestling scene for the breakout performances of Team SENDAI Girls' (Meiko, Sendai Sachiko, and DASH Chisako) during CHIKARA's King of Trios tournament. To the unaware, they seemingly came out of nowhere (defeating an established CHIKARA team as well as established veterans), putting on unreal performances, and looking like they were going to win the whole thing. So it was deflating when the heel Team ROH (Mike Bennett and The Young Bucks) beat them—even though Team ROH was more established in the States—to advance to the finals. However, four years later, Team Sendai (this time with Cassandra Miyagi in the place of Sendai Sachiko) won the whole thing, and the CHIKARA audience was more than ready. The following year, the reigning King of Trios made another tournament appearance, making it to the finals once more but falling to House Strong Style (Pete Dunne, Trent Seven, and Tyler Bate).

In March 2018, Meiko set out to take over the British wrestling scene the way she had the Japanese joshi scene, winning the Fight Club: PRO (FCP) Championship from Chris Brookes. (FCP was co-founded in 2009 by Trent Seven, one of Meiko's King of Trios opponents the previous year.) With that, Meiko is the first woman to win the FCP Championship. So with 23 years of experience under her belt, Meiko Satomura still doesn't look like she'll show any signs of letting up.

★ MELINA PEREZ ★

YEARS ACTIVE: 2000–2017

TRAINED BY: Dave "Fit" Finlay · Jesse Hernandez · School of Hard Knocks · OVW

BILLED FROM: Los Angles, California · Hollywood, California

ACCOMPLISHMENTS: 1x MCW Women's Champion · #3 in 2009 PWI Female 50 · 1x SWE Queen of Southside Champion · EWF Hall of Fame Class of 2016 · 2016 SWE Queen of the Ring · 3x WWE Women's Champion · 2x WWE Divas Champion

AKA: Kyra · Little Deer · Melina · 1/3 of MNM · "The A-List Diva" · "The Barracuda" · "The Gorgeous Grappler" · "The Hell Cat" · "The Lovely Latina" · "The Paparazzi Princess" · "The Red Carpet Diva" · "The Scream Queen" · "The Most Dominant Diva in WWE"

NOTABLE MATCHES: Melina vs. Trish Stratus (c) at WWE Survivor Series 2005, for the WWE Women's Championship (November 27, 2005) · Melina (with Johnny Nitro) vs. Trish Stratus at WWE *Monday Night RAW* (July 10, 2006) · Melina vs. Mickie James (c) at WWE *Monday Night RAW*, for the WWE Women's Championship (February 19, 2007) · Melina (c) vs. Mickie James at WWE Backlash 2007, for the WWE Women's Championship (April 29, 2007) · Melina vs. Mickie James (c) vs. Beth Phoenix at WWE Judgment Day 2008, in a Triple Threat match for the WWE Women's Championship (May 18, 2008) · Melina vs. Beth Phoenix at WWE One Night Stand 2008, in an "I Quit" match (June 1, 2008) · Melina vs. Beth Phoenix (c) at WWE Royal Rumble 2009, for the WWE Women's Championship (January 25, 2009) · Melina vs. Michelle McCool (c) at WWE Night of Champions 2009, for the WWE Women's Championship (February 19, 2009) · Melina (c) vs. Alex Windsor vs. Dahlia Black vs. Kay Lee Ray vs. Nixon Newell vs. Ruby Summers at SWE 6th Anniversary Show, in a Six Way match for the Queen of Southside Championship (October 29, 2016)

★ Despite her background in modeling and beauty pageants, Melina Perez dreamed of being a wrestler when she grew up. A Los Angeles native, she eventually got her start in professional wrestling in 2000, training at Jesse Hernandez's School of Hard Knocks wrestling school. While training at Hard Knocks, Melina was highly praised for her natural ability—so it was only a matter of time before she made it big-time. Melina started her in-ring as "Kyra" (with a submission finisher known as "The Kyrapractor") in 2002, mostly wrestling in the SoCal scene before she got signed to WWE developmental (OVW) at the end of 2003. (She had auditioned for the third season of *Tough Enough* in 2002, making it to the final 21 but not the final TV cut of 13.)

The majority of Melina's wrestling career—especially in WWE—has been as a heel, so it was only right for her to debut in OVW as one, aligning herself with John Hennigan (aka Johnny Nitro) as his love interest (which she already was in real life). Soon, Melina and Nitro joined forces for Joey Matthews (aka Joey Mercury), with their team eventually being known as "MNM." As rare as it is for a wrestler to have a firm grasp on their character right out the gate, that's what happened with Melina and MNM; even in OVW, with a lower budget for vignettes, MNM sold their roles as shallow Hollywood celebrities (the type famous for nothing, which would pay off tremendously years later when the Melina and Nitro characters became friends with Kevin Federline). While Melina would make a couple of solo main roster appearances toward the end of 2004—with the storyline reason being that Randy Orton hired her during a stint as guest General Manager—MNM officially made their debut in the spring of 2005. As MNM went for the WWE Tag Team Championship, Melina feuded with Trish Stratus in an attempt to win gold herself, but she came up short. In fact, it would be another couple of years before Melina got gold in WWE.

Following the split of MNM (well, Nitro and Mercury), Melina and Nitro were "fired" from SmackDown and sent to RAW, leading to Melina coming up short in a feud against Trish Stratus yet again (while Nitro won gold—the Intercontinental Championship—yet again). After that, however, Melina entered into a storyline with Mick Foley—based on their real-life friendship behind the scenes—seemingly turning Melina face, only for Melina to show her true colors and embarrass her "friend." After this storyline, things finally seemed to go Melina's way, as her next feud for the WWE Women's Championship— against then-champion Mickie James—resulted in her winning the championship for the first time. She also retained the championship in the first ever Divas Falls Count Anywhere match. She even got to go into (and come out of) WrestleMania XXIII as Women's Champion. However, a few weeks later, she lost the championship back to Mickie James . . . at an untelevised house show in Paris, proving that anything can happen in WWE. While WWE recorded the win and loss in the history books, it was actually a mistake on the referee's part, and upon receiving a rematch that same night, Melina officially became a two-time WWE Women's Champion.

Eventually, Melina lost the championship again (for real this time) to Candice Michelle, and she eventually teamed up with Beth Phoenix, a solid heel duo until multiple miscommunications led Phoenix to take all her aggressions out and turn on Melina. This made Melina face for the first time in her WWE career, which basically meant eliminating her piercing shriek and upping the emphasis on her intense flexibility. The latter came in handy during the former partners' matches—especially their "I Quit" match, another Divas division first featuring Melina—when Phoenix did everything she possibly could to literally bend and break Melina in half. After suffering from a legitimate heel injury a few weeks after the "I Quit" match (which she lost), Melina took time off from WWE until November, determined to get her Women's Championship back from Beth Phoenix. And months later, at the Royal Rumble 2009 pay-per-view, she did, winning the championship for the third time and retaining in the rematch.

A couple of months later, Melina was drafted to SmackDown with the Women's Championship, where she feuded with (and lost the championship to) #1 Contender Michelle McCool. According to Michelle McCool, she and Melina infamously got in trouble during their feud (specifically during their rematch, at Night of Champions 2009) for wrestling like the guys and their match "looking too good," something that was unfortunately considered a bad thing during this point in the Divas era.

By the fall of 2009, Melina had moved back to RAW again, winning the WWE Divas Championship almost immediately, but had to vacate the championship a couple of months later due to an ACL injury. Upon returning in August 2010, again, Melina won the Divas Championship almost immediately, only to be attacked by LayCool (co-WWE Women's Champion Layla and Michelle McCool) and proceeded with a title unification storyline and match (which LayCool won). By the end of the year, Melina was back to her default setting as a heel, and by the

first week of August 2011 she'd be out of WWE. Despite how highly decorated she became in the company, there were rumors swirling for years—without any true denial or confirmation either way—that she had the dreaded "attitude problems" behind the scenes. Post-WWE, she wrestled a few times in WSU, WWC (in Puerto Rico), FWE, SWE (in England, eventually winning the SWE Queen of Southside Championship), MCW, and even STARDOM. She has yet to make any promotion a permanent home—though she came pretty close with SWE.

★ MERCEDES MARTINEZ ★

YEARS ACTIVE: 2000–present

TRAINED BY: Jason Knight

BILLED FROM: Waterbury, Connecticut

ACCOMPLISHMENTS: 1x Defiant Pro Wrestling Women's Champion · 2x Green Mountain Wrestling (GMW) Women's Champion · 1x IWA-MS Women's Champion · 1x IndyGurlz Australia Champion · 1x IndyGurlz Champion · 1x NWA Midwest Women's Champion · 1x New England Championship Wrestling (NECW) Yoshimoto Ladies Pro North American Women's Champion · 1x NECW World Women's Champion · 2014 NHPW Global Conflict Shield Tournament · 2016 NHPW Global Conflict Shield Tournament · 2x nCw Femmes Fatales Champion · #2 in 2011 PWI Female 50 · Pro Wrestling Unplugged (PWU) Unified Women's Champion · 2x SHIMMER Champion · 1x SHINE Tag Team Champion (with Ivelisse) · 1x WSU All Guts, No Glory Champion · 3x WSU Champion · 1x WSU Tag Team Champion (with Angel Orsini) · 2008 WSU J-Cup · 2011 WSU/NWS King and Queen of the Ring (with Julio Dinero) · 1x WXW C4 Women's Champion · 1x WXW Cruiserweight Champion · 6x WXW Women's Champion ·

2006 WXW Elite 8 Tournament · 2008 WXW Elite 8 Tournament · WXW Hall of Fame Class of 2014 · WSU Hall of Fame Class of 2017

AKA: Maria Toro · member of The Vulture Squad · "Latina Sensation" · member of Las Sicarias · 1/3 of Trifecta

NOTABLE MATCHES: Sara Del Rey vs. Mercedes Martinez at SHIMMER Volume 1 (November 6, 2005) · Sara Del Rey vs. Mercedes Martinez at SHIMMER Volume 5, in a No Time Limit match (May 21, 2006) · Mercedes Martinez vs. Amazing Kong at SHIMMER Volume 23 (May 2, 2009) · Mercedes Martinez vs. Madison Eagles (c) at SHIMMER Volume 37, for the SHIMMER Championship (March 26, 2011) · Mercedes Martinez (c) vs. Lexxus at WSU Martinez vs. Lexxus, for the WSU World Championship (August 6, 2011) · Mercedes Martinez vs. Athena at SHIMMER Volume 45 (March 17, 2012) · LuFisto vs. Mercedes Martinez at nCw Femmes Fatales IX (July 7, 2012) · Mercedes Martinez vs. Shayna Baszler at the WWE Mae Young Classic, in a Mae Young Classic Semifinals match (September 6, 2017) · Toni Storm (c) vs. Mercedes Martinez at RISE 6: Brutality, for the World of STARDOM Championship (December 1, 2017) · Mercedes Martinez vs. Meiko Satomura at the WWE Mae Young Classic II, in a Mae Young Classic Second Round match (October 3, 2018)

⭐ With nearly 20 years of experience under her belt, Mercedes Martinez (born Jasmine Benetiz) has made the most of her time and done a lot in professional wrestling. After suffering a basketball injury in college, for Martinez, "Wrestling just came at the right time." It was the contact sport she craved, and, other than legitimate combat sports, what better way than professional wrestling? Also, she was admittedly just "bored." After training under former ECW star Jason Knight (who also trained former TNA Knockouts Champion Velvet Sky), Martinez made her in-ring debut a month into her studies. She then quickly—but not as quickly as her training—became a fixture in the New England independent wrestling scene, contributing to and helping to expand its burgeoning women's wrestling scene for her first few years as a wrestler.

By 2004, Martinez had wrestled in more than just her local indies; she'd wrestled in CHIKARA, TNA, and CZW. She'd proven her worth as a top talent, as well as her ability to maintain feuds (as she did with Japanese wrestler Sumie Sakai). Because of this, Martinez was booked on the inaugural SHIMMER show (Volume 1) in a match against Sara Del Rey that went to a 20-limit draw—something that would have been unheard of in WWE in 2005—which got a standing ovation. At SHIMMER Volume 5, Martinez and Del Rey had a rematch, this time with no time limit, and the fan reception remained impressed: something special was happening. While the early goings-on of SHIMMER certainly opened up the possibilities for Mercedes Martinez to get her name out there and wrestle in places like ROH (SHIMMER's sister promotion at the time), ChickFight, nCw Femme Fatales, and of course WSU (arguably Mercedes Martinez's home promotion), one must fast-forward to Mercedes Martinez's place in wrestling as a grizzled veteran for the real excitement.

Returning to SHIMMER after a two-year retirement would have been special enough. But to return to SHIMMER after a two-year retirement—with backup in the form of Heart of SHIMMER Champion Nicole Savoy and "The Queen of Spades" Shayna Baszler—and immediately win the SHIMMER Championship is next level. Which is exactly what Mercedes Martinez did at SHIMMER Volume 85, and Trifecta was born. After holding the SHIMMER Championship for nearly a year (for a second time, as she lost the championship to Kellie Skater for a day at SHIMMER Volume 87), her ego eventually got the better of her. Once Shayna left for WWE, Martinez attempted to add Aja Kong to the group—refusing to allow Nicole Savoy to move up in the ranks and become her "#2." In retaliation, Savoy challenged Martinez for the championship and defeated her at Volume 99 and at the rematch on Volume 100 (during WrestleMania Weekend, in front of the biggest possible audience).

The rest of 2017 was definitely a big year for Mercedes Martinez, as she was not only inducted in the WSU Hall of Fame, but she participated—alongside her Trifecta clan, pre-implosion—in the WWE's inaugural Mae Young Classic (and has since wrestled in a number of *NXT* TV matches). Martinez made it to the Semifinals, for a standout mentor-vs.-mentee match against Shayna; and while Shayna may have won, Mercedes proved she hadn't taught her protégé all of her tricks. Mercedes Martinez also became a two-time NHPW IndyGurlz Australia Champion, taking matters into her own hands when Shayna, her former stablemate, couldn't drop the title herself (due to WWE obligations)—because that's what a "true champion" does.

★ MIA YIM ★

YEARS ACTIVE: 2009–present

TRAINED BY: John Kermon · Mark Bravura · C.A. Elliot · Bobby Shields · Christian York · CZW · DJ Hyde · ROH Dojo · Daizee Haze · Delirious

BILLED FROM: San Diego, California · Fontana, California

ACCOMPLISHMENTS: 1x Big Time Wrestling (BTW) Women's Champion · 1x DDT Ironman Heavymetalweight Champion · 1x SHINE Champion · 1x SHINE Tag Team Champion (with Leva Bates) · 2014 SHINE Tag Team Championship Tournament · #6 in 2016 PWI Female 50 · 2016 TNA Queen of the Knockouts · 2016 TNA World Cup (with Jeff Hardy, Eddie Edwards, Jessie Godderz, & Robbie E) · 1x TNA Knockouts Champion · 1x SWE Queen of Southside Champion

AKA: Jade · 1/2 of Fly High WDSS · 1/2 of The Lucha Sisters · member of The Dollhouse · member of The Embassy · "Blue" · "The Blasian Barbie" · "The Blasian Baddie" · 1/3 of the #BRE (Best Roommates Ever)

NOTABLE MATCHES: Mia Yim vs. Mickie James at MCW Shane Shamrock Memorial Cup 2010 (July 31, 2010) · Mia Yim vs. Athena vs. Jessie McKay at SHIMMER Volume 42, in a 3-Way match (October 1, 2011) · Mia Yim vs. Allysin Kay (with Chest Flexor) at AIW Girls Night Out 6, in an Unsanctioned match for the vacant AIW Women's Championship (August 3, 2012) · Mia Yim vs. Serena Deeb at Pro Wrestling Syndicate (PWS) Bombshell Ladies of Wrestling 9 (March 22, 2014) · Mia Yim vs. Jessicka Havok at WSU United, in an Uncensored Rules match (July 12, 2014) · Mia Yim vs. Athena at SHIMMER Volume 71: The ChickFight Tournament, in a SHIMMER ChickFight Tournament First Round match (March 28, 2015) · Jade (with Marti Bell) vs. Brooke at TNA Impact Wrestling (June 3, 2015) · Fly High WDSS (Mia Yim & Kay Lee Ray) vs. The Kimber Bombs (Kimber Lee & Cherry Bomb) (c) vs. Team Slap Happy (Heidi Lovelace & Evie) vs. BaleSpin (KC Spinelli & Xandra Bale) at SHIMMER Volume 84, in a Four Corners Elimination match for the SHIMMER Tag Team Championship (June 26, 2016) · Jade (with Gail Kim) vs. Rosemary at TNA Impact Wrestling, in a Six Sides of Steel Cage match for the vacant TNA Knockouts Championship (December 1, 2016) · Jade vs. Rosemary (c) at TNA Impact Wrestling Genesis 2017, in a Monster's Ball match for the TNA Knockouts Championship (January 26, 2017) · Mia Yim vs. Keith Lee at Beyond All Day, in an Intergender match (May 27, 2018)

★ The self-proclaimed "Blasian Baddie" (as she is half-black and half-Asian—Korean, to be exact) has been a fan of professional wrestling since she was eight years old and made the serious decision to pursue a career in the sport at the ripe old age of 10. Of course, she—born Stephanie Bell—waited until she was 18 years old to *actually* pursue it as a career and follow in the footsteps of her inspirations, WWF/WWE Divas like Lita, Chyna, and Trish Stratus. Despite her father being the one who hooked her on wrestling in the first place, he didn't want her to make it her profession. But at least his daughter managed to complete her studies in college while she trained, which is a true rarity in the professional wrestling world. Training for 18 months in Virginia—starting as soon as she graduated from high school—Bell made her independent wrestling debut in August 2009 as "Mia Yim." Very early on in her wrestling career, Mia Yim got to work with Sara Del Rey—who Mia's credited as a "big sister type" for her generation of wrestling—and also got booked on JAPW shows. The former helped prove that Mia could hang with the best of the best on the independent scene (and in the world), while the latter allowed Mia to meet even more important people for her career, like Daizee Haze (Mia's in for training at and working in ROH) and DJ Hyde (Mia's in for training at and working in CZW).

Both Mia's times with ROH and CZW bore fruitful results, as she featured as the gorgeous-but-lethal valet for The Embassy stable in ROH and as the sleazy "Panama City Playboy" Adam Cole's valet and on-screen girlfriend in CZW. Both gimmicks started toward the end of 2010/beginning of 2011, and both allowed Mia Yim to show her range as a heel. They also provided Mia with more opportunities around the independent scene, and the next few years seemed like nothing but opportunities for Mia. By 2013, Mia Yim had toured Japan and Mexico, as well as having wrestled in prominent all-women's promotions like SHIMMER and SHINE and other indies like AIW, PWS, MCW, ACW, FIP, and CWF Mid-Atlantic.

By 2013, Mia Yim was also on the radar of TNA Impact Wrestling, having wrestled a dark match for the company all the way back in 2010. She'd make a few later appearances in various Impact Wrestling One Night Only pay-per-views, but she wouldn't make her official debut as a part of the roster until the spring of 2015: as "Jade," a member of a new heel Knockouts stable called "The Dollhouse." And as Jade, she would become the breakout star of The Dollhouse, turning face and winning the Knockouts Championship after just a year in the company. As a face, Jade immediately feuded with Maria Kanellis-Bennett and aligned herself with Impact's top face (and Jade's former rival), Gail Kim. However, Jade would lose the championship to Maria's muscle Sienna (aka Allysin Kay, someone Mia Yim was very familiar with in AIW) after an 87-day reign, thanks to a sneak attack from Marti Bell, Jade's former Dollhouse partner.

After getting past Marti (in a Street Fight, as Marti was very much obsessed with taking their feud "to the street"), Jade would enter into a Knockouts Championship feud with "The Demon Assassin" Rosemary (a feud known as "Red vs. Blue," due

to Rosemary and Jade's hair colors at the time), featuring star-making matches for both of them, in the form of Six Sides of Steel, Monster's Ball, and Last Knockout Standing. However, Jade lost all three of these matches, with the Last Knockout Standing match being her final match in Impact Wrestling (as she had not signed a new contract with the company). A few months later, Jade showed up on WWE TV—back to "Mia Yim"—as one of the 32 participants in the inaugural Mae Young Classic tournament. She was eliminated in the Second Round by Shayna Baszler (who would go on to compete in the finals).

Post-Mae Young Classic, Mia Yim continued to work non-stop on the indies, save for the leg injury she suffered at the end of 2017. Still, she returned to action just in time for WrestleMania Weekend in April, even getting to wrestle (and win) on SHIMMER's 100th show. At the end of May 2018, independent wrestler Keith Lee hand-picked Mia Yim as his final opponent in his farewell match (on his way to WWE developmental) at his home promotion of Beyond Wrestling. Despite the size difference, Mia defeated Lee, and he afterward put Mia over as one of the best wrestlers in the world—male or female.

★ MICHELLE MCCOOL ★

YEARS ACTIVE: 2004–2011

TRAINED BY: DSW · OVW · Dave "Fit" Finlay

BILLED FROM: Palatka, Florida

ACCOMPLISHMENTS: 2010 Slammy Award for Knucklehead Moment of the Year (LayCool loses to Mae Young, with Layla) · #1 in 2010 PWI Female 50 · 2010 PWI Woman of the Year · 2x WWE Divas Champion · 2x WWE Women's Champion · 2010 Slammy Award for Diva of the Year

AKA: 1/2 of LayCool · "The All-American Diva" · "The Leggy Lolita"

NOTABLE MATCHES: Michelle McCool (c) vs. Maryse at WWE Unforgiven 2008, for the WWE Divas Championship (September 7, 2008) · Michelle McCool (c) vs. Melina at WWE Night of Champions 2009, for the WWE Women's Championship (February 19, 2009) · LayCool (Michelle McCool & Layla) vs. The Divas of Doom (Beth Phoenix & Natalya) at WWE TLC 2010, in Divas Tag Team Tables match (December 19, 2010) · LayCool (Michelle McCool & Layla) & Dolph Ziggler vs. Trish Stratus, Nicole "Snooki" Polizzi, & John Morrison at WWE WrestleMania XXVII (April 3, 2011) · Michelle McCool vs. Layla at WWE Extreme Rules 2011, in a No Count-out No Disqualification Loser Leaves WWE match (May 1, 2011)

★ Like many Divas in Michelle McCool's—yes, that's her real name—era of WWE, she was a Diva Search competitor. But unlike other Diva Search competitors (as well as the majority of her future WWE colleagues), Michelle McCool came from quite the unique world. No, it wasn't the fact that she was a big fan of wrestling growing up: it's that prior to WWE, she was a middle school teacher for four years. In fact, she even has a master's degree, which isn't exactly the type of thing you expect of professional wrestlers (although she also had a past in fitness competitions, which is of course more expected). Despite only making it to seventh place in the Diva Search—like Maryse, whose career trajectory paralleled Michelle's in a lot of ways—McCool was soon signed to a three-year deal in November 2004.

Almost more surprisingly, Michelle McCool ended up on WWE almost immediately, with a gimmick as SmackDown's resident fitness trainer (a face character but perhaps the most unmemorable part of McCool's career) and a necessity to basically learn how to wrestle on the show. She wouldn't even make her way down to developmental (in DSW, and then OVW) until months later—after having a feud with Melina—in the summer of 2005. However, that was probably the best decision WWE could have made for McCool, assuming they saw the potential in her to be a star. In developmental, she worked on her in-ring work, pitched storylines, and worked as an interviewer, host, and commentator, making sure to soak up as much knowledge as she possibly could. Then she made her return to SmackDown a year after she'd been sent to developmental, this time as a heel—and this time accepting the concept of the best characters being yourself turned up to 11, as she portrayed a version of the "sexy teacher" gimmick. This eventually led to her valeting a tag team called The Teacher's Pets and then (as a face) Chuck Palumbo, with neither team-up actually complementing McCool's personality.

In the summer of 2008, Michelle McCool ended up competing against Natalya to become the inaugural WWE Divas Champion. She remained a face until the end of the year, when she lost the championship to Maryse; then, months later, she won the WWE Women's Championship for the first time, becoming the first Diva to have won both championships. After

McCool turned on Layla and attacked her. The two former friends eventually had a one-on-one match to settle their differences, but it ended in a double count-out; so at Extreme Rules, they had a No Count-out No Disqualification Loser Leaves WWE match, which Layla won.

Michelle McCool's loss ended up being due to the fact that she was legitimately retiring from WWE (which is why the LayCool break-up was so quick). The reason for Michelle's retirement was simple: despite a relatively short career, the wear and tear of a professional wrestling career had gotten to her. During her time in WWE, Michelle McCool had suffered a broken sternum, ribs, and nose, among other injuries, and at the end of her run she was working on a broken toe and a torn MCL. In her farewell to the WWE Universe on WWE.com, Michelle had some parting words: "Thank you for the love and the hate. Thank you for being you and for watching. Hopefully I'll see you around—not in the ring—but maybe someday."

However, in a case of "never say never," Michelle eventually did make an in-ring return—though for one night only—as a surprise participant in the inaugural Women's Royal Rumble match at the 2018 Royal Rumble pay-per-view. And she didn't just return: she did so in a big way, with the most eliminations of anyone that night (eliminating five other women). Some might call that simply "flawless."

that, Michelle McCool found the perfect complement for her character in the form of Layla (with the two forming the "flawless" heel duo known as "LayCool"). The duo ran roughshod over the Divas Division from 2009 to early 2011, feuding with Divas stars like Mickie James, Beth Phoenix, and Kelly Kelly, while also deeming themselves co-champions (and splitting the Women's Championship in half)—all with the support of SmackDown authority figure Vickie Guerrero. With their abilities to finish each other's sentences (as well a simultaneous speech), no one was more in sync than LayCool at the time.

However, the beginning of the end for the superficial mean girl party started at the 2011 Royal Rumble, when LayCool lost the Divas Championship (at that point, unified) to Eve Torres. LayCool attempted to get over their miscommunications and losing streak through couples therapy, but eventually Michelle

★ MICKIE JAMES ★

YEARS ACTIVE: 1999–present

TRAINED BY: The Funkin' Conservatory · Dory Funk Jr. · KYDA Pro Training School · Ricky Morton · Bobby Eaton · Maryland Championship Wrestling · ECW Dojo

BILLED FROM: Richmond, Virginia

ACCOMPLISHMENTS: 1x Covey Pro Women's Championship · Covey Pro Hall of Fame Class of 2014 · 1x CyberSpace Wrestling Federation (CSWF) Women's Champion · 1x DCW Women's Champion · 1x Ground Xero Wrestling (GXW) Champion · 1x Impact Championship Wrestling Super Juniors Champion · 1x IPW: UK Women's Champion · 1x MCW Women's Champion · 1x PREMIER Wrestling Federation (PWF) Universal Women's Champion · 2009 PWI Woman of the Year · 2011 PWI Woman of the Year · #1 in 2009 PWI Female 50 · 1x Southern Championship Wrestling Diva Champion · 3x TNA Knockouts Champion · 2013 TNA World Cup of Wrestling (with Christopher Daniels, Kazarian, James Storm, & Kenny King) · 1x Ultimate Wrestling Federation Women's Champion · 5x WWE Women's Champion · 1x WWE Divas Champion

AKA: Alexis Laree · Vickie Adams · member of The Gathering · member of La Sociedad · member of Sports Entertainment Xtreme (S.E.X.) · La Luchadora · 1/3 of Team In Your Dreams

NOTABLE MATCHES: Mickie James vs. Trish Stratus (c) at WWE WrestleMania 22, for the WWE Women's Championship (April 2, 2006) · Mickie James vs. Lita (c) at WWE Survivor Series, for the WWE Women's Championship (November 26, 2006) · Mickie James (c) vs. Beth Phoenix vs. Melina at WWE Judgment Day 2008, in a Triple Threat match for the WWE Women's Championship (May 18, 2008) · Mickie James vs. Mia Yim at MCW Shane Shamrock Memorial Cup 2010 (July 31, 2010) · Mickie James vs. Tara at TNA Turning Point 2010 (November 7, 2010) · Mickie James vs. Cherry Bomb at 2CW Christmas Chaos (December 27, 2014) · Mickie James (c) vs. Kimber Lee at MCW Autumn Armageddon Tour 2015 – Night 5, for the MCW Women's Championship (November 13, 2015) · Mickie James vs. Princess KimberLee at CHIKARA National Pro Wrestling Day (February 6, 2016) · Team Original Divas Revolution (Mickie James, Jazz, & Victoria) vs. Team SHIMMER (Candice LeRae, "Crazy" Mary Dobson, & Solo Darling) at CHIKARA King of Trios 2016 – Night 1, in a King of Trios First Round match (September 2, 2016) · Mickie James vs. Asuka (c) at NXT TakeOver: Toronto (November 19, 2016) · Mickie James vs. Becky Lynch at WWE Elimination Chamber 2017 (February 12, 2017) · Mickie James vs. Alexa Bliss (c) at WWE TLC 2017, for the WWE RAW Women's Championship (October 22, 2017)

As a kid, Mickie James used to watch WWF with her father, and she was hooked. But it wasn't until after high school that she learned from a friend that wrestling schools even existed. However, once she learned, she made up her mind: she was going to wrestling school to become a professional wrestler. So after training at KYDA Pro Wrestling, she made her debut (first as a valet) in early 1999 as "Alexis Laree." That March, she made her in-ring debut, but she continued to hone her skills by taking classes and attending training camps everywhere she possibly could. Her early career as Alexis Laree featured brief runs in ROH and TNA, but it was always obvious where Mickie James would end up: WWE.

After signing a developmental contract for OVW in the summer of 2003, Mickie James spent the entirety of her two years in development under the "Alexis Laree" ring name . . . only to debut on *RAW* in the fall of 2005 as "Mickie James." Not every future Hall of Famer has the chance for their first major storyline to be their most memorable, but in the case of Mickie James that's exactly what happened. Mickie James debuted on *RAW* as Trish

Stratus's #1 fan, an overenthusiastic—but well-meaning—face that came into the wrestling world because she wanted to be just like Trish. As Trish appreciated Mickie's fandom, she allowed the rookie to team with her and sit under the champ's learning tree. However, as weeks went by, Mickie James revealed herself to be more unhinged and truly obsessed with Trish Stratus, attempting to emulate Trish, becoming possessive of her, even costing herself a chance at winning the Women's Championship during a Battle Royal to make sure Trish retained. That December, in a backstage segment, Mickie James would spring a kiss on Trish under mistletoe, creating more confusion over whether she wanted to be *like* Trish or be *with* Trish. Even after losing a one-on-one shot for Trish's Women's Championship, James remained devoted to her, at which point Trish finally attempted to draw a line in the sand and get some space from Mickie, which only made Mickie more possessive, until she finally snapped and attacked Trish. Leading up to WrestleMania 22, it looked like a fired-up Trish would vanquish her stalker once and for all. But at WrestleMania 22—in arguably one of the greatest women's matches in the history of WrestleMania, if not *the* best at that time—Mickie James defeated Trish Stratus to become the WWE Women's Champion for the first time, eventually defeating her in the subsequent rematches to win the feud.

While there have been plenty of "crazy" angles in wrestling, especially among women in WWE, James's performance always stood out from the pack, with an undercurrent of sadness that came with most of what she was doing. Perhaps that is why Mickie James would later become such a popular face: if she could make even the craziest stalker character sympathetic, then the sky must be the limit.

Just a couple of months after Mickie James's feud with Trish Stratus ended, Trish retired from WWE and Mickie turned face against the also-soon-to-retire Lita. As an integral part of the farewell storylines of two of WWE's most popular Divas, Mickie James seemed primed to take their spot at the top. However, despite becoming Women's Champion five times

(putting her just behind Trish in terms of most reigns with this particular WWE Women's Championship) and Divas Champion once during the rest of her tenure in WWE, she never had a story or feud that quite lived up to James's potential. Then, following the "Piggy James" feud with LayCool, Mickie James was released from WWE in April 2010, the result of WWE's desire to "move in a new direction with their women's division." So Mickie James moved to the indies and back to TNA—this time as Mickie James—where she won the Knockouts Championship three times. However, a little over six years after Mickie was originally released from WWE, it appeared that they had finally moved in a direction more welcoming to James (especially post-Divas Revolution).

In the fall of 2016, WWE announced that Mickie James would be a one-time challenger to NXT Women's Champion Asuka's title, at NXT TakeOver: Toronto. James put up a great effort, proving that she could hang with the new blood—and that she wasn't just good for the era of WWE she had come up in—although she lost. By the end of the year, Mickie James had signed a full-time contract with WWE, returning in January 17 as a heel and ally of Alexa Bliss (who, in story, was one of the few new wrestlers who remembered Mickie James's accomplishments). Eventually, Mickie James turned face—due to Alexa Bliss refusing to give her the SmackDown title match she had promised—but months later, James and Bliss reunited as a heel duo once more.

During her original run in WWE, Mickie James was often called a victim of the era, as a Diva who could actually compete in the ring at the highest level despite the directive for Divas. Since returning to WWE, she's proved that on a regular basis—especially in history-making moments like the first-ever Women's Royal Rumble and Elimination Chamber matches—keeping up with the new era of women's Superstars both in the ring and on the mic. Surely, one can argue Mickie James never lost it, but this really does call for one specific chant: "YOU'VE STILL GOT IT!"

★ MILDRED BURKE ★

YEARS ACTIVE: 1935–1955

TRAINED BY: Billy Wolfe

BILLED FROM: Coffeyville, Kansas

ACCOMPLISHMENTS: 3x Women's World Champion · 1x NWA World Women's Champion · Professional Wrestling Hall of Fame Class of 2002 · 1x WWWA World Heavyweight Champion · Wrestling Observer Newsletter Hall of Fame Class of 1996 · WWE Hall of Fame Class of 2016 (Legacy Inductee)

NOTABLE MATCHES: Mildred Burke vs. Clara Mortenson (c), for the Women's World Championship (January 28, 1937) · Mildred Burke vs. June Byers, in a 2 Out of 3 Falls match for the NWA World Women's Championship (August 20, 1954)

★ Mildred Burke wanted to be in a world that didn't necessarily want her. Born Mildred Bliss, she had dreams of becoming a professional wrestler after her boyfriend took her to see professional wrestling in Kansas City, Missouri. The problem was—besides the fact that she was pregnant at the time, and the boyfriend-turned-husband had left her high and dry—women in professional wrestling wasn't so much a reality as it was a bit in a vaudeville routine. She was 19 when she started training—after she had given birth to her son—under Billy Wolfe, another hurdle in her quest to make the impossible possible. While Billy was training other women to be wrestlers, when Mildred came to him to ask for wrestling training herself, he turned her away, proclaiming "You ain't no bigger than a pint of piss" to the 5-foot-2 new mother.

But nevertheless, she persisted, so Wolfe tried to scare her away by having a larger male wrestler essentially rough her up (for the incentive of $2). The male wrestler was able to grab Mildred and airplane-spin her, but before he could body-slam her, she managed to reverse and end up pinning him. That wasn't enough to convince

Billy Wolfe to train her, though, so he made her do it all over again; and not only did she do it, she pulled the same airplane-spin and body-slam combination he'd tried on her. Only then would Billy Wolfe accept her, deciding to take this show on the road on the carnival circuit and have her take on male challengers. Somewhere in between that tryout and the carnival circuit, Mildred Bliss became "Mildred Burke"; then she became Billy Wolfe's wife. And they became "women's wrestling's power couple."

Life with Billy Wolfe was not a happy life for Mildred Burke, nor was it one of monogamy on Wolfe's part, as part of his approach to fostering female talent also involved engaging in affairs with them. But that didn't change the one fact that, in the 1930s, out of over 200 men she wrestled, Mildred Burke beat all but one. As far as her work against women went, in 1937 Mildred became the Women's World Champion, defeating Clara Mortenson (in controversial fashion) for the title and holding it for 17 years. Wrestling for two decades. Six days a week. 50 weeks a year. She might have even competed in the first mud-wrestling match somewhere during all that, and was arguably the first wrestler (male or female) to wear fancy robes to the ring. Her work was making women's wrestling something more than just a sideshow to a sideshow.

Then in 1949, Wolfe was able to join the NWA, which meant he could hire out his stable (or harem, depending on who you ask) of 30 women wrestlers to any promotion he wanted—and take a significant cut of their earnings as a "manager." Mildred Burke was making about $2,000 a night at her peak, but all those earnings went to Billy Wolfe. Three years later, Mildred finally filed for divorce—they hadn't even lived together for the past eight years—but Wolfe ended up getting her essentially blackballed from the NWA in the process, making it harder for her to wrestle in a time where it was already hard enough for her to wrestle. The thing is, this was technically a breach of their divorce settlement, in which Mildred would pay $30,000 for Wolfe's wrestling agency (which she would call Attractions, Inc.) and the right to the championship, and Wolfe would be banned from participating in wrestling for five years. She would also waive alimony with the deal.

The banning point was obviously the part that breached the settlement, but this time the NWA stayed out of it. Billy Wolfe and his stable started their own women's wrestling agency (Girl Wrestling Enterprises, Inc.), with the offer that talent would get 50% of their earnings. So Mildred's Attractions, Inc. offered talent 60% of their earnings . . . but Wolfe upped the ante with the promise of 75% of all earnings to the talent. In the case of Billy Wolfe, he had already become a wealthy man with his earlier work as manager; but for Mildred Burke, it all ended up being too much and Attractions, Inc. went bankrupt. Eight months later, Billy Wolfe was put in place as the administrator of the agency, and he put out a memo to wrestling promoters around the United States announcing that he was now the booker in charge (with Mildred Burke as one of the talents). All this was in absolute defiance of the deal they had struck after their divorce, and Mildred refused to wrestle for her ex-husband, an act that essentially got her blackballed from the

NWA, as no one would book her without Wolfe's okay. In September 1953, she attended the annual NWA conference to make this right; but since women were banned from these conferences, she had to sit in the lobby while these men had a closed-door meeting about her future. About her livelihood. And the only one whose side was heard was Billy Wolfe. After the meeting, the NWA simply declined to recognize or officiate over women's wrestling—because they were tired of dealing with what, at its simplest, was a marital dispute—but Billy Wolfe still won. The one bright side was in the case of the women who were loyal to Mildred and refused to wrestle for Wolfe, but that wasn't a fix at all. Especially as Wolfe continued to sabotage her chances at getting work and gaining steam anywhere in the business—she'd still have to work for him for two more years before she could leave.

This all came to a head when Mildred was forced to wrestle June Byers—Wolfe's daughter-in-law, whom he had made the champion during the split—in a 2 Out of 3 Falls match in August 1954. The cause of this match was the need for an undisputed champion (and a need to make June Byers more popular), and since Mildred wasn't going to relinquish the title, this match ended up being booked as a shoot match (meaning there would be no predetermined spots or finish). Naturally, Wolfe stacked the deck against Mildred, paying off the referee to call the match in June's favor. While June got the first fall in 16 minutes—which Burke later went on the record saying she allowed in order to start strong for the second fall—after 63 minutes during the second fall, officials stopped the match. Because there was no second fall (and she certainly didn't lose two falls), Mildred was under the assumption that she still had the title. Instead, Wolfe told the press that June Byers won the match and the championship, and the credibility Mildred Burke had in the business was swiftly destroyed.

Still, Mildred had her own wrestling promotion based in Los Angeles that she'd started in the early 1950s, the WWWA, in which she was the champion. In the fall of 1954, she even went on tour to Japan with the WWWA World Single Championship, a tour that would greatly affect the course of women's wrestling, as the All Japan Women's Pro-Wrestling Association would be formed the following summer. Then, after Mildred retired in 1956, AJW would make their top prize the WWWA World Single Championship, with Aiko Kyo winning it from champion Marie Vagnone. Mildred also founded International Women's Wrestlers, Inc., a booking agency/wrestling training center with offices in New York, San Francisco, and Sydney, Australia. She also started a wrestling school in California called The Mildred Burke School for Lady Wrestlers, a school from which former WWF Women's Champion Bertha Faye graduated.

Mildred Burke died of a stroke in 1989, but despite Billy Wolfe's attempts in his lifetime, her legacy did not die with her. She was posthumously inducted into the Professional Wrestling Hall of Fame in 2002 and the WWE Hall of Fame (as a Legacy Inductee) in 2016.

★ MISS ELIZABETH ★

YEARS ACTIVE: 1985–2000

TRAINED BY: "Macho Man" Randy Savage

BILLED FROM: Louisville, Kentucky

ACCOMPLISHMENTS: Pro Wrestling This Week Wrestler of the Week (October 4–10, 1987) · 1987 Slammy Award for Woman of the Year

AKA: "Ms. Elizabeth Macho" · "The First Lady of Wrestling" · member of Alliance to End Hulkamania · member of Millionaire Club · member of nWo · member of nWo Wolfpac

NOTABLE MATCHES: "The Match Made in Heaven" at WWF SummerSlam 1991 (August 26, 1991)

★ While plenty of people remember Miss Elizabeth, it's safe to say that it's not for her wrestling. However, that shouldn't be taken as a backhanded compliment, as Miss Elizabeth's contribution to professional wrestling showed the power of both a solid valet/wrestler relationship and the importance of emotional resonance in the entertainment part of "sports entertainment." In terms of "actual wrestling," Miss Elizabeth never even got into the ring in that type of fashion until her final year in the business, 2000—and that was only the result of an in-storyline grudge.

Elizabeth Hulette originally got involved in professional wrestling as a fan-turned-employee at International Championship Wrestling, her local wrestling promotion in Lexington, Kentucky. As her father ran the local TV station which aired International Championship Wrestling—and she worked as a camera operator at the station—Elizabeth was soon hooked on the wrestling promotion. Eventually, she met Randy Poffo, son of the wrestling promotion's owner Angelo Poffo and better known as "Macho Man" Randy Savage, and the two hit it off romantically. As a result, Elizabeth eventually became an announcer and host for International Championship Wrestling. And by the end of 1984, she and Savage were hitched. Then in the summer of 1985, she debuted in WWF as Savage's manager, concluding a storyline in which the company's various managers all attempted to sign him on as a client. As Savage would feud with wrestlers like George "The Animal" Steele and The Honky Tonk Man, Miss Elizabeth's character would have to deal with unwanted advances from these characters, men who attempted to get it into Savage's head (if they even had to try at all) that she would prefer them over him. Even after Savage's face turn and the team-up of him and Hulk Hogan as The Mega Powers, the eventual conclusion would revolve around Hogan's friendliness toward Elizabeth.

"Elegant" was the word often used to describe Miss Elizabeth, which was what made it such a shock when "Macho Man" Randy Savage introduced her to the WWF and its audience. She was the opposite of what a wrestling valet or manager was supposed to be; she wasn't flashy or loud. In a sense, she was the opposite of

event; after Hogan won, Savage replaced her with "Sensational" Queen Sherri. This on-screen separation would continue for the next couple of years—seeming even longer once Miss Elizabeth stopped making television appearances in 1990—until WrestleMania VII in spring of 1991. After Savage lost to Ultimate Warrior—in a match with retirement on the line—Sherri attacked him . . . and Elizabeth made her WWF return, disposing of Sherri, and reuniting with (a now face-again) Randy Savage. Months later, at SummerSlam, Elizabeth and Savage had an on-screen wrestling wedding, with their wedding reception leading to Savage's next feud, against Jake "The Snake" Roberts.

Despite the storybook romance on-screen, Elizabeth and Savage divorced about a year after their storyline wedding (known as "The Match Made in Heaven"). Speaking to how atypical the entire situation was to the era in which it took place—though it would make sense today—Savage even issued a statement in *WWF Magazine* about the divorce, breaking kayfabe to explain. This was revealed a couple of months after the end of Miss Elizabeth's time in WWF, post-Savage/Ric Flair feud, another feud where Savage's opponent tried to pretend Elizabeth was unfaithful—with Flair claiming Elizabeth was "damaged goods," as "she was mine before she was yours." (A good portion of the feud continued months after Elizabeth was done with WWF.)

Elizabeth would remain out of the professional wrestling limelight until 1996, when she joined rival wrestling company WCW. The Miss Elizabeth in WCW was somewhat indicative of the time period in wrestling then, as no more was she considered the same classy, quiet, "stand by her man" type as she had been in WWF. While she debuted as Savage and Hogan's valet once more, a few weeks later she turned on Savage to help Flair (and valet for him in the Four Horsemen), which would have been unheard-of in WWF. Despite this, according to Savage's brother (Lanny Poffo), bringing Elizabeth into WCW was Savage's version of getting closure in their real-life past relationship—as well as a way to get the fans excited. And it worked for Elizabeth as well, as she recalled:

professional wrestling as a whole concept, which instantly made her special. And if she was drawn to a character like the "Macho Man," then he must have been special too. Especially as Savage portrayed a heel character, while Elizabeth simply remained a sweet, patient woman. In fact, Elizabeth was considered "a calming influence" to Savage, a virtue which was credited for Savage winning the WWF Championship at WrestleMania IV.

As Tito Santana once described the relationship, "Elizabeth was different from any other woman in wrestling. The crowd felt very protective of her. When [the heel] Savage would make an angry move towards Elizabeth, the fans wanted to jump over the barricade and stand in front of him. She won the people over. [Later] their sympathy for her allowed them to see Randy as human. . . ."

At WrestleMania V (billed as "The Mega Powers Explode"), Elizabeth refused to pick sides in the Savage vs. Hogan main

I was so excited. I never thought I would come back to it. Because of my personal relationship with Randy, I didn't want to be involved if it would make him uncomfortable. Now we have a good relationship and he has a very sweet girlfriend and we all get on very well.

Later that year, she then joined the ultimate WCW heel stable—alongside Hogan—and the antithesis of class, the nWo. Elizabeth and Savage would again reunite, though, once he joined nWo, but by the summer of 1998 they found each other on opposite ends of the nWo faction wars. Miss Elizabeth's time in WCW sometimes felt like it was a bizarro world version of the same woman from WWF, as this heel version of Elizabeth was no longer the one who wrestlers created rumors about: *she* started the rumors, like in the storyline where she (on behalf of the nWo) claimed Goldberg was stalking her. And eventually, she found real love again with a wrestler, this time in the form of Lex Luger.

"ELEGANT" WAS THE WORD OFTEN USED TO DESCRIBE MISS ELIZABETH, SHE WASN'T WHAT A WRESTLING VALET OR MANAGER WAS SUPPOSED TO BE; SHE WASN'T FLASHY OR LOUD, WHICH INSTANTLY MADE HER SPECIAL.

However, this love story also didn't have a happy ending. Three years after leaving WCW (in August 2000) with Lex Luger, Elizabeth passed away, due to an overdose of alcohol and pain pills. (And Luger blamed himself for being such a negative influence on her at the time.) At just age 42, the onetime example of grace and class in WWF sadly became just another statistic in the long list of wrestlers and wrestling personalities who died young.

★ MOLLY HOLLY ★

YEARS ACTIVE: 1997–2005

TRAINED BY: Dean Malenko · Dave "Fit" Finlay · Memphis Championship Wrestling · Jeff Bradley · Tim Mahoney · Tracy Smothers · Madusa · WCW Power Plant

BILLED FROM: Forest Lake, Minnesota · Mobile, Alabama

ACCOMPLISHMENTS: 1x New Dimension Wrestling (NDW) Women's Champion · 1x World Professional Wrestling Federation (WPWF) Women's Champion · WSU Hall of Fame Class of 2010 · 2x WWE Women's Champion · 1x WWF Hardcore Champion

AKA: Mighty Molly · Nora Greenwald · Lady Ophelia · Lady Ophelia Bristol · Ophelia · Miss Madness · Mona · Sabotage · Starla Saxton · member of The Alliance · member of Team Madness

NOTABLE MATCHES: Molly Holly, Crash Holly, & Steve Blackman vs. T&A (Trish Stratus, Test, & Albert) at WWF Survivor Series 2000 (November 19, 2000) · Mighty Molly (Alliance) vs. Ivory (Alliance) vs. Trish Stratus (WWF) vs. Jacqueline (WWF) vs. Jazz (Alliance) at WWF Survivor Series 2001, in a 6-Pack Challenge for the vacant WWF Women's Championship (November 18, 2001) · Molly Holly & Jazz vs. Jacqueline & Ivory at WWE Sunday Night Heat (May 25, 2003) · Molly Holly & Gail Kim vs. Lita & Trish Stratus at WWE Unforgiven 2003 (September 21, 2003) · Molly Holly (c) vs. Ivory at Survivor Series 2003, for the WWE Women's Championship (November 16, 2003) · Molly Holly vs. Victoria (c) at WWE WrestleMania XX, in a Hair vs. Championship match for the WWE Women's Championship (March 14, 2004)

★ If there were an award for Most Underrated Women's Wrestler of All Time—and to be fair, there just might be—then Molly Holly would be a shoo-in. There is perhaps no professional wrestler (female or otherwise) who has been held in such high regard by peers as the woman known as "Molly Holly"; and in a business that can be cutthroat behind the scenes and bring

out the worst in people, it takes a lot for a wrestler to be lauded for quite the opposite . . . and to have still been quite successful despite this.

The woman behind Molly Holly, Nora Greenwald, originally wanted to be one of the American Gladiators. And after a co-worker suggested that she try wrestling (due to her "athletic" look), she only did it because it was fun, not something she actually thought would get her on TV. So at age 19 she began her training in Tampa, Florida—with only $200 to her name—under WCW wrestler Dean Malenko. She got her start with the ring name "Starla Saxton," which would also be the name she used in her earliest WCW and WWF appearances (as enhancement talent). And despite her not initially wanting to be a pro wrestler, as it turned out, it was something that came quite easy to her. (Not only was she the innovator of her finishing move, the Molly-Go-Round—a flipping seated senton, suggested by Malenko—she reportedly suggested Victoria's finishing move—the Widow's Peak—to her as its final form of a neckbreaker variation Gory Special, as opposed to the original form.)

Greenwald would officially get her big break in 1999, when she debuted in WCW as villain beauty queen "Miss Madness,"

one of "Macho Man" Randy Savage's valets—along with Gorgeous George, the female valet, not the male wrestling legend—and a member of the short-lived "Team Madness." Savage had originally asked Greenwald to teach Gorgeous George—his girlfriend at the time—to wrestle after seeing her work as Starla Saxton. They developed a friendship after that, leading to his getting her the gig at WCW. Post-Team Madness, Greenwald transitioned into "Mona," the face version of Miss Madness. Neither of these gimmicks set the wrestling world on fire; but, according to Greenwald, just a month as Miss Madness (before she had signed a contract) allowed a young wrestler like herself to get interest from WWF, which made WCW want her more; and, as a result, the two-year deal she eventually got from WCW during this time got her "good money" (the first year) and "amazing money" (the second year). However, while this was good for Greenwald—and for plenty of other talent in WCW at the time, making hand-over-fist money—this was bad for WCW. Without a true women's division and Savage by her side (as he'd since left the company), Greenwald spent the last six months of her time in the company getting paid to do nothing, and WCW finally released her for budgetary reasons. (Seven months later, WCW would crumble and be bought by WWF.)

Almost immediately—and thanks to Malenko introducing her to Jim Ross—WWF snatched her up. Greenwald had a temporary debut in WWF—after some time in their developmental territory in Memphis Championship Wrestling—as "Lady Ophelia" (manager to William Regal). But it wasn't until that November that she made her true debut, as "Molly Holly," the third (and female) Holly cousin (the other two being Hardcore Holly and Crash Holly). Her debut was an attack on Trish Stratus, leading to a Holly Cousins/T & A feud. Early 2001 would see the Holly Cousins feud with the Dudley Boyz—another tag team with a superfluous family member suddenly showing up, in the form of Spike Dudley—and with this feud Molly found on-screen love (with said superfluous family member). The Molly Holly/Spike Dudley on-screen pairing was the wrestling equivalent of *Romeo & Juliet* or *West Side Story*, but with tables (the Dudley Boyz's weapon of choice), and it eventually led to the dissolution of the Holly Cousins as a joint unit, with Molly choosing Spike over her family. This particular storyline—a "Disney romance" as it were—is the one Molly has called the "best time of her career."

But by the fall of 2001, Molly would dump Spike for the standard reason: she wanted to be a superhero. Becoming "Mighty Molly," the sidekick to WWF's resident superhero The Hurricane, Molly would play a "cheerier, dorkier version" of her real-life self. She'd also go on to win the WWF Hardcore Championship from Hurricane at WrestleMania X8, but as a result of the 24/7 rule of the championship—a comical aspect of the title—she'd end up losing it later that night to Christian. After the storybook romance and superhero origin story—in a way, Molly Holly's character was just going through Hollywood blockbuster genres, now wasn't she?—the otherwise upbeat Molly Holly that the WWF audience knew turned heel. According to Molly, her heel turn was the result of Jazz suffering an injury and the necessity for Trish Stratus and Lita to have competent competition (as well as someone experienced to put over and help the less-experienced female wrestlers). Despite a hesitancy to turn heel, Molly ran with her new gimmick, shedding her bubbly demeanor for self-righteousness and trading her blonde hairdo for a modest brunette. Molly's gimmick was the antithesis of the WWE Diva presentation, and she made sure every one of her opponents and the audience knew it, frequently reminding them she was "pure and wholesome."

However, despite her success as a heel at this time, behind the scenes Molly Holly found the transition rough. The combination of characters—including commentators—deriding her character for her physical attributes (mostly in the form of her weight) as well as her purity (as Nora Greenwald was legitimately a virgin, something that was mocked in terms of the character) took a toll on her, as it was difficult to separate the character from the real person, when the character was so heavily informed by the real person. This version of Molly Holly had a memorable feud with

Trish Status and won the WWE Women's Championship twice during this time, even getting to have a "WrestleMania moment" because of this gimmick. That would be the Hair (hers) vs. Championship (Victoria's) match at WrestleMania 20. Molly Holly actually pitched the match—and the fact that she would have to shave her head at all—as a way to guarantee a match at WrestleMania; she'd first pitched it to Vince McMahon eight months before WrestleMania 20, then again three months before it (to both Vince and Stephanie McMahon), getting the green light that time. But Molly Holly has also admitted it was a time when she was essentially absolutely miserable behind the scenes, with a bad attitude (the opposite of what anyone would expect) and no more drive for the business other than money. So in 2005, she asked for and was granted her release from the company—not necessarily because she didn't like that her character was a heel, but because she didn't like the way she was handling it. She left to reevaluate and reassess her life, to essentially recharge her batteries.

While Nora Greenwald technically retired in 2005—or went "on sabbatical," in her words—she continued to make appearances on the indies post-WWE and remained a fan of wrestling. In fact, Greenwald teaches wrestling now at The Academy School of Professional Wrestling in Minneapolis, Minnesota, alongside former WWE talents Ken Anderson (formerly known as Mr. Kennedy) and Shawn Daivari. And she remained on good terms with WWE, appearing on the *RAW* 15th anniversary show, in the "Miss WrestleMania" match at WrestleMania XXV, and other little things. On January 28, 2018, Holly made a surprise appearance as an entrant in the inaugural WWE Women's Royal Rumble match. (A true worker through and through, Holly gave an interview prior to the event, making clear that she wouldn't be a part of the event and wasn't even privy to WWE's inner workings anymore.) A few months later, she showed up again to induct Ivory into the WWE Hall of Fame. Now, when is Molly Holly going to be inducted into the WWE Hall of Fame?

★ NAOMI ★

YEARS ACTIVE: 2009–present

TRAINED BY: FCW

BILLED FROM: "Planet Funk" · Orlando, Florida

ACCOMPLISHMENTS: 1x (and inaugural) FCW Divas Champion · 2010 FCW Divas Championship Tournament · 2013 Slammy Award for Best Dance Moves of the Year (with Cameron, as The Funkadactyls) · #7 in 2015 PWI Female 50 · 2x WWE SmackDown Women's Champion · 2018 (and inaugural) WrestleMania Women's Battle Royal

AKA: Ms. Florida · Naomi Knight · Naomi Night · Trinity McCray · Trinity · Trinity Fatu · 1/2 of The Funkadactyls · member of Tons of Funk · 1/3 of Team B.A.D. (Beautiful and Dangerous) · 1/2 of Naomina · member of Team B.A.D. & Blonde · 1/2 of Day One Glow

NOTABLE MATCHES: Naomi Night vs. Serena at FCW, in a FCW Divas Championship Tournament Finals match for the inaugural FCW Divas Championship (June 20, 2010) · Naomi vs. AJ Lee at WWE *NXT* Season 3 (November 23, 2010) · Team B.A.D. (Naomi, Sasha Banks, & Tamina) vs. Team Bella (Brie Bella, Nikki Bella, & Alicia Fox) vs. Team PCB (Paige, Charlotte, & Becky Lynch) at WWE SummerSlam 2015 (August 23, 2015) · Naomi vs. Carmella vs. Becky Lynch vs. Alexa Bliss vs. Nikki Bella at WWE Backlash 2016, in a 6-Pack Challenge for the inaugural WWE SmackDown Women's Championship (September 11, 2016) · Naomi vs. Alexa Bliss (c) at WWE Elimination Chamber 2017, for the WWE SmackDown Women's Championship (February 12, 2017) · Naomi vs. Alexa Bliss (c) vs. Becky Lynch vs. Carmella (with James Ellsworth) vs. Mickie James vs. Natalya at WrestleMania 33, in a 6-Pack Challenge match for the WWE SmackDown Women's Championship (April 2, 2017)

★ In August 2009, it was announced that Orlando Magic cheerleader/dancer (and former Flo Rida background dancer) Trinity McCray had signed a WWE developmental contract at FCW. A couple of months later, she debuted as "Naomi Night" (eventually becoming "Naomi Knight"). (Despite her never actually wrestling on the main roster as "Naomi Knight," fans and wrestling media still continue using it as the character's kayfabe last name.) During her time in FCW, Naomi's biggest feuds were with Serena and AJ Lee, as she defeated the former to become the inaugural FCW Divas Champion and eventually faced the latter in a title vs. title match of her FCW Divas Championship against AJ's Queen of FCW crown.

Around the same time, Naomi technically made her main roster debut (alongside AJ and others) on the all-Diva third season of the game show version of *NXT*. With Kelly Kelly as her Pro mentor, Naomi was easily slotted into a face, fan favorite persona. And despite the constant derision and mockery that came during the third season of *NXT*—as many of the Divas-in-training had little to no in-ring experience before making their debuts on national television—Naomi's natural athleticism was something that couldn't be denied. The biggest example of this was during a one-on-one match between Naomi and AJ, in which the commentary team—who had taken to openly insulting the skills of the women and the general quality of the show—actually called the match and acknowledged its superior quality. Naomi would go on to place second in this *NXT* season, but she wouldn't return to WWE TV until early 2012 . . . as half of a dancing valet duo for "The Funkasaurus" Brodus Clay called "The Funkadactyls."

NAOMI'S NATURAL ATHLETICISM WAS SOMETHING THAT COULDN'T BE DENIED. DURING A ONE-ON-ONE MATCH BETWEEN NAOMI AND AJ, THE COMMENTARY TEAM ACKNOWLEDGED ITS SUPERIOR QUALITY.

Again, Naomi was put in as a fan favorite; but as one of the most promising Diva prospects in the developmental system at the time, her role as a valet to a comedy wrestler seemed like an improper use of her time and skill. (Even during her developmental days, Naomi was lauded for her athleticism.) However, being in The Funkadactyls (and the larger stable, known as "Tons of Funk") did allow Naomi to showcase her dancing ability, something that has been a key aspect of her character for nearly all of her time on the main roster. (At the same time, Naomi's mainstream popularity also factored into things, as she was cast as one of the stars of WWE's reality series, *Total Divas*, on E!. In fact, she was one of the few Divas who was put on the show with her real name instead of her character name.) Naomi and her dance/tag team partner, Cameron, did however get some opportunities to wrestle

in multi-woman matches, and feuded with The Bella Twins—in conjunction with "The Funkasaurus" and Sweet T feuding with the tag team Team Rhodes Scholars—during the build-up to an Eight-Person Mixed Tag Team match at WrestleMania 29. The match never happened, though, as it was reportedly cut due to time constraints. (This particular situation was also the focus of an episode of *Total Divas*, leading to the question of whether the WWE had really planned to have the match in the first place or if they'd manufactured the situation for reality show purposes.) By the end of 2013, Naomi (and Cameron) was more associated with *Total Divas* than she was with Tons of Funk, and the group broke up. Naomi and Cameron would continue to team together going into 2014, but Naomi would see more singles success, regularly chasing the Divas Championship (against AJ Lee and then Paige), leading to Cameron's heel turn on Naomi that summer.

Prior to the feud with Cameron, however, Naomi suffered an injury during a match against Aksana (who had also been on the game show *NXT* season with Naomi). Naomi suffered a fractured orbital bone, yet she surprisingly wasn't off TV for long (only a month), returning to the ring with various custom eye patches. And honestly, the eye-patch look was pretty badass. At the time, it appeared the eye patch would become a bigger part of Naomi's gimmick—she had at least three custom patches made, with promises of more—but after a few weeks, there was no more eye patch. (Despite no official confirmation on the matter, depth perception was probably the biggest reason.) Mid-Cameron feud, Naomi required minor surgery to fix issues regarding the orbital bone injury, but she came back to ultimately defeat her former Funkadactyl partner.

Following the Cameron feud, Naomi was involved in storylines with her husband Jimmy Uso ("Jon Fatu," in real life) and brother-in-law Jey Uso against The Miz, as *Total Divas* had opened the door for the acknowledgment of their characters' connection. (This would continue even during opposite heel/face character alignments, despite WWE typically avoiding such real-life connections in the past.) However, following WrestleMania,

Naomi turned heel for the first—and currently, only—time in her WWE career. She would go on to align with Tamina—a relative through marriage, on the Uso/Fatu side—as her muscle and backup. Naomi remained in title contention during this time, but continually fell short . . . and then the Divas Revolution happened. With the Divas Revolution, Naomi and Tamina would end up teaming with NXT call-up (and then-NXT Women's Champion) Sasha Banks, forming Team B.A.D. (Beautiful and Dangerous). The team lasted from the summer of 2015 to February 2016, when Sasha Banks left (and turned face) and Naomi and Tamina (subsequently calling themselves "Naomina") attacked her as a result. A few months after the split with Banks, both Tamina and Naomi suffered various leg injuries, effectively putting an end to the Naomina team-up.

Naomi's return from injury, however, proved to be the most important point in her career thus far. After being drafted to SmackDown LIVE in the 2016 brand extension, Naomi made her in-ring debut as a face again—this time with a whole new entrance, theme (a remix of the theme sung by Naomi during the Team B.A.D. days), and look. And thus began the "Glow" era of Naomi. According to Naomi, the "Feel The Glow" gimmick was something she'd originally come up with in 2014, but a combination of WWE officials not thinking the idea (inspired by "The Glow" from the 1985 film *The Last Dragon*) would work and timing prevented it before. "The whole philosophy and concept behind 'The Glow' [a mystical force that hero Bruce Leroy must unlock to achieve martial-arts mastery] is pretty much about believing in yourself and being confident, no matter what you go through or experience. The good times and the bad. You always have to believe in yourself and not let your confidence fade." Glowing shoes, glowing gear, glowing makeup—Naomi didn't just feel the glow, she *became* the glow. And the glow apparently paid off, when Naomi spent early 2017 feuding with WWE SmackDown Women's Champion Alexa Bliss and won the championship for the first time in her eight-year career. However, two days later she was—quite controversially—forced to vacate the championship after suffering a legitimate knee injury, as the assumption was that she wouldn't be able to perform at WrestleMania 33 to defend the championship. However, the injury turned out not to be as severe as originally assumed, and not only was she able to perform at WrestleMania—and compete in the championship match now as a challenger—she defied the odds and won the championship back in her hometown of Orlando.

Naomi held the SmackDown Women's Championship for 140 days before dropping it to Natalya; but since then, Naomi has remained a glowing star in the women's division. In January 2018, she competed in the inaugural Women's Royal Rumble match, which she didn't win, but she put on a memorable performance with her athleticism. She did, however, go on to win the inaugural WWE Women's Battle Royal at WrestleMania 34. From being underrated to making WWE history. . . .

★ NATALYA NEIDHART ★

YEARS ACTIVE: 2000–present

TRAINED BY: Bruce Hart · Hart Dungeon · Clive Lewellin · Ross Hart · Tokyo Joe · Tyson Kidd · DSW · FCW · OVW

BILLED FROM: Calgary, Alberta, Canada

ACCOMPLISHMENTS: 1x ECCW SuperGirls Champion · 2005 Stampede Wrestling Women's Wrestler of the Year · #4 in 2011 PWI Female 50 · 2x Stampede Wrestling Women's Pacific Champion · 1x WWE Divas Champion · 1x WWE SmackDown Women's Champion

AKA: Natalya · Nadia Hart · Nattie Neidhart · "Nasty Nattie" · member of Hart Foundation 2.0 · member of Next Generation Hart Foundation · 1/2 of The Divas of Doom · 1/3 of The Hart Dynasty · 1/3 of The Hart Trilogy · "The Anvilette" · "The Hart Dungeon Diva" · "Nattie By Nature" · "The Queen of (Black) Harts" · member of The Welcoming Committee

NOTABLE MATCHES: Nattie Neidhart vs. Cheerleader Melissa at ECCW SuperGirls Volume 1 (September 23, 2005) · Natalya & Beth Phoenix vs. LayCool (Layla & Michelle McCool) at WWE TLC 2010, in Divas Tag Team Tables match (December 19, 2010) · Natalya vs. AJ Lee (c) at WWE TLC 2013, for the WWE Divas Championship (December 15, 2013) · Natalya vs. AJ Lee (c) at WWE *Main Event*, for the WWE Divas Championship (March 11, 2014) · Natalya (with Bret Hart) vs. Charlotte (with Ric Flair) at NXT TakeOver, for the vacant NXT Women's Championship (May 29, 2014) · Natalya vs. Nikki Bella at WWE SmackDown LIVE, in a Falls Count Anywhere match (February 21, 2017) · Natalya vs. Carmella (with James Ellsworth) vs. Becky Lynch vs. Charlotte Flair vs. Tamina Snuka at WWE Money in the Bank 2017, in a Money in the Bank Ladder match, for the inaugural Women's Money in the Bank contract (June 18, 2017) · Natalya vs. Carmella vs. Becky Lynch vs. Charlotte Flair vs. Tamina Snuka at WWE SmackDown LIVE, in a Money in the Bank Ladder match, for the Women's Money in the Bank contract (June 27, 2017)

⭐ As a third-generation wrestler (and the first-ever female third-generation wrestler), Nattie Neidhart was born with an advantage in the wrestling industry. The daughter of Jim "The Anvil" Neidhart and niece of Bret and Owen Hart, as well as "The British Bulldog" Davey Boy Smith, she was always either destined for greatness or destined to constantly tell people she was destined for greatness. Nattie chose the former, even though it was the harder route; though there have certainly been times when her in-ring character has required her to play the latter. Luckily, she has both the pedigree and genuine ability to make both work.

After graduating from high school, Nattie officially began training—at the world-famous Hart Family Dungeon, for which she is known for being the first female graduate—for the business that was technically already in her blood. While she began her wrestling career mostly wrestling in her native Canada—for Stampede Wrestling, a promotion run by her uncles Bruce and Ross—she began to branch out around 2004, with wrestling tours in the United Kingdom and then Japan (where she faced

Amazing Kong, as "Nadia Hart"). The fall of 2006 then saw Nattie debut in SHIMMER, but her time there was only for one weekend—as, by the time the next set of tapings had come around, Nattie would already be signed to the WWE, as "Natalya Neidhart." Nattie signed with WWE (for developmental in DSW, then eventually FCW and then OVW) in January 2007.

Nattie originally debuted on the main roster as "Natalya Neidhart" (with that eventually being shortened to "Natalya") in the spring of 2008, as a heel aligned with the Diva veteran Victoria. This eventually led to Natalya facing off against Michelle McCool for the inaugural Divas Championship—falling short—as well as her first main roster feud against The Bella Twins—who she had feuded with in developmental and has continued to cross paths

with ever since. However, Natalya's more memorable early run in WWE was the follow-up to the Victoria alliance, as a third of The Hart Dynasty (one of the many forms of the team), along with her cousin David Hart Smith (son of British Bulldog) and her real-life boyfriend (now husband) Tyson Kidd. While originally a heel team, The Hart Dynasty turned face at WrestleMania XXVI during Bret Hart's match against Mr. McMahon (with Bruce Hart as the Special Guest Referee) and followed up by feuding with the heel, debuting Usos and Tamina Snuka. The team broke up by the fall of 2010—with Tyson turning heel—but face Natalya was able to return to the title conversation around this time, and after multiple attempts at LayCool and their "co-Divas" Championship, she defeated them (in a Handicap match) at Survivor Series 2010 to win the title for the first time. Immediately following her championship win, LayCool attacked her, leading to Beth Phoenix stepping in to help her—forming the alliance that would eventually be known as The Divas of Doom. All four of these women would then go on to make history, wrestling in the first-ever Divas Tag Team Tables match (which Natalya and Beth won).

After losing the Divas Championship to Eve at Royal Rumble 2011, Natalya transitioned into a mentor role (reflecting her own veteran status, as she has legitimately functioned as a mentor for the Bellas as well as Charlotte Flair) for The Chickbusters (AJ Lee and Kaitlyn), before turning heel in the summer with Beth Phoenix for the Divas of Doom gimmick. This eventually all ended in March 2012, with Natalya feuding with Kaitlyn for a bit on *NXT Redemption* before turning face again—and a comedic one, at that—due to an on-screen romance with The Great Khali, who she had been calling her secret crush. (Despite how short-lived it was, it's also worth noting that early 2012 also saw a baffling gimmick change for heel Natalya in the form of flatulence.) As Natalya was soon after announced as a cast member on the reality series *Total Divas*, though—which featured an in-depth look at her real life, which included her long-term relationship with TJ "Tyson Kidd" Wilson—the emphasis was eventually taken off this on-screen relationship. So when her storylines weren't specifically connected to her role as a member of the *Total Divas* cast, Natalya eventually became the valet to Tyson's tag team with Cesaro. With this role, she transitioned from oblivious face—specifically oblivious to how dismissive and disrespectful Tyson would be to her, like when he would arrive late to a double-date dinner and bring Cesaro with him because of "Canadian Doubles"—to voluntary heel. This team-up would end after Tyson suffered a career-ending spinal injury in the summer of 2015.

Post-Tyson's injury, Natalya has constantly vacillated between face and heel, with the latter alignment leading to some of the most memorable moments in her WWE career thus far, like her propensity to quote pop music lyrics while not realizing they're pop lyrics. She also continues to factor her intense love of cats into her gimmick, something she had been doing since the Tyson/Cesaro team-up, thanks to *Total Divas*. Despite being the butt of the joke at times—though without farting this time around—Natalya has had a second life of sorts as the in-ring veteran in WWE's Women's Evolution. And in the summer of 2017, after defeating Naomi at SummerSlam, Natalya won the SmackDown Women's Championship (becoming the first former Divas Champion to hold it).

★ NIA JAX ★

YEARS ACTIVE: 2015–present

TRAINED BY: WWE Performance Center

BILLED FROM: San Diego, California

ACCOMPLISHMENTS: 2016 PWI Rookie of the Year · #22 in 2017 PWI Female 50 · 1x WWE RAW Women's Champion

AKA: Lina · Zada · 1/2 of Team Rude · "The Irresistible Force" · "The Hybrid Athlete"

NOTABLE MATCHES: Nia Jax vs. Bayley (c) at NXT TakeOver: London, for the NXT Women's Championship (December 16, 2015) · Alexa Bliss vs. Carmella vs. Nia Jax at NXT, for the #1 Contendership to the NXT Women's Championship (May 25, 2016) · Nia Jax vs. Bayley (c) vs. Charlotte Flair vs. Sasha Banks at WWE WrestleMania 33, in a Fatal-4-Way Elimination match for the WWE RAW Women's Championship (April 2, 2017) · Nia Jax vs. Bayley vs. Alexa Bliss (c) vs. Emma vs. Sasha Banks at WWE No Mercy 2017, for the WWE RAW Women's Championship (September 24, 2017) · Nia Jax vs. Alexa Bliss (c) at WWE WrestleMania 34, for the WWE RAW Women's Championship (April 8, 2018)

⭐ She's not like most girls. At least, that's something Nia Jax's theme song would like you to be aware of. Standing at a billed height of 6 feet even and a billed weight of 272 pounds (which is only known because WWE makes sure Nia Jax's impressive and incomparable size is known, unlike her opponents'), Nia Jax is unlike most women in WWE today—or ever. The only thing that makes her like the others—other than her lineage, as part of the Fatu/Anoa'i wrestling dynasty—is that she's an absolutely stunning woman. Prior to her debut in professional wrestling, she was a plus-size model, and even as a monster heel in WWE, there's a reason why Nia Jax's debut vignettes in *NXT* pointed out that she could disarm her opponents "with just a smile."

After signing a WWE developmental deal to NXT in 2014, Savelina "Lina" Fanene made her in-ring debut in May the following year as "Zada"; but a few months later, she would be "Nia Jax." A month after the switch to Nia Jax, she got vignettes hyping her debut at *NXT*. In the vignettes, she posited that "Most girls take what they're given in life. . . . I'm not most girls. . . . Greatness is my destiny." Jax's debut on *NXT* in October 2015 quickly branded her as a dominant monster character who even more quickly dismantled her opponents, which led her into a feud with NXT Women's Champion Bayley. While Jax dominated Bayley for the majority of the feud—in which she also teamed up with Eva Marie, as something of her muscle—she couldn't get the W when it came to their title match at NXT TakeOver: London. In fact, despite her otherwise dominant nature, that somewhat defined Jax's time in NXT: While she could pull off the monster role on weekly television, come title match (whether it was against underdog Bayley or even more dominant Asuka), she couldn't get it done. And for quite a while, this also seemed to be Nia Jax's M.O. on the main roster as well, with Bayley and Asuka again, as well as with other wrestlers.

But Jax's time at NXT was at least not a failure behind the scenes. According to her, Bayley was her favorite rivalry in NXT.

She was the one who truly helped Jax grow as a professional wrestler and performer, as Bayley was already quite established and seasoned (as the only WWE Four Horsewoman not yet called up to the main roster at the time). This would be a necessary tool fairly soon into her professional wrestling career, as Jax would end up being called up to the main roster (RAW) in July 2016, a little over a year after her in-ring debut.

After debuting on *RAW* with a win streak, Nia Jax feuded with Alicia Fox—defeating her before she moved on to a feud against Sasha Banks. While Sasha came out on top in that victory, Nia was able to stay in title contention, competing in her first WrestleMania in a Fatal-4-Way Elimination match for the RAW Women's Championship (against Sasha Banks, Charlotte Flair, and the champion, Bayley). After Alexa Bliss became the RAW Women's Champion the following month, Nia Jax got more to do as a character, as she was written as Bliss's muscle/frenemy/friend—with the duo being affectionately known as "Team Rude"—playing off their real-life best friendship (which was also documented when the two joined the seventh season of *Total Divas*). During this partnership, Bliss would regularly promise Jax an opportunity at competing one on one for the championship, only to find some excuse or loophole not to have to defend it. This turned—as did Jax, into a face—during an episode of *RAW* in March 2018, during a backstage segment in which Alexa Bliss was caught body-shaming Nia Jax to Mickie James. This finally led to a match against Bliss for the championship, at WrestleMania 34; and here Nia Jax won, winning her first championship in WWE on the grandest stage of them all.

However, despite her new face turn—and the character's anti-bullying-focused promos—Jax returned to heel a month later, challenging Ronda Rousey to a title match and becoming a bully herself. No, wrestling doesn't always make sense. But luckily for Nia Jax, it's still quite early in her professional wrestling career: there's still time for more storylines that actually make sense.

★ NICOLE SAVOY ★

YEARS ACTIVE: 2011–present

TRAINED BY: Gillberg Pro Wrestling Academy · "Ramblin'" Rich Myers · Earl the Pearl · "Old School" Oliver John · Sacramento Wrestling Federation · Michael Modest

BILLED FROM: Sacramento, California

ACCOMPLISHMENTS: 2015 AWS Race For The Ring Women's Tournament · 1x AWS Women's Champion · 2016 GRPW Golden Thrones Tournament · #13 in 2016 PWI Female 50 · 1x PWR World Women's Champion · 1x (and inaugural) Heart of SHIMMER Champion · 1x SHIMMER Champion

AKA: Niki Savo · Niki Savoy · 1/3 of Trifecta · "Bay Area Bad Girl" · "The Queen of Suplexes" · "Sacramento Suplex Machine"

NOTABLE MATCHES: Nicole Savoy vs. Winter at BTW International Incident (July 19, 2013) · Nicole Savoy vs. Candice LeRae vs. Heidi Lovelace at SHIMMER Volume 80, in a Heart of SHIMMER Championship Tournament Finals 3-Way Elimination match for the inaugural Heart of SHIMMER Championship (April 2, 2016) · Nicole Savoy vs. Candice LeRae at the WWE Mae Young Classic, in a Mae Young Classic Second Round match (September 6, 2017) · Nicole Savoy & Hikaru Shida vs. Mercedes Martinez & Aja Kong at SHIMMER Volume 98 (November 12, 2017) · Nicole Savoy vs. Mercedes Martinez (c) at SHIMMER Volume 99, for the SHIMMER Championship (November 12, 2017) · Nicole Savoy (c) vs. Jungle Kyona at STARDOM Osaka Nighttime, for the SHIMMER Championship (February 24, 2018) · Nicole Savoy (c) vs. Mercedes Martinez at SHIMMER Volume 100, for the SHIMMER Championship (April 7, 2018)

★ Growing up a military brat, Nicole Matthias wasn't the type of kid who was obsessed with professional wrestling. On the contrary, she was the type of kid who pointed out to other kids just how "fake" it was. But one of her younger sisters was a wrestling fan, and it was only a matter of time before Nicole caught the wrestling bug too; at age 14, in 1999, she saw a WWF match between Ivory and Jacqueline and was interested. Twelve years later, she began her training to be a wrestler. She started at the Gillberg Pro Wrestling Academy (WCW personality Duane Gill's wrestling school)—which was the only training she had before her first match—in Maryland, where she learned from The Holy Rollers, "Ramblin'" Rich Myers and Earl the Pearl. Her debut match in Maryland—as "Nicole Savoy," borrowing the last name of one of her best friends—saw Nicole face off against (and defeat) a fellow Gillberg trainee, Jessie Kaye (better known these days as WWE's first full-time female referee Jessika Carr). Nicole moved back to California (one of the many places she had lived growing up) a year later, to train at Oliver John's Sacramento Wrestling Federation (SWF). It was the move back to California—specifically to increase her training—that proved to Nicole's friends and family that this whole wrestling thing wasn't just a phase she was going through: it was completely serious.

While Nicole's love of the popular Attitude Era of wrestling is one shared with many casual wrestling fans, she credited John with making her truly fall in love with wrestling outside of the mainstream eyes. According to her, "I was watching more and more wrestling. I was watching a lot of [joshi], Europe, anything I could watch, I was watching. He also pushed me to go outside of pro wrestling, to do jiu-jitsu, [Muay Thai], and even catch wrestling." This love of wrestling also led to a realization that if she wanted to break out as a wrestler, she would most likely need to move out of the Bay Area and either to the Midwest or even back to the East Coast. However, that all changed in 2014, as it was the year in which Savoy became more of a regular fixture on the independent scene—as well as the year in which she made her debut at SHIMMER, the premier North American promotion for women's professional wrestling. Making that debut meant officially ticking off a box on her mental checklist: "There were girls in my training class

that were saying, 'I wanna get signed by WWE' or 'I wanna go for TNA.' That's cool, but I wanted to wrestle for SHIMMER!" A little over a year later, she wouldn't just be wrestling in SHIMMER, she'd be a champion, defeating Kimber Lee, LuFisto, Candice LeRae, and Heidi Lovelace (WWE's Ruby Riott) all on her way to winning the inaugural Heart of SHIMMER Championship.

Even Savoy has acknowledged that things only went on an upturn as soon as she was booked on SHIMMER. Because of that, 2015 was the year that Savoy truly started turning heads on the independent scene. Women's wrestling-centric website Diva-Dirt proclaimed her one of their "Five To Watch" that year, calling her a "total package" of a professional wrestler.

> ## "THERE WERE GIRLS IN MY TRAINING CLASS THAT WERE SAYING, 'I WANNA GET SIGNED BY WWE' OR 'I WANNA GO FOR TNA.' I WANTED TO WRESTLE FOR SHIMMER!"

Nicole credits Winter (aka Katarina Leigh) with being one of the first wrestlers to teach her proper match psychology in the ring and connecting with the crowd. But as for her character—especially as a heel—she credits Wesley Snipes' character from *Demolition Man*, Simon Phoenix, as her inspiration there. That description certainly fits Savoy's character as the "Queen of Suplexes" in SHIMMER, a flamboyant bad guy who trash-talks their way through a fight and can back it up. This is especially as a member of Trifecta, a dominant SHIMMER heel faction including Savoy, Mercedes Martinez (as the veteran leader), and Shayna Baszler (as the one who approached both to join), which officially formed at SHIMMER Volume 85 (after Baszler interfered to help Savoy retain Volume 84).

After winning the Heart of SHIMMER Championship at Volume 80, the gold kept flowing in for Savoy, as she soon after won the PWR World Women's Championship as well as the AWS Women's Championship that September. However, a month after winning both of those titles, Savoy announced that she had a torn ACL in her right knee—which she just so happened to suffer while at a WWE tryout. (She had torn her ACL in her left knee 10 years ago—back in the military—playing basketball.) On the plus side, she wasn't forced to vacate any of her championships due to injury, but she was still out of in-ring action until July 2017, which was at least earlier than expected.

And while she was able to hold on to the Heart of SHIMMER Championship, still appearing on SHIMMER shows in crutches and antagonizing any member of the roster who wasn't in Trifecta (and appearing ringside at Trifecta matches due to a kayfabe manager's license), she did lose the championship to Shazza McKenzie in her first title defense post-recovery. But where one door closed, another one opened, as Savoy was competing in the tapings for the first-ever WWE Mae Young Classic Tournament a week later. Her promotional video package for the tournament even highlighted her difficult road to recovery and determination to be recovered in time for the tournament (which she was invited to be a part of by WWE). Falling in the second round to Candice LeRae, this was still the biggest opportunity of Savoy's career, with the most people watching her in her entire career.

By November 2017, Mercedes Martinez had been the SHIMMER Champion for nearly a year—and Trifecta had imploded due to Shayna Baszler leaving for WWE, with Savoy not accepting Martinez's decision to add Aja Kong to the group and keep treating Savoy as the "#3"—and at SHIMMER Volume 99, Nicole Savoy defeated Martinez for the title, ending her championship reign just one day of being a full calendar year. The following April, for the monumental SHIMMER Volume 100 during WrestleMania Weekend in New Orleans, Savoy defended the SHIMMER Championship in a rematch against Martinez and won, proving that she wasn't the weak link in Trifecta once and for all. By winning the SHIMMER Championship, Savoy became the first wrestler in company history to have held both it and the Heart of SHIMMER Championship. While that's really a statistic that's only been able to exist for a short time, it's still an achievement no one can ever take away from Savoy.

Savoy also eventually got to mark off another thing on her checklist, wrestling in Japan at the beginning of 2018 as part of STARDOM. She even got to successfully defend her SHIMMER Championship at a STARDOM event, as well as to (unsuccessfully) challenge for the Wonder of Stardom CHAMPIONSHIP. What Nicole Savoy's future in the wrestling industry will be remains to be seen, but as WWE themselves wrote about her in a profile from the Mae Young Classic: "[R]est assured, somebody's getting suplexed."

★ NIKKI CROSS ★

YEARS ACTIVE: 2008–present

TRAINED BY: Robbie Brookside · Finn Balor · Killian Dain · Johnny Kidd · Paul Tracey · Scottish Wrestling Alliance · WWE Performance Center

BILLED FROM: Glasgow, Scotland

ACCOMPLISHMENTS: 1x Scottish School of Wrestling (SSW) Diamonds Champion · 3x Pro-Wrestling: EVE Champion · 1x World Wide Wrestling (W3L) League Women's Champion · #40 in 2017 PWI Female 50

AKA: Nikki Storm · Nicola Glencross · Nikki Glencross · Nicola Storm · "The Best in the Galaxy" · "The White Chocolate Cheesecake of ICW" · "The White Chocolate Cheesecake of Sports Entertainment" · member of SAnitY · NXT's Twisted Sister

Cross vs. Asuka (c) at NXT, in a Last Woman Standing match for the NXT Women's Championship (June 28, 2017) · Nikki Cross vs. Ember Moon vs. Kairi Sane vs. Peyton Royce at NXT TakeOver: WarGames, in a Fatal 4-Way match for the vacant NXT Women's Champion (November 18, 2017)

⭐ When she was 10 years old, Nicola Glencross's sister forced her to start watching professional wrestling (the WWF Fully Loaded pay-per-view, to be exact), and something clicked. Nine years later, Nicole was training to become a professional wrestler herself, claiming "I had to scratch this itch." So after training with the Scottish Wrestling Alliance (SWA), she made her in-ring debut (as "Nikki Storm") in a Tag Team match against Sweet Saraya and Ricky Knight, arguably the matriarch and patriarch of British independent wrestling. (At the very least, the matriarch and patriarch of WWE Superstar Paige, their daughter.)

SWA was of course Nikki's home, but she had to branch out to bigger promotions. In early 2010, she debuted in Insane Championship Wrestling (ICW), and by the fall she was showing what she could do in Pro-Wrestling: EVE. The latter promotion (an all-women's promotion) is one where Nikki made her star power as she won the Pro-Wrestling: EVE Championship three times during her years on the indies. Her time on the indies would also feature her calling herself "The Best in the Galaxy," coming out to Backstreet Boys' "Larger Than Life" for her entrance theme—she was kind of a cocky one. (Plus, in her defense, everyone calls themselves "Best in the World.") In 2013, Nikki made her Japanese wrestling debut for the now-defunct JWP Joshi Puroresu and even got the chance to successfully defend her Pro-Wrestling: EVE Championship. Then that fall, America came calling, as Nikki debuted in SHINE (losing to Mia Yim), AIW (defeating Mia Yim at Girls Night Out 10), WSU (making it to the finals of the International J-Cup), and SHIMMER (winning three out of her four matches) all in one tour. Then back to Scotland and SWA it was.

NOTABLE MATCHES: Nikki Storm vs. The Alpha Female (c) at Pro-Wrestling: EVE Wrestle-Fever, for the Pro-Wrestling: EVE Championship (November 10, 2012) · Nikki Storm vs. Kana at SHIMMER Volume 65 (April 13, 2014) · Nikki Storm vs. Athena (c) at AIW Nuthin' But A G Thang, for the AIW Women's Championship (April 25, 2014) · Nikki Storm vs. Kay Lee Ray at SHIMMER Volume 71: The ChickFight Tournament, in a SHIMMER ChickFight Tournament First Round match (March 28, 2015) · Nikki Storm vs. Io Shirai at STARDOM Gold May 2015, for the vacant Wonder of STARDOM Championship (May 17, 2015) · Nikki Cross vs. Asuka (c) vs. Billie Kay vs. Peyton Royce at NXT TakeOver: San Antonio, in a Fatal 4-Way match for the NXT Women's Championship (January 28, 2017) · Nikki Cross vs. Asuka (c) vs. Ruby Riott at NXT TakeOver: Chicago, in a Triple Threat match for the NXT Women's Championship (May 20, 2017) · Nikki

As Nikki kept her workload up in 2014—working in both the United Kingdom and the United States and even Spain—she also had the opportunity for more exposure, participating in the second season of TNA's *British Boot Camp*, alongside wrestlers she worked with all the time on the indies, like Grado, Kay Lee Ray, and Viper. She advanced to the finals but didn't make it to the final six. Then in the spring of 2015, she tried out for the WWE when they were on their European tour. Immediately after the tryout, she went on another tour of Japan for the summer, this time making her wrestling debut in STARDOM. That same summer, Nikki got a call from WWE that they wanted to sign her to a WWE developmental contract.

Naturally, the first person Nikki told the news to when she officially got the contract was her sister.

In April 2016, it was officially announced that Nikki Storm had signed a contract with WWE, making her the first-ever Scottish female to sign to the company. She made her in-ring debut that same month on NXT house shows under her real name, which she kept until that August, when she became "Nikki Cross." (As is standard for NXT, though, she did make a soft NXT TV debut as "Nikki Glencross" first, without the actual character.) And Nikki Cross was markedly different from Nikki's previous Best in the Galaxy form, as she was, well, a rabid psychopath. That's at least one way to describe it. As

Nikki Cross, a member of the (originally heel) chaotic faction called SAnitY—which debuted on NXT TV that October—Nikki's particular brand of insanity quickly endeared her to the NXT audience, who couldn't wait to see what she'd do next and who she'd attack next, whether it was a female Superstar or a male Superstar.

In the beginning of 2017, Nikki found herself in the championship conversation for Asuka's NXT Women's Championship, as well as in a sense of limbo between being willing to help defend Asuka from attackers and attacking Asuka herself. Their championship feud saw Asuka defend her championship in multi-woman matches before she and Nikki finally had a one-on-one encounter in a main event Last Woman Standing match (which Asuka just barely won). However, considering Nikki's psychosis, the fact that she lost didn't really keep her down—she just moved on to a new obsession. Sometimes that obsession is wanting Ruby Riot to be her friend. Sometimes that obsession is just diving at wrestlers who try to interfere in matches. When her SAnitY brethren got called up to the main roster in the spring of 2018 (reportedly leaving Nikki behind so she could bolster NXT's women's division), Nikki decided again that she wanted to be the NXT Women's Champion . . . so she decided to just steal the belt from the current champion, Shayna Baszler. The question is, what will she do next?

 ★ ODB ★

YEARS ACTIVE: 2000–present

TRAINED BY: Midwest Pro Wrestling · Eddie Sharkey · Johnny Emerald · Shifty · OVW

BILLED FROM: Minneapolis, Minnesota

ACCOMPLISHMENTS: 1x (and inaugural) Midwest Pro Wrestling Cruiserweight Champion · 2x (and inaugural) OVW Women's Champion · 2007 Miss OVW · #14 in 2008 PWI Female 50 · 1x Steel Domain Wrestling Women's Champion · 1x Texas Wrestling Federation Women's Champion · 1x TNA Knockouts Tag Team Champion (with Eric Young) · 4x TNA Knockouts Champion · 2008 TNA Knockouts Gauntlet for the Gold · 2017 TNA Knockouts Gauntlet for the Gold · 2010 TNA New Year's Knockout Eve Tournament · 2014 TNA World Cup of Wrestling (with Bully Ray, Gunner, Eddie Edwards, & Eric Young) · 1x United States Wrestling Organization (USWO) Television Champion

AKA: "One Dirty Babe" · Jessica Dalton · Jessica James · Poison · Mekka The Warrior · "One Dirty Bitch" · "One Dirty Briscoe"

NOTABLE MATCHES: ODB & Gail Kim vs. Awesome Kong & Raisha Saeed at TNA Lockdown 2008, in a Six Sides of Steel Cage match (April 13, 2008) · ODB vs. Raisha Saeed at TNA Impact Wrestling (September 4, 2008) · ODB & Eric Young vs. Gail Kim & Madison Rayne (c) at TNA Impact Wrestling, for the TNA Knockouts Tag Team Championship (March 8, 2012) · ODB (c) vs. Brooke vs. Gail Kim at TNA Bound For Glory 2013, in a 3-Way match for the TNA Knockouts Championship (October 20, 2013) · ODB vs. Brittany at TNA Xplosion (April 29, 2014) · ODB vs. Kelly Klein at ROH, in a Women of Honor match (December 12, 2016)

★ Jessie Kresa, better known as "ODB," had sort of planned to be an American Gladiator. Sure, she was always a fan of professional wrestling as a kid—she and her brothers were fans of wrestlers like The Killer Bees and Buck Zumhoffe, with her all-time favorite being "Macho Man" Randy Savage—and had known that that's what she'd wanted to become since she was five years old. But she never actually thought she could pull off the over-the-top, larger-than-life characters that professional wrestlers could. Her 17+ year career has obviously proven that she sold herself short with that belief.

So despite not thinking she could put the entertainment into "sports entertainment," she eventually looked into professional wrestling schools in her native Minneapolis. But not wanting to embarrass herself before she even set foot in a ring, Kresa hired a personal trainer first, to make sure she was in proper shape. Around the same time, a casting call for the first season of WWF *Tough Enough* came through, and Kresa pressed her luck and tried out, making it to the top 25. Getting cut, however, didn't deflate her; it only made her hungrier, and she finally enrolled in wrestling school (Midwest Pro Wrestling). Wrestling in the Midwest, Kresa—as ODB, the name that was there from the character's inception—would also get the opportunity to work in intergender matches, teaming with and facing off against her future TNA Impact colleagues Ken Anderson and Shawn Daivari (who went by Sheik Abdul Bashir in TNA). (All three eventually ended up in WWE developmental, although ODB was there after Ken—as Mr. Kennedy—and Daivari had been called up to the main roster.)

ODB's first big break of sorts was in TNA—which would eventually become the promotion she's most remembered for—during its weekly pay-per-view days and in dark matches, but in 2006 she signed a developmental contract with WWE at OVW. She got to keep the ODB name in developmental, and debuted as a heel. After debuting in OVW in the summer of 2006, by that fall ODB essentially willed the OVW Women's Championship into existence. . . . In fact, she willed herself into being the inaugural OVW Women's Champion—claiming to have won it in Rio de Janeiro—constantly cutting promos about it until OVW owner Danny Davis gave the okay and allowed it to be so. Surely if all wrestlers knew you could just proclaim your championship status in this way, most would do so, right? Now, with the "official" lineage of the OVW Women's Championship beginning in August 2006, ODB had to defend the championship, which she successfully did at first. However, after a couple of title defenses, ODB lost her championship the following month after its original recognition, in a 4-Way match with Serena (the winner), Beth Phoenix, and Katie Lea.

Perhaps speaking to the talent of these four women—even without the knowledge that the other three eventually made it to the WWE main roster—they took turns holding the OVW Women's Championship, before ODB finally won it back (from Katie Lea) in June 2007. A few months prior to winning the Women's Championship for the second time, ODB was also crowned "Miss Ohio Valley Wrestling." Yes, "ODB" was "Miss OVW." However, despite this declaration, by that September ODB would drop the OVW Women's Championship to Milena Roucka (better known as WWE's Rosa Mendes) and was released from her WWE developmental contract. According to ODB, during her time in OVW, WWE officials had always told her she didn't have the "Diva look," so she wasn't surprised they never called her up to the main roster. In her eyes, she never really got a fair chance, even if she was successful in OVW itself.

Plus, WWE was in the process of going TV-PG, and ODB was a boob-grabbing (with the catchphrase to go with it: "BAM!"), flask-carrying (and drinking) . . . well, everything the opposite of TV-PG, basically. What WWE saw as the opposite of what they wanted, however, TNA Impact Wrestling saw as something else and contacted her. "When I got to TNA, they said they wanted to see what I did in OVW. WWE wanted to go PG, but TNA wanted to take me as I was." And so ODB re-debuted in TNA as a fully-fledged character at Bound For Glory 2007, in a Gauntlet Match for the inaugural TNA Knockouts Championship. ODB was eliminated third to last, an impressive showing right out the gate. During her time in TNA, the loud-and-drunk ODB quickly became a fan favorite, feuding with The Beautiful People and Awesome Kong and Raisha Saeed. Months after winning the Knockouts Championship

in the summer of 2009—thanks to the help of her manager, Cody Deaner—however, ODB turned heel, dropping the championship to Tara. ODB and Tara traded the championship back and forth (making ODB a two-time Knockouts Champion at the time), before ODB left Impact (something she would do on more than one occasion).

While ODB eventually went on to win the Knockouts Championship two more times, her most memorable championship run and storyline was perhaps the one eventually surrounding the Knockouts Tag Team Championship, in a team with the eccentric but sweet Eric Young (who, you may have figured, was not a Knockout). The impetus of the team was a Wild Card Tournament at the end of 2011, in which the eight teams in the tournament were (in storyline) picked at random. Eric Young was paired with ODB, who also happened to be the only Knockout in the tournament. While ODB/Eric Young didn't win the tournament, they did make it to the Semifinals, losing to the eventual winners (Samoa Joe/Magnus).

Post-tournament, ODB and Eric Young (who ODB only referred to as "E.Y.") would make their intentions known—in the romantic sense—becoming an on-screen couple in addition to a competing tag team. In the case of the latter business, ODB/Young would feud with Angelina Love and Winter (a romantic couple in their own right), on their way to winning the TNA Knockouts Tag Team Championship (to reiterate, despite Young's not being a Knockout). Immediately following the match, Young dropped down on one knee and proposed to ODB—which the Impact Wrestling crowd loved, chanting for her to "SAY YES"–only for ODB to get down on one knee herself and propose to him. He said yes. While the duo's Knockouts Tag Team Championship reign eventually ended—with an authority figure finally calling out the fact that one half of the champions was a man—it lasted a record-setting 478 days. Also, despite its essentially killing the Knockouts Tag Team division, the duo's popularity with the fans in the Impact Zone seemingly justified it. Plus, Eric Young took a few months off from TNA in the summer of 2012 in order

to film an *Animal Planet* show—which ODB even appeared on—written off by having ODB send him out to get some beer and fried chicken. (Upon his return, he did bring the beer and fried chicken.)

For all of professional wrestling's continuity issues and dropped storylines, one thing that always remained unsullied in TNA—even when they just flat-out forgot about the Knockouts Tag Team Championship—after this storyline began was the simple fact that ODB and Eric Young were wife and husband. Even post-TNA Impact Wrestling, in interviews outside of kayfabe, ODB still refers to E.Y. as her "hubby."

ODB left TNA again in the spring of 2014—appearing in a tape-delayed One Night Only pay-per-view in the fall—showing up a couple of times since then, but nothing in terms of a full-time story or contract. In 2015, she made her ROH debut as a female partner for the Briscoe Brothers—calling herself "One Dirty Briscoe"—as a problem solver in their feud against The Kingdom (with her matching up against Maria Kanellis). She even participated in a few of ROH's Women of Honor matches in 2016. But in the spring of 2017, while not confirming that she had officially retired from in-ring competition, Kresa admitted that she'd been out of the wrestling scene for the past few years, focusing instead on bartending, as well as her food-truck business—The Meat and Great—in Daytona Beach (in conjunction with WWE Hall of Famer Jimmy Hart's bar), which spawned from her successful brand of whiskey-based barbecue sauces.

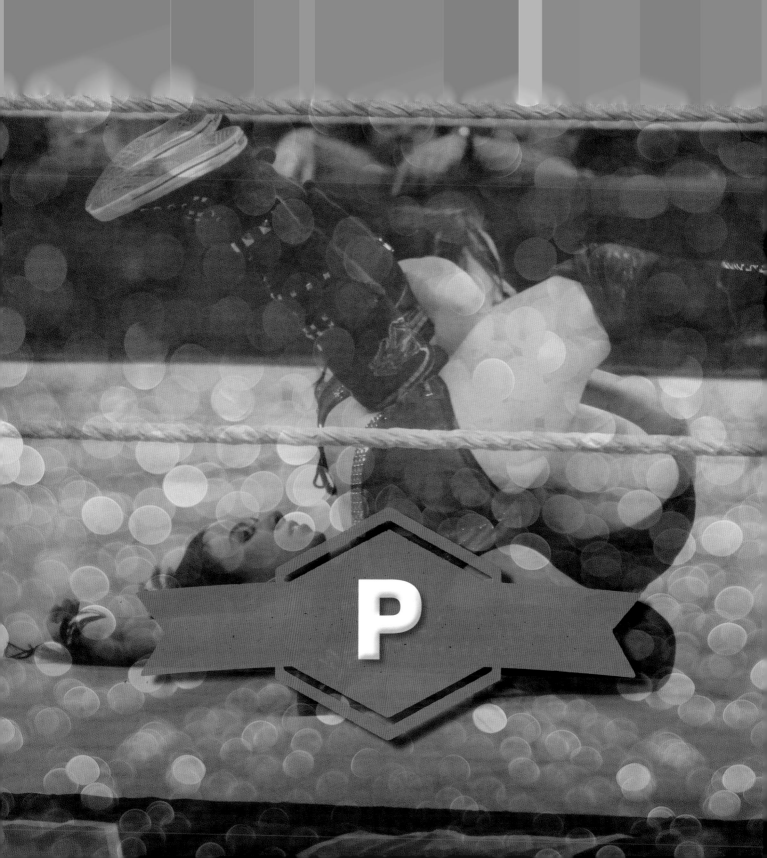

 ★ PAIGE ★

YEARS ACTIVE: 2005–2018

TRAINED BY: Jason Cross · Ricky Knight · Roy Bevis · Sweet Saraya · Zak Zodiac · WAW Academy · FCW · Dusty Rhodes · Norman Smiley · Joey Mercury · Bill DeMott · WWE Performance Center

BILLED FROM: Norwich, England

ACCOMPLISHMENTS: 1x German Stampede Wrestling (GSW) Ladies Champion · 2x Herts & Essex Wrestling (HEW) Women's Champion · 1x PWF Tag Team Champion (with Sweet Saraya) · 1x Pro-Wrestling: EVE Champion · #1 in 2014 PWI Female 50 · 1x Real Deal Wrestling (RDW) Women's Champion · 1x Real Quality Wrestling (RQW) Women's Champion · 2014 *Rolling Stone* Diva of the Year · 1x Swiss Championship Wrestling Ladies Champion · 1x World Association of Women's Wrestling (WAWW) British Ladies Champion · 1x WAWW British Tag Team Champion (with Melodi) · 1x WAWW Ladies Hardcore Champion · 1x (and inaugural) NXT Women's Champion · 2013 NXT Women's Championship Tournament · 2x WWE Divas Champion

AKA: Britani Knight · Saraya · 1/2 of the Anti-Diva Army/The Anti-Divas · 1/3 of Team PCB · 1/3 of Absolution · 1/2 of The Knight Dynasty · 1/2 of The Norfolk Dolls · "The Anti-Diva" · "The Diva of Tomorrow" · "The Raven-Haired Renegade"

NOTABLE MATCHES: The Knight Dynasty (Britani Knight & Saraya Knight) (with Rebecca Knox) vs. Hiroyo Matsumoto & Misaki Ohata (c) SHIMMER Volume 38, for the SHIMMER Tag Team Championship (March 26, 2011) · Britani Knight (c) vs. Blue Nikita vs. Miss Mina at GSW Ultimate Spirit, in a 3-Way No Disqualification match for the GSW Ladies Championship (April 7, 2011) · Britani Knight vs. Saraya Knight at SHIMMER Volume 44, in a No Disqualification match (October 2, 2011) · Paige vs. Emma at NXT, in the NXT Women's Championship Tournament Finals, for the inaugural NXT Women's Championship (July 24, 2013) · Paige (c) vs. Emma at NXT ArRival, for the NXT Women's Championship (February 27, 2014) · Paige vs. AJ Lee (c) at WWE *Monday Night RAW*, for the WWE Divas Championship (April 7, 2014) · Paige vs. Nikki Bella (c) at WWE *Monday Night RAW*, for the WWE Divas Championship (March 23, 2015)

★ When telling the story of the WWE's Paige, the first thing anyone ever notes is that she was wrestling before she was even born. And for good reason, as she was literally in her mother's—British women's wrestler Sweet Saraya—womb while her mother was wrestling a match, before the woman even knew she was pregnant with her daughter. Born Saraya-Jade Bevis, she made her official in-ring professional wrestling start in 2005—at age 13, as she'd been trained when she was 10/11 by her brothers and father, known as "Ricky Knight"—at her family's World Association of Wrestling (WAW) promotion in their hometown, Norwich, England. At the time, Saraya-Jade was just supposed to be filling in for another wrestler. But the unconventional life of a wrestler appealed to her, and by age 14 she (as "Britani Knight") was sending her resume out to any promotion she could think of, eventually wrestling all over Europe, as well as the United States—by herself.

While it may be hard to believe, while Britani eventually worked in SHIMMER—along with her mother as "The Knight Dynasty," who were managed by Rebecca Knox—it was only for a short time in 2011. After failing to win the SHIMMER Tag Team Championships on a number of occasions, this led to the story of Sweet Saraya blaming Britani for the losses and disowning her daughter, leading to a No Disqualification match between mother and daughter at SHIMMER Volume 44—one that Britani won, thus ending the SHIMMER losing streak she had been on. This would end up being Britani's final SHIMMER match.

When she was still only 17, a WWE talent scout met with Saraya-Jade at one of her family shows and invited her for a tryout the next time WWE came to England that November. The way she tells it, she assumed that WWE would only be interested in her if she looked like the cookie-cutter model-turned-Diva they typically looked for, so the fair-skinned girl got a tan, dyed her hair blonde, took out her piercings, and wore a colorful dress (as opposed to her usual all-black look). However, at the tryout, WWE officials told her the fact that she obviously wasn't being herself meant that she wasn't ready to be in WWE. And they were right, as Saraya-Jade's second chance at a tryout—the following April—featured her signature pale, pierced, and all-black-everything look. And if that didn't make her stand out as it was, the fact that she was the only woman in her tryout (with 15 men, including her brother) certainly did. At the end of the tryout, she was told that she was signed, reporting to WWE's then-developmental territory FCW (in Tampa, Florida) at the beginning of 2012 with her new ring name (after a brief moment as just "Saraya"): "Paige."

As Paige, she originally formed a heel team in FCW with Sofia Cortez (Ivelisse Vélez) called the "Anti-Diva Army." The self-proclaimed Anti-Divas only lasted for a few months, no longer together once FCW rebranded into NXT (with Cortez released fairly soon after that). The rebrand to NXT also saw a rebrand in WWE's Divas division—at least on the smaller level, at first—with the now fan favorite Paige pushed as one of the stars of the division. Eventually, she took part in a tournament to crown the inaugural NXT Women's Championship (yes, "Women's," not "Divas") and made it to the finals in June 2013, against Emma. The match was lauded at the time for its difference from main roster Divas matches, as it was both over 10 minutes and didn't feel like the directive called for the women to avoid fighting like the guys. It was a sign that Paige's goals for women's wrestling in WWE were coming true:

"I came into FCW thinking, 'I'm going to create change.' That's what I always wanted to do. I wanted to be the different Diva. I'm not trying to mold myself into what a Diva is supposed to be. I'm going to be different. Eventually, there were more girls coming in with the same attitude, which was great, but it was hard because at that point in time, people were classifying the Divas as the 'toilet break.' It was really hard to overcome that and to get the respect from the WWE Universe and even from

some of the guys in the business. So we were struggling with those obstacles at the time."

This mentality came along with Paige's run on the main roster as well, as Paige ended up being called up to *Monday Night RAW* in April 2014, the *RAW* after WrestleMania XXX. Here, Paige entered into an impromptu Divas Championship match with champion AJ Lee, defeating Lee and officially become the youngest WWE Divas Champion in WWE history (at age 21)—as well as the only woman to hold both the NXT Women's Championship and the Divas Championship at the same time, though Paige was forced to vacate the former later that month (after a 274-day reign). On the main roster, despite going up against capable talent (like AJ Lee, Nikki Bella, Natalya, and eventually her NXT rival-turned-ally Emma),

Paige found herself wrestling in the type of short WWE Divas matches that her NXT run subverted. This, however, began to change with the summer of 2015, with the announcement of "The Divas Revolution" and the beginning of Divas faction rivalry (with new NXT call-ups Charlotte, Becky Lynch, and Sasha Banks). With Charlotte and Becky Lynch by Paige's side to form "Team PCB" (after the original name, "Submission Sorority," proved to lead to NSFW search results), they faced off against Team Bella (The Bella Twins and Alicia Fox) and Team B.A.D. (Sasha Banks, Naomi, and Tamina), with Team PCB as the definitive face team of the three. This eventually changed, however, when Charlotte eventually defeated Nikki Bella for the Divas Championship, with a heel Paige turning on her PCB brethren for a chance at the gold.

SARAYA-JADE'S SECOND CHANCE AT A TRYOUT FEATURED HER SIGNATURE PALE, PIERCED, AND ALL-BLACK-EVERYTHING LOOK. IF THAT DIDN'T MAKE HER STAND OUT, THE FACT THAT SHE WAS THE ONLY WOMAN DID. SHE WAS TOLD THAT SHE WAS SIGNED.

Despite losing the feud against Charlotte—both as a heel and in early 2016, with the alignments reversed and the championship renamed the WWE Women's Championship—Paige remained a popular member of the WWE's Women's division. (She had even gotten more mainstream popularity, having joined the cast of the WWE/E! reality series *Total Divas* in its third season, as well as served as a judge on the latest season of WWE *Tough Enough*.) Things, however, took a turn after

the 2016 WWE draft, as a combination of neck injury (with her undergoing neck surgery in October 2016), wellness policy suspensions (two back-to-back), and tabloid fodder took place while she was on hiatus from WWE for well over a year. Against all odds and despite rumors that Paige's WWE career was over, she was officially cleared to return to WWE in September 2017—and she did just that, a couple months later, in an episode of *Monday Night RAW*. Despite the WWE Universe's excitement to see Paige, she returned as heel, alongside debuting NXT Superstars Sonya Deville and Mandy Rose—who both had a past with Paige, as competitors in the season of *Tough Enough* she'd judged—as a trio known as "Absolution."

However, Paige's in-ring return was short-lived, as by the end of the year she'd suffer an impact injury to her neck during a house show match. While she still managed Absolution for months after, WWE waited until the *RAW* after WrestleMania 34 to allow Paige to announce her official in-ring retirement (and to announce the injury at all, which had been kept quiet, despite her obvious inability to compete). The following night on SmackDown LIVE, Paige replaced Daniel Bryan—who ironically had just been cleared to compete after his own career-ending injury—as the brand's General Manager, becoming face and leaving Absolution in the process.

While the idea of ending an in-ring career at 25 certainly wasn't the plan for Paige, it's hard to argue that she didn't make the most of her time as an active competitor. And her legacy won't even just be contained to memories within the squared circle: in early 2017, it was announced that Dwayne "The Rock" Johnson and Stephen Merchant were producing a feature biopic adaptation of *The Wrestlers: Fighting With My Family*, a 2012 documentary chronicling Paige's family and the lead-up to her departure for WWE.

Paige's career-ending injury prevented her from participating in things like the first-ever Women's Elimination Chamber and Royal Rumble matches, but her career as a whole certainly helped allow these things to even exist in WWE in the first place.

★ PEYTON ROYCE ★

YEARS ACTIVE: 2009–present

TRAINED BY: PWA Australia Training School · Lance Storm · Storm Wrestling Academy · WWE Performance Center

BILLED FROM: Sydney, Australia

ACCOMPLISHMENTS: 2014 Melbourne City Wrestling Vera and Jenny Memorial Cup · 1x Prairie Wrestling Alliance Women's Champion · 2016 NXT Year-End Award for Breakout Star(s) of the Year (with Billie Kay)

AKA: KC Cassidy · Cassie · 1/2 of The Iconic Duo · "The Venus Fly Trap" · 1/2 of The IIconics

NOTABLE MATCHES: KC Cassidy vs. Jessie McKay (c) at PWA Only The Strong 2010, for the PWWA Championship (March 5, 2010) · KC Cassidy vs. Madison Eagles at Melbourne Championship Wrestling Final Battle 2014 (December 13, 2014) · Peyton Royce, Billie Kay, & Daria Berenato vs. Aliyah, Ember Moon, & Liv Morgan at NXT (November 23, 2016) · Peyton Royce vs. Asuka (c) vs. Billie Kay vs. Nikki Cross at NXT TakeOver: San Antonio, in a Fatal 4-Way match for the NXT Women's Championship (January 28, 2017) · Peyton Royce vs. Ember Moon vs. Kairi Sane vs. Nikki Cross at NXT TakeOver: WarGames, in a Fatal 4-Way match for the vacant NXT Women's Champion (November 18, 2017) · The IIconics (Peyton Royce & Billie Kay) vs. Naomi & Asuka at WWE Super Show-Down (October 6, 2018)

★ Like her other half in NXT, Billie Kay, Peyton Royce grew up a huge wrestling fan in Australia. (It remains to be seen if they ever did determine which one of them was "the biggest WWE fan" in their youth, however.) She actually credits her mother with getting her into professional wrestling—as well as becoming a huge fan of Eddie Guerrero, as the first wrestling program her mother ever showed her was an episode of *WWE*

SmackDown—when she was nine years old. From 2006 on, her mother would always take her to go see WWE whenever they'd come to Australia. But Billie Kay was actually her inspiration for becoming a professional wrestler: upon seeing a poster for a PWA show on her 16th birthday, she realized that she recognized one of the wrestlers as a girl she'd gone to high school with. (That would be Billie Kay, who was wrestling as Jessie McKay at the time.) A few weeks later, she'd sign up to train at PWA as well.

As for her athletic background:

> [Dancing] took up most of my time as a kid. I did some sports in school, but dancing had a really big place in my heart. Because of it, I found the transition to pro wrestling quite easy. Dancing really teaches you to be aware of your body, and that transitioned well into wrestling. The footwork came easy to me. The rolls came easy to me. The basics made sense quicker to me than maybe someone without that type of background.

She'd debut as KC Cassidy a few months later in PWWA, PWA's all-woman brand), in a Mixed Tag Team match with Robbie Eagles (against Madison Eagles and Mike Valuable). She would also go on to feud with Jessie McKay, unsuccessfully challenging her for the PWWA Championship. After starting her professional wrestling career in Sydney, Cassidy moved to Melbourne, where she eventually became one of the faces (if not the face) of Melbourne City Wrestling, a promotion she debuted in during the summer of 2011. In Melbourne, she also eventually became the assistant trainer at Vicious Pursuit Pro Wrestling and Performance Academy. In 2012, Cassidy moved to Calgary, Alberta, Canada temporarily to train at Lance Storm's Storm Wrestling Academy for three months. She even won the Prairie Wrestling Alliance (in Edmonton, Albert, Canada) Women's Championship during her time in Canada.

Of the experience training under Storm, Cassidy stated: "Best decision I could have ever made for my career at this point was definitely going to Calgary to get trained by Lance."

Then, when WWE came to Australia for a tour in the summer of 2014, Cassidy attended a two-day tryout they were holding. Seven weeks later—when she was questioning if she should just pop in and say hello at the Performance Center on her upcoming trip to Florida—she finally received the email from WWE informing her that they wanted to sign her. (Jessie McKay/Billie Kay was also signed at the same time.) Her final match on the independent scene would be a singles match against Madison Eagles at Melbourne Championship Wrestling's Final Battle 2014, a match Cassidy would win on her way out. Three weeks after she officially signed with WWE, she had her first NXT TV match (as "Cassie") against the NXT Women's Champion at the time, Sasha Banks, something she considered an "insane achievement." She'd get the new name "Peyton Royce" that August, and after plenty of televised matches as a face (on the losing end of said matches), Peyton turned heel at the end of 2015.

In October 2016, she and Billie Kay formed the heel tag team "The Iconic Duo." As *the* mean girls of NXT, The Iconic Duo quickly became one of the highlights of the show—even when they were often being humiliated because of their hubris, especially by Ember Moon and Asuka. Still, despite their win-loss record and often writing checks their mouths couldn't cash—and all the Superstars they would pester backstage, from Johnny Gargano to Hideo Itami—The Iconic Duo were voted Breakout of the Year in the 2016 NXT Year-End Awards. She and Billie even competed together in a Fatal 4-Way match for the NXT Women's Championship (against champion Asuka and Nikki Cross) at the start of 2017, though neither one of them came out as champ. Despite not capturing the title,

Peyton and Billie of course still believe they were at the top of the food chain known as NXT's Women's Division.

In an interview with WWE.com, Peyton spoke of her goals for her future in NXT:

> This is my dream. There's nothing else I want to do with my life. Being here in NXT, I want to be the leader, the top girl. Jessie and I have a dream of creating a division within the division, for tag teams. We really would love to introduce a women's tag team division and get that rolling in NXT. I can't wait to see what the future holds. It's really exciting to think about.

It really was exciting to think about at the time. Who could have imagined they'd debut together (now as "The IIconics") on the main roster (SmackDown LIVE) two days after WrestleMania 34, attacking SmackDown Women's Champion Charlotte Flair? Imagine that.

IN OCTOBER 2016, SHE AND BILLIE KAY FORMED THE HEEL TAG TEAM "THE ICONIC DUO." AS THE MEAN GIRLS OF NXT, THE ICONIC DUO QUICKLY BECAME ONE OF THE HIGHLIGHTS OF THE SHOW—EVEN WHEN THEY WERE OFTEN BEING HUMILIATED BECAUSE OF THEIR HUBRIS.

★ RACHAEL ELLERING ★

YEARS ACTIVE: 2015–present

TRAINED BY: Lance Storm · Storm Wrestling Academy

BILLED FROM: St. Paul, Minnesota

ACCOMPLISHMENTS: 1x PWM Women's Champion · 2016 RPW Championship Tournament · 1x RPW Women's Champion · 1x (and inaugural) WrestleCircus Lady of the Ring Champion

AKA: Rachael Evers · "The One Woman Minnesota Wrecking Crew" · Rachael Fazio · "The Queen of Strong Smile" · "One in a Million" · "The One in One in a Million"

NOTABLE MATCHES: Rachael Ellering vs. Sexy Dulce vs. Chelsea Green at WrestleCircus Taking Center Stage, in a 3-Way Elimination match for the vacant WrestleCircus Lady of the Ring Championship (February 19, 2017) · Rachael Ellering (c) (WrestleCircus Lady of the Ring) vs. Tessa Blanchard (c) (WrestleCircus Sideshow) at WrestleCircus The Squared Ring Circus, for the WrestleCircus Lady of the Ring Championship/WrestleCircus Sideshow Championship (July 22, 2017) · Rachael Evers vs. Marti Belle at the WWE Mae Young Classic, in a Mae Young Classic First Round match (August 28, 2017) · Rachael Ellering vs. Allysin Kay at AAW Seize The Day, in an AAW Women's Championship Tournament First Round match (October 7, 2017) · Rachael Ellering vs. Ivelisse Vélez vs. Jessicka Havok at AAW Legacy, in an AAW Women's Championship Tournament Finals Elimination 3-Way match (December 2, 2017)

★ Despite having only a little over three years of wrestling experience under her belt, Rachael Ellering makes up for that lack of experience by being a quick learner and having wrestling in her blood. The daughter of WWE Hall of Famer "Precious" Paul Ellering—best known for managing the Road Warriors—Rachael Ellering attended Lance Storm's Storm Wrestling Academy in Calgary, Alberta, Canada, something

she's since considered "the best decision I could have made to start my career off on the right foot."

But despite being a second-generation entrant into the wrestling world, Rachael Ellering didn't even start watching professional wrestling until she was 16 years old. (And it wasn't until she was 18 that she even truly grasped her father's impact on the business, as that was when he was inducted into the WWE Hall of Fame.) In fact, she wasn't allowed to watch, nor did her father allow her to go to live wrestling events. According to Rachael, a stealth YouTube moment was what hooked her on the sport her father shielded from her, as she stumbled upon the WWE *Monday Night RAW* from a 2004 main event between Trish Stratus and Lita (who Rachael immediately gravitated to). That was when she knew she had to become a professional wrestler, even if her father didn't approve.

After three months of training under Lance Storm, Rachael had her first match at the end of November 2015, wrestling

in a Prairie Wrestling Alliance show against fellow Storm trainee Gisele Shaw. The following year, Rachael hit the ground running on the independent scene, not just wrestling in Prairie Wrestling Alliance and local Alberta promotions but going back to Florida to wrestle in smaller indies Championship Wrestling Entertainment (CWE) and Coastal Championship Wrestling (CCW) before debuting in all-women's promotion SHINE. She then moved on to North Carolina for Queens of Combat and NWA Mid-Atlantic Wrestling, and by the end of the year, she'd end up in promotions in the Midwest (like Chicago's RPW) and the West (like WrestleCircus). In November 2016, a year after she made her wrestling debut, Rachael won her first championship ever, at RPW, becoming their Women's Champion.

DESPITE HAVING ONLY A LITTLE OVER THREE YEARS OF WRESTLING EXPERIENCE, RACHAEL ELLERING MAKES UP FOR THAT BY BEING A QUICK LEARNER AND HAVING WRESTLING IN HER BLOOD.

The only month in 2016 Rachael Ellering wasn't booked to wrestle was March, which is practically unheard-of for such a new wrestler who isn't signed by WWE. And speaking of WWE, that spring, Rachael made her debut as enhancement talent for *WWE NXT* (its developmental territory and weekly show), appearing three times that year. In her first appearance, she appeared as "Rachael Ellering"; in her second, she was "Rachael Fazio"; and in her third, she was "Rachael Evers," the ring name she'd come to be known by in WWE/NXT, despite not even being signed. The choice in surname was a tribute to trainer Lance Storm, whose real last name is "Evers" and who

Rachael regularly refers to as "family." This would continue even during her time as a competitor in the inaugural WWE Mae Young Classic tournament—in the summer of 2017, where Rachael made it to the second round—despite acknowledgment that she was in fact the actual daughter of Paul Ellering.

Early in 2017, Rachael competed in a 3-Way Elimination match for the vacant WrestleCircus Lady of the Ring Championship, defeating both *Lucha Underground*'s Sexy Star (as Sexy Dulce) and Impact Wrestling's Laurel Van Ness (as Chelsea Green) to win it. This win led to a WrestleCircus feud between Ellering and Tessa Blanchard, as Blanchard believed her pedigree as a third-generation wrestler was greater than Ellering's as "only" a second-generation wrestler. (The feud also extended outside WrestleCircus, to SHINE and other indy promotions that booked the two multi-generational women.) After Ellering defeated Blanchard in her first title defense as Lady of the Ring Champion, this culminated in a Championship vs. Championship match—as Blanchard had won the Sideshow Championship a month before her rematch with Ellering—which Blanchard won. Despite the loss, this was still an important match, as this was the first time women had main-evented a WrestleCircus show.

Through the fall and winter of 2017, Rachael participated in another tournament, this time in the form of independent promotion AAW's tournament to crown the inaugural AAW Women's Champion. While she didn't win this tournament either, she did make it to the finals—another Elimination 3-Way match—which main-evented the show. Despite not making it to the gold, Rachael at least got to live another dream, as she finished out the year (and began 2018) wrestling in Japan, for STARDOM—debuting in Korakuen Hall, one of the many goals Rachael had in her professional wrestling career. Before her tour of Japan was through, Rachael also got the chance to challenge STARDOM ace Io Shirai to the Wonder of STARDOM Championship, though she came up short.

Upon returning to the States, Rachael got the chance to face off against fellow former Storm Academy graduate Tenille Dashwood, fresh off her stint in WWE as "Emma," with Lance Storm as the Special Guest Referee. But that wasn't her only encounter with a former WWE female Superstar that month, as she also got to face against Celeste Bonin (formerly known as WWE's Kaitlyn) in Bonin's first wrestling match in over four years. Despite still being a young wrestler and working on the independent scene, it feels like, no matter where she goes, WWE is somewhere around Rachael Ellering. Only time will tell if that becomes a more official proximity.

★ ROSEMARY ★

YEARS ACTIVE: 2007–present

TRAINED BY: Can-Am Wrestling School · Johnny Devine · Scott D'Amore · Tyson Dux

BILLED FROM: Winnipeg, Manitoba · The Valley of Shadows

ACCOMPLISHMENTS: 1x Acclaim Pro Wrestling Tag Team Champion (with KC Spinelli) · 1x Acclaim Pro Wrestling Women's Champion · 1x AWE Women's Champion · 1x Bellatrix Female Warriors World Champion · 1x GCW W.I.L.D. Champion · 1x nCw Femmes Fatales Champion · #8 in 2014 PWI Female 50 · 1x Pure Wrestling Association Canadian Elite Women's Champion · 1x SHIMMER Tag Team Champion (with Sara Del Rey) · 1x TNA Knockouts Champion · 1x TCW Women's Champion

AKA: Courtney Rush · PJ Tyler · Casey Maguire · El Tigre Diablo · "The Demon Assassin" · "The Death Dealer" · "The Canadian Assassin" · "The Leader of The Hive" · "Queen of the Hivelings" · "Red" · 1/2 of The Queens of Winning · 1/3 of Decay · 1/2 of Demon Bunny · 1/2 of Ontario's Top Team

NOTABLE MATCHES: Courtney Rush & Vanessa Kraven vs. The Kimber Bombs (Cherry Bomb & Kimber Lee) at SMASH Wrestling Super Showdown III (August 23, 2015) · Courtney Rush vs. Kimber Lee (with Cherry Bomb) at SMASH Wrestling SMASH vs. CZW (January 16, 2016) · Courtney Rush vs. Cherry Bomb at SMASH Wrestling Any Given Sunday 4 (March 20, 2016) · Courtney Rush vs. Cherry Bomb vs. Leah Vaughan at SMASH Wrestling Forest City Rampage (April 9, 2016) · Courtney Rush vs. Allie at SMASH Wrestling Super Showdown IV, in a No Disqualification match (August 21, 2016) · Rosemary (CANADA) vs. Allie (USA) at SMASH Wrestling CANUSA Classic 2016, in a Steel Cage match (October 22, 2016) · Rosemary vs. Jade (with Gail Kim) at TNA Impact Wrestling, in a Six Sides of Steel Cage match for the vacant TNA Knockouts Championship (December 1, 2016) · Rosemary (c) (TNA) vs. Nixon Newell (c) (BEW) vs. Toni Storm at BEW Britain's Rising IV, in a 3-Way No Rules Purge match for the TNA Knockouts Championship/ BEW Woman's Championship (December 4, 2016) · Rosemary (c) vs. Jade at TNA Impact Wrestling Genesis 2017, in a Monster's Ball match for the TNA Knockouts Championship (January 26, 2017) · Rosemary vs. Sienna (c) at GFW Impact Wrestling, in a Last Knockout Standing match for the GFW Knockouts Championship (July 27, 2017) · Rosemary vs. Sexy Star (c) vs. Ayako Hamada vs. Lady Shani at AAA TripleMania XXV, in a 4-Way match for the AAA Reinas de Reinas Championship (August 26, 2017)

★ Before she was known as the Demon Assassin—or an assassin of any kind—Holly Letkeman was just a wrestling fan in Manitoba, Canada. She grew up with wrestling in the household, with her father and his friends; she would wrestle her cousins all around the house; her bedroom was essentially a shrine to all things WWF and WCW. And once she got to high school, she and a friend had decided they were going to be wrestlers sooner rather than later. They found a school, but thankfully cut and run after the sketchy trainer expected them to have a wrestling match immediately after a single training session. After graduating from college (with a film and theatre degree), Holly remained obsessed

Wrestling, Scott D'Amore's Border City Wrestling, and the now-defunct Pro Wrestling Xtreme, among others. She began breaking out on the indy scene in the beginning of 2010, debuting in both nCw Femme Fatales (where she'd go on to win the nCw Femme Fatales Championship in the summer of 2014) and SHIMMER. In SHIMMER, she originally debuted as part of the SPARKLE Division (the pre-show dark match, a tryout for SHIMMER proper) in 2010 and not officially joining the roster until a year later—as Courtney Rush. The following year, the quirky up-and-comer would team with the heel veteran Sara Del Rey, eventually going on to win the SHIMMER Tag Team Championship. (It wouldn't end up that well, though, once Del Rey got tired of her and abandoned her during a title defense, for the loss.)

September 2013 saw Rush suffer a fractured collarbone, putting her on the shelf until March 2014, the year in which she'd make her debut in SMASH Wrestling, arguably the most important wrestling promotion of her career. By that fall, Rush had gotten the negative attention of Cherry Bomb, one-half of SMASH Wrestling's (and independent wrestling as a whole, as they would be a thorn in Rush's side in SHIMMER as well) resident mean-girl duo, The KimberBombs (with Kimber Lee). After finally getting an opportunity to face off against The KimberBombs in tag team action (alongside Vanessa Kraven), The KimberBombs ended up beating Rush up until she was unconscious, only for Cherry Bomb to add insult to injury by cutting Rush's hair as well.

After this, SMASH Wrestling posted a series of videos, featuring a bizarre, unhinged—honestly, possessed—version of Courtney Rush, now with odd writing all over her arms and hands (and eventually facial makeup). During her matches, she would snap at times, seeing Cherry Bomb in her opponents and reacting accordingly. And while she couldn't get her hands on Cherry Bomb at the time—as Cherry Bomb broke her collarbone (in a bizarre bit of similarity between the two) soon after the inciting incident—that didn't stop her from mocking

with wrestling, but it wasn't until Eddie Guerrero's untimely passing in 2005 that she made the decision to chase her dreams before it was too late.

So she contacted Scott D'Amore about training at his Can-Am Wrestling School; and once she had the money, she moved to Ontario in 2007, to start her professional wrestling career. She began her training that May, but she wouldn't make her in-ring debut until January 2008, under the ring name "Casey Maguire." That lasted one match before she became "PJ Tyler," a wannabe "rock 'n' roll chick" (and a tip of the hat to Aerosmith's Steven Tyler). The PJ Tyler gimmick and name remained a surprisingly long time, as she wouldn't become "Courtney Rush" until October 2010. As she began wrestling in local independents, she regularly wrestled at Great Canadian

Rush in pre-tapes, carrying around her ponytail as a trophy. As this story progressed, Cherry Bomb—despite her obvious heel status—became vehement that she was the good guy that was going to slay the demon, carrying a stake/cross, Buffy-style. So Rush carried a weapon of her own: a cleaver. February 2015 saw Courtney Rush finally able to face Cherry Bomb in a match, but the feud wouldn't be over until October 2016—when after pull-apart brawls, No Disqualification matches, and mind games, the two faced off in a main event featuring SMASH Wrestling's first-ever Steel Cage match. Only it wasn't Courtney Rush versus Cherry Bomb at that point: It was Rosemary (the demon possessing Rush, as well as her Impact Wrestling name) and Allie (Cherry Bomb's Impact Wrestling name). And the demon prevailed over the slayer.

Despite "Rosemary" not debuting in SMASH Wrestling until August 2016, she had already debuted as the character—as something of a demonic brainwashing valet—in Impact Wrestling that January. Together with Crazzy Steve and Abyss, they formed the heel trio Decay and immediately cemented their macabre brand of dominance in Impact. Stealing championships, attempting to kidnap babies, poison mist, disappearing wrestlers—nothing was too over-the-top or dark for Decay. By the end of 2016, Rosemary was the Knockouts Champion, feuding with Jade (the "Blue" to her "Red") to start 2017 in standout matches. Rosemary and Jade were getting people talking about the Knockouts Division again, and it was only a matter of time before Impact Wrestling accepted Rosemary's position as a fan favorite, despite the horror aspect. Yes, despite the fact she's a fricken demon, Rosemary quite easily became one of the most popular members of the Impact Wrestling roster, regardless of gender, with children dressing up like her. And Impact fully accepted this at the end of May 2017 (a month after Decay "died"), with Rosemary coming to the aid of Allie—who in Impact Wrestling was the exact opposite of her Cherry Bomb persona on the indies. Rosemary would go on to explain that "the hive" (the demon that controls

her) wanted her to protect Allie, who she would then take to calling her "bunny." And the duo of "Demon Bunny" was born. It's certainly a long way from a gimmick based on being a fan of Aerosmith.

★ RUBY RIOTT ★

YEARS ACTIVE: 2010–present

TRAINED BY: Billy Roc · The School of Roc · OVW · WWE Performance Center

BILLED FROM: Lafayette, Indiana · Edwardsburg, Michigan

ACCOMPLISHMENTS: 1x AIW Women's Champion · 1x AAW Heritage Champion · 1x Alpha-1 (A1) Wrestling Alpha Male Champion · 1x Channel Islands World Wrestling World Heavyweight Champion · CHIKARA Young Lions Cup XI · 1x OVW Women's Champion · #20 in 2016 PWI Female 50 · 1x Revolution Championship Wrestling (RCW) Heavyweight Champion · 1x SHIMMER Tag Team Champion (with Evie)

AKA: Heidi Lovelace · "The Punk Rock Ragdoll" · Dori Prange · Heidi Douglas · Miss Heidi · Heidi the Riveter · Sally Stitches · member of Daffney's All-Star Squad (Daff's A.S.S.) · 1/2 of The Buddy System · 1/3 of The Riott Squad · Ruby Riot · 1/2 of Brutally Heartless · 1/2 of Team Slap Happy · member of Dasher's Dugout · member of Oedo Tai

NOTABLE MATCHES: Heidi Lovelace vs. Matt Cage (c) at AAW All Hail, for the AAW Heritage Championship (August 15, 2014) · Heidi Lovelace vs. Missile Assault Ant at CHIKARA Tomorrow Never Dies, in a CHIKARA Young Lions Cup XI Finals match (December 6, 2014) · Heidi Lovelace vs. Athena (c) at AIW Faith No More, for the AIW Women's Championship (September 11, 2015) · Heidi Lovelace vs. Nicole Savoy vs. Candice LeRae at SHIMMER Volume 80, in a Heart of SHIMMER Championship Tournament Finals 3-Way Elimination match for the inaugural

Heart of SHIMMER Championship (April 2, 2016) · Heidi Lovelace vs. Nicole Matthews at SHIMMER Volume 80, in a Heart of SHIMMER Championship Tournament Semifinals match (April 2, 2016) · Heidi Lovelace vs. Josh Alexander (with Seleziya Sparx) (c) at A1 Immortal Kombat, for the A1 Alpha Male Championship (May 15, 2016) · Team Slap Happy (Heidi Lovelace & Evie) vs. The Kimber Bombs (Kimber Lee & Cherry Bomb) (c) vs. BaleSpin (KC Spinelli & Xandra Bale) vs. Fly High WDSS (Kay Lee Ray & Mia Yim) at SHIMMER Volume 84, in a Four Corners Elimination match for the SHIMMER Tag Team Championship (June 26, 2016) · Heidi Lovelace vs. Jessicka Havok at AAW Windy City XII, in an I Quit match (November 26, 2016) · Ruby Riot vs. Asuka (c) vs. Nikki Cross at NXT TakeOver: Chicago, in a Triple Threat match for the NXT Women's Championship (May 20, 2017)

⭐ While "The Punk Rock Ragdoll" got her start in professional wrestling in 2010—debuting for RCW as "Miss Heidi," in her hometown of South Bend, Indiana—it wasn't until 2013 that things got interesting for the wrestler formerly known as Dori Prange. Now as "Heidi Lovelace," she began wrestling at OVW (as a face) in a storyline with heel Taeler Hendrix (who was in OVW as part of TNA developmental at the time). In the storyline, after months of Hendrix receiving gifts from a secret admirer, it was revealed Lovelace was the secret admirer and had romantic feelings for Hendrix. Despite the lack of mainstream attention, the storyline did get some buzz among hardcore fans, as it portrayed a potential female same-sex relationship in wrestling as an actual, complicated situation, instead of just some titillating content. Of course, as Taeler remained a heel the whole time, she ended up using Heidi's feelings as a way to manipulate her (with Heidi clinging to the hope that their relationship wasn't "one-sided," though it was) and even used her as a human shield when necessary. Heidi eventually saw reason, but they never had the chance to have a blow-off match as a result. Heidi Lovelace's time in OVW ended in August 2013, after failing to win the OVW Women's Championship for the second time (as she had won it from Hendrix in 2012, prior to their major storyline).

Heidi had also made her SHIMMER and SHINE debuts back in the summer of 2012, eventually becoming SHIMMER Tag Team Champion with Evie (as "Team Slap Happy") and forming the tag team "The Buddy System" in SHINE with Solo Darling (although they didn't make it to championship status). But in all Heidi Lovelace's work wrestling other female competitors—eventually making her Japanese debut in joshi promotion STARDOM in early 2015—she really made a name for herself on the independents due to her work as an intergender wrestling specialist. Making her CHIKARA debut in 2013, Lovelace was instantly thrown into the intergender wrestling deep end. In December 2014, she became the first female wrestler ever to hold the CHIKARA Young Lions Cup (defeating Missile Ant in the Young Lions Cup XI tournament finals) and the wrestler with the second longest reign with the cup, at 429 days (trailing Hallowicked's record 602 days). The following year (and CHIKARA season), she joined the stable Dasher's Dugout as part of the Challenge of the Immortals tournament, who were set to win until it was revealed that "Mr. Touchdown" had rigged the tournament, leading to Dasher Hatfield forfeiting their points and wins that entire season. In the spring of 2016, Heidi then went after the CHIKARA Grand Championship, challenging champ (and friend, as well as intergender wrestling star) Princess KimberLee. Unfortunately, she couldn't beat KimberLee and failed to win her next Grand Championship match later that year (that time, against Hallowicked).

After it first was reported in December 2016, WWE officially announced Lovelace as one of the newest developmental signees. Prior to her official debut, she appeared at live events under her name; but in February it was revealed that she'd be known as "Ruby Riot" from then on. Ruby debuted in *NXT* that March as a face, helping to even the odds for a face tag team against SAnitY (as the female competition to Nikki Cross). Ruby would then go on to compete for title contention, wrestling for the NXT Women's Championship at NXT TakeOver: Chicago but coming up short. Riot's time in developmental was honestly relatively short, as she made her main roster debut—

alongside Sarah Logan and Liv Morgan, all characters with no real interaction back in *NXT*—on *SmackDown* in November 2017. Now known as "Ruby Riott," Ruby led this trio known as "The Riott Squad," making her main roster presence known as a heel attacking faces and heels alike in the Women's Division. Proving the cream rises to the top, Ruby fairly quickly found herself in title contention here, challenging Charlotte Flair for the SmackDown Women's Championship at Fastlane in February, Ruby's first singles pay-per-view match. (Her first pay-per-view match was at the Royal Rumble, in the inaugural Women's Royal Rumble match.)

RUBY LED A TRIO KNOWN AS "THE RIOTT SQUAD," MAKING HER MAIN ROSTER PRESENCE KNOWN AS A HEEL ATTACKING FACES AND HEELS ALIKE IN THE WOMEN'S DIVISION.

After WrestleMania—where she and The Riott Squad also competed—The Riott Squad were drafted to RAW, immediately going after top stars again, this time in the form of Sasha Banks and Bayley. Ruby would then go on to beat both Sasha Banks and Bayley in singles competition, continuing her consistent push in a company many people wouldn't have thought a punk rock girl like her would ever have gotten signed by.

★ SABLE ★

YEARS ACTIVE: 1996–2004

TRAINED BY: Marc Mero

BILLED FROM: Jacksonville, Florida

ACCOMPLISHMENTS: 1x WWF Women's Champion · 1997 Slammy Award for Dressed to Kill · 1997 Slammy Award for Diva of the Year · 1998 PWI Rookie of the Year · 1999 PWI Woman of the Year

AKA: Rena Mero · "The Diva of the World Wrestling Federation" · member of The Oddities · Rena Lesnar

NOTABLE MATCHES: Sable & Marc Mero vs. Luna & Goldust at WrestleMania XIV, in an Intergender Tag Team match (March 29, 1998) · Sable vs. Jacqueline (c) at WWF Survivor Series 1998, for the WWF Women's Championship (November 15, 1998) · Sable (c) vs. Luna at WWF Royal Rumble 1999, in a Strap match for the WWF Women's Championship (January 24, 1999)

★ Considering how popular she was, you would think Sable held the WWF Women's Championship more than just once in her career. However, at the time, the crowning achievement for a WWF Diva was a *Playboy* cover, not the gold. In that case, Sable was Attitude Era Royalty.

After marrying WCW wrestler Johnny B. Badd (real name Marc Mero) in 1994, Rena Mero went from the flashing lights of the modeling world to the flashing lights of the squared circle, joining her husband as he made his 1996 debut in WWF under his real name. She originally made her debut as "Sable" at WrestleMania XII, as Hunter Hearst Helmsley's valet, leading into a backstage segment where Marc Mero saved damsel-in-distress Sable from a furious Helmsley later that night (in his official debut as well). A couple of weeks later, she officially became his valet and stood by his side. Until he injured his ACL in early 1997, that is. While Mero was out for six months due

to the injury, Sable remained on television, accruing popularity through things like modeling the latest WWE merchandise and competing in bikini contests on *RAW*. This led to a heel turn on Mero's part when he returned in November, as he grew notably jealous over Sable's increased attention and greater popularity. The jealousy led to controlling and possessiveness, with him even forcing her to wear a potato sack to the ring at one point. At that, Sable engaged in an act of defiance—removing the sack, revealing a tiny bikini—to Mero's dismay, but she would remain with him for a few more months. As they feuded with Luna Vachon and Goldust heading into WrestleMania XIV, Sable would now actually have to get into the ring and wrestle. During this match, she introduced her version of the powerbomb, the "Sable Bomb"—which was considered impressive because she would go on to give the move to men—as well as her version of Marc Mero's patented TKO, before pinning Luna and winning, allowing her popularity to continue to rise.

The last straw for Sable when it came to Mero was a month later, after the Unforgiven pay-per-view, when a distraction from Mero allowed Luna to win an Evening Gown match. She challenged Mero to a Loser Leaves WWF match at the next pay-per-view, where she was supposed to pick someone to face Mero—with the stipulation of Sable leaving the WWF forever if Mero won, and Mero letting her free if her representative won. Instead, she decided to wrestle him for herself (having already shown the ability to Sable Bomb him) which Mero quickly won after toying with her and pretending he would let her win. A couple of weeks after this match, WWF played a career video tribute for Sable, really selling the idea that she was out of the WWF for good. Then the next week, Sable returned, with a simple explanation that Vince McMahon had rehired her. Sable would continue to feud with Marc Mero—and his new valet, Jacqueline—interfering in his matches and causing him to lose. It was during this feud that Sable participated in the infamous Bikini Contest against Jacqueline, revealing her bikini top as body paint (in the form of two hands painted onto her breasts). With the help of Edge, Sable eventually went on to defeat Mero and Jacqueline in a Mixed Tag Team match, effectively closing the book on Sable/Marc Mero.

However, Sable did have one last bit of unfinished business, in the form of the reinstated WWF Women's Championship. While Mero helped Jacqueline beat Sable to win the championship, Sable would win the championship a couple of months later at Survivor Series, Sable-Bombing both Mero and Jacqueline out of her orbit.

However, while Sable held the WWF Women's Championship for 176 days, only three of those days featured title defenses. (And the final defense featured her losing to Debra, who also was more a character than a wrestler.) She was still featured on the shows weekly, but if she was in a match at all, it was usually a Tag Team match (Mixed or otherwise). But naturally, her popularity with the rowdy Attitude Era audience translated into her getting more outside opportunities, guest-starring on an episode of USA Network's *Pacific Blue* and then achieving the wrestling holy grail at the time of being the cover girl for *Playboy*—an issue that, at the time, was the highest-selling *Playboy* in 15 years and still remains one of the top-selling issues. In the aftermath of this success, Sable turned heel, introducing a new hip-swiveling "dance" called "the grind" into her character and a catchphrase that she'd say during promos and in the ring before matches: "This is for all the women who want to be me and all the men who come to see me."

Given her skill level, even more than the usual for the Attitude Era, the key to the rare Sable match—besides heel Sable compulsively doing "the grind" in between moves and as a taunt—was a litany of distractions and interferences (so the focus wasn't actually on her in-ring work) and the fact that the Sable Bomb still seemed impressive compared to the rest of her arsenal. Luna arguably got the best wrestling possible out of Sable, but the ultimate takeaway years later was that Sable wanted nothing to do with actually wrestling in a match, especially the part about taking any bumps or potentially getting truly physical—as she didn't want to endanger her breast implants. And she wasn't forced to by WWF either, due to her popularity. In fact, there was reportedly a mandate in the company not to "hurt" Sable in the ring, which Luna tried her hardest to abide by but couldn't quite do. Sable was called "The Diva" of the WWF, and she set the template for what the WWF/WWE Divas would be for a long time, with dreams of *Playboy* covers and Lingerie matches in their heads. With Sable's popularity, it was proof that a model-turned-wrestler could work, given the proper veteran experience surrounding her. Trish Stratus perhaps perfected this theory, though, in terms of actually filling the wrestler part instead of just playing it.

However, because of Sable's popularity and status in the company, that Diva attitude seemingly bled into her behind-the-scenes situation, with her losing the Women's Championship to Debra in an Evening Gown match as the result of backstage drama with the company. (Allegedly, she would regularly claim she was the reason for the company's success.) So while she technically won the match the proper way, by removing Debra's evening gown, the storyline made the rules so the dress loser actually won. And in stripping Sable of the championship off-screen, it was the company's way of ensuring that she wouldn't leave with the title. And leave she did, the following month, filing a $110 million sexual harassment and unsafe working conditions lawsuit, while Vince McMahon countersued over her continuing to use the ring name Sable. The suit was settled out of court a couple of months later, with Sable—as Rena Mero—posing in *Playboy* for the second time the following month.

Proving that money is thicker than bad blood in professional wrestling, Sable returned to WWE in the spring of 2003 as a heel, to feud with new *Playboy* cover girl Torrie Wilson on *SmackDown*. The Torrie/Sable feud was somewhat of a new guard vs. old guard storyline—with Bikini contests and gratuitous girl-on-girl action—which eventually led to a face team-up between the two once they became joint *Playboy* cover girls. Sable also entered into a feud with Stephanie McMahon, where she was Vince's mistress as well as Stephanie's personal assistant. In August 2004, Sable left WWE again for good, this time on good terms, with Sable wanting to spend more time with her family.

★ SARA DEL REY ★

YEARS ACTIVE: 2001–2012

TRAINED BY: Bryan Danielson · Donovan Morgan · Robert Thompson · Pro Wrestling IRON · APW Boot Camp · Roland Alexander · ARSION Dojo · Mariko Yoshida · AKINO

BILLED FROM: Martinez, California

ACCOMPLISHMENTS: 1x Canadian Wrestling Revolution (CWR) · 2011 CHIKARA Torneo Cibernetico · 1x Impact Zone Wrestling (IZW) Women's Champion · 1x JAPW Women's Champion · 1x OCW Women's Champion · #4 in 2012 PWI Female 50 · #430 in 2012 PWI 500 · 1x Pro Wrestling WORLD-1 SUN Champion · 1x Remix Pro Wrestling Women's Champion · 1x (and inaugural) SHIMMER Champion · 1x SHIMMER Tag Team Champion (with Courtney Rush)

AKA: "Death Rey" · Sara Amato · "The American Angel" · Nikki · Nic Grimes · 1/2 of The Queens of Winning · "The Queen of Wrestling" · "Sara Death Rey" · member of BDK · 1/2 of Dangerous Angels · member of Sweet 'n' Sour Inc.

NOTABLE MATCHES: Sara Del Rey vs. Mercedes Martinez at SHIMMER Volume 1 (November 6, 2005) · Sara Del Rey vs. Mercedes Martinez at SHIMMER Volume 5, in a No Time Limit match (May 21, 2006) · Sara Del Rey vs. Cheerleader Melissa at SHIMMER Volume 9 (April 7, 2007) · Sara Del Rey vs. Lacey at SHIMMER Volume 12, in a SHIMMER Championship Tournament Finals match for the inaugural SHIMMER Championship (June 2, 2007) · The Dangerous Angels (Sara Del Rey & Allison Danger) vs. Cheerleader Melissa & MsChif at SHIMMER Volume 17 (April 26, 2008) · Sara Del Rey vs. Jessie McKay vs. Ayako Hamada at SHIMMER Volume 34, in a 3-Way match (September 11, 2010) · BDK (Sara Del Rey & Claudio Castagnoli) vs. Manami Toyota & Mike Quackenbush at CHIKARA Through Savage Progress Cuts The Jungle Line (September 19, 2010) · Sara Del Rey (c) vs. LuFisto at JAPW 13th Anniversary Show – Night 2, for the JAPW Women's Championship (December 11, 2010) · Sara Del Rey vs. Madison Eagles at CHIKARA Clutch of Doom (February 20, 2011) · Sara Del Rey vs. Kana at CHIKARA Klunk In Love (October 8, 2011) · Sara Del Rey & The Canadian NINJAS (Nicole Matthews & Portia Perez) vs. Christina Von Eerie, MsChif, & Athena at AAW Epic: The 8th Anniversary Show (March 16, 2012) · Sara Del Rey vs. El Generico at CHIKARA Hot Off The Griddle (April 28, 2012)

★ Like so many kids, Sara Amato loved professional wrestling—and then she grew out of it, before falling back in love with it in high school, hard. However, unlike Hulk Hogan and Ultimate Warriors—the kind of flamboyant guys she loved when she'd originally started watching wrestling—Amato was shy by nature. She didn't think she had what it takes to make it as a professional wrestler, so she dropped the silly notion—until she didn't, opting to drop out of college instead to finally make her dream become a reality. So she attended her local wrestling school, APW Boot Camp, and learned under APW owner Roland Alexander.

At first, Amato wrestled for APW as "Nikki." Yes, just "Nikki." After a couple of months in APW, she'd meet "The American Dragon" Bryan Danielson (WWE's Daniel Bryan), a wrestler who

would become integral on her path to becoming the best women's wrestler in the world. She'd also wrestle Cheerleader Melissa—a lot—creating less of a feud or rivalry and more of a reason for Nikki to branch out in the wrestling world. In the summer of 2003, she did just that, leaving APW to become "Sara Del Rey." And Sara Del Rey wrestled on the debut PWG show (PWG Debut Show). Sara Del Rey wrestled in Big Time Wrestling. And Sara Del Rey wrestled outside of California as, about two-and-a-half years into her career, she got the chance to tour in Japan as part of the AtoZ women's wrestling promotion, as she was one of the only *gaijin* (foreigners) training there (the other was LuFisto).

In 2005, Sara Del Rey's wrestling made it to the Midwest, debuting at IWA-MS and facing off against women who would define the women's indy scene around this time, along with her: women like Mickie Knuckles, Daizee Haze, MsChif, and Cheerleader Melissa. She'd also return to Japan (getting the opportunity to face Kana), before heading to Mexico, where she would have another (yet temporary) name change: "The American Angel," a patriotic American gimmick in LLF which required her to wear a mask. Del Rey truly began to break out in 2005, especially toward the end. She had a dark match against Lacey in ROH; she tore the house down with Mercedes Martinez, Lacey, and Daizee Haze in the first two volumes of SHIMMER; she rekindled the Cheerleader Melissa feud in APW into an actual feud, as Sara Del Rey, not Nikki. So in 2006, if you knew women's independent wrestling, you knew Sara Del Rey. And if you didn't, you were going to.

SHIMMER, CHIKARA, ROH, AAW, Mexico. Then by the summer of 2007, she became the inaugural SHIMMER Champion and defended the championship on an ROH card. Naturally, the cockiness over her accomplishments and accolades started to get to the character. She would refer to herself as "The Queen of Wrestling," joining forces with an egotistical crew like Larry Sweeney's Sweet 'n' Sour Inc. (As a member of the crew, Sara is also a one-time ROH Undisputed World Intergender Heavyweight Tag Team Champion with Chris Hero, but the championship was never officially recognized by ROH or any wrestling promotion featuring the two. It was only recognized by their fellow Sweet 'n' Sour Inc. members.) By a certain point, she was regularly considered the best women's wrestler in the world, both from her character's perspective and just from fans and critics' perspectives. In 2012, she became the fourth-ever woman to make it onto the PWI 500.

Then in 2013, Del Rey retired from professional wrestling in order for Sara Amato to take on a role as one of the head trainers for (and the first female coach at) WWE's Performance Center in Orlando, Florida. While it was disheartening to see the best women's wrestler in the world sign to the big time, but not to wrestle, everything about Sara and her natural shyness (which she made up for in her wrestling character) says that she's more content being behind the scenes, away from the bright lights. But it would be nice just to see her bully someone on-screen—even if it's just at the Performance Center—just for old time's sake. Since being hired, Amato has also moved up to working as a producer and agent for the main roster Superstars, and in 2015 she was promoted to Assistant Head Coach, second to Head Coach Jason Bloom. Regarding Sara's ability as a trainer, WWE Superstar Bayley put it like this: "She's very good at taking her time to teach, and she's very patient. She's like no other. She's the greatest female wrestler in the world, and she knows what she's doing." In another life, a compliment like that might have gotten to Sara's head.

★ SARAH STOCK ★

YEARS ACTIVE: 2002–2015

TRAINED BY: Top Rope Championship Wrestling · Eddie Watts · Phil Lafon · Diluvio Negro I · El Satánico

BILLED FROM: Winnipeg, Manitoba, Canada via Mexico City, Mexico

ACCOMPLISHMENTS: 2007 Alianza Universal de Lucha Libre (AULL) Copa Internacional Femenil · 1x Beauty Slammers Champion · 1x Can-Am Wrestling Women's Champion · CMLL Bodybuilding Contest (2006–2012, 2014) · Federación Internacional de Lucha Libre (FILL) Women's Champion · Lucha Libre Feminil (LLF) Juvenil Champion · #14 in 2011 PWI Female 50 · 2x TNA Knockouts Tag Team Champion (1x Taylor Wilde, 1x with Rosita) · 2009 TNA Knockouts Tag Team Championship Tournament (with Taylor Wilde) · 1x Wonder of STARDOM Champion · 1x Nuevo León State Women's Champion · 1x Can-Am Wrestling Women's Champion

AKA: Sarita · Dark Angel · Canadian Dark Angel · Natasha Graves · Sarah Stone · Sarah Swayze · Sweet Sarah · "Sara la Canadiense" ("Sara the Canadian") · member of Mexican America · 1/3 of El Sexy Team · member of Los Un-Mexicans

NOTABLE MATCHES: Dark Angel, Diana La Cazadora, & Marcela vs. Hiroka, Mima Shimoda, & Princesa Sujei at CMLL Super Viernes, in a 2 Out of 3 Falls match (May 18, 2007) · Sarah Stock vs. Cheerleader Melissa at SHIMMER Volume 18 (April 26, 2008) · Sarita vs. Alissa Flash at TNA Impact Wrestling (July 16, 2009) · Sarita & Taylor Wilde vs. The Beautiful People (Madison Rayne & Velvet Sky) at TNA No Surrender 2009, for the inaugural TNA Knockouts Tag Team Championship (September 20, 2009) · Sarita & Taylor Wilde (c) vs. Hamada & Awesome Kong at TNA Impact Wrestling, for the TNA Knockouts Tag Team Championship (January 4, 2010) · Dark Angel (c) vs. Act Yasukawa at STARDOM Season 14 Goddesses In Stars 2013 – Night 4, for the Wonder of STARDOM Championship (November 4, 2013) · Dark Angel vs. Princesa Sujei at CMLL 82nd Anniversary Show (September 18, 2015) · Dark Angel vs. Io Shirai (c) at STARDOM Appeal The Heat 2015, for the Wonder of STARDOM Championship (October 11, 2015)

★ Originally competing in kickboxing, Sarah Stock felt like she wasn't getting booked for as many fights as she wanted and needed a change. And despite a previous lack of interest and enjoyment in the sport, professional wrestling just so happened to be that change. After five weeks of training at Top Rope

Championship Wrestling—under Eddie Watts—in her native Winnipeg, Manitoba, Canada, that change led to her in-ring debut at a Can-Am Wrestling Federation (CAWF) show, as "Sarah Stone." Sarah was awarded the Can-Am Wrestling Women's Championship on her debut show, though she lost it later that same month.

If only things could be as decisive when it came to her ring name. Because while she was "Sarah Stone" at CAWF, she was "Sarah Swayze" back at Top Rope and then "Canadian Dark Angel" at Premier Championship Wrestling and "Sweet Sarah" at Real Action Wrestling and MainStream Wrestling, before she was "Sarah Griffin" at ECCW. All of those were in just her first year as a wrestler, and all of those were also just promotions in Canada, not all over the world. She was also "Sarah Griffin" in Connecticut's World Xtreme Wrestling at the time. It wasn't until 2003 that Stock began wrestling under her real name; and it spread, although her nicknames all stayed around the Canadian independent scene for a while. But the goal was to wrestle overseas, in Japan. And in order to do that, she knew she had to improve her in-ring work tremendously.

So in the fall of 2003—and after some proper introductions by Eddie Watts—Sarah Stock made her wrestling debut in (and moved down to) Monterrey, Mexico (for the Lucha Libre Femenil promotion) and added another ring name to her arsenal: "Dark Angel," a masked wrestler. This wasn't the first time she wore a mask, as she would walk to the ring with a mask (which she would take off before the match) and wings as Sarah Griffin. But she went forth with the masked-wrestler gimmick, settling on the name Dark Angel, again thanks to Eddie Watts. Stock also had to learn how to speak Spanish, a necessity for getting through her matches with her opponents without feeling "like [she was] being thrown to the wolves." While living and wrestling in Mexico, Stock would still make trips to the States and Canada, however, making her debut in ROH (in a dark match, only for the live crowd and tryout purposes) and OVW (as enhancement talent, during its WWE developmental days). Early in her LLF

career, she'd win the LLF Juvenil Championship from Simply Luscious, though she would lose it back to her two days later.

While Dark Angel would participate in plenty of multi-person Tag Team matches, she would also find herself in a feud against Princesa Sujei, leading to a Mask vs. Mask match in April 2004. She would lose this match—and therefore lose her mask. According to Stock, "After I lost my mask, I realized that there were a lot of opportunities for me without the mask, for people to see my face, to get to know me better and for me to show them a different side of my personality." And after that, she moved to Mexico City to wrestle for a bigger Mexican promotion, AAA. However, they only booked her as a host/valet, and she eventually signed with their rival promotion, CMLL, instead, as it was reestablishing its women's division. During her time in CMLL,

Stock also worked in other promotions—such as SHIMMER—allowing her to continue her rivalry with Princesa Sujei in Federación Internacional de Lucha Libre (FILL), defeating her to win the FILL Women's Championship. The two rivals eventually found mutual respect for each other; and years later, when Princesa competed in the inaugural WWE Mae Young Classic, it was reported that Stock (a WWE trainer at that point) had recommended her for one of the 32 slots.

During her time in CMLL, Stock got the opportunity to appear in commercials, as well as to be the basis for a comic book series. Her time in Mexico also led to her getting the chance to wrestle in Japan, just like she had hoped it would. She took her first tour in 2005, with later tours in 2009 and 2010, before spending most of her 2012–2013 there (in STARDOM). In STARDOM, Dark Angel became the Wonder of STARDOM Champion, holding it for 189 days before dropping it to Act Yasukawa. She also became good friends with Io Shirai and Kairi Hojo (WWE's Kairi Sane), two of the promotion's top stars at the time, regularly teaming with Io and also teaming up with Io and Kairi (as well as Mayu Iwatani) in Mexico in 2014, in a match at Último Dragón's wrestling promotion. Stock's time in STARDOM also wasn't without its controversy for a bit, as they were worried CMLL would blacklist her from wrestling in Mexico for wrestling in a joshi promotion unassociated with CMLL. (CMLL's sister promotion is REINA.) However, once she came back from her tour in 2012, she went right back to work at CMLL, suggesting that everything was just fine.

In all this, Sarah Stock was also becoming a more well-known name in the States and globally, as she joined TNA's roster in the spring of 2009 as "Sarita." Debuting as a face—and as a Mexican—Sarita teamed with Taylor Wilde to compete for the inaugural Knockouts Tag Team Championship, and they won. They'd lose the titles to Awesome Kong and Hamada at the beginning of 2010, however, and months later Sarita turned heel on Wilde. Their feud led to a Street Fight, which Sarita won, but Stock had to take a couple of months off after that to tend to a torn triceps. Upon returning, she temporarily appeared to be face again, before revealing her true colors in a feud with Velvet Sky.

The Canadian Sarita joined a heel stable eventually known as "Mexican America," a team mostly remembered for its lazy similarity to original TNA stable LAX and the seemingly little it did for its female stars, Sarita and her kayfabe cousin Rosita (Thea Trinidad, now known as Zelina Vega in WWE and also not Mexican). In the spring of 2011, Sarita and Rosita won the Knockouts Tag Team Championship from Angelina Love and Winter—and Sarita proclaimed this the start of a "Mexican takeover," thus officially beginning Mexican America. A few months after winning the championship, Sarah Stock would suffer from legitimate facial paralysis, eventually wearing a protective mask to the ring (which unfortunately didn't protect them from losing the championship) for a few months. Sarita and Rosita would go on to spend the rest of their time in TNA fighting for the Knockouts Tag Team Championship, falling short each time and silently disappearing from weekly television in the spring of 2012. After working one house show that June, in January 2013 it was reported that Sarah's TNA contract had expired and she had been released.

In the spring of 2015, Stock spent a week working at WWE's Performance Center, working as a guest trainer for the developmental talent. That then translated into her working as an extra at NXT TakeOver: Unstoppable, as one of Tyler Breeze's models in his ring entrance. Then, in September, it was reported that Sarah had signed fulltime with WWE as a trainer for the WWE Performance Center, teaching talent for NXT and a future on the main roster in WWE. Following this announcement, she wrestled two farewell matches in STARDOM, the first a tag team match (as Dark Angel) with Mayu Iwatani against Candy Crush (Chelsea Green and Kairi Hojo), and the second a one-on-one match between Dark Angel and her good friend Io Shirai, for Io's Wonder of STARDOM Championship. Stock won the tag match but came up short in the championship match.

★ SARAYA KNIGHT ★

YEARS ACTIVE: 1990–present

TRAINED BY: Ricky Knight · Jimmy Ocean

BILLED FROM: Norwich, Norfolk, England

ACCOMPLISHMENTS: 1x GSW Women's Champion · 3x HEW Women's Champion · 1x IndyGurlz Australia Champion · 1x PWF Ladies Tag Team Champion (with Britani Knight) · #3 in 2013 PWI Female 50 · 1x Queens of Chaos Champion · 1x RQW Women's Champion · 1x SHIMMER Champion · 1x TNT Extreme Wrestling Women's Champion · 1x WAWW British Champion · 1x WAWW World Champion

AKA: "Sweet Saraya" · 1/2 of The Knight Dynasty

NOTABLE MATCHES: The Knight Dynasty (Saraya Knight & Britani Knight) (with Rebecca Knox) vs. Hiroyo Matsumoto & Misaki Ohata (c) at SHIMMER Volume 38, for the SHIMMER Tag Team Championship (March 26, 2011) · Saraya Knight vs. Britani Knight at SHIMMER Volume 44, in a No Disqualification match (October 2, 2011) · Saraya Knight vs. Cheerleader Melissa (c) at SHIMMER Volume 48, for the SHIMMER Championship (March 18, 2012) · Saraya Knight (c) vs. Cheerleader Melissa at SHIMMER Volume 53, in a Steel Cage match for the SHIMMER Championship (April 6, 2013) · Saraya Knight (with Rhia O'Reilly & Sammi Baynz) vs. Allysin Kay at SHINE 30, in a Falls Count Anywhere Anything Goes match (October 2, 2015) · Saraya Knight vs. Mia Yim at SWE Nothing To Lose, for the vacant Queen of Southside Championship (July 1, 2017)

★ When you look into her backstory, it's baffling that Saraya Knight (born Julia Hamer) isn't the Saraya in her family who's had a feature film made about her life. (The Saraya in question would be Saraya-Jade, aka WWE's Paige. *Game of Thrones*' Lena Headey plays Sweet Saraya, though.) A childhood full of abuse, rape, homelessness, addiction—all before the age of 18, which was when she finally decided to get clean. Two years later, she met professional wrestler Ricky Knight; and from then on, they were inseparable (and married almost immediately).

Julia would go from working ring crew and making wrestling gear (as well as cleaning up after wrestlers and generally just taking care of them) to being Ricky's manager, "Saraya" (originally inspired by a drunk mishearing of the name of Slayer frontman Tom Araya)—and a fairly successful one at that, as she became in demand by both promoters and magazines. Everybody wanted a piece of "Sweet Saraya." And it wouldn't be until 1993 that wrestling actually entered her mind, thanks to Ricky's suggestion. From then on, Saraya would wrestle all over the British independent circuit—during somewhat of a slump period, with no TV time and, in a way, memories lost to time—while also wrestling for Ricky's World Association of Wrestling

(WAW) from its inception in 1994. She also infamously once wrestled while she was pregnant with her daughter—seven months pregnant, even—though she wasn't aware at the time. There truly isn't anything Saraya hasn't seen or done.

Yet somehow it wouldn't be until 2011 that she'd make her United States wrestling debut, debuting in SHIMMER along with her daughter (Britani Knight/Paige/Saraya-Jade). After Britani left for WWE—and after Britani defeated Saraya in a feud that her mother had started—Saraya set her sights on Cheerleader Melissa's SHIMMER Championship, continuing a years-long feud between the two. The inciting incident was during a match in 2007 at RQW, where an outside-the-ring brawl between the two led to a fan's soda can slicing through Saraya's knee and severing her main tendon—putting her on the shelf for eight months and almost ending her career completely. So at SHIMMER Volume 48, five months after SHIMMER fans had finally witnessed Cheerleader Melissa win the big one at SHIMMER Volume 44, they were stunned when Saraya took it away from her. However, Saraya held on to it until Volume 54, when Melissa won in back in a Steel Cage match, putting an end to the 384-day reign of misery.

Wrestling blogger Tom Holzerman once described Saraya Knight's character as "cantankerous, miserable, volatile, and violent." That pretty much sums it up. For fear of Holzerman's safety if she reads that, he also added that everything he's heard about the real person is the opposite of the character, "sweet as a Hershey's Kiss®." Reportedly, that's how Saraya's always been behind the scenes in SHIMMER, as well as everywhere else she wrestles. In fact, just looking at the list of opponents Saraya has had—especially the younger wrestlers—shows you how much she cares about helping out the industry.

In 2006, she founded the Bellatrix Female Warriors (originally as World Association of Women's Wrestling) women's promotion and school in the United Kingdom, as an offshoot and sister promotion to Ricky's World Association of Wrestling. There's nothing more cantankerous than ensuring the future of professional wrestling for years to come, right?

★ SASHA BANKS ★

YEARS ACTIVE: 2010–present

TRAINED BY: Brian Milonas · Brian Fury · Hanson · Chaotic Wrestling · WWE Performance Center

BILLED FROM: Cambridge, Massachusetts · Boston, Massachusetts

ACCOMPLISHMENTS: 1x Chaotic Wrestling Women's Champion · 1x Independent Wrestling Entertainment (IWE) Champion · 1x Ring Wars Carolina (RWC) No Limitz Champion · 2015 PWI Match of the Year (vs. Bayley, at NXT TakeOver: Respect) · 2015 PWI Woman of the Year · 2015 NXT Year-End Award for Match of the Year (vs. Bayley, at NXT TakeOver: Brooklyn) · #2 in 2016 PWI Female 50 · 2015 *Rolling Stone* Future Divas of the Year · 2015 *Rolling Stone* NXT Match of the Year (vs. Bayley, at NXT TakeOver: Brooklyn) · 2015 *Rolling Stone* Title Feud of the Year, NXT (vs. Bayley, for the NXT Women's Championship) · 2016 PWI Feud of the Year (vs. Charlotte Flair) · 4x WWE Women's/RAW Women's Champion · 1x NXT Women's Champion

AKA: "The Boss" · Mercedes KV · Mercedes · Miss Mercedes · 1/3 of Team B.A.D. (Bad and Dangerous) · "The Boss" · "The Legit Boss" · 1/3 of The BFFs (Beautiful Fierce Females) · 1/2 of Team B.A.E. · 1/4 of The Four Horsewomen (WWE) · 1/2 of the Boss & Hug Connection

NOTABLE MATCHES: Sasha Banks vs. Charlotte (c) at NXT TakeOver: R Evolution, for the NXT Women's Championship (December 11, 2014) · Sasha Banks vs. Charlotte (c) vs. Bayley vs. Becky Lynch at NXT TakeOver: Rival, in a Fatal 4-Way match for the NXT Women's Championship (February 11, 2015) · Sasha Banks (c) vs. Becky Lynch at NXT TakeOver: Unstoppable, for the NXT Women's Championship (May 20, 2015) · Sasha Banks (c) vs. Bayley at NXT TakeOver: Brooklyn, for the NXT Women's Championship (August 22, 2015) · Sasha Banks vs. Bayley (c) at NXT TakeOver: Respect, in a 30-Minute Ironman match for the NXT Women's Championship (October 7, 2015) · Sasha Banks vs. Becky Lynch vs. Charlotte, in a Triple Threat for the vacant WWE Women's Championship at

WrestleMania 32 (April 3, 2016) · Sasha Banks vs. Charlotte (c), for the WWE RAW Women's Championship (October 3, 2016) · Sasha Banks vs. Charlotte Flair (c) at WWE Monday *Night RAW*, in a Falls Count Anywhere match for the WWE RAW Women's Championship (November 28, 2016) · Sasha Banks vs. Alexa Bliss (c) vs. Bayley vs. Emma vs. Nia Jax at WWE No Mercy 2017, for the WWE RAW Women's Championship (September 24, 2017)

★ As WWE commentator Michael Cole would say, "It's Boss time!" As one of the Four Horsewomen of the WWE—and arguably the most popular of the quartet—Sasha Banks is also recognized as one of the most important figures in WWE's Divas Revolution and subsequent Women's Evolution.

Born Mercedes Kaestner-Varnado, before she was a boss she was just a girl who loved Eddie Guerrero and AJW matches on YouTube, while her family moved around a lot. All she'd wanted to be since she was 10 years old was a professional wrestler. So while she began training at Chaotic Wrestling when she was 16, she officially made her in-ring debut two years later, in the fall of 2010, as "Mercedes KV" (and sometimes as "Miss Mercedes"). However, because of the prominence of Mercedes Martinez on the independent circuit—especially in the Northeastern territory where KV was working—this eventually led to an awkward situation in the summer of 2012, when reports had come out that Martinez had attended a WWE tryout and was possibly getting signed . . . only for her to have to release a statement that it wasn't her, it was KV.

Because of the Diva style and objectification of women in WWE—and a belief that she wouldn't be given the time of day if she tried out—KV's original plan was to end up wrestling in Mexico or Japan instead. But KV did in fact get signed by WWE after that tryout, forcing her to have to vacate the Chaotic Wrestling Women's Championship—during a reign in which she had broken the record for title length, which was 182 days—after 260 days. KV debuted at NXT house shows in the fall of 2012 as Mercedes KV, before becoming "Sasha Banks" that November. Sasha's original NXT TV debut (in December 2012) was as a nice-girl, AJ Lee-esque character (right down to her gear), and it wasn't until the fall of 2013 that everything changed. After weeks of Summer Rae getting into Sasha Banks' head, trying to tell her she had the answers to relevancy for Sasha—other than just in the case of a happy-to-be-here face that the crowd likes well enough but doesn't care about—Sasha turned heel and joined forces with Summer Rae to become The BFFs (Beautiful Fierce Females). And from that point on, Sasha would also be known as "The Boss." Behind the scenes, Tyler Breeze had helped Sasha come up with a list of characters, and "The Boss" character was one inspired partially by her real-life cousin, Snoop Dogg—with a little bit from Keke Wyatt of *R&B Divas*—as well as her legitimate frustration with the lack of fan connection at the time.

The BFFs would soon add Charlotte to their ranks, and when Summer spent time on the main roster, Sasha and

Charlotte would end up changing the wrestling world, all from developmental. While Charlotte would become NXT Women's Champion during Summer's absence, things would implode after Summer temporarily returned. Champion Charlotte would turn face (teaming with Bayley, who had been The BFFs' punching bag), and Sasha would feud with her for the title. Sasha would also turn Becky Lynch heel (the same way Summer had originally turned her), to form Team B.A.E. (Best At Everything), though Lynch always made clear that the partnership was professional (as opposed to the mean-girls friendship The BFFs had). On her fourth shot at Charlotte's title, Sasha Banks won at NXT TakeOver: Rival, in a Fatal 4-Way including Bayley and Becky Lynch—a match including all of the WWE's Four Horsewomen. Sasha would then go on to defend her championship against plucky underdog Alexa Bliss, Becky Lynch (in a match at NXT TakeOver: Unstoppable that arguably made Lynch a star), and eventually Charlotte (where they shared a hug post-match, as they had been called up to the main roster and it was the end of an era).

However, while Sasha Banks was called up to the main roster in the summer of 2015 to take part in the Divas Revolution (as part of Team B.A.D.), she still had some unfinished business in the form of Bayley, who wanted her NXT Women's Championship. At NXT TakeOver: Brooklyn that August, Sasha dropped the championship to Bayley, in a match that has often been called (even by WWE) the best women's match in WWE history. Then their rematch—which Bayley also won, but Sasha can at least say she intentionally made a child, aka Bayley's super-fan Izzy, cry during the match—at NXT TakeOver: Respect was the first Women's 30-Minute Ironman match in company history.

While Sasha's main roster 2015 was mostly Team B.A.D.-related, she stepped back into the singles spotlight (and into a face role) in the beginning of 2016, focused on winning the Divas Championship. This culminated in a mini-feud between Sasha Banks and Becky Lynch to determine who would challenge heel Charlotte for her title at WrestleMania 32, resulting in a Triple Threat between three of the Four Horsewomen. And even better, the match was no longer going to be for the Divas Championship: it was going to be for the newly reinstated WWE Women's Championship. (And women in WWE would no longer be "Divas," they'd be "Superstars," just like the men.) While Charlotte won the championship—which she and Sasha would eventually trade back and forth, leading to Sasha becoming a four-time WWE Women's/RAW Women's Champion—these women's points had been made and women's wrestling in WWE had been changed for the better. During her championship feud with Charlotte, Sasha would participate in main event RAWs as well as pay-per-views (Hell in a Cell 2016 marked the first-ever women's Hell in a Cell match as well as the first-ever women's pay-per-view main event in WWE), with the one sour note being that Sasha would lose in every title defense she had.

Sasha Banks has said before that WWE wasn't interested in her, as she didn't have the "Diva look," and that it was William Regal who made the big push for her to be signed in the first place. According to Regal, the people who were in charge of talent scouting for NXT at the time thought she was "useless." But Sasha Banks has more than proven herself to be a solid investment, as—even without the "Diva look"—Sasha Banks has helped usher in a new direction for women in the WWE. Sure, once she did get signed, she was also told to wrestle girlier, "like a Diva"; but that clearly didn't end up sticking. It looks like Sasha's perspective was right: if you're gonna do it, do it like a boss.

★ SERENA DEEB ★

YEARS ACTIVE: 2005–2015 · 2017

TRAINED BY: OVW · Terry Taylor · FCW · Al Snow · Rip Rogers · Nightmare Danny Davis · Robert Gibson · Greg Gagne · "Dr. Death" Steve Williams · Lance Storm · Les Thatcher · Dr. Tom Prichard

BILLED FROM: Fairfax, Virginia · Seattle, Washington

ACCOMPLISHMENTS: 1x Queen of FCW · 1x Great Lakes Championship Wrestling (GLCW) Ladies Champion · 1x NWA France Women's Champion · Memphis Championship Wrestling Women's Champion · 6x OVW Women's Champion · #16 in 2011 PWI Female 50 · 1x Wrestling New Classic (WNC) Women's Champion · 2013 WNC Women's Championship League

AKA: Serena · Serena Mancini · Mia Mancini · Paige Webb · "The Anti-Diva" · "The Extreme Diva" · member of The Insurgency · member of The Straight Edge Society · member of Valkyrie · "Female Terminator" · "The Deebius One"

NOTABLE MATCHES: Serena vs. Naomi Night at FCW, in a FCW Divas Championship Tournament Finals match for the inaugural FCW Divas Championship (June 20, 2010) · The Straight Edge Society (Serena & Luke Gallows) vs. Kelly Kelly & The Big Show at *WWE SmackDown*, in a Mixed Tag Team match (August 20, 2010) · Serena Deeb & Sara Del Rey vs. Daizee Haze & Amazing Kong at ROH Final Battle 2010 (December 18, 2010) · Serena Deeb & Sara Del Rey vs. Ayumi Kurihara & Hiroyo Matsumoto at ROH Honor Takes Center Stage, Chapter 1 (April 1, 2011) · Serena vs. Kana at SMASH.21, in a SMASH Diva Championship Finals match (September 8, 2011) · Serena Deeb vs. Mickie James at TNA One Night Only: Knockouts Knockdown 2013 (September 6, 2013) · Serena Deeb vs. Mia Yim at PWS Bombshells Ladies of Wrestling 9 (March 22, 2014) · Serena Deeb vs. Ivelisse (c) at SHINE 20, for the SHINE Championship (June 27, 2014) · Serena Deeb vs. Piper Niven at the WWE Mae Young Classic, in a Mae Young Classic Second Round match (September 6, 2017)

⭐ As soon as an 11-year-old Serena Deeb saw wrestling for the first time—through an episode of WWF programming—she was in love. So when she turned 18, she decided to turn that love into a reality. After graduating from high school in Virginia, she took all the money she had saved up and moved to Kentucky, to train at OVW (from March to November 2005).

Serena spent most of her time at OVW as a face, as well as somehow earning the ire of Beth Phoenix. While OVW was a developmental territory for WWE at the time, Serena was not a WWE developmental talent, unlike her rivals Beth Phoenix, ODB, and Katie Lea. So it was certainly a surprise when Serena ended up beating those three women in a Fatal-4-Way match for the OVW Women's Championship. In fact, despite the fact that Serena was pushed as the top woman in OVW's women's division—winning the championship six times during her tenure there—she eventually got a nose job and breast implants, reportedly to actually get on WWE's radar at the time. (She'd later get the implants removed, post-WWE.)

Deeb also wrestled in SHIMMER during this time, eventually feuding with Sara Del Rey in an underdog story on her way to challenge MsChif for the SHIMMER Championship, despite a consistent losing streak in the promotion. However, in order to get to MsChif—who had come to respect Deeb's persistence and fire—Deeb had to beat Del Rey. That was easier said than done, as Del Rey had beat Deeb two times prior; but at SHIMMER Volume 22, the third time was the charm. Unfortunately, Deeb couldn't beat MsChif in the promised SHIMMER Championship match, at the following volume. On the bright side, a few weeks after Volume 23, Serena was seen on WWE TV (ECW) as a background extra, and after much speculation of the state of her relationship with the company, it was announced in July 2009 that WWE had signed her to a developmental deal at FCW.

During her time in FCW, Serena soon became "Serena Mancini" and then "Mia Mancini" (before becoming just "Serena" again), a mob daughter character, and feuded with April "AJ" Lee for the Queen of FCW crown. However, the Mancini character ended up having nothing to do with Serena's finished product when she debuted on the main roster in January 2010, as a new member (originally as an audience plant) of CM Punk's Straight Edge Society. Part of the gimmick required Serena to be shaved bald (despite her gorgeous head of hair) on national television, an opportunity she jumped at: "It was a really unique opportunity. Seeing a woman getting her head shaved was so rare, you don't see it all that often in the history of wrestling. Getting to do it as my debut was really, really cool, and really powerful. I was also very scared about what I was going to look like. There were a lot of uncertainties, but it ended up being really, really great for my career." Serena also had no idea whether WWE had asked other Divas on the main roster or in developmental to fulfill this role, but she was going to make the most of the opportunity. However, despite working on the main roster for eight months, Serena only wrestled one match on WWE TV before she was released. Reports at the time claimed that WWE released her for not "living out" the straight-edge persona she had assumed on-screen—with her being drunk in front of fans out in public—but considering that this was wrestling in 2010 and not wrestling in the 1980s, that kind of adherence to kayfabe never quite made sense. In reality, it was perhaps mostly a softening of the truth, as Serena later revealed that she had a drinking problem.

Post-WWE, Serena returned to SHIMMER and ROH (teaming with rival Serena Del Rey in her return match); she also began wrestling in indies like Pro Wrestling Syndicate, WSU, SHINE, and France's Queens of Chaos. She also finally toured in Japan like she had always wanted to, losing to Kana (now known as WWE's Asuka) in the finals to crown the inaugural SMASH Diva Champion. And while she made some appearances in TNA Impact Wrestling, she never signed a full-time contract as did so many of her fellow WWE alums. Instead, in the summer of 2015, Deeb announced her retirement from professional wrestling, choosing to focus instead on her newfound career as a yoga instructor.

Surprisingly, Deeb briefly returned to professional wrestling (in an in-ring sense) and WWE two years after her final match, as one of the 32 participants in the inaugural WWE Mae Young Classic tournament. While she was eliminated in the Second Round, she made an impression, especially as she opened up about how her past mistakes had ruined things her first go-around in WWE. Then in February 2018, news broke that Deeb had signed a coach's contract at the WWE's Performance Center.

★ SEXY STAR ★

YEARS ACTIVE: 2006–present

TRAINED BY: Humberto Garza Jr. · Mr. Lince · Gran Apache · Abismo Negro

BILLED FROM: Monterrey, Nuevo León, Mexico

ACCOMPLISHMENTS: 3x AAA Reina de Reinas Champion · 1x AAA World Mixed Tag Team Champion (with Pentagon Jr.) · 1x FILL Women's Champion · 1x FILL Mixed Tag Team Champion (with Humberto Garza Jr.) · 1x Lucha Underground Champion · 1x Lucha Underground Gift of the Gods Champion · Lucha Underground Aztec Warfare III · #9 in 2016 PWI Female 50 · 1x The Crash Femenil Champion

AKA: Sexy Dulce · Dulce Poly · Dulce Garcia · Dulce Star · 1/3 of Las Gringas Locas · member of La Legión Extranjera · member of La Sociedad · member of La Nueva Sociedad

NOTABLE MATCHES: Sexy Star vs. Aero Star vs. Bengala vs. Big Ryck vs. Fenix vs. Jack Evans vs. King Cuerno at Lucha Underground Ultima Lucha Part 2, in a Seven-Way match for the Gift of the Gods Championship (August 5, 2015) · Sexy Star vs. Mariposa at Lucha Underground, in a No Mas match (May 4, 2016) · Aztec Warfare at Lucha Underground, in a 20 Man Aztec Warfare match for the Lucha Underground Championship (November 16, 2016) · Sexy Dulce vs. Rachael Ellering vs. Chelsea Green at WrestleCircus Taking Center Stage, in a 3-Way Elimination match for the vacant WrestleCircus Lady of the Ring Championship (February 19, 2017) · Sexy Star (c) vs. Ayako Hamada vs. Lady Shani vs. Rosemary at AAA TripleMania XXV, in a Four-Way match for the AAA Reinas de Reinas Championship (August 26, 2017)

★ As "Dulce Poly," a student of Humberto Garza Jr.'s, Dulce Garcia Rivas began her professional wrestling career as an unmasked wrestler in Mexico's Federacion Internacional de Lucha Libre (FILL) promotion. Dulce's rise to the top in FILL was a

this, Sexy Star went from being a top star in AAA—dropping the Reina de Reinas Championship in a Six-Person Mixed Tag Team match—to wrestling on the undercard for months, as apparent punishment. However, by the end of 2011, she was Reina de Reinas Champion for the second time—a reign that only ended when she vacated the championship in February 2013 because of her pregnancy.

The thing about *Lucha Underground* and Sexy Star is, as Sexy Star was one of the top *ruda* (the lucha libre approximation of "heel") wrestlers in the women's division (starting in 2009), it was somewhat surprising to realize that in *Lucha Underground* she would be a *tecnica* ("face"). And not just a *tecnica*, but an underdog with a backstory just primed for audiences to love and get behind her. In *Lucha Underground*, Sexy Star's origin story was that of a victim of abuse who became "Sexy Star" "for every girl out there who needs a hero." Making her way through adversity, over the first three seasons of *Lucha Underground*, Sexy Star faced harassment, male competitors not taking her seriously, kidnapping—and came through it all eventually becoming the first female Lucha Underground Champion. And even before that, after the No Mas match against Mariposa in *Lucha Underground* season two, it looked like the sky was the limit for Sexy Star, with articles arguing that she embodied professional wrestling's women's revolution. However, Sexy Star's behavior outside of *Lucha Underground* and the carefully scripted version of the character became more difficult to reconcile.

After Sexy Star returned to AAA in December 2013 after giving birth, she went on to win the AAA World Mixed Tag Team Championship with fellow *Lucha Underground* star Pentagon Jr. the following April. They held the championship until February 2016, when Sexy Star relinquished the championship and quit AAA. At the time, it was reported that she had retired from professional wrestling—to focus on a boxing career instead—but Sexy Star has denied ever saying that, instead claiming that things got lost in the translation. Instead, long-term fans of AAA and Lucha Libre noted Sexy Star's propensity to

quick one, as she won the FILL Women's Championship mere months after making her professional wrestling debut (though she did lose the title two months later). However, just a few weeks after she'd lost the championship, she made her AAA debut as "Sexy Star." It wasn't until 2009, though, that she'd get a real storyline, in a love triangle between real-life husband-and-wife wrestlers Billy Boy and Faby Apache. The love triangle would eventually turn into a feud for Apache's AAA Reina de Reinas Championship, with Sexy Star winning the championship for the first time thanks to the help of AAA's top heel group, La Legión Extranjera.

In August 2010, Sexy Star participated in a paid WWE tryout (paying $1,000 to try out) for a contract at the developmental territory FCW. She wasn't signed, and reports at the time said it was a combination of her in-ring skill, her poor English, and not being "pretty enough to be in *Playboy*." Months after the failed tryout, it was also reported that Sexy Star was in the doghouse with AAA for trying to leave for WWE in the first place, leading to her getting into even more hot water with the company when she attempted to look for a new job in rival promotion CMLL (while still contracted with AAA). After drop championships by relinquishing them, presumably to avoid looking weak and putting other wrestlers over. This was highlighted even more once she made her surprise return to AAA (despite that "retirement"), winning the vacant Reina de Reinas Championship weeks after her *Lucha Underground* colleague Taya Valkyrie was stripped of the championship in a deceptive manner.

Then came AAA TripleMania (the biggest show of the year) XXV, in which Sexy Star defended the championship in a Four-Way against Ayako Hamada, Lady Shani, and Impact Wrestling's Rosemary (as part of Impact Wrestling's global partnership with AAA). During this match, Sexy Star won by putting Rosemary down with an armbar submission. Only it was a legitimate armbar, and Sexy Star wouldn't stop even after the match ended, forcing the referee to pull her away. Prior to the match, there had allegedly been legitimate conflict between Hamada, Shani, and Sexy Star; then during the match itself, the former were trading actual blows with Sexy Star. However, Rosemary had no prior relationship or beef with Sexy Star, which made the whole situation even more bizarre. While Rosemary's injury ended up not being as severe as expected—it was a strained tricep and bicep, instead of the presumed tear—Sexy Star still suffered the consequences of her actions. After this, wrestlers and wrestling promotions from all corners spoke up about Dulce's unprofessionalism, making it clear that they either refused to work with her or refused to book her. Dulce eventually spoke out about the situation, saying that she had been "confused" at the time and only referring to Rosemary as "the girl"—even questioning whether Rosemary had actually been injured.

While AAA didn't release Sexy Star for her actions, they did strip her of the championship a few days after the incident (and she was written off the fourth season of *Lucha Underground*, off-screen). A few days after that, Sexy Star released another statement claiming that Rosemary had lied about the extent of her injuries altogether.

★ SHAYNA BASZLER ★

YEARS ACTIVE: 2015–present

TRAINED BY: Josh Barnett · Mercedes Martinez · WWE Performance Center

BILLED FROM: Sioux Falls, South Dakota

ACCOMPLISHMENTS: 1x AIW Women's Champion · 1x DDT Pro-Wrestling Ironman Heavymetalweight Champion · 1x NHPW IndyGurlz Australia Champion · 2017 NHPW Global Conflict Shield Tournament · 1x PREMIER Women's Champion · #12 in 2017 PWI Female 50 · 1x Quintessential Pro Wrestling (QPro) Women's Champion · 2x NXT Women's Champion

AKA: 1/3 of Trifecta · "The Submission Magician" · "The Queen of Spades" · "The Mother of Dragons" · 1/4 of The Four Horsewomen (MMA)

NOTABLE MATCHES: Shayna Baszler (with Marina Shafir) vs. Nicole Matthews at ECCW Ballroom Brawl 5, in a Knockout or Submission match (January 16, 2016) · Shayna Baszler vs. Heidi Lovelace (c) at AIW Bloodsport, for the AIW Women's Championship (September 9, 2016) · Shayna Baszler vs. Io Shirai (c) at STARDOM of Champions, for the World of STARDOM Championship (February 23, 2017) · Shayna Baszler vs. Nicole Matthews (c) at ECCW Last Women Standing, in a Last Woman Standing match for the ECCW Championship (May 13, 2017) · Shayna Baszler vs. Madison Eagles (c) at NHPW Global Conflict 2017 – Night 2, in a NHPW Global Conflict Tournament Finals match for the IndyGurlz Australia Championship (May 27, 2017) · Shayna Baszler vs. Mercedes Martinez at the WWE Mae Young Classic, in a Mae Young Classic Semifinals match (September 6, 2017) · Shayna Baszler vs. Kairi Sane at the WWE Mae Young Classic, in a Mae Young Classic Finals match (September 12, 2017) · Shayna Baszler vs. Ember Moon (c) at NXT TakeOver: New Orleans, for the NXT Women's Championship (April 7, 2018) · Shayna Baszler (c) vs. Kairi Sanat NXT TakeOver: Brooklyn IV, for the NXT Women's Championship (August 18, 2018) · Shayna Baszler vs. Kairi Sane (c) at WWE

Evolutions for the NXT Women's Championship (October 28, 2018) · Shayna Baszler vs. Kairi Sane st NXT TakeOver: War Games 2018: in a 2 Out of 3 Falls Match for the NXT Women's Championship (November 17, 2018)

⭐ Shayna Baszler's background before becoming a professional wrestler is a lot different from most women's professional wrestling origin story. For starters, Shayna was already 35 years old, which isn't exactly the norm in a sport where competitors start young (and, especially in the case of female competitors, tend to retire relatively young as well). But also, she came from the world of MMA—mixed martial arts—and catch wrestling. In fact, Baszler is the only American female certified as a competitive catch wrestler, thanks to the training of British catch legend Billy Robinson during her amateur wrestling career. In MMA (and now in wrestling), she became known as "The Queen of Spades," and not just because of her ability to work as a "submission magician" in her fights: Josh Barnett literally gave her the nickname because of her ability to perform card magic tricks.

As for the transition from MMA to professional wrestling, it wasn't as surprising as one might think, in Shayna Baszler's eyes. Not just because her MMA trainer Josh Barnett had made the transition from MMA to wrestling—and had a hand in Baszler's wrestling training as well—but because of the teachings of Billy Robinson. According to Baszler, the similarities between catch wrestling and professional wrestling are what she considers the secret behind her quick success in professional wrestling: "If you look at the history of professional wrestling, it started out as shoot fighting until they figured out they could make more money working fights [and fixing results] and people would watch. Catch wrestling is pro wrestling, if you look at the ground moves and the rule set. It's just about learning the art of it for yourself." Plus it helped that Baszler was already a professional wrestling fan, as she and her inner circle in the world of MMA

(including Ronda Rousey, Marina Shafir, and Jessamyn Duke) named themselves "The Four Horsewomen," after the Ric Flair and Arn Anderson–led wrestling stable (and with Flair and Anderson's blessing).

Baszler's first actual appearance as part of the professional wrestling world was as the valet for the ROH Tag Team Champions ReDRagon (Kyle O'Reilly and Bobby Fish) at ROH's 13th Anniversary Show in March 2015. (However, since 2014, Baszler and the rest of the Four Horsewomen had been known to show up in the audience of and backstage at PWG in Reseda, California.) In a post-match promo, ReDRagon referred to Baszler as the "Ringo" (with Fish as their "John," O'Reilly as their "Paul," and "Filthy" Tom Lawlor as their "George") and "The Mother of Dragons" of their team. Training under Josh

Barnett again, Baszler made her in-ring debut that September, against veteran women's wrestler Cheerleader Melissa. And from that point on, Baszler was on the fast track in her professional wrestling career, debuting for STARDOM (during a USA tour in California) the following month. Soon after, Baszler made her Canadian wrestling debut in ECCW, immediately entering into a feud with Nicole Matthews.

In the spring of 2016, Baszler debuted in Ohio interdependent promotion Absolute Intense Wrestling (AIW)–which would be her home promotion—and debuted in SHIMMER (at Volume 81) that same summer. At SHIMMER Volume 85, Baszler joined forces with Heart of SHIMMER Champion Nicole Savoy (who Baszler had failed to defeat for the title back at SHIMMER Volume 83) and a returning Mercedes Martinez—coming out of retirement after two years—to help Martinez take the SHIMMER Championship from Madison Eagles. There, Trifecta was born, the brainchild of Baszler, who wanted to be where the power in SHIMMER was. Meanwhile, that same September in AIW, Baszler defeated Heidi Lovelace to win the AIW Women's Championship. At the end of that month, she also participated in a WWE tryout alongside 35 other wrestlers, including Lovelace and fellow Trifecta member Savoy. Still showing no signs of slowing down, Baszler made her official Japanese in-ring debut for STARDOM in January 2017, a tour in Japan in which she unsuccessfully challenged Io Shirai and Toni Storm for the World of Stardom Championship and the SWA World Championship, respectfully. Upon returning to North America, Baszler remained dominant in AIW and even temporarily rekindled her feud with Nicole Matthews in ECCW, before making her Australian wrestling debut with NHPW. At NHPW, Baszler added more gold to her collection, beating dominant Australian champion Madison Eagles for the IndyGurlz Australia Championship.

In the summer of 2017, Shayna Baszler competed alongside 31 other women (including her Trifecta teammates) in the inaugural WWE Mae Young Classic. Throughout the tournament, Baszler proved herself to be a bloodthirsty competitor who cared about nothing but the win, even when going against her friend Mercedes Martinez in the Semifinals. Making it to the live finals that September, however, Baszler's cockiness finally got the better of her, coming up short against Kairi Sane. While Baszler had worked WWE NXT house shows that summer and had even previously been featured on WWE TV before (on *Total Divas*, helping Nikki Bella train), it wasn't until that October that WWE announced that she had officially signed a developmental contract to NXT and had reported to the Performance Center in Orlando.

Just barely two years into her professional wrestling career, Baszler had already wrestled in four different countries and had been signed to a WWE contract. Her final AIW match happened on July 17, right after Mae Young Classic tapings, in an AIW Women's Championship defense against Mia Yim (who was Baszler's first AIW opponent ever) at Absolution XII . . . in which Baszler retained. Since then, the title has yet to be vacated, despite Baszler's commitments to WWE. (As for the IndyGurlz Australia Championship, while she was not able to lose the title in a match, in her absence her former stablemate and mentor Mercedes Martinez—a former IndyGurlz Australia Champion herself—took matters into her own hands and filled in as NHPW's "true champion.")

In December 2017, *NXT* began airing vignettes for Baszler's official debut, and by the end of the month she was debuting with two things on her mind: revenge over Kairi Sane beating her in the Mae Young Classic, and the NXT Women's Championship. After attacking Kairi Sane upon making her debut, all she had to do next was convince NXT Women's Champion Ember Moon to face her. To do that, Baszler set her sights on NXT underdog Dakota Kai, attacking after their wrestling match, injuring her at practice—anything to goad Ember Moon into playing the hero and putting her championship on the line. Which she did, at NXT TakeOver: Philadelphia (at the end of January 2018), just barely eking out a win (getting a desperate pin while Baszler still had her in a submission hold). Longtime followers of both women's careers jokingly called the match the one for the AIW Women's Championship, as Ember Moon was a former AIW Women's Champion (as Athena) and Shayna Baszler was of course still technically the current AIW Women's Champion.

However, in a rematch at NXT TakeOver: New Orleans that April (during WrestleMania Weekend), Baszler was able to beat Ember Moon by technical submission. The following Monday, Ember Moon made her debut on the WWE main roster—at *RAW*—an act Baszler essentially called an attempt to run away for the embarrassment of losing the championship to her. As NXT Women's Champion, Baszler continued to bully her way through the female roster—calling herself the official locker room leader—with Dakota Kai remaining the thorn in Baszler's side, not exactly a threat but also not exactly someone who would just take Baszler's threats and attacks lying down. But considering Baszler's M.O., those threats just happened to end with Kai lying down. And backup—if needed—wasn't too far away, as Ronda Rousey made her WWE main roster debut in January 2018, while both Marina Shafir and Jessamyn Duke reported to the Performance Center on NXT developmental contracts in May 2018.

★ SHERRI MARTEL ★

YEARS ACTIVE: 1978–2006

TRAINED BY: Donna Christanello · The Fabulous Moolah · "Mr. Personality" Butch Moore

BILLED FROM: New Orleans, Louisiana

ACCOMPLISHMENTS: 3x AWA World Women's Champion · 1x AWA Superstars of Wrestling World Women's Champion · 1994 Cauliflower Alley Club Honoree · 1x IWA Women's Champion ·

Professional Wrestling Hall of Fame Class of 2014 · Southern States Wrestling Kingsport Wrestling Hall of Fame Class of 2003 · WSU Hall of Fame Class of 2009 · 1x WWF Women's Champion · WWE Hall of Fame Class of 2006 · 1991 Wrestling Observer Newsletter Manager of the Year

AKA: "Scary" Sherri · "Sensational" Sherri · Sister Sherri · "Sensational" Queen Sherri · "Sensuous" Sherri · Sherri Martine · Peggy Sue

NOTABLE MATCHES: Sherri Martel vs. Candi Devine (c) at AWA SuperClash, for the AWA World Women's Championship (September 28, 1985) · Sherri Martel vs. The Fabulous Moolah at WWF, for the WWF Women's Championship (July 24, 1987) · "Sensational" Sherri, Dawn Marie, Donna Christianello, & The Glamour Girls (Judy Martin & Leilani Kai) (with Jimmy Hart) vs. Velvet McIntyre, Rockin' Robin, The Fabulous Moolah, & The Jumping Bomb Angels (Itsuki Yamazaki & Noriyo Tateno) at WWF Survivor Series 1987, in a 5-on-5 Survivor Series Elimination match (November 26, 1987) · Sherri Martel, Amber O'Neal, Krissy Vaine, & Peggy Lee Leather vs. Wendi Richter, Bambi, Jenny Taylor, & Malia Hosaka at WrestleReunion (January 29, 2005)

★ At 16 years old, Sherri Russell asked Grizzly Smith (father to Jake "The Snake" Roberts and Rockin' Robin) for advice on becoming a professional wrestler. He didn't take her seriously— not only was she just 16, but she was a girl trying to become a professional wrestler—but told her to come back when she was 21 if she was really interested in becoming a wrestler. But by age 20, she had just gone through her second divorce and decided to move to Memphis—which is where she found the wrestling school run by "Mr. Personality," Butch Moore. With $500 and a dream, Sherri entered that wrestling school, gave her money to Moore, and got the taste slapped out of her mouth as a result. According to Sherri, however, it was her alleged response that sealed the deal for her future in this business: "Is that all you got?"

Getting her official in-ring debut in the fall of 1980, Sherri originally went by "Sherri Martine." However, after attending

The Fabulous Moolah's wrestling school for supplemental training—based on a recommendation from Grizzly Smith, once she did in fact come back to him when she was 21—Moolah did perhaps the best thing she could have for Sherri and changed her name to "Sherri Martel." (She also eventually kicked Sherri out of her wrestling school, for partying too much.) After a tour of Japan in 1981 (through Moolah's school), Sherri went back to Memphis, where she was the first wrestler legendary wrestling manager Jim Cornette ever managed. However, about two weeks into their run, Sherri suffered an injury, putting her on the shelf. Sherri would eventually bounce back, though, making her debut in the Minneapolis-based territory AWA in 1985 and winning the AWA World Women's Championship three times in the time she was with the promotion.

Sherri Martel was still on her third AWA World Women's Championship when she officially debuted (having worked some shows with Moolah in 1982) in the WWF—though she immediately vacated it once she defeated Moolah (who she subsequently developed a rivalry with) for the Women's Championship in said debut. After winning the championship, Sherri was now "Sensational" Sherri, and she held the championship for 15 months before dropping it to Rockin' Robin.

Over her entire career, Sherri managed a veritable who's who of professional wrestlers: "Macho Man" Randy Savage, "Million Dollar Man" Ted DiBiase, "The Heartbreak Kid" Shawn Michaels (as the one who originally sang his "Sexy Boy" entrance theme), Harlem Heat (Booker T and Stevie Ray), Ric Flair—and the list goes on. And with her flamboyant makeup—Gorilla Monsoon once asked if Helen Keller did her makeup—she could be just as loud and larger-than-life as her clients. Sherri forced people to look at her, all so she could then force them to look at her client. So when WWF phased out its Women's Division in 1990, Martel was naturally able to adapt before eventually being released in 1993. She then went on to work as (primarily) a manager in SMW, ECW, and WCW. Her time in WCW saw the introduction of "Sensuous" Sherri—looking for a man worthy of her services and

able to win the WCW World Heavyweight Championship—and then "Sister Sherri" during her time with the Harlem Heat.

In terms of just how effective and tough Sherri was, Booker T once recalled how well she did the job of getting him and his brother Stevie Ray over: "I remember one time Sherri slapped Jim Duggan so hard, he stopped selling. Sherri almost started riots in certain towns. She was our ace that made us." Stevie Ray added, "You cannot mention Harlem Heat without mentioning Sherri Martel at the same time." Post-breakup with the Harlem Heat in the summer of 1997, Sherri made intermittent appearances in WCW as well as indies like IWA Mid-South. In 2005, she made an appearance in WWE as part of the Shawn Michaels/Kurt Angle buildup to WrestleMania 21.

Sherri died in 2007 at age 49 due to an apparent drug overdose, after years of struggling with substance abuse. She had just been inducted into the WWE Hall of Fame (by Ted DiBiase) the year before. Her last televised appearance on a wrestling show would be in September 2006, as one of the many managers Bobby Roode was considering for his brand. As she reminded Roode, "Behind every successful man is a strong, successful woman."

★ STACY KEIBLER ★

YEARS ACTIVE: 1999–2006

TRAINED BY: WCW Power Plant

BILLED FROM: Baltimore, Maryland

ACCOMPLISHMENTS: 2004 WWE Babe of the Year

AKA: "The Legs of WCW" · "The Legs of WWE" · Super Stacy · Miss Hancock · Skye · "The Duchess of Dudleyville"

NOTABLE MATCHES: Stacy Keibler & Torrie Wilson (Alliance) vs. Trish Stratus & Lita (WWF) at WWF InVasion 2001, in a Bra and Panties Tag Team match (July 22, 2001) · Stacy Keibler (with Reverend D-Von & Deacon Batista) vs. Trish Stratus (c) (with Bubba Ray Dudley) at WWE Judgment Day 2002, for the WWE Women's Championship (May 19, 2002) · Stacy Keibler & Test vs. Chris Jericho & Christian at WWE *Monday Night RAW* (February 24, 2003) · Stacy Keibler vs. Trish Stratus (c) at WWE *Monday Night RAW*, for the WWE Women's Championship (October 11, 2004)

★ Stacy Keibler grew up with a background in dance (ballet, jazz, and tap), and that just so happened to be the skill set that brought her into professional wrestling—along with her naturally long legs, which became her calling card in the business.

After entering WCW's "Nitro Girl Search" contest (something of a proto-Diva Search) to become a *WCW Monday Nitro* Girl dancer, Keibler defeated 300 other girls—and won a cool $10,000—to close out the year. As a Nitro Girl, she was known as "Skye," and the 20-year-old Keibler considered it just one thing on her plate: At a certain point, she was working as a Nitro Girl, cheerleading for her hometown football team (the Baltimore Ravens), and attending college.

But upon becoming a Nitro Girl, Skye wasn't just expected to dance—as the Nitro Girls were in a feud at the time—and was immediately thrust into a role as a heel character upon joining WCW. Only two years earlier, Keibler had reluctantly started watching WCW with her boyfriend. But with acting as her true passion, Keibler dove in head-first, and in early 2000 she was promoted from a Nitro Girl to full-blown character: "Miss Hancock." Valeting for the team known as "Standards and Practices's," out was the spandex and in were the fantasy-fulfilling business suits and briefcases. Miss Hancock served as Standards and Practices "secretary," basically meaning she would distract opponents with a little dance to help lead her hypocritical censorship-driven team to victory. Miss Hancock eventually left Standards and Practices (and ended up using her distraction abilities against them) and soon embarked on a romantic storyline with David Flair, which ended with a pregnancy scare . . . instead of the rumored shark-jumping reveal that she was pregnant with

Ric Flair's (David's father) or Vince Russo's (the WCW head writer) child. With the storyline simply dropped, Miss Hancock was taken off of WCW TV, returning four months later under her real name, alongside Shawn Stasiak. If this sounds confusing, that's because it was: as this was during the dying days of WCW, there was no telling where any storyline would go on any given week.

A few months later, however, that wouldn't be a problem, because WWF would buy WCW, and Keibler would become a WWF talent (as well as a heel, as a member of The Alliance in the WCW/ECW Invasion storyline). Upon debuting in WWF, Keibler was paired with friend and former WCW colleague Torrie Wilson, as they feuded with top WWF Divas Trish Stratus and Lita. Despite Keibler and Wilson's teamwork early on as part of The Alliance, they ultimately became rivals in their WWF/WWE careers, eventually only separated by the inaugural WWF/WWE brand split in April 2002; Keibler stayed on RAW (with a brief detour in SmackDown), while Wilson went to SmackDown for the majority of her career (then they switched in 2005). Keibler's first non-Invasion feud was as a heel, against Wilson—and with the Dudley Boyz by her side, she was able to have Wilson put through a table. The feud ended up with a one-on-one match on pay-per-view (No Mercy 2001), with what in retrospect seems like a false equivalency after the table bump: the first-ever Lingerie match. However, Wilson got her revenge on Stacy in a way, as the Dudley Boyz eventually turned on Keibler and put her through a table too (for costing them the WWF Tag Team Championship). To this day, Keibler says she still feels neck pain as a result of the table bump.

Eventually, WWE seemed to realize that it could make a sympathetic face in Stacy Keibler by constantly putting her in abusive relationships with male wrestlers. Test, Scott Steiner, and Randy Orton all fit the bill, and by the summer of 2005 it was time for something new. So instead of another doomed romance for Keibler, WWE teamed her up with The Hurricane and his "Super Hero In Training" (yes, "S.H.I.T.") Rosey, giving her a superhero alter ego of her own: "Super Stacy." This only lasted for a few months, however, before Keibler was traded to SmackDown. A few months after that, Keibler took a break from WWE to compete on the second season of *Dancing With The Stars* (in which she placed third). However, the break turned into an official departure, as Keibler never returned to WWE, officially parting ways with the company in 2006. The next time Keibler was seen on WWE TV of any kind, it was as a special guest in the 2011 season of WWE *Tough Enough*.

★ STEPHANIE MCMAHON ★

YEARS ACTIVE: 1999–present

BILLED FROM: Greenwich, Connecticut

ACCOMPLISHMENTS: 1x WWF Women's Champion · 2000 PWI Woman of the Year · 2002 PWI Feud of the Year (vs. Eric Bischoff) · 2013 Slammy Award for Insult of the Year (for insulting Big Show) · 2013 PWI Feud of the Year (vs. Daniel Bryan, as a member of The Authority) · 2013 PWI Most Hated Wrestler of the Year (as a member of The Authority) · 2014 PWI Most Hated Wrestler of the Year (with Triple H) · 2014 Slammy Award for Rivalry of the Year (The Authority vs. Daniel Bryan)

AKA: Stephanie McMahon-Helmsley · "The Billion Dollar Princess" · "The Billion Dollar Baroness" · member of the McMahon-Helmsley Faction · member of The Authority · member of The Alliance · "The Queen of Queens"

NOTABLE MATCHES: Stephanie McMahon (c) vs. Lita at WWF *Monday Night RAW*, for the WWF Women's Championship (August 21, 2000) · Stephanie McMahon vs. Trish Stratus at WWF No Way Out 2001 (February 25, 2001) · Stephanie McMahon vs. Brie Bella at WWE SummerSlam 2014 (August 17, 2014)

★ Behind the scenes, Stephanie McMahon is currently the Chief Brand Officer of WWE, having worked as Executive VP of Creative for years before that and a handful of other jobs, from the bottom up. And as the boss's daughter, Stephanie McMahon could have just stayed behind the scenes, the face of corporate WWE. Especially when you consider how many times she's been embarrassed on both live TV and pay-per-view. In fact, her early years on WWF television were almost exclusively that.

The world's first exposure to Stephanie McMahon was in 1999 as Mr. McMahon's sweet—the antithesis of her father—daughter who got wrangled into her father's issues with The Undertaker. As these things are wont to do, escalation led Stephanie being kidnapped by The Undertaker, tied to his cross-like symbol, and almost being forced to partake in a "Black Wedding" with him. Her father's biggest rival, "Stone Cold" Steve Austin, would rescue her just in the nick of time. Soon it was revealed that Mr. McMahon was actually the puppet master behind Undertaker the whole time, including the orchestration of his daughter's abduction. Despite something like this being the perfect reason in real life to cut someone out of your life, in wrestling—especially during the Attitude Era—the only viable option is to fire back with an even more insane plot. Which is what led to the courtship of Stephanie and the wrestler Test and the eventual wrestling wedding segment—after Stephanie's brother Shane tried to stop Test from dating his sister through the power of a gimmick match called "A Love Her or Leave Her" match—and the arrival of Triple H as a wedding crasher. At the wedding, Triple H played a video of him and a drugged and passed-out Stephanie at a drive-through chapel in Vegas, meaning Stephanie was already married to him.

Triple H would then go on to feud with Mr. McMahon, with Stephanie seemingly rooting for her father . . . until Triple H won. Then the big swerve happened, with the reveal that Stephanie had been in on it with Triple H the whole time, as revenge for the Undertaker/kidnapping/Black Wedding thing her father was responsible for. As a storyline in the Attitude Era, the hindsight concept is always a reminder that Stephanie seemingly fell in love with the man who drugged her, married her as a result, and implied he had date-raped her; *but* the storyline did eventually acknowledge that Stephanie had been in on it the whole time and it wasn't actually as repugnant (on Triple H's end) as it first seemed. All it meant was that Stephanie McMahon was a sociopath, which is really the only baseline you need to know when it comes to the character. This feud then ushered in the "McMahon-Helmsley Era" of WWF to close out 1999; and despite the origins of the entire thing, Mr. McMahon and Shane joined Stephanie and Triple H's the heel empire in the spring of 2000, because the McMahon characters are all varying levels of sociopaths, even matriarch Linda.

Since then, the evolution of the Stephanie McMahon character (and everyone around her) has seen love triangles, divorce (as the real Stephanie and Triple H were getting more serious about their relationship), ECW, WWF becoming WWE, her father's libido getting the better of him, the guest host era of *RAW*—really, just about anything, considering how weird professional wrestling can be. Despite not even being a wrestler by trade, she also saw the WWF Women's Championship during her time in the McMahon-Helmsley Faction, though it took a lot of interference from Triple H's D-Generation X buddies for it to happen.

In 2007, after years of winking and nudging about their marriage still existing off-screen despite divorcing on-screen, WWE continued to acknowledge their on-screen pairing again. In 2008–2009, this was a factor in the McMahons/Triple H vs. Legacy feud, which heated up when Randy Orton—Triple H's former protégé—kissed an unconscious (due to a Sledgehammer shot) Stephanie on the lips, all while a handcuffed Triple H struggled to break free. Of course, a heel McMahon is always better than a face McMahon, and post-Legacy feud, that's exactly what the WWE Universe got.

That's when The Authority angle began—playing up even more Stephanie and Triple H's roles as a legitimate WWE power couple—and Stephanie got to do some of her best work. It was always one thing for her to play the spoiled princess and get heat by being bratty, but it was another to represent what wrestling fans already felt about the McMahons and their particular corporate choices (whether it be which wrestlers got pushed as stars or WWE going from TV-14 to TV-PG). And while The Authority always spoke about what was "best for business," they met their match in the form of Daniel Bryan, the ultimate underdog, beloved by the WWE Universe . . . and supposedly a "B+ player," according to Stephanie and Triple H. And it all led to the feel-good moment of WrestleMania XXX, with Bryan main-eventing the entire show and proving to The Authority that he was anything but a B+.

This storyline in particular proved the importance of a good heel, as it began the realization that Stephanie McMahon is the closest thing to a clone of Vincent Kennedy McMahon in WWE. On-screen, Stephanie has transitioned mostly into the role of authority figure; but come WrestleMania, she tends to get her hands dirty . . . and gets a little comeuppance from the wrestlers, whether she's actually in a match or just on the sidelines for Triple H (as she was at WrestleMania XXX, reacting in a way that proves wrestling really is live theater). And unlike so many other women mentioned in this book, as the boss's daughter she really didn't have to do any of this.

★ SUMMER RAE ★

YEARS ACTIVE: 2011–present

TRAINED BY: FCW · Bill DeMott · Steve Keirn · WWE Performance Center

BILLED FROM: Raleigh, North Carolina

ACCOMPLISHMENTS: #14 in 2014 PWI Female 50

AKA: 1/3 of The BFFs (Beautiful Fierce Females) · "The First Lady of NXT" · Hot Summer · 1/2 of The SLayers · 1/2 of Team Red & Gold · member of Team B.A.D. & Blonde · Danielle Moinet

NOTABLE MATCHES: Summer Rae vs. Emma at NXT, in a Dance-Off (August 7, 2013) · Summer Rae vs. Paige at NXT (May 1, 2013) · Summer Rae & Fandango vs. Emma & Santino Marella at NXT, in a Mixed Tag Team match (October 2, 2013) · Summer Rae vs. Kaitlyn at WWE Superstars (December 20, 2013) · Summer Rae vs. Paige at NXT (October 30, 2013) · Summer Rae (with Charlotte & Sasha Banks) vs. Emma (with Bayley) at NXT (February 18, 2014) · Summer Rae vs. Charlotte (c) at NXT, for the NXT Women's Championship (July 24, 2014) · Summer Rae vs. Paige at *WWE Main Event* (February 16, 2016)

In all the talk of who started WWE's Divas Revolution, Summer Rae's name often gets lost in all the chatter. However, anyone who followed her work during her time in developmental —especially during NXT—probably couldn't have foreseen that at all, considering her integral role in the character development of each member of WWE's Four Horsewomen. In fact, if anything, that could arguably make Summer Rae the honorary fifth Horsewoman. (Or at least a Mini-Horse.)

Prior to WWE, Danielle Moinet was a quarterback in the Lingerie Football League (LFL)—as well as a big WWE fan, whose dream was to become a WWE Diva. In November 2011, months after her final LFL game, it was announced that she would be reporting to FCW, having signed a developmental deal with WWE. Originally, she was going to have the ring name "Kylie Summer," until WWE legend Dusty Rhodes stepped in and personally vetoed the name. Instead, "Summer Rae" was born. And Summer Rae quickly became an integral part of FCW, first as a ring announcer, then as a manager, and finally as the FCW General Manager. As FCW's authority figure, she took a different approach to her heel work, instead acting like a vain young woman put in an authority position with power she didn't deserve, bossing around a subservient assistant (Rob Naylor, the actual FCW/NXT Creative Assistant), and refusing to learn the names of talent who worked for her (she had Rob for that). It was also in FCW where Summer Rae began the recurring bit where she believed WWE SummerSlam was named after her.

As more of an on-screen personality, Summer Rae really only had a couple of matches in FCW during her time there. That changed with the transition from FCW to NXT. While she started off as a ring announcer again, she was regularly wrestling NXT house shows by the fall of 2012 and was a full-fledged competitor on NXT TV as soon as 2013 began. Summer Rae's first two feuds in NXT were against Paige and Emma, the two women who went on to wrestle in the finals of the inaugural NXT Women's Championship Tournament. Both of these women got under Summer Rae's skin, with Emma especially

getting to her due to her spacey, bubbly nature (in addition to her terrible dancing). The Emma feud led to a Dance-Off segment—and at this time, Summer Rae had simultaneously been called up to the main roster, as the dance partner/valet to dancing WWE Superstar Fandango—which could have been a black mark on the feud. There was a time in the WWE during the 2010s where Dance Contests were bafflingly pervasive, which made the segment between Summer Rae and Emma particularly interesting. Flipping the script, it wasn't just bad dancing for cheap heat; the dancing was informed by both characters' gimmicks and actually drove the story along, leading audiences to crown the competition "the only good dance contest in WWE history." (There would be a couple of main-roster reduxes of this segment in 2014, but the original couldn't really be duplicated.) The feud would also involve some old-school heel heat, as Summer would end up blinding Emma with bubble solution (Emma was really into bubbles).

But acknowledging the aforementioned connection that Summer Rae had to WWE's Four Horsewomen, there is a direct link that can be made between Summer and each member of that crew, beginning with Sasha Banks. After getting into Sasha Banks's head for weeks in backstage segments—trying to show Banks that she needed a change if she was going to be relevant—Banks joined forces with Summer and turned heel, officially becoming the character she's known for, "The Boss." Together, the two formed The BFFs (Beautiful Fierce Females) and continued Summer's feud against Emma and Paige. They then feuded with Bayley, after convincing Charlotte to join their team and turn on her friend at the end of 2013.

Then things got iffy, as Summer Rae spent more time on the main roster as Fandango's dance partner/valet. Because of this, she was absent from NXT for four months—while Banks and Charlotte quickly became top stars, while paying lip service to their missing leader by carrying a popsicle stick with a picture of Summer's head on it—finally returning after her on-screen relationship had ended. By that point, Charlotte had also become NXT Women's Champion, but the death knell of Summer Rae leading the BFFs was neither Charlotte nor Sasha Banks wanting to help her during her match against a debuting Becky Lynch. (Upon the split of The BFFs, Sasha Banks would then indoctrinate Becky Lynch in the same way Summer Rae had done to her.) There's an argument to be made that getting promoted to the main roster first was the worst thing that could have happened to Summer Rae, as her absence from NXT at a critical time allowed the people she had originally mentored on-screen to become superstars and change women's wrestling in the WWE greatly for the better. Especially since in future storylines between Sasha Banks and Charlotte (as well as Becky Lynch), WWE's revisionist history would always gloss over or flat-out ignore Summer Rae's involvement (at the very least) in The BFFs.

GETTING PROMOTED TO THE MAIN ROSTER FIRST WAS THE WORST THING THAT COULD HAVE HAPPENED TO SUMMER RAE, AS HER ABSENCE FROM NXT AT A CRITICAL TIME ALLOWED THE PEOPLE SHE HAD ORIGINALLY MENTORED ON-SCREEN TO BECOME SUPERSTARS.

In 2015, *Rolling Stone* awarded Summer Rae (along with Rusev, Dolph Ziggler, and Lana) the title of "Worst Storyline" of the year. The storyline began as an already frustrating love triangle between Rusev, Lana, and Ziggler—as it hinged on Lana's face turn throwing away everything audiences had liked about her—but then it reached all-time ridiculous levels when Summer joined. Summer joined forces with Rusev, trying to help him get over Lana—and bringing the amazing nicknames "RuRu," "Hot Summer," and "Dog Ziggler" into the wrestling fan lexicon—but instead wound up becoming subservient to Rusev and turning into an original Lana clone to please him. The storyline lasted until the fall, mercifully being put to an end after the real-life Rusev/Lana engagement was leaked to TMZ and WWE decided to acknowledge it on TV the following *RAW*. During this storyline, Summer was praised for at least being able to "sell" the weak story, as was Rusev for his comedic timing. But at the same time, it was kind of definitive of Summer Rae's time on the main roster.

Post-Rusev, Summer Rae temporarily went on to valet for a main roster-debuting Tyler Breeze, only for that storyline to fizzle out when the two decided to amicably split at the end of 2015. She then returned to in-ring competition as 2016 rolled around (as she had not wrestled—not even on house shows—since mid-July 2015), attempting to insert herself into Naomi and Tamina's Team B.A.D. in a humorous storyline that didn't really get traction other than a Team B.A.D. & Blonde multi-women's Tag Team match at WrestleMania 32. After April 2016, Summer was no longer featured in any storylines and disappeared completely from WWE live events and shows that September. As it was later revealed, Summer Rae was dealing with injuries to the neck, back, and elbow and had been taking time off even before. Summer Rae was inactive in WWE for over a year before she was released from her contract, despite reportedly being cleared to wrestle in May 2017.

Post-release, the assumption was that Summer Rae—or, more honestly, Danielle Moinet—would move on from professional wrestling and focus on modeling or possibly even acting (having co-starred in *Total Divas* and *The Marine 4: Moving Target* during her time in WWE). In a pleasant turn of events, in May 2018—a year after she'd been cleared to wrestle in the first place—it was announced that Moinet would be making her independent wrestling debut in Australia, at Battle Championship Wrestling. While she ended up losing the match, fans can only hope this isn't the last wrestling sees of this beautiful fierce female.

★ TAMINA SNUKA ★

YEARS ACTIVE: 2009–present

TRAINED BY: Afa Anoa'i · Sika Anoa'i · Wild Samoan Training Center · FCW

BILLED FROM: The Pacific Islands

ACCOMPLISHMENTS: #19 in 2012 PWI Female 50

AKA: Tamina · 1/3 of Team B.A.D. (Beautiful and Dangerous) · 1/2 of Naomina · Sarona Snuka · member of The Welcoming Committee

NOTABLE MATCHES: Tamina & The Usos (Jimmy Uso & Jey Uso) vs. The Hart Dynasty (Natalya, David Hart Smith, & Tyson Kidd) at WWE Fatal 4-Way 2010 (June 20, 2010) · Tamina vs. Carmella (with James Ellsworth) vs. Becky Lynch vs. Charlotte Flair vs. Natalya at WWE Money in the Bank 2017, in a Money in the Bank Ladder match, for the inaugural Women's Money in the Bank contract (June 18, 2017) · Tamina vs. Carmella vs. Becky Lynch vs. Charlotte Flair vs. Natalya at *WWE SmackDown LIVE*, in a Money in the Bank Ladder match, for the Women's Money in the Bank contract (June 27, 2017) · WWE Royal Rumble 2018, in the Women's Royal Rumble match (January 28, 2018)

★ The daughter of "Superfly" Jimmy Snuka, Tamina Snuka (born Sarona Snuka) naturally had some big, high-flying shoes to fill. Prior to wrestling, she was a divorced mother of two, trying to get a college degree and make ends meet as a janitor. In 2009, she became the first person (and first woman) to win the Lia Maivia Scholarship to train at the Wild Samoan Training Center, under Afa and Sika Anoa'i (The Wild Samoans). After wrestling under her real name at World Xtreme Wrestling (Afa's promotions) for a few matches, she was signed to WWE under a developmental deal at FCW. There she became "Tamina."

While her FCW debut saw her immediately feuding with AJ Lee (Tamina's future tag team partner) and Naomi Night (Tamina's future tag team partner and future family member), Tamina was simultaneously called up to the main roster pretty quickly as well, as part of a heel team with The Usos (her cousins). The Usos and Tamina feuded with The Hart Dynasty as their introduction to the main roster, a feud which they eventually lost after a couple of months. After that, Tamina turned face and began an on-screen romance with Santino Marella through the rest of 2010, to her cousins' dismay. However, after being drafted to SmackDown in 2011, she was back to the heel side of things, until she picked a feud back up with Natalya—feuding with her again post-Usos/Hart Dynasty—in which they would try to determine which wrestling family was better. Around this time, WWE made sure to bill her as "Tamina Snuka," really hammering in the fact that she was the daughter of a legend (which she also did too, every time she hit the Superfly Splash). Tamina would also go for Divas Championship gold around this time, falling short; and she has yet to win a championship in WWE despite a nine-year career.

In August 2012, Tamina took time off from WWE after suffering a back injury, and returned three months later as a heel (again looking for gold, and again coming up short). After spending some time off TV (but still working the live events), Tamina joined Divas Champion AJ Lee as her bodyguard until Lee took time off in the spring of 2014. A couple of months later, Tamina suffered a torn ACL and meniscus, ending up off TV for 11 months. Upon her return, she aligned herself with her cousin-in-law, the now-heel Naomi against The Bella Twins as well as Sasha Banks once the Divas Revolution began that summer. Together, they formed Team B.A.D. (Beautiful and Dangerous), and the trio lasted until Banks' face turn in the beginning of 2016. Tamina would remain by Naomi's side, though, until May 2016, when she had to take time off again for surgery to repair torn ligaments.

While she'd then be cleared in February 2017, she wouldn't make her return to WWE (and debut on SmackDown LIVE) until that April. This time, as a heel, she'd be on opposite sides with Naomi. A few months later, Tamina would be a participant in the inaugural Women's Money in the Bank Ladder match (as well as in the do-over two weeks later) but would come up short in securing the contract. She would also join a heel faction with Natalya, Carmella, Lana, and James Ellsworth, known as The Welcoming Committee of SmackDown LIVE. January 2018 saw Tamina compete in another first for the Women's Division, in the inaugural Women's Royal Rumble match.

But the following month—like clockwork—Tamina had to take time off again to have surgery on a torn rotator cuff. In May, Tamina posted on social media that she would be "getting into prime form" for her next return from injury.

★ TARYN TERRELL ★

YEARS ACTIVE: 2008–present

TRAINED BY: FCW · Dusty Rhodes · Steve Keirn · Dr. Tom Prichard · OVW

BILLED FROM: New Orleans, Louisiana · Orlando, Florida

ACCOMPLISHMENTS: 1x OVW Women's Champion · #10 in 2015 PWI Female 50 · 1x TNA Knockouts Champion

AKA: Tiffany · 1/2 of The Blondetourage · "Skirt Tiffany" · "Hot Mess" · member of The Dollhouse

NOTABLE MATCHES: Taryn Terrell vs. Gail Kim at TNA Slammiversary XI, in a Last Knockout Standing match (June 2, 2013) · Taryn Terrell vs. Gail Kim at TNA Impact Wrestling, in a Ladder match for the #1 Contendership to the TNA Knockouts Championship (July 11, 2013) · Taryn Terrell vs. Havok (c) vs. Gail Kim at TNA Impact Wrestling, in a 3-Way match for the TNA Knockouts Championship (November 19, 2014) · Taryn Terrell (c) vs. Awesome Kong vs. Gail Kim at TNA Impact Wrestling, in a 3-Way Dance match for the TNA Knockouts Championship (March 20, 2015)

★ It's probably safe to assume that no one thought WWE ECW's Tiffany would be as important to a specific time in women's professional wrestling as she ended up being. In fact, despite the fact that she was on WWE television, it would most likely be difficult to find anyone who truly remembers the Tiffany character at all.

Taryn Terrell had tried out for the 2007 edition of the WWE Diva Search—which she'd gotten inspired to do after going to her first live show—making it to the final eight and finishing fourth. So, despite losing, like most Diva Search contestants, she was offered—and signed—a WWE developmental contract (to FCW). She debuted in February 2008 under her real name for the first few months, before she officially became "Tiffany." That June—while still training in FCW—she also made her main-roster debut on ECW, as Teddy Long's Assistant General Manager. Why an authority figure would participate in costume competitions and multi-Diva matches was never truly answered, but by April 2009 she was promoted on-screen to ECW General Manager, so it seemed the game plan worked out.

However, once ECW ended in February 2010, Tiffany was out of her position of power and onto SmackDown as a member of its roster. Here, she found herself the victim of LayCool's bullying (as they called her "Skirt Tiffany," because she wore a skirt to the ring), leading to a team-up with Kelly Kelly (called "The Blondetourage") where they sadly came out on bottom. A month after losing the feud against LayCool, Taryn Terrell was legitimately suspended indefinitely from WWE, following an arrest and criminal charge of domestic assault. While she was cleared of all charges the following month, Taryn never made it back to WWE TV, and she was released from the company that November.

Post-WWE, Taryn Terrell arguably could have given up on professional wrestling. Outside of wrestling, she has quite the prolific career in stunt work. However, after a few independent dates, Taryn signed with TNA in the summer of 2012. Introduced as the official referee of the Knockouts Division, there wasn't much fanfare about her addition to the Impact Knockouts roster. But that changed pretty quickly, as she began to feud with Gail Kim, who grew frustrated with Taryn's calls in the ring and physically confronted her for it. And Taryn would come back at Gail, interfering in her matches and attacking her backstage. That March, Taryn Terrell transitioned into a full-fledged Knockout, leading to a Last Knockout Standing match at Slammiversary XI, one of the most memorable matches in the history of the Knockouts division and one that defied expectations. (No one was expecting Taryn Terrell to give Gail Kim a cutter off the entrance ramp, that's for sure.) They would then follow the match up with another memorable one-on-one

encounter, in the form of a Ladder match, but Taryn would take time off after it due to her pregnancy.

When she returned, she and Gail Kim aligned, based on mutual respect—even keeping it civil as Taryn unsuccessfully challenged Gail for the Knockouts Championship—which was necessary if they were going to survive the debuting monster Havok. And they did, as Taryn was able to win the Knockouts Championship for the first time in a 3-Way match against Gail and Havok. Taryn then went on to feud with another one of Gail Kim's rivals, Awesome Kong, surviving once more to retain the championship and eventually setting the record for longest reign (279 days). It was during the feud with Kong, however, where Taryn Terrell turned heel for the first time in her career—again, defying expectations and knocking it out of the park—as the leader of a new heel faction in Impact, The Dollhouse. Gail Kim eventually cost Taryn the championship, and while The Dollhouse continued (with Taryn off TV, occasionally appearing via pre-taped segments on the Titantron), Taryn Terrell left the company at the beginning of 2016 and retired from wrestling for personal reasons. She made an appearance later that year for Gail Kim's induction into the TNA Hall of Fame, though.

And then she made a more official return in August 2017—as a heel again—attacking Gail Kim and vowing to help send her off to retirement quickly. The storyline was supposed to culminate in a Four-Way match at Bound For Glory; but two weeks before the match, she pulled out and left the company again. In storyline, it was concussion issues, but a follow-up report claimed the real reason was an inability to travel into Canada (where Bound For Glory took place) because of the previous domestic assault, even though the charges had been dropped. It remains to be seen if this is officially the end of the road for Taryn Terrell in the squared circle, but she certainly made some lasting memories.

★ TESSA BLANCHARD ★

YEARS ACTIVE: 2014–present

TRAINED BY: George South · Highspots Wrestling School · Tully Blanchard · Magnum T.A.

BILLED FROM: Charlotte, North Carolina

ACCOMPLISHMENTS: 1x American Pro Wrestling Alliance (APWA) World Ladies Champion · 1x Canadian Wrestling Federation Women's Champion · 1x ECWA Women's Champion · 2014 ECWA Super 8 ChickFight Tournament · 1x Exodus Wrestling Alliance (EWA) Florida Heavyweight Champion · 1x EWA Heavyweight Champion · 1x Impact Wrestling Knockouts Champion · 2015 Lucky Pro Wrestling Kings and Queens Tournament (with Anthony Greene) · 1x Pro Wrestling eXpress Women's Champion · #38 in 2016 PWI Female 50 · #43 in 2017 PWI Female 50 · 1x Remix Pro Wrestling Fury Champion · 1x SHIMMER Tag Team Champion (with Vanessa Kraven) · 1x WOW: Women of Wrestling Champion · 1x WrestleCircus Sideshow Champion · 1x WrestleCircus Lady of the Ring Champion · 1x (and inaugural) PCW ULTRA Women's Champion · 1x Zelo Pro Women's Champion

AKA: "The Queen of the Carolinas" · "Tessie Two Belts" · member of Valkyrie · 1/2 of Mount Tessa · Tessa B · "The Undeniable" Tessa Blanchard

NOTABLE MATCHES: Tessa Blanchard vs. Deonna Purrazzo at ECWA 2nd Annual Super 8 ChickFight Tournament, in a Super 8 ChickFight Tournament Finals match for the vacant ECWA Women's Championship (October 17, 2015) · Tessa Blanchard vs. Ricochet at Beyond Wrestling Midas Touch (October 2, 2016) · Mount Tessa (Tessa Blanchard & Vanessa Kraven) vs. Team Slap Happy (Evie & Heidi Lovelace) (c) at SHIMMER Volume 89, for the SHIMMER Tag Team Championship (November 13, 2016) · Tessa Blanchard (c) (WrestleCircus Sideshow) vs. Rachael Ellering (c) (WrestleCircus Lady of the Ring) at WrestleCircus The Squared Ring Circus, for the WrestleCircus Sideshow Championship/WrestleCircus Lady of the Ring Championship (July 22, 2017) · Tessa Blanchard vs. Kairi Sane at the WWE Mae Young Classic, in a Mae Young Classic First Round match (August 28, 2017) · Tessa Blanchard, Jazzy Gabert, & Kay Lee Ray vs. Marti Belle, Santana Garrett, & Sarah Logan at the WWE Mae Young Classic – Road To The Finals (September 11, 2017) · Mount Tessa (Tessa Blanchard & Vanessa Kraven) (c) vs. Tubular Tag Team (Leva Bates & Delilah Doom) at SHIMMER Volume 97, for the SHIMMER Tag Team Championship (November 11, 2017) · Tessa Blanchard vs. Vanessa Kraven at SHIMMER Volume 99, in a Lumberjack match (November 12, 2017) · Tessa Blanchard (c) (WrestleCircus Sideshow) vs. Brian Cage (c) (WrestleCircus Ringmaster) at WrestleCircus The Show Must Go On, for the WrestleCircus Sideshow Championship/WrestleCircus Ringmaster Championship (February 17, 2018)

★ It's hard to believe Tessa Blanchard only has four years of professional wrestling experience under her belt; but on the other hand, she was born into this world. The daughter of Four

Horseman Tully Blanchard (and granddaughter of Joe Blanchard), as well as the stepdaughter of Magnum T.A., if Tessa Blanchard never got into professional wrestling at some point in her life, it seems like something would have went very, very wrong. As a kid, seeing her father get hurt in a match was the type of thing that scared her; but after seeing him inducted into the WWE Hall of Fame with the rest of the Four Horsemen in 2012, that's when Tessa finally "got" professional wrestling and why anyone in her family would want to do it. That included herself.

So after her freshman year of college, Tessa began training under George South at Highspots Wrestling School (aka RINGS Pro Wrestling Training School) in North Carolina. She didn't tell her family she was training at the time, as she wanted to get by on her own (as much as she possibly could with the last name "Blanchard"). So, naturally, Tessa's character—which is typically heel—is obsessed with letting everyone know her last name is Blanchard and that she has a certain pedigree that just makes her better than her opponents. She is a diamond, and diamonds are forever, after all. Even when she's a face, she exudes this as well. But the point is that she can also back up her words in the ring.

Tessa officially got her in-ring start in June 2014, debuting (and losing) at a QOC event. While she wrestled her first few shows locally in North Carolina—with a quick detour in Georgia in her second month—by the fall of 2014 Tessa had broken into the Midwest scene at AIW (wrestling on Girls Night Out 13 and 14) as well as the East Coast for ECWA (in their Super 8 ChickFight Tournament) and WSU. The latter was a taste of just how quickly success would come to Tessa, as she ended up winning the tournament, as well as her first wrestling championship (the ECWA Women's Championship). By the end of 2014, Tessa had also faced a former WWE Women's Champion, Mickie James, in front of her local crowd at QOC. She'd also had a tryout in WWE, at just 19 years old, and though it was unsuccessful, WWE began using her as an extra and as enhancement talent—as well as eventually featuring her as one

of the 32 female competitors in the inaugural Mae Young Classic tournament in the summer of 2017.

The year 2015 saw Tessa make her debuts in SHIMMER, SHINE, and AAW, with her forming a new team in SHIMMER: Mount Tessa. The pairing of Tessa Blanchard and 6-feet-tall Vanessa "The Mountain" Kraven provides Tessa (who would continue to make her presence known in every new promotion with a mouth much bigger than her small stature would suggest) with some much-needed backup in the ring, to finally have someone to write the checks that Tessa's mouth would attempt to cash. And it would finally pay off, as two years after the formation of Mount Tessa—and Vanessa Kraven putting up with a lot of Tessa's cowardly behavior—the duo would win the SHIMMER Tag Team Championship.

But of course, Tessa wasn't just having success in the tag-team realm, as her status as a singles star got her a dark-match tryout in Lucha Underground, as well as a summer touring Japan in STARDOM (returning the following spring).

Tessa's character has also made her the perfect foil for Rachael Ellering—daughter of WWE Hall of Famer "Precious" Paul Ellering—on the independent scene, as the two have wrestled for multi-generational wrestling superiority in SHINE, WrestleCircus, and PCW ULTRA, among other promotions. The WrestleCircus arm of the feud featured Ellering defeating Tessa in her first defense of the WrestleCircus Lady of the Ring Championship, only for Tessa to come back at her harder in a Championship vs. Championship (Ellering's Lady of the Ring Championship vs. Blanchard's newly-acquired Sideshow Championship) a month before her rematch with Ellering—and winning in the first female main event of WrestleCircus. Months later, Tessa would main-event a WrestleCircus show again, this time in an attempt to win the highest WrestleCircus championship (the Ringmaster Championship) in an Intergender, Championship vs. Championship (her Sideshow Championship on the line) match against "The Machine" Brian Cage. While Tessa put up a valiant effort and often looked like she could possibly (and believably, despite the size difference) win, she ended up losing to Cage and losing one of her championships.

In 2018, Tessa made a few notable promotional debuts, first in CZW, competing in the annual Best of the Best tournament—as the first female to ever compete in the tournament—and making it to the Semi Finals. Then in PCW ULTRA, where she debuted to become the inaugural PCW ULTRA Women's Champion. And last but not least—as it marked her official debut as a contracted wrestler on a nationally broadcast wrestling show—in Impact Wrestling. Here, she quickly staked her claim over the Knockouts Division due to her third generational pedigree. When she debuted, she made sure to put the entire Knockouts Division on notice, letting them know just who and what she is: "Dirty as it gets; clean as they come."

★ TONI STORM ★

YEARS ACTIVE: 2009–present

TRAINED BY: Dean Allmark · Mason Childs · Impact Pro Wrestling (IPW) Australia Training School

BILLED FROM: Gold Coast, Australia

ACCOMPLISHMENTS: 1x All Action Wrestling Women's Championship · 1x BEW Woman's Champion · 1x IPW Australian Women's Champion · 1x IPW Australian Cruiserweight Champion · 1x IPW Australian Hardcore Champion · 2x PWAQ Women's Champion · #24 in 2017 PWI Female 50 · PROGRESS Wrestling Natural Progression Series IV · 1x (and inaugural) PROGRESS Women's Champion · 2017 wXw Femmes Fatales · 1x SWA World Champion · 1x World of STARDOM Champion · 2017 STARDOM 5☆STAR GP · 2017 STARDOM Cinderella Tournament · 2013 STARDOM MVP Award · 1x wXw Women's Champion · WWE Mae Young Classic II

AKA: Storm

NOTABLE MATCHES: Toni Storm vs. Kay Lee Ray at STARDOM 5☆STAR Grand Prix 2016 – Night 4, in a Block A match (September 3, 2016) · Toni Storm vs. Nixon Newell (c) (BEW) vs. Rosemary (c) (TNA) at BEW Britain's Rising IV, in a 3-Way No Rules Purge match for the BEW Woman's Championship/TNA Knockouts Championship (December 4, 2016) · Toni Storm vs. Jinny vs. Laura Di Matteo at PROGRESS Chapter 49: Super Strong Style 16 Tournament 2017 – Night 2, in a Natural Progression Series IV Finals 3-Way match for the inaugural PROGRESS Women's Championship (May 28, 2017) · Toni Storm (c) vs. Kay Lee Ray at PROGRESS Chapter 50: I Give It Six Months, for the PROGRESS Women's Championship (June 25, 2017) · Toni Storm vs. Piper Niven at the WWE Mae Young Classic, in a Mae Young Classic Quarterfinals match (September 6, 2017) · Toni Storm vs. Kairi Sane at the WWE Mae Young Classic, in a Mae Young Classic Semifinals match (September 6, 2017) · Toni Storm (c) vs. Dahlia Black at PROGRESS Chapter

55: Chase The Sun, for the PROGRESS Women's Championship (September 10, 2017) · Toni Storm vs. Wesna at wXw Femme Fatales 2017, in a Femme Fatales 2017 Semifinals match (October 7, 2017) · Toni Storm (c) vs. Mercedes Martinez at RISE 6: Brutality, for the World of STARDOM Championship (December 1, 2017) · Toni Storm vs. Meiko Satamura at the WWE Mae Young Classic II, in a Mae Young Classic Semifinals match (October 24, 2018) · Toni Storm vs. Io Shirai at WWE Evolution, in a Mae Young Classic Finals match (October 28, 2018)

⭐ The thing you have to understand about Toni Storm is that, by the age of 22, she already had eight years of wrestling experience under her belt and had accomplished more in her professional wrestling career than wrestlers—women or men—years older. She also did so outside of WWE but with WWE's eyes planted firmly on her. Few wrestlers can say these things about themselves, but Toni Storm is a unique situation with the potential to have a Hall of Fame career before she even turns 25.

At 13 years old, an Australian girl called Toni Rossall began her wrestling career, training at IPW Australia. She had decided she wanted to become a professional wrestler three whole years earlier, so it made sense for her to get to work; and get to work she did, as she made her in-ring debut 10 days before her 14th birthday as "Storm." (That 10-year-old had some good ideas after all, as it was her 10-year-old desire to be a "wrestling rock star" that eventually helped Toni land on her gimmick.) However, once she got older and had more experience under her belt, Toni knew that if she wanted to be the best in professional wrestling, she had to get serious—even more serious than just the general concept of being a 13-year-old professional wrestler—and at the end of 2014/early 2015, she persuaded her mother to allow her to move to Liverpool (to live with her grandmother), where she could continue her professional wrestling training in the more bustling UK scene. While she eventually got the chance to wrestle talents

like Madison Eagles, Shazza McKenzie, and Kellie Skater—some of the biggest names in Australian independent women's wrestling who also branched out—there was only so much she could accomplish and only so many promotions in Australia. Then she soon found Dean Allmark, who she calls "a magician." As Toni explains, "Without that experience I got from England, I wouldn't be where I am today."

Just being in England as a wrestler, it was like the floodgates opened up for Toni. While she had had a couple of UK matches in mid-2014 (around the time she began wrestling as "Toni Storm"), actually living and training in the United

Kingdom allowed her to wrestle British independent wrestling legend "Sweet Saraya" Knight fairly early on; get featured at indy promotions like BEW, Preston City Wrestling (PCW), and SWE; and branch out even further in Europe to wrestle in Spain and Germany (wXw, becoming an integral part of their burgeoning women's division). In 2015, Toni Storm was finally wrestling the people she's currently always thought of in connection with, people like Kay Lee Ray, Viper, Nixon Newell, WWE's Tegan Nox, and Lana Austin.

BY THE AGE OF 22, SHE ALREADY HAD EIGHT YEARS OF WRESTLING EXPERIENCE UNDER HER BELT

If 2015 was the year that Toni Storm's name first really got heard on the scene, then 2016 is the year she became the Toni Storm everyone actually knows. Upon making her first tour in Japan for STARDOM that summer, Toni defeated Io Shirai for the SWA World Championship (a championship created earlier that year, during a STARDOM European tour where Toni had originally fallen short to Io in the tournament to crown the inaugural champion). Closing out the year and upon returning to the United Kingdom—after a quick detour in Germany for wXw—Toni then won the BEW Women's Championship from Nixon Newell. Then by the end of 2017, Toni Storm was on nearly every wrestling fan's "best of the year" lists, as she not only became the inaugural PROGRESS Women's Champion but also proved she was on WWE's radar (after trying out back in 2014 and 2015), wrestling at both WrestleMania Axxess (making her United States debut that WrestleMania Weekend) and as a competitor in the inaugural Mae Young Classic tournament (making it to the Semi Finals before falling to eventual winner, Kairi Sane). And during a summer tour in STARDOM, Toni won the promotion's annual STARDOM 5☆STAR GP. She also won the top prize in the company—the World of STARDOM Championship; however, of all the success she'd proven to have in such a relatively short time, this was the one that didn't sit right. Unfortunately, Storm's success in winning came in the form of Mayu being physically unable to continue to compete, due to a freak accident (dislocating her elbow two minutes into the match) instead of an actual, decisive win.

Toni was very clearly unhappy with how it happened—and she knew she'd have quite the uphill battle to prove just how much she actually deserved the championship. (Six months later, Toni would get some semblance of peace of mind as she defeated a recovered Mayu in the rematch to retain the championship.)

Toni would immediately start 2018 by winning the wXw Women's Championship, something expected—as it was expected she would be the inaugural champion in the first place—and just another championship for a young woman who seemingly had every championship possible. But then she lost the SWA World Championship to Viper in March. Then she lost the PROGRESS Women's Championship to Jinny at the end of May, and the World of STARDOM Championship at the beginning of June. This could have all been a string of bad luck for the rising Aussie star, or it could have signaled something else: that she was going to WWE. In fact, weeks before she lost the PROGRESS Women's Championship, it was announced that Toni would be competing on the upcoming *WWE United Kingdom Championship Tournament* show; but that didn't necessarily mean she had signed with WWE, because Jinny was also announced for the same WWE show, and she'd just won the championship from Toni. A few weeks later, however, it was reported that Toni Storm had signed a WWE UK deal, which isn't a full-time WWE contract, meaning she can still wrestle at PROGRESS (but time will tell where else she'll be allowed to wrestle).

All this before the age of 23.

★ TORRIE WILSON ★

YEARS ACTIVE: 1999-2008

TRAINED BY: WCW Power Plant · Madusa · Dave "Fit" Finlay · John Laurinaitis · Billy Kidman

BILLED FROM: Boise, Idaho

ACCOMPLISHMENTS: WWE Hall of Fame Class of 2018

AKA: Samantha · member of The Alliance · member of The Filthy Animals · member of The New Blood · 1/3 of Ladies in Pink · 1/3 of Vince's Devils

NOTABLE MATCHES: Torrie Wilson & Stacy Keibler (Alliance) vs. Trish Stratus & Lita (WWF) at WWF InVasion 2001, in a Bra and Panties Tag Team match (July 22, 2001) · Torrie Wilson vs. Dawn Marie at WWE Royal Rumble 2003, in a Stepmother vs. Stepdaughter match (January 19, 2003) · WWE Royal Rumble 2018, in the Women's Royal Rumble match (January 28, 2018)

★ Torrie Wilson's professional wrestling origin story is kind of like the stories one hears about actors being discovered while doing something as innocuous as walking their dogs: after attending a WCW house show in 1999, she and her boyfriend (the wrestling fan of the two, as she would often make fun of him for his wrestling fandom) went backstage . . . and then she was asked if she wanted to be Scott Steiner's valet to the ring for the night. That's it. At the time—she had moved to Los Angeles just six months prior—Wilson was an aspiring actress, so technically it was the classic mundane acting origin story. Only, in the case of professional wrestling, it led to a combination career of her two loves: athletics (as she got her start in fitness competitions, having won the 1998 Miss Galaxy competition) and, of course, entertainment. ("Sports Entertainment" just rolls off the tongue better than "Athletics Entertainment," though.) Plus, unlike in her acting auditions, the chances of the wrestling world telling Wilson she was too muscular were probably slim.

The following week, Kevin Nash—who was booking WCW at the time—called her and asked if she'd be interested in doing a storyline with David Flair for a couple of months. As "Samantha," Wilson's role was as a hired nWo spy (meaning, she was immediately working with top talent), seducing David Flair to turn to the dark side against his father, Ric Flair (who was feuding with the nWo). As Wilson's time in WCW was during the dying days of the company, it was probably no surprise that she was hired without any actual wrestling experience; in fact, Wilson confirmed post-WCW that at times she wasn't even privy to what her character was supposed to be or whether she was heel or face. As for the in-ring aspect of things—as she eventually entered into Mixed and Intergender Tag Team matches with Kidman and his brethren—while she had gotten some rudimentary training at the WCW Power Plant, Wilson has mused that she mostly only recalls Madusa dropping her on her head. Eventually, "Samantha" left David Flair, aligning herself with Billy Kidman and his team, The Filthy Animals, as their manager (under her actual name). (Wilson and Kidman would develop a real-life relationship, eventually getting married in 2003 and divorced in 2008.)

TORRIE WILSON'S PROFESSIONAL WRESTLING ORIGIN STORY IS LIKE THE STORIES ONE HEARS ABOUT ACTORS BEING DISCOVERED. SHE WAS ASKED IF SHE WANTED TO BE SCOTT STEINER'S VALET TO THE RING FOR THE NIGHT. THAT LED TO A COMBINATION CAREER OF HER TWO LOVES: ATHLETICS AND ENTERTAINMENT.

As a former WCW talent, Wilson debuted as a heel in WWF as part of The Alliance (in the WCW/ECW) invasion storyline, after WCW had officially ceased to exist. Upon signing with WWF, Wilson was given a more formal wrestling training, with "Fit" Finlay and John Laurinaitis (with some additional help from Kidman, who'd also signed with WWF). However, as part of the Attitude and Ruthless Aggression eras of WWF/WWE, Torrie Wilson was a Diva known more for her edgy, sexy, and shocking storylines than for her actual wrestling ability. (Wilson was part of the first-ever Lingerie match in WWF.) Alongside Stacy Keibler (WCW's "Miss Hancock"), Wilson made her in-ring debut in

WWF in a Bra and Panties match against more established WWF Divas Trish Stratus and Lita—which was one of the rare times that these former WCW women faced off against these WWF women for storyline purposes, despite the popularity all four would achieve in WWF/WWE. Also, despite the initial partnership with Stacy Keibler—thanks to the common thread of the Alliance, as former WCW talents—Wilson/Keibler were ultimately considered rivals in their WWF/WWE careers, eventually only separated by the inaugural WWF/WWE brand split in April 2002, as Wilson went to *SmackDown* for most of her career and Keibler went to *RAW* (then, in 2005, Wilson went to RAW . . . only for Keibler to go to SmackDown). During this brand split, Torrie Wilson was one of the faces of the SmackDown brand, regularly featured in storylines at any given point.

Wilson's most memorable feud and storyline of her career in WWF/WWE was perhaps one that was most indicative of the over-the-top nature of the time, against former ECW valet Dawn Marie. In this storyline, Dawn Marie seduced Torrie Wilson's actual father, Al Wilson, as a way to blackmail Torrie Wilson into spending the night with her in exchange for ending the relationship. While Torrie accepted, Dawn Marie turned out to be lying and aired the hotel footage of their tryst on a WWE pay-per-view. Eventually, Dawn Marie and Al Wilson got married on an episode of *SmackDown*. However, the night of the wedding, Al Wilson died (in kayfabe) of a heart attack, due to all the sex—which led to a "Stepmother vs. Stepdaughter" match at Royal Rumble 2003. This storyline was a nine-month feud.

Torrie Wilson's time in WWE led to her becoming a two-time *Playboy* cover girl, which also became the stuff of storyline fodder. After her first cover in the spring of 2003, Wilson feuded with SmackDown Diva Nidia (and her on-screen boyfriend Jamie Noble), who was jealous for not being picked by Hugh Hefner. This cover also led to the return of former WWF Diva Sable, who was a *Playboy* cover girl herself and arguably the top Diva of the Attitude Era. The Torrie/Sable feud was somewhat of a new guard vs. old guard storyline, which eventually led to a team-up between the two (especially once they became joint cover girls the following year).

Upon moving to *RAW* in the summer of 2005, Torrie Wilson turned heel and joined forces with Candice Michelle and Victoria (the enforcer, as the more established in-ring competitor of the trio) to form the "Ladies in Pink," who eventually became known as "Vince's Devils." The trio began to leave their mark on the RAW brand by targeting 2005 Diva Search winner Ashley Massaro, who eventually got backup in the form of Trish Stratus. After losing that feud, Wilson took a few weeks off from WWE TV, eventually returning with her dog Chloe (who she had been known to travel with during her time in the company) as their team mascot. However, eventually *Playboy* struck again, this time with Candice Michelle getting the cover. As the newfound attention got to Candice's head, Torrie Wilson eventually became face again, leaving the trio behind.

Wilson's final couple of years in WWE saw her in romantic, valet storylines again—having gotten her *SmackDown* start in such a storyline with Tajiri—first with Carlito and then with Jimmy Wang Yang (when she moved back to SmackDown in 2007). At the end of November 2007, Wilson took time off from WWE TV again to nurse a back injury, though this time she didn't return: in May 2008, WWE officially released Wilson, as she had made the decision to retire from the wrestling industry after nine years on the road. The following month, Wilson got back surgery. While Wilson didn't come back to WWE full-time post-surgery, she did make an appearance in WrestleMania XXV's "Miss WrestleMania" Battle Royal in 2009.

Torrie Wilson then made her surprise in-ring return to WWE nine years later—after an appearance at *Monday Night RAW*'s 25th anniversary show—as one of the 30 participants in the company's inaugural women's Royal Rumble match. She also competed in the women's battle royale at WWE's first-ever all-women's pay-per-view, *Evolution*. These days, Wilson has her own online fitness and wellness site—Torrie Wilson Fit—continuing to combine athletics and entertainment, just like the good old days.

★ TRISH STRATUS ★

YEARS ACTIVE: 2000-2006

TRAINED BY: Ron Hutchison · Dave "Fit" Finlay

BILLED FROM: Toronto, Ontario, Canada

ACCOMPLISHMENTS: 2016 Cauliflower Alley Club Iron Mike Mazurki Award · 2006 *Fighting Spirit* Magazine Double X Award · 2006 *Fighting Spirit* Magazine Three Degrees Award · 2017 Ontario Sports Hall of Fame Sandy Hawley Community Service Award · 2002 PWI Woman of the Year · 2003 PWI Woman of the Year · 2005 PWI Woman of the Year · 2006 PWI Woman of the Year · PWI Woman of the Decade (2000s) · 7x WWF/WWE Women's Champion · 1x WWF Hardcore Champion · 2001 WWF Babe of the Year · 2002 WWE Babe of the Year · 2003 WWE Babe of the Year · WWE Diva of the Decade (2000s) · WWE Hall of Fame Class of 2013

AKA: "The Quintessential WWE Diva" · "The Queen of Queens" · "Canada's Greatest Export" · 1/2 of Team Bestie

NOTABLE MATCHES: Trish Stratus vs. Stephanie McMahon at WWF No Way Out 2001 (February 25, 2001) · Trish Stratus (WWF) vs. Ivory (Alliance) vs. Jacqueline (WWF) vs. Jazz (Alliance) vs. Mighty Molly (Alliance) at WWF Survivor Series 2001, in a 6-Pack Challenge for the vacant WWF Women's Championship (November 18, 2001) · Trish Stratus vs. Victoria (c) at WWE *Monday Night RAW*, for the WWE Women's Championship (November 25, 2002) · Trish Stratus vs. Victoria (c) (with Steven Richards) at WWE *Monday Night RAW*, in a Chicago Street Fight for the WWE Women's Championship (January 27, 2003) · Trish Stratus vs. Victoria (c) (with Steven Richards) vs. Jazz at WWE WrestleMania XIX, in a Triple Threat match for the WWE Women's Championship (March 30, 2003) · Trish Stratus & Lita vs. Molly Holly & Gail Kim at WWE Unforgiven 2003 (September 21, 2003) · Trish Stratus & Lita vs. Chris Jericho & Christian at WWE Armageddon 2003, in a Battle of the Sexes match (December 14, 2003) · Trish Stratus & Christian vs. Chris

Jericho at WWE Backlash 2004, in an Intergender Handicap match (April 18, 2004) · Trish Stratus (c) vs. Lita at WWE *Monday Night RAW*, for the WWE Women's Championship (December 6, 2004) · Trish Stratus (c) vs. Mickie James at WrestleMania 22, for the WWE Women's Championship (April 2, 2006) · Trish Stratus vs. Melina (with Johnny Nitro) at WWE *Monday Night RAW* (July 10, 2006) · Trish Stratus & Carlito vs. Lita & Edge at WWE *Monday Night RAW* (August 7, 2006) · Trish Stratus vs. Lita (c) at WWE Unforgiven 2006, for the WWE Women's Championship (September 17, 2006) · Trish Stratus & Lita vs. Mickie James & Alicia Fox (with Alexa Bliss) at WWE *Evolution* (October 28, 2018)

⭐ When it comes to discussing the greatest WWE Divas of all time, one can't possibly have a conversation without mentioning Trish Stratus. Having gotten her start as a fitness model and then as a co-host on Live Audio Wrestling (a Canadian sports talk radio show) in Toronto, WWE officials were drawn to Patricia Stratagias after seeing her on the covers of multiple fitness magazines. And her love of wrestling is most likely what helped her swim instead of sink like so many other models-turned-wrestlers at the time. After signing her to a multi-year contract at the end of 1999, WWF officials sent Patricia—who would of course be known as "Trish Stratus" from that point forward—to Ron Hutchison to learn how to wrestle; and with less than half a year of training under her belt, it was time for her to swim.

The Attitude Era (when Trish Stratus made her debut) was obviously the most popular time in the WWF's/WWE's history, but it was also a time where looks were the most important part for any female talent. And Stratus already had the looks in spades, starting off as a heel valet for the entendre-laden tag team T & A (Test & Albert) and soon transitioning into a more sexually charged storyline with WWF Chairman Vince McMahon. The affair storyline with Vince McMahon infamously led to his degrading Trish and making her bark like a dog in her bra and panties in the center of the ring; but once

Trish stood up for herself and turned face (at WrestleMania X-Seven), it was the beginning of one fundamental truth: the WWF audience would always be invested in Trish Stratus.

At the same time that Trish was developing popularity—as well as genuine in-ring skills—so was her alternative Diva counterpart, Lita. After first working on opposite sides in the Hardy Boyz vs. T & A, the two joined forces for the side of good (and WWF) in the WCW/ECW invasion storyline. Trish and Lita ended up teaming against Torrie Wilson and Stacy Keibler—two former WCW women who weren't known for their wrestling—in a Tag Team Bra and Panties match. Now, while neither Trish nor Lita was opposed to their sexuality being on display during this era of WWF, there was a line. For example, in 2001, Stratus won the WWF Women's Championship for the first time at the Survivor Series pay-per-view, only to lose it three months later on an episode of *Monday Night RAW*. The predominant theory, even from Stratus herself, was that she lost the title so soon—and on free television—because of a refusal to partake in an on-screen kiss with Torrie Wilson (a role that was eventually taken up by Stacy Keibler):

> "So, was I being punished? Who knows? I was never told that's why I lost, but it was a little strange that WrestleMania in my hometown of Toronto was coming up, and all of a sudden I wasn't going in as champion."

But that was just a momentary setback, as Stratus's popularity with the crowds never waned and she went on to make waves as the face of the women's division—whether it was as a fan favorite babyface or an absolutely despicable heel, shattering the glass ceiling in the male-dominated WWE. Stratus was never content to simply let her looks do the talking—despite it being a time when plenty of Divas were portrayed as chasing *Playboy* covers—and she quickly improved in the ring to go with her good (and eventually superb) mic skills. And while it was always nice to see Trish and Lita as allies, as the years went on it was even better to see them on opposite sides. Trish, especially, worked as the anything-goes heel to Lita's pissed-off face, and both women arguably did the best work of their lives when feuding and wrestling against each other.

Outside of her work with Lita, Trish had memorable feuds with Molly Holly, Jazz, Chris Jericho, and of course her two stalkers: Victoria and Mickie James. (It spoke to the talent of both women that their takes on the crazy stalker trope never overlapped.)

THE ATTITUDE ERA (WHEN TRISH STRATUS MADE HER DEBUT) WAS THE MOST POPULAR TIME IN THE WWF'S/ WWE'S HISTORY, BUT ALSO A TIME WHERE LOOKS WERE THE MOST IMPORTANT PART FOR ANY FEMALE TALENT.

Today, the concept of becoming "the next Trish Stratus" is just as coveted in women's wrestling as becoming "the next The Rock" or "the next Hulk Hogan" is for male wrestlers, though the success rate is more proof that Trish Stratus is a once-in-a-lifetime talent. Stratus held the WWE Women's Championship a record seven times. Stratus also won the WWE Women's Championship from Lita in her hometown, Toronto, in her final match as a professional wrestler (in a storyline with the rare combination of Lita being the heel and Trish being the face). It was just as much of a storybook ending as anyone could ask for in professional wrestling, especially on as big a stage as WWE.

Even after retiring in 2006, Trish made surprise returns and appearances at major events in WWE. In 2013, Trish Stratus joined WWE's Hall of Fame in a class alongside wrestling legends Bob Backlund, Booker T, and Mick Foley. She was inducted by Stephanie McMahon. The following year, she inducted Lita. Then in 2018, Trish wrestled as a surprise entrant in the inaugural Women's Royal Rumble match, at the coveted #30 spot.

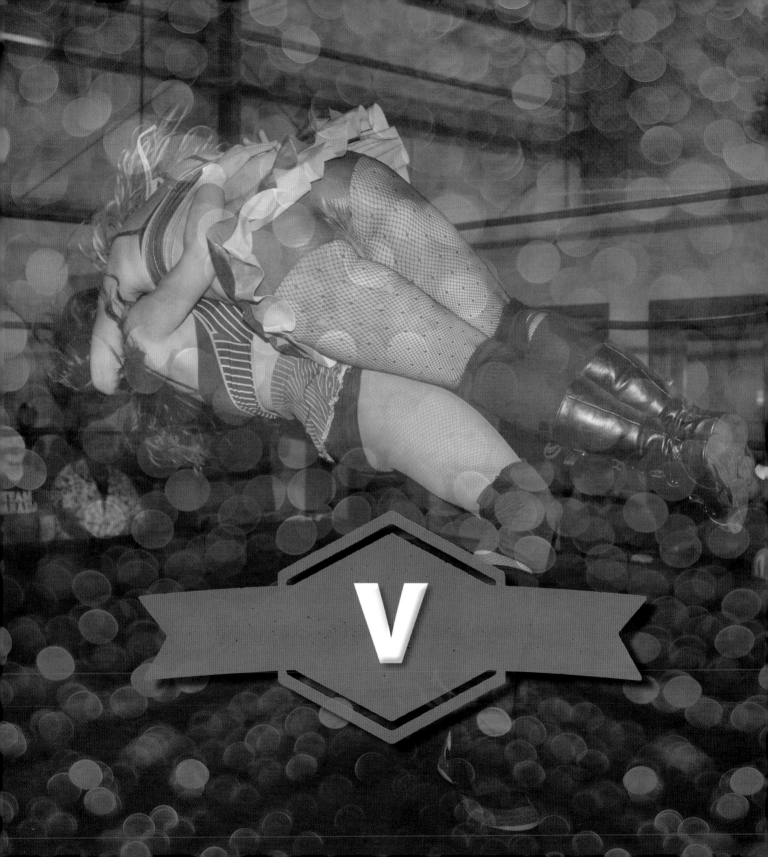

★ VEDA SCOTT ★

YEARS ACTIVE: 2011-present

TRAINED BY: Daizee Haze · Delirious · ROH Wrestling Academy

BILLED FROM: Providence, Rhode Island

ACCOMPLISHMENTS: 1x AIW Women's Champion · 1x AIW Tag Team Champion (with Gregory Iron) · 1x DDT Pro-Wrestling Ironman Heavymetalweight Champion · 1x FWE Women's Champion · 1x Inspire Pro Wrestling XX-Division Champion · 1x Legacy Wrestling Women's Champion · 2012 PWI Rookie of the Year · #43 in 2013 PWI Female 50

AKA: Member of The Embassy · 1/2 of Pop Culture · 1/2 of Hope and Change

NOTABLE MATCHES: Veda Scott vs. "Crazy" Mary Dobson at ROH Road to Best in the World, in a Women of Honor match (June 5, 2016) · Hope and Change (Veda Scott & Gregory Iron) (with Southside St. Clair) vs. The Batiri (Kodama & Obariyon) (with Veronica) (c) at AIW Hell on Earth 8, for the AIW Tag Team Championship (November 23, 2012) · Veda Scott vs. Jimmy Lloyd vs. Arik Cannon vs. Bryan Idol vs. Crazy Boy vs. Dink vs. Ethan Page vs. Façade vs. Flip Gordon vs. Glacier vs. Jervis Cottonbelly vs. John Silver vs. The Invisible Man at Game Changer Wrestling (GCW) Joey Janela's Spring Break, in a 13 Man Clusterfuck match (March 30, 2017) · Veda Scott vs. Gregory Iron at AIW Absolution IX (June 29, 2014) · Veda Scott vs. Gregory Iron at AIW Battle of the Sexes, in a Steel Cage match (July 26, 2014)

★ While wrestling has had its fair share of profession gimmicks—garbage men, goalies, dentists, Mounties—it's not as common for these types of gimmicks to truly represent the wrestler who has them. That's not exactly the case for independent wrestler Veda Scott, a Bar-certified lawyer who brought just that to her wrestling character (in addition to her natural charm and charisma). While training at the ROH Wrestling School and eventually making her professional wrestling debut in 2011—against one of her trainers, Daizee Haze, at Horizon Wrestling Alliance in Maryland—she also attended the Drexel University School of Law (graduating in 2012). And apropos of nothing, she'd probably also want everyone to know that, as far as her accomplishments go, she is currently 5-0 in SMASH Wrestling's annual CANUSA Classic tournament—undefeated since the tournament began in 2013.

After training at their wrestling school, Veda Scott made her official debut in ROH in 2012, as a backstage interviewer. She eventually expanded her duties to commentary for the company's women's matches. Veda would become best known for her role as a manager to various talent in the ROH from

2014 to 2016—although she wrestled in dark matches and as part of the promotion's Women of Honor Division after it was relaunched as its own brand in 2015. As a manager, she'd still use her legal skills to her advantage in storylines, never shy to go after ROH for "unsafe work conditions."

A SMALL PART OF WHAT GAINED VEDA SCOTT NOTORIETY ON THE INDEPENDENT SCENE WAS HER WILLINGNESS TO WRESTLE BOTH WOMEN AND MEN.

The first ROH wrestler she managed was RD Evans, a scrawny wrestler best known for his comedy; Veda would set Evans up with easy-to-win matches against jobbers, so he would rack up the wins and she could sing the praises of her undefeated and unbeatable client. Comparing him to WCW legend Goldberg (with a historic undefeated streak of 173-0), Veda Scott would call this "The New Streak," and for the wrestlers Evans would have to face who were legitimate, serious contenders, Veda would make sure he beat them by disqualification. This would eventually lead to Scott managing another talent on the roster by the name of Moose, using him as the muscle to continue Evans's win streak—and this partnership would end when Moose turned face and finally caused Evans to lose, bringing the streak of over a year to an end at 167-1. Veda would then go on to manage Cedric Alexander during his heel turn, leading to her getting some semblance of revenge against Moose by having Alexander in turn end Moose's own undefeated streak in the company. But after Cedric left ROH in May 2016—and soon ended up WWE-bound—ROH seemingly had nothing new for Veda to tackle. On December 1, 2016, Veda requested and received her release from ROH.

Outside of ROH, Veda Scott also debuted in AIW in 2011, but it wasn't until the fall of 2012 that she had her first major storyline. Again, she brought her legal acumen into her character, working as the legal counsel to "The Handicapped Hero" Gregory Iron in order for AIW to "accommodate his affliction." In this particular case, that meant making it so all of his matches had the stipulation that his opponents could only beat him via pinfall with a four-count instead of the standard three. Veda claimed it was her "mission to right these wrongs" against her client and promised that change would be coming to the promotion. This would then lead to the duo becoming a tag team called "Hope and Change," with the four-count rule coming into play to win them the AIW Tag Team Championship in November 2012. The next June, the two lost the championship, and a few months later they began feuding with each other. As a result, the two eventually main-evented an AIW show in a Steel Cage match (full of tables and thumbtacks, to make things worse). According to Gregory Iron, this was his favorite storyline, as fan investment in the feud and his and Veda's work boosted it from a mid-card storyline to a main-event program.

In 2012, Veda was named PWI Rookie of the Year, making her the second woman ever to earn that honor; the first was Madusa Miceli, in 1988. Her alma mater even wrote about the achievement, as one of their own had (at the time) wrestled in 15 states and toured Japan while simultaneously attending law school and preparing for the Bar Exam.

A small part of what gained Veda Scott notoriety on the independent scene was her willingness to wrestle both women and men. In 2017, she even wrestled an invisible man! But it's undeniable that her character work and mic skills go above and beyond the call of duty, which is what makes her stick out even more than her red hair and signature glasses. That and her lack of hesitance to simply "sue" her opponents and the companies she works for, that is.

★ VICKIE GUERRERO ★

YEARS ACTIVE: 2005–2014

BILLED FROM: El Paso, Texas

ACCOMPLISHMENTS: 2008 Slammy Award for Couple of the Year (with Edge) · 2012 Slammy Award for LOL! Moment of the Year (with The Rock) · 1x WWE Miss WrestleMania · 2009 *Wrestling Observer* Newsletter Best Non-Wrestler · 2010 *Wrestling Observer* Newsletter Best Non-Wrestler

AKA: "The Cougar" · "Queen Diva" · member of La Familia

NOTABLE MATCHES: Vickie Guerrero, Edge, & The Edgeheads (Curt Hawkins & Zack Ryder) vs. The Undertaker at WWE *SmackDown* (May 16, 2008) · Vickie Guerrero, LayCool (Layla & Michelle McCool), Alicia Fox, & Maryse vs. Beth Phoenix, Eve Torres, Gail Kim, Kelly Kelly, & Mickie James, in a 10-Diva Tag Team match at WWE WrestleMania XXVI (March 28, 2010) · Vickie Guerrero & Dolph Ziggler vs. Trish Stratus & John Morrison at WWE *Monday Night RAW*, in a Mixed Tag Team match (April 4, 2011) · Vickie Guerrero & John Cena vs. AJ Lee & Dolph Ziggler at WWE *Monday Night RAW*, in a Mixed Tag Team match (December 10, 2012) · Vickie Guerrero vs. Stephanie McMahon at WWE *Monday Night RAW*, in a Mud Pool match (June 23, 2014)

★ Vickie Guerrero's full-time entry into the world of professional wrestling is a story of tragedy-turned-triumph. The wife of wrestling legend and WWE Hall of Famer Eddie Guerrero, Vickie first truly became a part of the business—outside of just coming to watch shows or being part of Eddie-based video packages—in July 2005, when she became part of a heel in Eddie's extremely personal feud with longtime friend Rey Mysterio. While the majority of her role in the storyline was simply to try to talk sense into her husband, she got physically involved at that year's SummerSlam, preventing Eddie from winning his Ladder match with Rey by pushing him off the ladder and holding him down. (A case of her greenness, however, is that she initially missed her cue for this particular spot, causing Eddie to break kayfabe and shout as he climbed the ladder, "WHERE THE FUCK IS VICKIE?!?" during the match.)

While he was on the road with WWE, Eddie would pass away in his sleep that November. He'd then be inducted posthumously into the WWE Hall of Fame in 2006, and Vickie would return to accept the induction in his honor. Vince McMahon promised to financially support Vickie and her children "forever"—and had even helped with the planning of the funeral—but Vickie still wanted to earn that paycheck. So about seven months after Eddie passed, Vickie received a phone call from WWE, asking her to participate in another quick angle. Obviously, "quick" gained a whole new definition, as Vickie would become a fixture in the company for a decade. And surprisingly, despite her sympathetic existence, she'd soon become heel—and after a very brief reprieve into being a face again, remain heel for the entirety of that decade. It would begin when she'd align herself with Chavo Guerrero—Eddie's nephew and former tag team partner—in his feuds against Rey Mysterio and Chris Benoit. Both feuds were with men who were extremely close with Eddie, and for some fans, Vickie and the company were disrespecting Eddie's legacy in the way they approached the situation.

Vickie went on to become the on-screen assistant to the SmackDown General Manager, Teddy Long, and when Teddy suffered a kayfabe heart attack, she was put in charge as the new GM. This is when her on-screen relationship with Edge began, with her abusing her power to get him World Heavyweight Championship (held by The Undertaker) opportunities—and in some cases, the World Heavyweight Championship itself. During this time, a wheelchair-bound—thanks to a Tombstone Piledriver from The Undertaker, a move Vickie personally thanked Undertaker for hitting her with in her farewell letter to WWE—Vickie formed the heel stable La Familia, composed of Edge, Chavo, and the tag team The Edgeheads (Curt Hawkins and Zack Ryder, who Edge would regularly use in his matches as decoys). Despite everything she said and did during this phase in her career, it became clear that all Vickie really needed to do to get heat from the WWE Universe from this point on was say two words: "Excuse me!" As for how these two words that became her catchphrase came about:

"That was just a fluke. I think I probably forgot my lines one night and just kept saying 'excuse me' to remember what I had to say next, and the fans just got louder. I tried it a couple more times and we thought, let's stay with it and see where it goes. Now I sign all my autographs with 'excuse me.'"

It was also during her La Familia phase that Vickie Guerrero "wrestled" her first match, against The Undertaker . . . in a Handicap match where her partners were also Edge and The Edgeheads. Vickie and Edge would eventually get "married," but as with all WWE weddings, the honeymoon phase would soon be over. (That is, assuming the wedding even fully takes place.) At their wedding reception, it was revealed that Edge cheated on Vickie with their wedding planner, Alicia Fox. With this, Vickie would turn on Edge and give The Undertaker the chance to get his revenge on her husband . . . but even that wasn't enough to actually turn Vickie face. In fact, despite having moments in her career where most wrestlers or wrestling personalities would officially have face turns as a result, Vickie's character would always remain so petty and vindictive that the crowd couldn't help but keep booing her—it's that type of consistency that was impressive, especially coming from someone who had only been doing this for a short time.

In June 2009, Vickie took a break from WWE to focus on raising her daughters—one of whom eventually went on to be known as Raquel Diaz in WWE developmental—a choice that led to her being written out by having Edge "apologize" for using her but also requesting a divorce. She returned to the company and SmackDown that October for the *SmackDown* 10th Anniversary. After a brief storyline with her new "boyfriend," short-tenured wrestler Eric Escobar, and being named "SmackDown Consultant" by Vince McMahon, Vickie got involved with the heel, mean-girl Diva tag team known as LayCool. Like Edge and Eric Escobar before them, they of course merely used Vickie and her position of power for what she could provide them. Although, in the case of LayCool, the other shoe never dropped—making it a surprisingly rare example of real female friendship in WWE, though the friends were all vindictive, egomaniacal heels. Plus, the LayCool storyline lead to Vickie Guerrero wrestling at WrestleMania—WrestleMania XXVI—in a 10-Diva Tag Team match, with Vickie getting the win. She also received her true "WrestleMania moment," as she won the match by doing her version of her late husband's signature finish, the Frog Splash. (She even pointed to the sky before she hit the move.) WWE referred to her splash as the "Hog Splash"—though she later named it herself the "Cougar Splash"—as there were unfortunately a lot of weight jokes at Vickie's expense when she was in the company. It was especially frustrating, since she had lost quite a bit of weight before she returned at the *SmackDown* 10th anniversary show—and because WWE was highly touting its anti-bullying campaign, Be a STAR, at this time. However, Vickie has gone on the record plenty of times claiming it didn't really bother her over the years.

Then came Dolph Ziggler, and if you could imagine, his love for Vickie Guerrero fell under the same manipulative jurisdiction as all those times before. It was during this pairing that Vickie's added character trait as WWE's resident "cougar" began. She even started wearing a necklace with the word "COUGAR" on it. Not only did she use Ziggler as a tool to get payback on Edge, but like Edge before him, Ziggler also strayed, this time with Vickie's NXT rookie Kaitlyn; but Vickie wasn't going to let history repeat itself, and she made sure to keep the two of them separated. Vickie would also eventually manage the tag team of Ziggler and Jack Swagger, though Swagger would not be one of her romantic entanglements. Instead, Swagger actively pursued Vickie specifically for her managerial services, comparing her to past greats. But unfortunately for her and her relationship with Ziggler, he would eventually leave her for AJ Lee—and again, this betrayal of Vickie didn't lead to her turning face. (Though, in this case, Ziggler also didn't turn face either.) From that point on, Vickie would continue to have a vendetta against AJ Lee, which would be the context for the Vickie Guerrero Divas Invitational for the Divas Championship at WrestleMania XXX, in which AJ would be forced to defend her Divas Championship against 13 other women.

Vickie left WWE in June 2014 to focus on furthering her education and starting the next chapter of her life, both professionally (with a career in medical administration) and personally (she remarried in 2015). She was written out on an episode of *Monday Night RAW*, in a Mud Pool (actually pudding) match with Stephanie McMahon, with Vickie's job on the line. Vickie of course lost the match, but she still got to hold her head up high by throwing Stephanie into the pudding as well—and then officially turned face in her exit by mouthing "I love you" to Eddie and doing his signature taunt one last time on her way out. From the sympathetic widow of Eddie Guerrero to one of the most hated heel figures in WWE, Vickie Guerrero impressed millions of WWE fans—who loved to hate her and hated to . . . hate her—on a weekly basis. Chris Jericho would even coin the type of heel heat that Vickie Guerrero got as "Vickie heat," an aspirational concept for a heel. And when she'd dance—and during this era of WWE, it seemed a dance-off was always right around the corner—she channeled the gesticulation-based, thumb-heavy dance moves of Elaine Benes. She was very clearly in on the joke of her character, which only made her more entertaining. Like her late husband, Vickie Guerrero arguably deserves to be a part of the WWE Hall of Fame one day.

★ VICTORIA ★

YEARS ACTIVE: 2000–present

TRAINED BY: Ultimate Pro Wrestling (UPW) · Memphis Championship Wrestling · OVW · Jim Cornette · Danny Davis · Dave "Fit" Finlay

BILLED FROM: Chicago, Illinois · Los Angeles, California · Louisville, Kentucky

ACCOMPLISHMENTS: 2004 PWI Women of the Year · #5 in 2009 PWI Female 50 · 5x TNA Knockouts Champion · 1x TNA Knockouts Tag Team Champion (with Brooke Tessmacher) · 2x WWE Women's Champion

AKA: Tara · "Head Bitch in Charge" · "HBIC" · Queen "Tara" Victoria · Lisa Marie Varon · "The Vicious Vixen" · 1/3 of Ladies in Pink · 1/3 of Vince's Devils · 1/2 of TnT

NOTABLE MATCHES: Victoria (c) vs. Trish Stratus at WWE *Monday Night RAW*, for the WWE Women's Championship (November 25, 2002) · Victoria (c) (with Steven Richards) vs. Trish Stratus at WWE *Monday Night RAW*, in a Chicago Street Fight for the WWE Women's Championship (January 27, 2003) · Victoria (c) (with Steven Richards) vs. Jazz vs. Trish Stratus at WWE WrestleMania XIX, in a Triple Threat match for the WWE Women's Championship (March 30, 2003) · Victoria (c) vs. Molly Holly at WWE WrestleMania XX, in a Hair vs. Championship match for the WWE Women's Championship (March 14, 2004) · Tara vs. Awesome Kong at TNA Turning Point 2009, in a Six Sides of Steel Cage match (November 15, 2009) · Tara vs. Mickie James at TNA Turning Point 2010 (November 7, 2010) · Tara vs. Miss Tessmacher (c) at TNA Bound For Glory 2012, for the TNA Knockouts Championship (October 14, 2012) · Team Original Divas Revolution (Victoria, Jazz, & Mickie James) vs. Team SHIMMER (Candice LeRae, "Crazy" Mary Dobson, & Solo Darling) at CHIKARA King of Trios 2016 – Night 1, in a King of Trios First Round match (September 2, 2016) · Lisa Marie Varon vs. Candice Michelle at House of Hardcore (HOH) 36: Blizzard Brawl 2017 (December 2, 2017)

⭐ If there's one definitive way to describe Lisa Marie Varon, it's probably this: she ain't the lady to mess with. Best known as "Victoria" from her time in WWE, Varon (née Sole) was a professional bodybuilder and fitness competitor who was debating what to do with her future when she saw WWF wrestler Chyna at her local gym in Los Angeles. The way the story goes, Varon approached Chyna—with the icebreaker being that she herself was friends with female professional wrestlers Trish Stratus and Torrie Wilson—and Chyna told Varon she had a good look for wrestling and should try to pursue it. As Varon was best friends with Torrie Wilson at the time, she admitted that she watched the shows for her and

that she believed she could hang with the guys in the squared circle. (Wilson had previously attempted to get Varon a job at WCW.) After meeting with Chyna and getting the information for WWF's Talent Relations, Varon made a demo tape, sent it to WWF and heard back from them two days later—WWF was coming to Los Angeles in a month, and they wanted to meet with her.

So Varon trained at UPW (at the same time as John Cena) in Los Angeles to get prepared so she'd at least know the basics of being a wrestler before she met *the* people to know as a wrestler, since despite the fact that her older brothers were serious amateur wrestlers, she had no in-depth wrestling knowledge of any kind. Varon began training at UPW in June 2000, where she eventually wrestled under the ring name "HBIC" ("Head Bitch In Charge")—a riff on WCW's Nitro Girl Miss Hancock, aka Stacy Keibler—and impressed WWF talent scout Bruce Prichard. By that August, she had technically been introduced to WWF audiences as The Godfather's "Head Ho" during the "Save The Hos" storyline—which lasted for four months and ended with The Godfather's new Right To Censor persona "The Goodfather" powerbombing her through the table. After this, Varon was sent to WWF developmental, where she alternated between the ring names "Victoria" and "Queen Victoria" before officially being called up to the main roster as the former.

Victoria debuted on an episode of WWE *Sunday Night Heat* against Trish Stratus in July 2002 in what appeared to be a standard enhancement match—with Stratus defeating Victoria after a fairly back-and-forth match. Soon, however, it became clear there was nothing standard about this: Victoria's backstory was that of a woman psychotically obsessed with Trish Stratus from their fitness competition days, under the belief that Stratus had "double-crossed" her back in the day. The feud was even based on a small kernel of truth, as she and Trish legitimately had known each other pre-WWE through the fitness competition circuit. (Also, proving the power of entrance music and videos, Victoria's theme from December 2002 to May 2004 was t.A.T.u's "All The Things She Said.") Feuding for months, Victoria eventually won the WWE Women's Championship (for the first time) from Stratus in a Hardcore match at Survivor Series. Adding to Stratus's struggles, WWE Superstar Steven Richards soon revealed himself to be kayfabe involved with Victoria, accompanying her to the ring and getting involved in her brawls with Stratus. Victoria feuded with Stratus and held the Women's Championship until March 2003, when she lost the championship to Status in a Triple Threat match at WrestleMania XIX.

Post-Stratus, Victoria feuded with Lita, which eventually led to the first-ever women's Steel Cage match in WWE history. But her true follow-up storyline with the championship took place toward the end of 2003, with her turning face against the heel champion Molly Holly. This feud led to their championship match at WrestleMania XX, a Hair vs. Title match, which Victoria won (giving her the championship and the chance to shave Molly Holly bald). Face Victoria wasn't exactly the same as the heel unstable Victoria, as evidenced by her eventual music change ("Don't Mess With," as rapped by Nicki Minaj) and choreographed dancing to go along with it. And in a twist from her official debut, Victoria ended up losing the Women's Championship to heel Trish Stratus. She also ended up having her matches interrupted by a surprise Steven Richards—dressed in drag at first—as he hadn't turned face when she had.

After a return to heel status in 2005, Victoria went through many more phases, including her role as one of Vince's Devils (alongside Candice Michelle and Torrie Wilson) and even a vicious heel with a checklist of every Diva she'd defeated. However, in her last few years in WWE, she was used more in the veteran role to put newer or more inexperienced Divas over. In January 2009, Victoria announced her retirement from WWE (though she later appeared in the "Miss WrestleMania" Battle Royal at WrestleMania XXV that year).

A month after Victoria's last appearance in WWE, she debuted on TNA Impact Wrestling as "Tara," immediately feuding with heel stable The Beautiful People (Madison Rayne, Velvet Sky, and then-TNA Knockouts Champion, Angelina Love) and introducing a new aspect to her gimmick: a tarantula (which was also what "Tara" was short for . . . as the spider was named "Poison"). That July, Tara won the Knockouts Championship from Angelina Love, only to lose it back to Love later that month due to the referee being on the take. Varon remained in TNA until July 2013—when she was released—becoming a five-time Knockouts Championship as well as a one-time Knockouts Tag Team Champion (with Brooke Tessmacher, as they formed TnT) during her time there. Despite these achievements, Varon later stated that a TNA return "is out of the question" and that TNA "made her appreciate WWE a lot."

LISA MARIE VARON AIN'T THE LADY TO MESS WITH. BEST KNOWN AS "VICTORIA" FROM HER TIME IN WWE, VARON WAS A PROFESSIONAL BODYBUILDER AND FITNESS COMPETITOR.

Since TNA, Varon has been working the independent scene, typically under her real name; though in 2016, she teamed with Jazz and Mickie James as Victoria once more for CHIKARA's King of Trios tournament, as Team Original Divas Revolution. At the end of 2017, at a House of Hardcore show, she wrestled against her former Vince's Devil teammate Candice Michelle in Michelle's official retirement match. And in 2018, Varon appeared in an episode of the Netflix original series *Love*— surprisingly not *GLOW*, the Netflix original show about women's wrestling—as an independent wrestler, where she competed against another independent wrestler, played by her former WWE and TNA colleague Gail Kim.

★ WENDI RICHTER ★

YEARS ACTIVE: 1979-2005

TRAINED BY: The Fabulous Moolah · Judy Martin · Leilani Kai · Joyce Grable

BILLED FROM: Dallas, Texas

ACCOMPLISHMENTS: 1x AWA Women's Champion · 1993 Cauliflower Alley Club Honoree · 2x NWA Women's World Tag Team Champion (with Joyce Grable) · 1x National Wrestling Federation Women's Champion · 2x WWC Women's Champion · 2x WWF Women's Champion · WWE Hall of Fame Class of 2010 · Professional Wrestling Hall of Fame Class of 2012

AKA: Wendy Richter · 1/2 of The Texas Cowgirls

NOTABLE MATCHES: Wendi Richter vs. Jaguar Yokota (c) at AJW, for the WWWA Championship (October 5, 1982) · Wendi Richter vs. The Fabulous Moolah (c) at WWF The Brawl To End It All, for the WWF Women's Championship (July 23, 1984) · Wendi Richter vs. Leilani Kai (c) at WWF WrestleMania, for the WWF Women's Championship (March 31, 1985) · Wendi Richter (c) vs. Spider Lady at WWF on MSG Network, for the WWF Women's Championship (November 25, 1985) · Wendi Richter, Bambi, Jenny Taylor, & Malia Hosaka vs. Sherri Martel, Amber O'Neal, Krissy Vaine, & Peggy Lee Leather at WrestleReunion (January 29, 2005)

★ When rock and roll meets wrestling, you might think anything is possible. But really, you get Wendi Richter. Prior to professional wrestling, Richter was almost a stereotypical Texan girl, working on her family's ranch and competing in the rodeo. At 18 years old, she trained at The Fabulous Moolah's wrestling school—a choice that would actually end up being quite ironic—under the tutelage of Judy Martin, Leilani Kai, and Joyce Grable. Once she made her in-ring debut in 1979, in her first couple of years she often found herself in the ring with her trainers—as well as Moolah—forming The Texas Cowgirls with Grable,

teaming with Moolah in WWF, and feuding with Martin (as well as a woman who ended up being one of Richter's long-term rivals in the territories, Velvet McIntyre).

In 1984—two years after Vincent Kennedy McMahon had bought the company from his father—the WWF began its "Rock 'n' Wrestling Connection" campaign, which was built on a cross-promotion between the organization and the music industry. Many remember WWF manager Captain Lou Albano as Cyndi Lauper's father in the "Girls Just Want To Have Fun" video, which was reportedly the start of this newly formed relationship with the pop star after meeting on a flight to Puerto Rico. As Vince McMahon realized the key demographic the burgeoning MTV was garnering, he jumped at the opportunity presented to him when Lauper's boyfriend-cum-manager suggested a feud between Lauper and the heel Albano. So while Lauper functioned as Richter's manager on the way to the ring at The Brawl To End It All—a WWF Madison Square Garden show broadcast live on MTV on July 23, 1984—Albano was The Fabulous Moolah's. It was also the only match on the entire 11-match card that aired on MTV—the rest was solely a live event for the Madison Square Garden audience. And in this match, Richter defeated Moolah (after an interference from Lauper) to win the WWF Women's Championship and end what is considered the longest championship reign in professional wrestling—male or female—history. (WWF/WWE recognized it as a 28-year reign, not acknowledging the times Moolah had lost the title between 1956 and 1978, meaning that technically, Richter ended what was approximately a seven-year reign . . . which was still pretty impressive.) A ratings success, this was the match that officially began the Rock 'n' Wrestling Connection era, with "150 pounds of twisted steel and sex appeal" Wendi Richter playing a key role.

Lauper would also appear in Richter's corner during a title defense against Moolah protégé Leilani Kai (with Moolah in Kai's corner), a match that would put an end to Richter's 210-day title reign. (During that reign, Richter constantly defended the title either against Moolah or Judy Martin.)

Wendi was considered one of the faces of the first Wrestle-Mania alongside Cyndi Lauper, Hulk Hogan, Muhammad Ali, and Liberace. Given Hogan's pop culture status as a breakout professional wrestler, that should provide more context as to how big Richter was or could have been, as the only other wrestler in this bunch alongside these A-listers. In fact, as the Rock 'n'

Wrestling era led to Saturday morning cartoons in the form of *Hulk Hogan's Rock 'n' Wrestling* (which aired for two seasons, 1985–1986), Richter was one of the wrestlers who ended up being a character on the show. Wendi Richter would also show up in Lauper's "She Bop" and "Goonies R Good Enough" music videos, though the former hit (and also "Girls Just Want to Have

Fun") would function as Richter's entrance theme at one point in her wrestling career. So at the inaugural *WrestleMania*—aired on closed-circuit television in March 1985—Richter (with Lauper again in her corner) challenged Kai (with Moolah) for the WWF Women's Championship and won the title back for the second and final time.

This second reign would last 239 days, but the way it ended was quite controversial, considered "The Original Screwjob" in WWF/WWE history. The way the story goes, WWF had offered Richter a new contract and wanted her to sign it right away, but Richter wanted to be paid more (a point she would regularly make to Vince) and put off signing until an agreement could be made. However, Vince McMahon reportedly didn't want to wait or come to an agreement and instead decided to screw her out of the title, at least ensuring that WWF wouldn't get screwed out of keeping their title. Unfortunately, after that betrayal, Richter quit the WWF. The match took place at Madison Square Garden in November 1985, with Richter defending her championship against a masked opponent called "The Spider Lady." When the Spider Lady had Richter in a pinning predicament, the referee (who was aware of the Screwjob) quickly counted to three, despite Richter kicking out at one. Richter attacked the Spider Lady post-match and unmasked her to confirm (as Richter had already had her suspicions) that it was The Fabulous Moolah.

"I was so angry that I just walked right out of the building right in my wrestling suit, wrestling boots. I grabbed my bag, went out and hailed a cab—and it was cold; it was in November—and went to the airport in my wrestling outfit and got my ticket. And then I went in the bathroom and put my clothes on at the airport."

WHEN ROCK AND ROLL MEETS WRESTLING, YOU MIGHT THINK ANYTHING IS POSSIBLE. BUT REALLY, YOU GET WENDI RICHTER.

Post-WWF, Richter never achieved the same kind of wrestling or pop culture superstardom she'd had there. She'd wrestle for a few more years in Japan, Canada, Germany, and Puerto Rico (in Carlos Colón's WWC, where she held the WWC Women's Championship twice), as well as returning to her old stomping grounds at the AWA, winning the AWA Women's Championship. But after the '80s, Richter's wrestling matches became few and far between, and by 1996 she was basically done . . . until she wrestled in a couple of legends events for WrestleReunion (and WrestleReunion 2) in 2005.

In 2010, WWE announced that they would be inducting Wendi Richter into their Hall of Fame, apparently burying the hatchet between the two parties and shocking everyone who thought it would never happen. (Just a few years earlier, Richter was anything but happy when it came to talking about WWE in shoot interviews.) Naturally, Richter ended her speech—in which she spoke fondly about the days of Rock 'n' Wrestling—by quoting "Girls Just Want To Have Fun." Two years later, on the 1000th episode of *Monday Night RAW*, Richter made another appearance in the WWE, this time alongside Cyndi Lauper and fellow Hall of Famer "Rowdy" Roddy Piper, again celebrating her contributions to the wrestling industry.

INTERNATIONAL
WRESTLING
THE VILLA MARINA
MONDAY AT 8 P.M

STUPENDOUS
LADIES CONTEST
VIV
MARTELL
46-25-36 SEX SYMBOL
V.
BLACKFOOT
SIOUX
SENSATIONAL INDIAN SQUAW

75p   65p   50p

Advance Booking: Ernest Roberts, Dops Cafe,
The Maes, Pwllheli

"PIN-DOWN
GIRL"

★ Abbreviations ★

The following are abbreviations used throughout the book.

A1	Alpha-1 Wrestling
AAA	Lucha Libre AAA Worldwide
AAAW	All Asian Athlete Women's
AAW	AAW: Pro Wrestling Redefined
ACW	Anarchy Championship Wrestling
AIW	Absolute Intense Wrestling
AJW	All Japan Women's Pro-Wrestling
ALF	Association de Lutte Feminine
APW	All Pro Wrestling
AWA	American Wrestling Association
AWF	Apocalypse Wrestling Federation
AKE	Azteca Karate Extremo
BCW	Border City Wrestling
BCWA	Blue Collar Wrestling Alliance
BEW	British Empire Wrestling
BTW	Big Time Wrestling
CWR	Canadian Wrestling Revolution
CAPW	Cleveland All Pro Wrestling
CAWF	Can-Am Wrestling Federation
CWF	NWA Championship Wrestling from Florida
CCW	Coastal Championship Wrestling
CMLL	Consejo Mundial de Lucha Libre
CSWF	CyberSpace Wrestling Federation
CZW	Combat Zone Wrestling
CWE	Championship Wrestling Entertainment
CWF	Championship Wrestling from Florida
DDT	Dramatic Dream Team
DSW	Deep South Wrestling

ECCW	Elite Canadian Championship Wrestling
ECW	Extreme Championship Wrestling
ECWA	East Coast Wrestling Association
EWE	Empresa de Wrestling Europea
ECW	Empire Wrestling Federation
FCW	Florida Championship Wrestling
FIP	Full Impact Pro
FWE	Family Wrestling Entertainment
GFW	Global Force Wrestling
GLCW	Great Lakes Championship Wrestling
GLOW	Gorgeous Ladies of Wrestling
GSW	German Stampede Wrestling
GWF	German Wrestling Federation
GXW	Ground Xero Wrestling
HEW	Herts & Essex Wrestling
HWA	Heartland Wrestling Association
ICW	Insane Championship Wrestling
ICWA	International Catch Wrestling Association
IPW	Impact Pro Wrestling
IWA	International Wrestling Association
IWA-MS	Independent Wrestling Association Mid-South
IWCCW	International World Class Championship Wrestling
IWC	International Wrestling Cartel
IWE	Independent Wrestling Entertainment
IWF	International Wrestling Federation
JAPW	Jersey All Pro Wrestling
LFL	Lingerie Football League
LLPW	Ladies Legend Pro-Wrestling

LMLW	Ladies Major League Wrestling	SMW	Smoky Mountain Wrestling
LSC	Ladies Sports Club	SSW	Scottish School of Wrestling
		SWA	Scottish Wrestling Alliance
MCW	Maryland Championship Wrestling	SWE	Southside Wrestling Entertainment
MEWL	Main Event World League	SWF	Sunshine Wrestling Federation
NBWA	New Breed Wrestling Association	TNA	Total Nonstop Action (now Impact Wrestling)
nCw	Northern Championship Wrestling	TWA	Tri-State Wrestling Alliance
NHPW	New Horizons Pro Wrestling		
NJPW	New Japan Pro Wrestling	USWA	United States Wrestling Association
NWA	National Wrestling Alliance	UWA	Universal Wrestling Association
NWS	National Wrestling Superstars		
		VWAA	Vanguard Wrestling All-Star Alliance
OAC	Ontario Athletics Commission		
OVW	Ohio Valley Wrestling	WAWW	World Association of Women's Wrestling
OWIE	Ontario Wrestling's Indy Elite	WCW	World Championship Wrestling
		WEW	Women's Extreme Wrestling
PCW	Preston City Wrestling	WSU	Women Superstars Uncensored
POWW	Powerful Women of Wrestling	W3L	World Wide Wrestling
PWA	Pro Wrestling Alliance	WWC	World Wrestling Council
PWE	Pro Wrestling Entertainment	WWE	World Wrestling Entertainment
PWF	PREMIER Wrestling Federation	WWF	World Wrestling Federation
PWG	Pro Wrestling Guerilla	WWL	World Wrestling League
PWWA	Pro Wrestling Women's Alliance	WWN	World Wrestling Network
PWI	Pro Wrestling Illustrated	WWOW	Wild Women of Wrestling
PWR	Pro Wrestling Revolution	WWWA	World Women's Wrestling Association
		WWWD	World Woman Pro-Wrestling Diana
QOC	Queens of Combat		
QPro	Quintessential Pro Wrestling	wXw	Westside Xtreme Wrestling
RCW	Revolution Championship Wrestling		
ROH	Ring of Honor		
RPW	Resistance Pro Wrestling		
RQW	Real Quality Wrestling		
RTC	Right to Censor		

★ Glossary ★

babyface: The intended hero or "good guy" in a wrestling feud or match. (Also known as "face" for short, "*técnico*" in lucha libre.)

blow-off match: Technically, the final match in a feud. Although feuds can be rekindled, in terms of the original feud, the blow-off match is the one to which the wrestlers and their wrestling promotion are building, the one that will make the most money and have the most audience investment.

booker: The person who writes the wrestling show and is responsible for the storylines, the talent on the show (meaning: who gets booked), and even who wins or loses and how the matches themselves end.

dark match: A nontelevised/nonaired match on a wrestling card (primarily on a TV taping or a pay-per-view, but a dark match can also be one that doesn't appear on the DVD for a wrestling show). Dark matches usually happen before or after the show, with those before the show functioning as a tryout or training match for talent and those after often serving to please the live audience with a match that doesn't quite fit into the inner continuity of the story on the current TV product.

developmental: In WWE, specifically, developmental (or, hearkening back to the olden days, a "developmental territory") is a branch of the company specifically for the development of potential future stars on the main roster (RAW, SmackDown). Developmental is essentially the "minor leagues" to WWE's majors.

enhancement talent: Typically, wrestlers local to whatever city a show is in, getting a quick look from the company when they stop by. (Also known as "jobbers." See *jobbing*.) An "enhancement match" is one in which an established wrestler—or one who a wrestling promoter wants to become an established, dominant wrestler—faces said enhancement talent, typically in very short fashion.

heat: In terms of heel work, "heat" is what you want to get. It's the boos and jeers from the crowd, evidence that a heel is doing her job. However, heat can also be garnered from a wrestler working sloppily or poorly; it can come from backstage, if a wrestler or personality does something to offend or upset a colleague behind the scenes; even a face can get heat with the crowd if they intentionally play up an antagonistic crowd or just aren't liked for whatever reasons; the heat of the match overall is also the enthusiasm of the crowd, good or bad.

heel: The intended villain or "bad guy" in a wrestling feud or match. (Also known as "*rudo*" in lucha libre.)

house shows: Live events, specifically for the entertainment of the live crowd in attendance ("the house"), not for television or pay-per-view. House shows are typically more relaxed than a typical weekly on-air show—both in terms of the wrestling itself and the general storytelling—as well as ground zero for wrestlers (and their company) to test out new feuds and/or character directions and motivations.

jobbing: To "do the job" in professional wrestling is to lose. Someone whose job is simply to lose in a promotion is considered a "jobber" (as well as "performance enhancement," because her role is to make the other talent in the ring look good or better).

joshi puroresu: *Puroresu*—aka "pro-wres," based on the Japanese pronunciation of "professional wrestling"—is a term used to describe Japanese professional wrestling. *Joshi puroresu* (aka *joshi puro* or simply *joshi*) is the women's subset of Japanese professional wrestling.

kayfabe: This goes back to the carnival days of professional wrestling, as "kayfabe" was part of the secret jargon and code between those in the know. Kayfabe is basically its own fake reality. To "break kayfabe" is to break character or to let outsiders (potential "marks") in on the tricks of the trade, which was a big no-no years ago, when wrestling was still looked upon as real.

mark: The target audience for wrestling, the fans. Originating in the carnival days of professional wrestling—and the confidence trick aspect of it all—the term "marks" refers to the paying customers who buy into the world of professional wrestling. (To "mark out" is to get excited over something in wrestling, to invest in that suspension of disbelief.)

over: In professional wrestling, "to get over" is to connect with the crowd on a consistent basis, whether it's as a face (with cheers from the crowd) or as a heel (with boos and heat from the crowd).

putting over: Allowing an opponent to win—typically, "clean," without any shenanigans—as well as look good. This can also be a verbal or visual cue during a promo or after the match, if the opponent makes clear to the audience—win or lose—that she is or was up against quite the performer.

the rub: When a wrestler gives another wrestler "the rub," that also constitutes as putting them over. Especially when the former is the more established, popular of the two: The rub is essentially a sign of faith from both the established wrestler and the higher-ups in the company.

shoot: A wrestling term for "real, legitimate." (For example, MMA or even boxing would be considered "shoot fighting.") Despite professional wrestling being a "work"—with planned attacks and moves—sometimes, whether it was a wrestler's original plan or not, shoots can occur. With a shoot, a wrestler is really attempting to hurt her opponent.

shoot interview: A candid, out-of-character, (typically) one-on-one interview focusing on a wrestling talent, personality, or behind-the-scenes figure.

sports entertainment: The blanket term for professional wrestling, as dubbed by WWE chairman and CEO Vince McMahon back in the 1980s. It's also a term that has allowed wrestling to avoid certain regulations that it would incur were it an actual sport.

squared circle: The wrestling ring. Because a ring is traditionally a circle, but a wrestling ring is a square (well, a rectangle).

title: A championship distinction, in the form of the championship belt. In WWE, reportedly one of the company directives for branding purposes (as first seen from a set of WWE commentary notes) is not to call any of its championships "belts," as the belts themselves are representative of the titles.

work: The entire point of sports entertainment, as well as the opposite of a shoot. Wrestling is "a work," as kayfabe says the whole point is to deceive the crowd and get them to believe in the stories and character being presented. To "work the crowd" is to play to them under the guise of kayfabe, to stay in character with actions both inside and outside of the ring. (Wrestlers are also called "workers.")

★ Photo Credits ★

Alamy: The Advertising archives: 260 middle right; Allstar Picture Library: 246; Christian Bertrand: 179; Nacho Calonge: 260 top right; Stephen M. Dowell/Orlando Sentinel/TNS/Alamy Live News: 62; dpa picture alliance archive: 35; Everett Collection, Inc.: 260 bottom center; Globe Photos/ ZUMAPRESS.com: 176; © Yukio Hiraku/AFLO/Alamy Live News: 3, 33, 53, 98, 152, 159; MARKA: 96, 261 top right, middle left bottom, bottom left; © Jeff Moore/ZUMAPRESS.com: 190; © Matt Roberts/ZUMA Press: 251; F. Sadou/AdMedia/ZUMAWire/Alamy Live News: 230; © San Gabriel Valley tribune/ZUMA Wire/Alamy Live News: iv; 91, 260 middle center bottom; Jan Sochor: 260 top center; Birdie Thompson/AdMedia/ZUMAWire/ Alamy Live News: 184; WENN Ltd.: 6, 93, 169, 193; Rachel Worth/WENN: 69; Greg Zoe/MediaPunch: 71

Everett Collection: Mirrorpix: 260 bottom right, 266

Getty Images: B Bennett: 174; Tommaso Boddi: 237; Jeff Bottari/ Zuffa LLC: 224; Dick Darrell/Toronto Star: 87; Myron Davis/The LIFE Picture Collection: 172; Focus on Sport: 88, 261 middle left; John Giamundo: 227; Lynn Goldsmith/Corbis/VCG: 258; Philippe Huguen/AFP: 12; Hulton Archive: 268; Icon Sport: 131, 156; Jeff Katz: 209; KMazur/WireImage: 148; Michael Norcia/New York Post Archives/© NYP Holdings, Inc.: 256; Francine Orr/ LA Times: 222; George Pimentel: 228; Lukas Schulze/Bangarts: 38

Harvard University, Schlesinger Library, RIAS: 260 middle left; 261 bottom center

Ladies Professional Wrestling Association: 260 top left and bottom left; 261 top center and middle right

Library of Congress: viii

Cory Lockwood: 150

Mary Evans Picture Library: 260 middle center

Oli Sandler: 160, 241

Shutterstock.com: Alinari: ii, 261 top left; Broadimage: 20

Courtesy of Wikimedia Commons: Airman 1st Class Nicholas Pilch: 243; Anton: 182; felipe bascunan: 48; Jonathan Byrne: 114; daysofthundr46: 208, 214; Miguel Discarts: 9, 41, 45, 82, 103, 196, 218, 234, 235, 261 bottom right; Robby Green: 126; Mike Kalasnik: 117, 201; KnightEphrite: 261 middle center; Megan Elice Meadows: 78, 194; Mshake3: 168; Paparazzo Presents: 145; Shamsuddin Muhammad: 162; shstrng: 73; Staff Sgt. James Selesnick: 85; Simon: 123; Tabercil: xiv, 14, 23, 29, 54, 55, 64, 77, 107, 111, 135, 147, 166, 178, 188, 200, 204, 206, 212, 216, 239, 248, 249; Ed Webster: 120

★ Index ★

Numbers in **bold** indicate wrestler profiles.

★ About the Author ★

★ **LaToya Ferguson** is a writer living in Los Angeles. She is best known for her writing at *The A.V. Club*, where she spearheaded the publication's wrestling (WWE, Lucha Underground) coverage from 2015 to 2017 and reviews television shows like *GLOW*, *Brooklyn Nine-Nine*, and *Lucifer*; Uproxx, where she writes about film and TV and wrote about Impact Wrestling for Uproxx's WithSpandex vertical; and *Paste Magazine*. From 2016 to 2017, she was also a part of *The Story of Wrestling* podcast with her fellow A.V. Club colleagues Alasdair Wilkins and Kyle Fowle. Her work as a TV and film critic has also been featured in *Entertainment Weekly*, *The Guardian*, *Variety*, *IndieWire*, and more. In the summer of 2018, she became the Managing Editor of UFC Hall of Famer and WWE Superstar Ronda Rousey's newly launched official website.

When it comes to professional wrestling, you'll never meet anyone who has more in-depth opinions about some of its most niche aspects, whether it's the game-show version of *NXT* (specifically season five, *NXT Redemption*), WWE web series *The JBL & Cole Show*, and Impact Wrestling's Paparazzi Production video series (starring Alex Shelley and Kevin Nash).

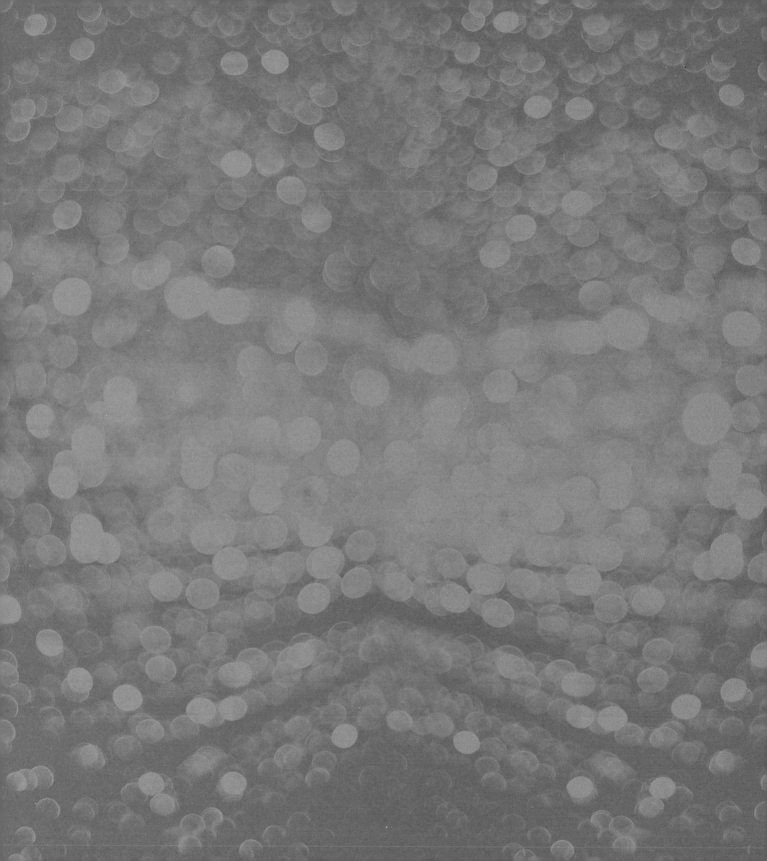